"A Right to Childhood"

The U.S. Children's Bureau and Child Welfare, 1912-46

Kriste Lindenmeyer

University of Illinois Press Urbana and Chicago

Manufactured in the United States of America
1 2 3 4 5 C P 5 4 3 2 1

This book is printed on acid-free paper.

Library of Congress Cataloging-in-Publication Data

Lindenmeyer, Kriste, 1955-
A right to childhood : the U.S. Children's Bureau and child welfare, 1912-46 / Kriste Lindenmeyer.
p. cm.
Includes bibliographical references and index.
ISBN 0-252-02275-0 (acid-free paper). —
ISBN 0-252-06577-8 (pbk. : acid-free paper)
1. United States. Children's Bureau—History. 2. Child welfare—United States—History. I. Title.
HV741.L525 1997
362.7'1'0973—dc20 96-10031
CIP

"A Right to Childhood"

For Michael and Vanessa

Contents

Acknowledgments

This project began as an undergraduate senior thesis in Roger Daniels's history methods course at the University of Cincinnati in 1984. Since I was searching for a women's history topic, Laura Struminger suggested that I take a look at the Cincinnati Babies' Milk Fund Association, a philanthropic organization begun in the late nineteenth century to benefit poor women and children. That small beginning led to a twelve-year journey examining the history of child welfare policy in the United States in the first half of the twentieth century. Various parts of this work have come to life as a master's thesis, doctoral dissertation, and now a book. I have incurred an enormous debt to those who helped me along the way. However, while I gratefully credit these individuals for their contributions, I take sole responsibility for all errors of interpretation or fact.

Many organizations graciously provided funding for my research. The American Historical Association's Littleton-Griswold Research Grant covered expenses for work conducted at the Library of Congress. I also benefited from generous dissertation grants from the Franklin and Eleanor Roosevelt Institute, the Mary Lizzie Saunders Fund of the Schlesinger Library, the Herbert Hoover Library Association, Chicago's Newberry Library, and the University of Cincinnati's Friends of Women's Studies. The University of Cincinnati's History Department helped to defray the cost of conducting research at the National Archives. The Charles P. Taft Memorial Fund, a Daughters of the American Revolution Neff Fellowship, and University of Cincinnati Graduate Studies scholarships funded my stipends and paid graduate school tuition while I wrote the dissertation. The University of Cincinnati Research Council underwrote fellowships during the summers of 1986 and 1987. My current home institution, Tennessee Technological University, provided released-time grants during the past four academic years that freed me to spend time revising and extending the dissertation for publication as this book.

I have also benefited from the insight of numerous individuals who have read parts or all of this work. My graduate school colleagues, particularly Michael Anderson, Robert Burnham, Andrea Kornbluh, Melanie Millspaugh, Nina Mjagkij, Robert Miller, and Mathew Sauer will recognize their thoughts offered in the many hours we shared together in graduate seminars. Also while I was in graduate school, Saul Benison, Bruce Levine, Gene Lewis, Zane Miller, Barbara Ramusack, David Sterling, and Henry Winkler provided keen insight and instruction that helped to shape my historical interpretations. Gale Evans's willingness to share her own work on the turn-of-the-century conservation history contributed greatly to my analysis of the early child welfare movement and its links to Progressive Era reforms. Molly Ladd-Taylor, Ruth Crocker, Wali Kharif, Larry Whiteaker, and Patrick Reagan also offered comments and suggestions that sharpened my work. Members of my own dissertation committee, Hilda Smith, Susan Hartmann, and Joanne Meyerowitz, provided welcome advice and encouragement. In addition, I am indebted to Joseph Hawes, who read the entire manuscript twice and painstakingly offered invaluable line-by-line suggestions. I would also like to thank Walter Trattner for his reader's comments on the early manuscript. B. F. Jones and Richard Hepler did not live to see the final product, but each were helpful to the completion of this work. My advisor, mentor, and friend, Roger Daniels, has been the single greatest influence on my scholarship. He has unselfishly read these pages in their various stages more times than I am sure he would like to know. He is an exacting, generous, and talented scholar and teacher, to whom I am eternally grateful.

Unfortunately I cannot name all the librarians and archivists who generously guided me through my research. However, I would like to gratefully acknowledge the special assistance I received from Sally Moffit at the University of Cincinnati's Langsam Library, Aloha South at the National Archives, and Linda Mulder and Eloise Hitchcock at Tennessee Technological University's library.

The staff at the University of Illinois Press deserve my gratitude, particularly Veronica Scrol, who helped me negotiate the path to publication, and Patricia Hollahan, whose skilled copyediting saved me from many embarrassing mistakes. Paul Deepan helped construct the index, a dreaded task, for which I am very grateful.

Of course, I am also indebted to my mother, Rebecca Lynne; my father, Rueben Walter Lindenmeyer; and my stepmother, Doris Lindenmeyer, for their unfailing support. My husband, Michael Dick, lovingly weathered the many years of graduate school and manuscript revision that it took to finally complete this project. My stepchildren, Aaron and Andrea Dick, were patient and understanding as they tried to balance their own lives while shuttled between their mother's and father's homes. I was also lucky enough to share eighteen months with a foster child, Tammy S. Key, whose very presence in our home provided another perspective on the difficulties faced by many American children. My daughter and friend, Vanessa Dick, has spent much of her childhood waiting for her mother to finish this book. I humbly hope that it is worth the wait and offers some insight into how to protect "a right to childhood."

Introduction

In her 1905 publication, *Some Ethical Gains through Legislation,* Progressive Era reformer Florence Kelley wrote that "a right to childhood . . . follows from the existence of the Republic and must be guarded in order to guard its life." Using rhetoric appealing to many Americans of the period she continued, "the noblest duty of the Republic is that of self-preservation by so cherishing all its children that they, in turn, may become enlightened self-governing citizens." One year later Kelley and New York reformer Lillian D. Wald formulated plans for a federal agency mandated to investigate, report, and advocate this "right to childhood." After six years of lobbying, on April 9, 1912, President William Howard Taft signed legislation establishing the U.S. Children's Bureau (37 *Stat.,* 79). With an initial appropriation of $25,640, Congress instructed the new agency to report "on all matters pertaining to the welfare of children and child life among all classes of our people." Taft named former Hull-House resident Julia Lathrop Children's Bureau chief, thereby making her the first woman to head a federal agency. From 1912 to 1946 the U.S. Children's Bureau acted as the primary "voice" for children.

In this role the Children's Bureau evolved from an agency limited to research and promotion to an administrator in what Michael Katz has called the "semiwelfare" state.[1] Under Lathrop and her successors the bureau focused on reducing infant and maternal mortality, improving child health, abolishing child labor, and advocating care for children with "special needs." As the primary authors of child welfare policy, the Children's Bureau's staff and supporters argued that a single agency could best serve the needs of the "whole child." However, as the federal government expanded and reorganized along functional rather than constituency lines, the bureau and its supporters watched the agency's influence and "blueprint" for reform fade in the wake of bureaucratic change. While other constituencies gained attention in the expanding federal bureaucracy, the only agency mandated to lobby solely for children lost power and influence.

Although it was popular with the general public and most women's organizations, from its inception the Children's Bureau confronted powerful political opponents. Some criticized the agency as innately socialistic; others contended that its "whole child" philosophy was impractical. Traditionalists argued that families needed no "help" from the federal government. According to these critics the Children's Bureau threatened rugged individualism and interfered in the lives of families. On the other hand, Children's Bureau supporters maintained that family life was so important and in such danger that children needed a single federal agency to lobby on their behalf. Entitled to "a normal homelife," every child needed the protection, or at least advocacy, of a federal agency mandated to serve the "whole child."

Although the Children's Bureau was the target of heated public policy debate, its leadership held very traditionalist views. The agency's definition of "normal homelife" was the same middle-class family ideal held by its critics: the two-parent family in which the father served as the sole breadwinner and the mother devoted her attention solely to the home and her family. As a result, the agency's blueprint, devised and implemented during its first four decades of work, resulted in a national child welfare policy that left few options for those unable to meet this middle-class ideal. In addition, the bureau placed the primary authority for implementing child welfare programs with the states in an era of legislated racial segregation, powerful ethnic prejudice, and few civil liberties protections. This practice often placed the "best" interests of children after those of parents and communities, thereby leading to disparate standards for children. By 1946, the agency's narrow approach to policy development coupled with its critics' relentless opposition led to the dismantling of the Children's Bureau's "whole child" philosophy. Despite the fact that many find it hard to "oppose" children, minors are a particularly vulnerable constituency who have little power in a government controlled by adults. Hence, the Children's Bureau's limited child welfare reforms increasingly had to compete with the interests of an expanding adult population.[2] Furthermore, the most defenseless children tend to come from socioeconomic groups with little political voice. Prohibiting welfare benefits to illegal immigrants or single teenage mothers might discourage what many view as undesirable adult behavior, but the children who are products of such circumstances suffer for the actions of their parents. By 1946, the Children's Bureau's network of supporters, largely consisting of women's organizations and Progressive Era child welfare reformers, was unable to thwart the agency's "dismemberment." Children no longer had a single voice within the federal government mandated to advocate on their behalf.

However, despite these and other limitations, the Children's Bureau contributed significantly to the growing recognition of childhood as a period of life demanding special attention and protection.[3] Bureau studies were often the first "scientific" investigations into the circumstances of particular groups of children. The information revealed in such efforts led to the nation's first maternal and infant health care education program (the 1921 Sheppard-Towner Act), child labor regulation, the inclusion of children's programs in the 1935 Social Security Act, and the extensive World War II Emergency Maternity and Infancy Care program (EMIC). In addition, a history of the Children's Bureau's first four decades provides one way to examine changing values concerning women, children, and social welfare. As Walter Trattner contends, "despite its limited function and modest initial appropriation, the Children's Bureau was extremely significant; it soon became the central, and in some cases the sole, source of authoritative information about the welfare of children and their families throughout the United States."[4]

Several historians investigating social welfare policy mention the Children's Bureau's creation as a watershed in public policy history.[5] For example, scholars examining the history of child labor legislation cite its important role as an initiator, however, there is little written about the bureau's role in implementing national policy. Walter Trattner's study of the National Child Labor Committee, *Crusade for the Children,* gives the Children's Bureau only a subordinate role. In *Constitutional Politics in the Progressive Era* Stephen B. Wood skillfully traces the legal history of child labor reform, but likewise pays only minimal attention to the Children's Bureau.[6] The bureau administered the nation's first federal child labor law, the 1916 Keating-Owen Act; helped to write the 1922 Child Labor Amendment; and contributed to the development of child labor codes in the 1933 National Recovery Act and 1938 Fair Labor Standards Act.

The Children's Bureau also played a primary role in the drive to reduce the nation's high infant and maternal mortality rates. Richard Meckel's *Save the Babies* provides an excellent examination of the early infant welfare movement in the United States and includes a valuable analysis of the Children's Bureau's 1921-29 Sheppard-Towner Act.[7] Molly Ladd-Taylor's book *Mother-Work: Women, Child Welfare, and the State, 1890-1930* traces the infant welfare movement's influence on the changing ideology surrounding motherhood.[8] Nevertheless, neither author details the Children's Bureau's overall "baby saving" campaign. Joseph Chepaitis's 1968 dissertation, "The First Social Welfare Measure: The Sheppard-Towner Maternity and Infancy Act," is a thorough legislative history of this important law and shows the Children's Bureau's influential role. Nevertheless, none of the aforementioned works explains how this law linked maternal and child health policy from the Progressive Era through World War II.[9]

The 1930s New Deal is viewed as a turning point in the history of social welfare policy. But here again studies generally neglect the Children's Bureau's role, especially as related to the 1935 Social Security Act.[10] Although most historians focus on the old age pension provisions of Social Security, the bureau's contributions include some of the most controversial programs in this epochal legislation.[11]

A similar story is true of the Children's Bureau's work during World War II.[12] In general the agency mandated to lobby on behalf of children developed strategies designed to lessen the war's impact on the everyday lives of young people. In addition, as part of an effort to boost morale among U.S. servicemen, millions of women and children received health care through the bureau's Emergency Maternity and Infant Care program. Although it looked as if the Children's Bureau was gaining influence, the war only camouflaged the agency's diminished role within the federal bureaucracy. In 1946 government reorganization plans transferred the bureau to the newly formed Federal Security Agency. Though the move was resisted by supporters of the bureau, it put an end to the Children's Bureau's "whole child" philosophy by shifting several administrative responsibilities to other agencies and by lowering the Children's Bureau's status within the federal hierarchy.

I, along with others who have written about the Children's Bureau, have been influenced by its pioneer historians, Nancy Pottishman Weiss and Louis J. Covotsos, whose logical organization I follow. Weiss's 1974 dissertation, "Save the Children: A History of the Children's Bureau, 1903-1918," gives an insightful overview of the origins of the agency and its first six years of work. In addition, Weiss focuses on the women involved in formulating and implementing the bureau's programs. Louis J. Covotsos's 1976 dissertation, "Child Welfare and Social Progress: The United States Children's Bureau, 1912-1935," outlines an institutional history of the agency. These dissertations pointed to important sources and proved to be invaluable in helping me conceptualize the vast amount of material relevant to this study. However, even though the organization and sources are similar, this analysis and that undertaken by Weiss and Covotsos contain some very important differences. Obviously Weiss's examination traces the bureau's creation and first six years of work. Further, Weiss's dissertation was written at a time when women's historians were just beginning to utilize gender as a viable element in the study of public policy and politics. Covotsos's overview is more extensive and primarily examines the bureau's organizational structure. But it is does not closely investigate the inclusion of children's provisions in the Social Security Act or the Fair Labor Standards Act. He recognizes that the Children's Bureau offered women expanded roles in the development of public policy. However, he criticizes the female administrators and supporters of the bureau for being more interested in maintaining control and power for themselves than in developing an effective comprehensive child welfare policy. This judgment seems somewhat harsh. By examining the years immediately following the New Deal, we find that the agency undertook some of its most aggressive reform efforts during World War II. However, it was too little too late. By 1946 the Children's Bureau's diminished status left it weakened and unable to thwart the kinds of criticism that had been condemning its "whole child" philosophy since 1912.[13]

In general, the Children's Bureau has received more attention from historians of women than from any other group of specialists. In *Woman's Proper Place: A History of Changing Ideals and Practices, 1870 to the Present,* Sheila Rothman cites the establishment and subsequent programs of the Children's Bureau as evidence of women's changing role during the early twentieth century. J. Stanley Lemons and Theda Skocpol recognize the significant role of women reformers in the passage of the 1921 Sheppard-Towner Maternity and Infancy Act. Each argues for the existence of Progressive Era reform into the 1920s. Similarly, Robyn Muncy, in *Creating a Female Dominion in American Reform, 1900-1935,* maintains that many women reformers during the first four decades of the twentieth century worked to establish the field of child welfare as an area of social welfare policy dominated by women. She argues that the Children's Bureau was at the center of this effort and that by 1935 women had lost control of child welfare policy as males increasingly entered the child welfare field.[14] Molly Ladd-Taylor discusses each of these contentions and argues that the bureau's policies were not only shaped by women administrators and middle-class supporters, its efforts were also affected by the thousands of letters the agency received each year from women and children.[15] In *Pitied but Not Entitled: Single Mothers and the History of Welfare, 1890-1930,* Linda Gordon includes a thoughtful gender-based analysis of mothers' pensions and the inclusion of the aid-to-dependent-children program (now called Aid to Families with Dependent Children, AFDC) in the 1935 Social Security Act. She clearly shows how "the stigmas of 'welfare' and of single motherhood intersect" and continue to contribute to the national debate about welfare and federal responsibility.[16]

This study has benefited from the work of these and many other scholars. Part of its significance rests in an attempt to synthesize the varied viewpoints of social welfare, children's, and women's historians. There has been no previous scholarly effort examining federal child welfare policy from the Progressive Era through World War II solely from the Children's Bureau's perspective. This is a significant void because the strategy developed by the Children's Bureau from 1912 to 1946 has served as the primary blueprint for child welfare policy to the present day. Although the agency brought attention to problems previously ignored by most Americans, its effectiveness was limited by both internal and external factors. First, the bureau's "whole child" philosophy was never embraced by its critics or, perhaps more importantly, by policy makers in Washington. This failure placed the agency in an ever more vulnerable position as the federal government's social welfare bureaucracy expanded during the 1930s and 1940s. Second, the Children's Bureau's reliance on the states to implement and assist in the funding of child welfare programs led to a wide variance in standards. Third, the Children's Bureau's effectiveness was also limited by its unquestioning promotion of the middle-class family ideal. This narrow definition of a "normal homelife" left women and children dependent upon men and offered little room for innovative programs designed to protect the interests of children. Fourth, concerns about the proper role of the federal government forwarded by the Children's Bureau's opponents and its own staff and supporters hindered the agency's reform agenda. And finally, the bureau's promotion of child welfare as a "woman's issue" left many, perhaps most, men disinterested.

This study follows a chronological organization within a topical framework. As previously described, it centers on the programs undertaken by the Children's Bureau during its first four decades. The first two chapters discuss the origins, establishment, and early work of the agency. Chapters 3 through 6 examine the bureau's work in its three most significant areas of interest: infant and maternal mortality and the promotion of child health care, child labor reform, and the protection of children with "special needs." Chapter 7 analyzes the effects of the Great Depression on Children's Bureau policies and children living in the United States. In addition, this chapter traces the links between the bureau's Progressive Era reforms and those implemented under the Social Security and the Fair Labor Standards Acts. Chapter 8 examines bureau policies during World War II. The final chapter traces the agency's "dismemberment" under the 1946 reorganization and discusses the Children's Bureau's successes and failures in the light of its primary goal, to promote "a right to childhood."

In a 1914 editorial the American Federation of Labor's organ, the *American Federationist,* maintained that a federal policy which placed more importance on appropriations for military weapons than child welfare would "destroy child life." It urged increased appropriations for the Children's Bureau because "the future of the nation is wrapped up in the lives of the children."[17] A 1991 *Time* magazine article contended that policy makers and citizens had "misplaced priorities." The editorial charged that "when it comes to buying weapons, cost is no object and logic goes out the window. But when it comes to saving infants' lives, penury is the rule." "Why," asked the magazine, "has [the United States] been so shortsighted about investing in its children?"[18] This study attempts to contribute to the effort to answer such questions by examining the origins, design, and transformation of child welfare policy from the Progressive Era through the World War II. It is intended as a bridge between policy history and social history. Perhaps a linking of these two perspectives will result in a better understanding of policy development and how such efforts affect the lives of children in the United States.

1

The Origins of a Federal Bureau for Children, 1900-1912

The proposal for a federal agency for children was representative of Progressive Era reform. What Robert Wiebe has called the "search for order" included the protection of "a right to childhood" for every child.[1] To many living in the United States at the turn of the century, the circumstances of many children—barely subsisting in poverty; laboring in the nation's factories, streets, tenements, mines, and fields; and dying as infants from preventable disease—represented the worst consequences of unregulated modernization. Children's rights advocates also believed that this situation offered the greatest opportunity for change. A federal agency designated to investigate and report on the best means for protecting "a right to childhood" seemed to be an obvious response in an era that redefined the role of the federal government in social welfare and celebrated "scientific investigation." Nonetheless, the proposal for a U.S. children's bureau faced apathy and some philosophical criticism. The effort took nearly ten years of work by a coalition of male and female activists who drew largely on women's reform networks to mobilize public support.

Historians disagree on the exact details concerning the origins of the U.S. Children's Bureau but all credit Lillian D. Wald and Florence Kelley with the idea.[2] As early as 1900, Kelley posited the need for a federal commission on children in a series of lectures eventually published in her 1905 volume, *Some Ethical Gains through Legislation.* She proposed a body consisting of "both male and female social work and health care professionals representing various areas of the country [to] correlate, make available, and interpret the facts concerning the physical, mental and moral condition and prospects of children of the United States, native and immigrant." Accordingly, the group should focus its concern on ten specific areas: infant mortality, registration of births, orphaned children, desertion, illegitimacy, degeneracy, delinquency, offenses against children, illiteracy, and child labor; thereby promoting "the vital and social efficiency of the children" by making accessible "the latest work of science and the latest method of applying it." Protecting "a right to childhood" was a moral and practical endeavor that should be undertaken by all citizens and their government. "The noblest duty of the Republic is that of self-preservation by so cherishing all its children that they, in turn, may become enlightened self-governing citizens. . . . For if children perish in infancy they are obviously lost to the Republic as citizens. If, surviving infancy, children are permitted to deteriorate into criminals, they are bad citizens; if they are left devitalized in body and mind, the Republic suffers the penalty of every offense against childhood."[3]

Kelley's friend and associate, Lillian D. Wald, also believed that the community and the government were responsible for protecting "a right to childhood." The two women probably had several conversations concerning children's welfare, but Wald remembers that she brought up the idea for a permanent federal children's bureau one morning in 1903 as she and Kelley shared breakfast. Wald argued that Kelley's suggestion for a government commission, while a positive step, was not a sufficient solution. Instead, only a bureau designated solely to collect and disseminate "scientific" information concerning *all* children, not just the poor or those in greatest need, could adequately promote child protection. Wald maintained, "if the Government can have a department to look after the Nation's farm crops, why can't it have a bureau to look after the Nation's child crop."[4] This call for a federal children's bureau can best be understood by considering the climate of reform opinion in the early twentieth century.

The Progressive Child Welfare Movement and the Children's Bureau Proposal

By the turn of the century there was an increasing awareness of the transformed structure and function of childhood and family life. According to Steven Mintz and Susan Kellogg, the idealized home "had become a private place, a shelter for higher redeeming values and a shelter from the temptations and corruptions of the outside world. . . . Marriages were . . . more based on romantic love, relations between husbands and wives had grown increasingly affectionate and egalitarian, children stayed at home longer than before, and parents devoted increased attention to the care and nurture of their offspring."[5] However, this popular image of family life was far from reality for many children. Writings by Progressive Era activists such as Homer Folks, Emma O. Lundberg, and John Spargo pointed out that an increasingly industrial and urban society placed special stress on families. Such critics argued that the social problems of "hunger, disease, vice, crime, and despair," so common to the nation's turn-of-the-century cities, hit children the hardest and would be perpetuated if the patterns of poverty were not broken among society's youngest members. In his influential 1890 condemnation of New York City's tenement districts, *How the Other Half Lives,* journalist Jacob Riis lamented that "the problem of the children [and] their very number . . . in these swarms" is enough to "make one stand aghast." Riis wrote that "nothing is now better understood than that in the rescue of children is the key to the problem of city poverty."[6]

Cultural changes and shifting attitudes about the nature of poverty and childhood also contributed to the growing emphasis on children as the heart of reform. As Robert H. Bremner and others have shown, although poor adults and children had always lived in the United States, there was a popular "discovery" of poverty in the years after the Civil War. Unemployment, low wages, discrimination, and crowded unhealthy living conditions in urban centers contributed to high infant mortality and child morbidity rates. Although national infant mortality rates were not gathered until 1915, it was clear by the turn of the century that urbanization threatened babies' lives. In Massachusetts, birth and death registration records kept since 1851 showed that infant mortality rates had actually risen in that state during the late nineteenth century. From 1851 to 1854 131.1 babies under one year of age died for every 1,000 live births. The death rates rose to 170.3 for the years 1870-74. Thereafter, the infant mortality rate fluctuated but remained 16.8 percent higher (153.2) from 1895 to 1899 than from 1851 to 1854.[7] To many it seemed inconsistent that death rates for society's most vulnerable members, children, were climbing as adult life expectancy rose.

Children's susceptibility to disease and exploitive labor practices was not new. Nonetheless, the modern argument that the United States was progressing at the expense of many of its youngest members fueled the growing child welfare movement. Wald, Kelley, and other reformers worked to make modern society more equitable. Felix Adler, a founding member and chair of the National Child Labor Committee (NCLC), probably the most visible child welfare interest group during the Progressive period, defined the motivations behind child labor reform as chiefly sympathetic, spiritual, and political: sympathetic because many individuals felt "pity for the abused child—pity and shame combined. It seemed intolerable" and spiritually bereft; and political because of "concern for the future of our democracy. In ten or fifteen years the children of today would be American citizens. On them would rest the responsibility for conducting the great experiment to which Lincoln referred in his Gettysburg speech." Adler asked how children with "weakened bodies, with minds uncultivated" would be able to "continue the economic prosperity of the country, or to conceive worthily of the public good." Child labor reformers argued that children who spent their hours working for wages instead of in school were inadequately prepared to be productive adults. In addition, children laboring for low wages in mines, glass factories, textile mills, canneries, at homework, and as street vendors seemed especially brutalized. As Adler suggested, altruism and social control were simultaneously a part of the growing child welfare movement. The Progressive Era arguments formulated in humanitarian and practical language became a lasting part of twentieth-century U.S. political and philanthropic rhetoric.[8]

A new emphasis by physicians, sociologists, and psychologists on childhood as a special period of life with specific needs also highlighted the predicament of many children in the United States. For example, in 1880 the American Medical Association organized a pediatric section, which became the foundation for the autonomous American Pediatric Society, organized in 1889. Illinois created the nation's first juvenile court in 1899.[9] G. Stanley Hall's influential two-volume work, *Adolescence: Its Psychology and Its Relations to Physiology, Anthropology, Sociology, Sex, Crime, Religion, and Education,* published in 1904, stimulated much public debate and scholarly investigation. A 1909 article in the *Pedagogical Seminary* celebrated this new attention to childhood by maintaining that despite the desperate situation of many young people there was a "New World for Children" illustrated by the trend that "there has come to American life within the past decade a change in the social attitude of mind toward children the like of which is not true of any other country or of any previous period."[10]

Interestingly the identification of childhood as a period of special need occurred at the same time that the proportion of young people in the total population diminished. In 1860 persons nineteen years of age and under constituted 52 percent of the U.S. population. By 1900, because of declining birth and death rates, that proportion fell to 45 percent. The result, argues Bremner, was that "as children became relatively less numerous, they became more visible and the particular needs of their condition were more easily recognized." Children were "economically worthless [but] emotionally priceless" and groups formed to advocate child protection. Private organizations such as the Massachusetts Society for the Prevention of Cruelty to Children (1878) and the NCLC (1904) lobbied municipal and state governments in what they believed to be the best interests of children.[11]

At the same time, a cultural glorification of motherhood, closely associated with the international "baby saving" movement, emerged in the United States. Public health reformers emphasized that access to physician-directed medical care coupled with the education of "modern" mothers in up-to-date child hygiene methods would reduce infant mortality rates. In 1908 New York City established the country's first division of child hygiene in its health department. The office directed educational and health care efforts at mothers and their children living in the city's working-class neighborhoods. As Wiebe maintains, "if humanitarian progressivism had a central theme, it was the child. . . . The child," he explains, "was the carrier of tomorrow's hope whose innocence and freedom made him singularly receptive to education in rational, humane behavior." Led by progressives, the "child rescue" work of the nineteenth century evolved into a more "secularized" and "scientific" approach.[12]

Concurrently, women began to gain influence in the political and professional arena. Sara Evans identifies this transformation as the new field of "domestic politics." In increasing numbers women attended college, worked outside of the home, and formed voluntary community service and reform associations. Such activities redefined the "proper role" for women both inside and outside of the home. Some occupations became "feminized" and women constituted the bulk of professional social workers and activists concerned with social welfare. These female advocates of "maternalist politics," contend Seth Koven and Sonya Michel, "envisioned a state in which women displayed motherly qualities and also played active roles as electors, policymakers, bureaucrats, and workers."[13] This circumstance further contributed to the attention placed on children and their families as the keystone of life in the United States.

Reformers involved in the female-dominated settlement house movement sat at the forefront of "maternalist politics." Settlements such as Wald's Henry Street and Jane Addams's Hull-House gained national attention and supplied direction for child welfare reform. Wald and Kelley used their association with Addams and the extensive network of social workers and child welfare reformers surrounding Hull-House to further their idea to establish a federal children's bureau.[14] They would need such connections to successfully promote their idea. Although rooted in earlier child welfare work, the call for a federal bureau for children differed from the programs sponsored by existing humane societies and child protection organizations. Reaching beyond the "child rescue" approach, the call for a federal children's bureau included the notion that the federal government, not just local communities, had a responsibility to promote the protection of children. Further, this responsibility included all children, not just the destitute or those dependent on their communities for support due to poverty or orphanage.

At first glance it might seem that a children's bureau arose with little effort. The proposal stood squarely within Progressive Era concerns. Wald and Kelley were situated at the heart of reform activism, and had close links with key policymakers. Furthermore, the idea mirrored the already existing women's protective labor legislation movement. Protective legislation and federal advocacy, argued supporters, gave women and children equal access to the "pursuit of happiness" through the recognition of their special needs in an increasingly modern society. Massachusetts and Connecticut had enacted the nation's first protective child labor legislation in 1842, limiting the working day for children under twelve to ten hours. In 1884 New York outlawed contract labor of children residing in reform schools. Alabama limited children under fourteen to an eight-hour workday in 1887, but the law was repealed in 1894. In 1893 Illinois passed a law prohibiting the employment of children under fourteen or for more than eight hours or at night. New York passed similar legislation in 1903 and required working children to register for certificates attesting to their age and good health. The New York law also prohibited children under fourteen from working during school hours. Penalties were light, twenty dollars for employing children without proper age certification, and poorly enforced,[15] but the historical precedent for child protection had been set. To Wald, Kelley, and like-minded reformers a federal children's bureau designed to gather and disseminate information about children seemed a logical step in the move to expand social welfare protection from the private sphere to the state.[16]

But, despite their membership in the settlement movement and the appeal of popular humanistic, scientific, and conservation arguments, Wald and Kelley knew that establishing a federal bureau for children would not be an easy task. New ideas were often difficult to implement. Anticipated opponents might contend that care for children was not a governmental function but a family one; others might insist that it was a state but not a federal concern; and some might maintain that existing government bureaus were already equipped to gather information on childhood. To counter such possible objections Kelley lamented that "if lobsters or young salmon become scarce or are in danger of perishing, the United States Fish Commission takes active steps in the matter. But infant mortality continues excessive, from generation to generation . . . yet not one organ of the national government is interested." She maintained that the Bureau of the Census or other government agencies with broadly defined mandates could not sufficiently provide professionals with the data and recommendations necessary to progress social work for children. In addition, according to Kelley, local officials responsible for decreasing infant mortality rates needed the information and criticism that only a federal agency designated to focus on "the whole child" could supply.[17]

Further complicating the issue, some local child welfare officials, such as John D. Lindsay, president of the New York Society for the Prevention of Cruelty to Children, protested that a federal bureau would deal "with matters exclusively of State concern, and under circumstances which would inevitably interfere with the work of our Societies." However, such protests from child welfare activists were rare. Apparently, most did not feel threatened by a federal bureau established only to collect, interpret, and distribute information concerning children.[18]

Kelley and Wald realized that they needed a powerful lobby and the support of President Theodore Roosevelt for the plan. Their settlement work and child labor reform experience had taught them that political success necessitated cooperation with men. Although not always harmonious, this strategy was particularly important in an era before women gained national suffrage or congressional membership. In addition, it sometimes brought attention to issues generally neglected by men.

In 1903 Kelley presented the children's bureau idea to Edward T. Devine, a Columbia University sociologist, child labor reform activist, general secretary for the New York Charity Organization, and founding editor of the influential *Charities* journal. Devine enthusiastically responded, saying that "the plan seems to me an excellent one . . . [and] is not the first step to get the plan and some evidence in need of it into print?" He proposed using *Charities* as a means to gain public support for the measure. In addition, Devine, a close political associate of Theodore Roosevelt from his days in New York, wired the president that Wald had an idea she wanted to discuss. Thanks to the introduction from his close friend, Roosevelt responded, "Bully, come down and tell me about it." Wald, accompanied by Devine, Jane Addams, and Mary McDowell (a former Hull-House resident and founder of the University of Chicago Settlement in 1894) visited the president in Washington on March 31, 1905, and gained his private endorsement for a federal children's bureau.[19]

Settlement workers and child welfare reformers felt that Roosevelt generally supported their efforts. Even though the president sometimes seemed uncomfortable with "radical" reformers, he liked those he believed to be "moderate." As he explained to Jane Addams in a 1906 letter, he admired her "eminent sanity, good-humor and judgment in pushing matters you have at heart. . . . I have such awful times with reformers of the hysterical and sensational stamp, and yet I so thoroughly believe in reform, that I fairly revel in dealing with anyone like you." Likewise, familiar with Lillian Wald from his days as New York City's police commissioner (1895-97), Roosevelt admired the Henry Street Settlement founder. In return for a report Wald sent him, President Roosevelt had given the Henry Street Settlement the unusual gift of a "pair of deer heads with locked antlers."[20] Wald might not have chosen such a gift, but it did effectively express Roosevelt's gratitude for her and her work. Although Roosevelt's reputation as a reformer was much stronger than his performance, he firmly supported the idea of a federal children's bureau.

Consistent with his "Square Deal" philosophy, Roosevelt included rhetoric supporting child labor laws, playgrounds, compulsory schooling, and juvenile courts in his annual message sent to Congress almost four months prior to the Wald-Addams-McDowell-Devine visit. On the issue of establishing a juvenile court in the District of Columbia he argued that "no Christian and civilized community can afford to show a happy-go-lucky lack of concern for the youth of to-day; for if so, the community will have to pay a terrible penalty of financial burden and social degradation in the tomorrow." He also urged that "there should be severe child labor and factory inspection laws." And consistent with the traditionalist nature of progressive reform, Roosevelt argued that "it is desirable that married women should not work in factories." This was true, insisted the president, because "the prime duty of the man is to work to be the breadwinner; the prime duty of the woman is to be a mother, the housewife."[21] To Roosevelt, a federal children's bureau would protect the family and the democratic rights of individualism and equal opportunity through regulation and public education. It would also act as a conservator of children as a natural resource, preserved for the future in much the same way as the regulation of wilderness and wildlife. In addition, some of Roosevelt's concern for children was rooted in eugenic ideas. He feared that the middle class was committing "race suicide" through a declining birthrate. His attitudes on Japanese in California reflect his nativist and racist sentiments. But whatever his motivations, Roosevelt's support was important to the success of a children's bureau plan and Devine lauded the president as "the most potent social force [for reform] in America."[22]

Armed with Roosevelt's endorsement, Wald, Kelley, and Devine took the proposal to fellow members of the recently formed NCLC. Established April 15, 1904, by uniting the New York and Alabama Child Labor Committees, the national organization worked to abolish child labor throughout the United States and acted as "a great moral force for the protection of children." Wald and Kelley were founding members of the New York committee. In addition, Kelley and Devine served on the newly created NCLC executive committee (renamed the board of trustees in 1905). Kelley and Devine urged the NCLC to accept advocacy of a federal children's bureau as the organization's primary legislative goal. With little persuasion board members enthusiastically accepted the idea.[23] At the group's second annual membership meeting, held in Washington in December, 1905, Wald, Kelley, Addams, and Samuel McCune Lindsay drafted and presented a bill calling for the establishment of a children's bureau in the Interior Department. Members of the NCLC gained President Roosevelt's approval of the drafted legislation in a private meeting. Devine predicted optimistically that Congress would surely pass the bill in the next session.[24]

The NCLC enlisted Senator Winthrop Murray Crane (R-Mass.) and Representative John J. Gardner (R-N.J.) to introduce identical bills in Congress on January 10 and May 9, 1906. But no action was taken on these measures in committee and each died. Since the bills faced little opposition, their failures seem due most likely to inertia. Politicians found it easy to stand in support of a bureau designed to promote child welfare, but more traditional government issues received Congress's primary attention.[25] At least in 1906, anticipated opposition from states' rights advocates did not materialize. An editorial in the *Providence Journal* stated that the bills should face little resistance because they limited the bureau to investigation and publicity. Furthermore, asked the editor, "may it not be that in this proposed union of national research and publicity with State autonomy many of the most trying of the great modern evils will be cured? If such should be the fortunate result, good laws would not mean curtailing in the slightest degree the liberty of the several States."[26]

Adding to the inertia, President Roosevelt failed to publicly advocate passage of the measure in any of his prolix messages to Congress. As several historians have shown, Roosevelt was cautious about publicly supporting social legislation. Consequently, as is often the fate of new ideas, lack of attention rather than open opposition contributed significantly to failure. Wald observed, although this is likely overstated, "not one dissenting voice has it been possible to discover."[27] At least dissenting voices would have made the issue controversial and brought public attention to the proposal.

Between 1906 and 1908 efforts to establish a federal children's bureau continued to achieve little progress.[28] Kelley's frustration level was so high that at one point she threatened to have the National Consumers' League take over from the NCLC as chief advocate of a federal children's bureau. Perhaps the NCLC's resources were poorly divided between its goals to secure child labor legislation in the states and that of establishing a federal children's bureau. Whatever the reason for the organization's ineffectiveness, the children's bureau plan continued to receive little attention in Congress or the press.

In the meantime, the National Consumers' League, the General Federation of Women's Clubs, the Daughters of the American Revolution, the National Congress of Mothers, and other women's organizations tried to publicize the proposal. Women seemed to be natural advocates for a children's bureau and many believed they held the primary responsibility for demanding one. Lindsay, then NCLC secretary, contended in a 1906 talk before a national meeting of the General Federation of Women's Clubs that a children's bureau was possible "only if you women want it earnestly enough to work for it." He compared the protection of children to the advancement of women. Child welfare, recognized as an acceptable women's political issue, drew increasing national attention and strengthened the perceived link between the interests of women and children. By late 1908, the idea gained momentum in the popular press and the NCLC again focused attention on the children's bureau proposal. On December 15, 1908, Herbert Parsons (R-N.Y.) introduced a new bill in the House and on January 11, 1909, Crane reintroduced his earlier proposal. The following February the National Congress of Mothers initiated a "better babies" campaign that further stimulated popular interest in child welfare and drew attention to the Parsons-Crane bills.[29]

The 1909 White House Conference on the Care of Dependent Children

The publication of a 1904 congressional report concerning the number and circumstance of institutionalized and dependent children in Washington, D.C., also focused attention on child welfare. In response, James E. West, a lawyer and secretary of the Washington-based National Child-Rescue League, urged President Roosevelt to call a White House conference to consider the problems of orphans and other dependent children throughout the United States.[30] West had intimate knowledge of the plight of dependent children. His father died before or shortly after his birth, and his mother, a seamstress, died of tuberculosis before his seventh birthday. West spent the balance of his childhood in a Washington, D.C., orphanage. As an adult, West advocated foster homes in place of institutions, catching President Roosevelt's attention. West's work on this issue in cooperation with Theodore Dreiser, editor of the *Delineator,* served as the impetus for the 1909 White House Conference.[31]

Roosevelt agreed to West's request for a White House conference as long as the organizers could insure the participation of "Catholics, Hebrews, and Protestants." West felt that this provision caused him some difficulty, but on December 22, 1908, he and eight other men prominent in the child welfare field sent a letter to the president formally requesting the conference. Their letter praised Roosevelt for his support of juvenile courts, but also argued that children "who make no trouble but are simply unfortunate . . . certainly deserve as much consideration and help as those who, by reason of some alleged delinquency, enforce the attention of the State and become objects of its care." They maintained that a conference focusing on the needs of the estimated 92,887 orphaned and abandoned children living in institutions and the 50,000 dependent children residing in foster homes would show that "the problem of the dependent child is acute; it is large; it is national [and] worthy of national considerations."[32] As he had promised, Roosevelt, in letters dated December 25, 1908, invited two hundred and sixteen individuals prominent in both private and public child welfare work to a White House Conference on the Care of Dependent Children to be held in Washington, D.C., on January 25 and 26, 1909.[33]

West explained that the "very purpose of this conference is to call the attention of the world to the fact that the dependent child has been neglected." By focusing on the plight of orphans and other needy children, the conference followed the patterns of nineteenth-century "child saving" or "child rescue." Nonetheless, the discussions and recommendations of those attending the meeting reveal a continuing shift away from nineteenth-century ideas. Instead, twentieth-century-style child welfare techniques emphasizing prevention, government regulation, aid to families so that children might stay within their own homes, and foster care as preferable to institutionalization prevail in the conference's official report. For example, attendees declared that poverty should not be considered indicative of immorality and maintained that children must be separated from "worthy" parents or placed in orphanages only as a last resort. The primary debate focused on placing dependent children in institutions or using state or local aid to enable them to remain in their own homes or in foster care. Further evidence of the shift from nineteenth-century child rescue concerns is clear in the other questions addressed by the conference: should state inspection and licensing of child-caring institutions be mandatory, should foster homes replace institutions where possible, should institutions where necessary be limited to cottage units not exceeding twenty-five children, how can dependency be eliminated, and should child placing extend across state lines?[34]

Roosevelt's condition requiring religious diversity also symbolized the shift from earlier approaches to child welfare advocacy. Attendees called for cooperation among the many "local child-caring agencies" and the establishment of "joint bureaus of information." They recommended that "agencies . . . be incorporated" and that states should "inspect the work of all agencies which care for dependent children." Nevertheless, despite the effort to diversify the conference's participants, little attention focused on black children or the needs of specific ethnic or religious groups. Booker T. Washington did address the meeting, but he downplayed the needs of dependent black children. He stated that there were about 31,000 black children living in institutions in the United States, but contended that "the number of dependents among my own race in America is relatively small as compared with the number of dependents among the white population." Washington argued, "this condition exists because . . . the negro, in some way, has inherited and has had trained into him the idea that he must take care of his own dependents." However, Washington failed to pointedly suggest to his white audience that the low number of black children in institutions might also be due to discrimination and racism rather than a lack of need.[35] But the shift from nineteenth-century policy was clearly a part of every other aspect of the meeting. This circumstance benefited children's bureau advocates. NCLC members Lillian Wald, Samuel McCune Lindsay, Edward Devine, and Owen R. Lovejoy championed the children's bureau idea in this friendly atmosphere.

Alluding to the pending Parsons-Crane bills, Wald urged that those present should "focus all of our attention . . . upon making the Government itself responsible for informing and giving education to all the people who are already interested in the children." Her remarks came in response to suggestions by some conference participants to create simultaneously a federal bureau and a private committee to collect and disseminate information concerning children. Some feared a government agency alone would be unable to utilize propaganda techniques, directly urge enactment of children's protective legislation, or, as one participant noted, "to accept voluntary assistance . . . [which] is a disability . . . the government bureau would have under the law."[36]

Homer Folks and James West aggressively promoted the idea to establish both a private committee and a federal bureau. One of the most highly respected leaders of the child welfare movement, Folks maintained that "the federal bureau would be strengthened . . . by the existence of a voluntary group of citizens, free to express their views on all subjects at all times." West cautioned bureau advocates that they encouraged opposition to their plan by suggesting that only a federal children's bureau encompassed "a scope large enough to do things which some of us want." He urged the proposal's supporters to keep in mind that "there is a clear distinction between what can be done by a bureau which is part of the United States Government and an organization which is supported by private funds and by private charity." Despite anticipated limitations, West concluded, "I heartily agree with Miss Wald, and all of the other good people who have been working for the children's bureau, and I was glad that this conference had the opportunity of indorsing [*sic*] the movement, and I will want to work for it."[37]

The disagreement between Wald and private committee advocates was a "friendly" split and in the end she agreed to the provision for a private committee. It is possible that men such as Folks and West, advocates who held high level positions in already existing and nationally recognized child welfare agencies, did not have the same degree of desire for a federal children's bureau as women such as Wald, Kelley, and Addams, whose influence came largely from outside of the established male-dominated child welfare associations. However, this circumstance should not diminish the acknowledgment of the support Folks and West gave the bureau idea. Moreover, inspired by their endorsement the conference passed a resolution stating that the "establishment of a federal children's bureau is desirable, and enactment of [the] pending bill [in Congress] is earnestly recommended." Attendees included this statement in a letter sent to President Roosevelt summarizing the meeting's conclusions. Conference records indicate unanimous support for the idea. The deck was stacked—it seems that organizers did not invite anyone who might object; for example, child welfare activists such as John Lindsay and other humane society members are conspicuously missing from invitation lists.[38]

According to Walter Trattner, the 1909 White House Conference on the Care of Dependent Children "had far reaching practical effects." Its recommendation that "home life is the highest and finest product of civilization . . . [and that] children should not be deprived of it except for urgent and compelling reasons" encouraged the development of adoption agencies, foster homes, and smaller "cottage"-style institutions for orphaned and neglected children. The group's endorsement of state regulation brought about higher standards of care, but also resulted in a wide disparity between the states. Conference resolutions also stimulated child welfare work encompassing the entire family rather than simply "rescue" of the needy child. A recognition of governmental responsibility for the welfare of children, at least at the state level, rested at the foundation of these changes.[39] But the conference's conclusions also assumed a narrowly defined "traditional" family as the ideal circumstance for all children, including those dependent on the state to protect their welfare. This middle-class ideal decreed that every child was entitled to a family consisting of a father who served as breadwinner and a mother who worked at home.

As intended, the meeting's resolutions and discussions brought national attention to the children's bureau legislation pending in Congress. Several conference participants remained in Washington to testify in behalf of the children's bureau plan before House and Senate committee hearings.[40] Alexander J. McKelway, NCLC assistant secretary for the southern states and chief Washington lobbyist for the organization, coordinated an impressive collection of children's bureau supporters. At the same time, women's groups and child welfare organizations deluged the committees with "hundreds of letters, petitions, and resolutions from all parts of the country . . . urging the establishment of [the] bureau."[41]

Formal support lent by S. N. D. North, director of the census; Charles P. Neill, commissioner of labor; and Elmer E. Brown, commissioner of education, further strengthened the proposal. These men denied that a children's bureau would duplicate programs undertaken by their own departments. Neill and Brown explained that child welfare research and data interpretation were beyond their bureaus' capabilities. Since their own departments already engaged in research and education work, Neill's and Brown's endorsements also undermined possible criticism that a federal children's bureau infringed on states' rights.[42] Other witnesses discounted possible objections related to economy in government or states' rights by specifically citing numerous areas where the federal government already acted as a collector of data and distributor of information. Florence Kelley rationalized that "if any stupid illiterate farmer up near Catskill in New York wants to know something about raising artichokes on his farm all he has to do is to get his son or the village school master to write to the Department of Agriculture, and he will be supplied with information not only about artichokes but about everything relating to agriculture in the most compendious way . . . but how different is the situation with regard to the children?" Edward Devine worked to quiet possible states' rights objections by assuring the committee that "all the Federal Government can do in such a field as this, we fully realize, is research and publicity." The Senate Committee on Education and Labor held similar hearings. A "view of the minority" written by Robert N. Page (D-N.C.) and Rufus Hardy (D-Tex.) for the House Committee report incorporated two opposition arguments anticipated by children's bureau supporters. Page and Hardy contended that "it is clear to us that already there exists in governmental departments for the gathering of all necessary information desired by the advocates of the bill . . . therefore the establishment of this bureau will mean a duplication of work." Furthermore, according to the legislators, the states were already engaged in child welfare work and "we believe this to be specifically the work of the various States and that the entrance of the National Government into this field would be followed by a loss of interest and cessation of the effort on the part of the States." But the majority did not accept such objections and both the Senate and House committees reported favorably on the respective bills.[43]

The 1909 Parsons-Crane bills stated that "there shall be established in the Department of the Interior a bureau to be known as the Children's Bureau . . . under the direction of a chief, to be appointed by the President, by and with the advice and consent of the Senate."

> That bureau shall investigate and report upon all matters pertaining to the welfare of children and child life, and shall especially investigate the questions of infant mortality, the birth rate, physical degeneracy, orphanage, juvenile delinquency and juvenile courts, desertion and illegitimacy, dangerous occupations, accidents and diseases of the working classes, employment, accidents affecting children . . . and such other facts as have a bearing on the health, efficiency, and training of children, and that the results of these investigations be published.[44]

Unlike Kelley's original plan, the 1909 proposal did not specifically identify illiteracy as a threat to children, apparently to avoid possible conflicts with the Bureau of Education. But otherwise, the 1909 Parsons-Crane bills echoed Kelley's original design. To implement the strategy, the Parsons-Crane bills provided for a staff of thirty-three with a total payroll of $49,820 and $2,000 for office space. The House committee reported that the total allotment of $51,820 was "a wise, just, and warranted expenditure" if compared to the amounts allocated for already existing federal bureaus using similar methodology in agricultural and conservation work. For example, the committee noted that approximately $4,500,000 was allocated to the Bureau of Animal Industry, $1,500,000 to the Bureau of Plant Industry, and $4,500,000 to the Forestry Service. Relying solely on McKelway's recommendations, no one testified in opposition to the children's bureau proposal during the House or Senate hearings.[45]

At last, on February 15, 1909, less than a month before leaving office, President Roosevelt sent a special message to Congress urging passage of the children's bureau proposal.

> Each of these children represents either a potential addition to the productive capacity and the enlightened citizenship of the nation, or, if allowed to suffer from neglect, a potential addition to the destructive forces of the community. The ranks of criminals and other enemies of society are recruited in an altogether undue proportion from children bereft of their natural homes and left without sufficient care.
>
> The interests of the nation are involved in the welfare of this army of children no less than in our great material affairs.[46]

Everything seemed to be in place. But despite Roosevelt's public endorsement, popular support, an absence of organized criticism during the hearings, and the favorable recommendations of the House and Senate committees, the 1909 children's bureau bills did not come up for a vote before Congress adjourned on March 4. Political manipulation behind the scenes by Humane Society leaders such as John Lindsay and a few southerners who opposed child labor reform stopped the bill from coming to a vote in either the House or Senate.[47] As in the past, lack of attention doomed the effort. Vocal support by some powerful congressmen might have overcome the limited reservations expressed by some at the time, but advocates never got the chance to speak in support of the bills.

Compromise and Success

A children's bureau proposal was reintroduced during the second session of the Sixty-first Congress and again reported favorably out of committee (H.R. 23259). Although essentially the same as its predecessors, the proposal included two exceptions. First, at the suggestion of the secretary of the interior and with the consent of the proposal's supporters, the planned children's bureau would be located in the Department of Commerce and Labor rather than the Interior. Second, to keep from appearing to be "class"-oriented legislation the new bill eliminated the direct reference to "the working classes." Some believed that this guaranteed the bureau could focus on the problems of all youth, thereby attracting support from rural as well as urban legislators. Again a new strategy seemed to work. The final committee report stated that "no one has appeared before us opposed to the bill [and the] field of child-helping service is handicapped for lack [of information] concerning the various problems of child life in the nation." Further, "the need for such a bureau has been proved, and . . . the scientific investigation and publication in popular form of the facts . . . will tend to the saving of human life and [the prevention of] suffering."[48] Although reported to the full Senate and successfully passed with little debate, the 1910 bill too was killed without a floor debate or vote in the House of Representatives. Perhaps, as Louis Covotsos contends, the failure was due to lack of support from President William Howard Taft, who instead wanted a Department of Health. However, as indicated in the NCLC minutes, members of the NCLC did not believe that Taft's support of a Department of Health eliminated his approval of a federal children's bureau. Taft had a cordial relationship with several members of the NCLC, even after the Republican party's split during the 1912 presidential election. In addition, some of the same reformers who advocated the creation of a children's bureau also supported the Department of Health proposal.[49]

Defeated again, children's bureau supporters did not give up. Senator William E. Borah (R-Idaho) introduced another children's bureau proposal on April 6, 1911, and Representative Henry A. Barnhart (R-Ind.) followed with an identical bill five days later.[50] This time the new head of the Bureau of Education, P. P. Claxton, hindered the proposal by suggesting that the new agency should be located in his bureau instead of the Department of Commerce and Labor. Alexander McKelway expressed disappointment at Claxton's remarks and felt that such power struggles only served to weaken the focus on the bill's passage. Lillian Wald apparently did not feel as strongly as McKelway about the issue and she quietly convinced Claxton to drop his suggestion. She explained that Claxton ultimately supported the idea of a children's bureau and wrote that "the advocates of the Bill have never had any preference in the matter, feeling that any re-adjustment of its permanent place in the Federal Government could easily be determined later."[51]

However benign such splits among supporters might have been, they encouraged a small group of critics to surface in Congress. Objections included the expected arguments about government economy and states' rights. Some also feared that a federal children's bureau might violate parental and individual rights. But supportive pressure from child welfare activists and women's organizations overrode such objections. A symbolic turning point occurred on January 31, 1912, when Senator Elihu Root (R-N.Y.) urged the bill's passage during a floor debate. Root may have been influenced by the fact that one of his constituents, Mrs. A. A. Anderson, sent him a personal note urging support for the bill and reminding the senator of his "promise to serve her in any way." It is likely that Anderson's request had special weight because she had contributed one million dollars to an institutional charity of personal interest to Root. As Lillian Wald speculated, "I am sure that must have sent Senator Root to the floor." When it appeared that the proposal would pass despite protests, Senator Charles A. Culberson (D-Tex.) successfully attached an amendment providing that "no official or agent or representative of said bureau shall, over the objection of the head of the family, enter any private family residence under this act." This addition helped put the children's bureau bill over the top and the legislation passed the Senate on January 31, 1912 (54-20).[52]

After the Senate's vote, Owen Lovejoy expressed the emotional relief felt by those intimately involved in the children's bureau fight. "I wept (& felt like an idiot!). . . . Now for the House! We *shall* get it but it will be a big fight." But Lovejoy's prediction was only partially correct. Only two months later, the House passed the bill on April 2 (177-17) and achieved final congressional action three days later. There was no big fight. Apparently once it received sufficient attention, the children's bureau proposal passed easily. The fact that 1912 was a hotly contested presidential election year when all major candidates identified themselves as progressives may have also contributed to the bill's final passage. As was noted earlier, although politicians found it easy to ignore the problems of children, it was difficult for them to actually vote against babies and children once a proposal reached the House and Senate floors. Public attention, political rhetoric, and a heightened Progressive Era reform crescendo finally joined to gain passage of the children's bureau proposal. President William Howard Taft signed the legislation into law on April 9, 1912 (Stat. L., 79) and presented the signature pen to NCLC lobbyist Alexander McKelway.[53]

The final act mandated that the Children's Bureau "investigate and report . . . upon all matters pertaining to the welfare of children and child life among all classes of our people." Thus, it closely followed the language of the first bill written by Kelley, Wald, Addams, and Lindsay in 1906. On the other hand, the act seemed vague when compared to the 1906 version listing ten specific aspects of child welfare. Kelley reported that she remembered "haggling with Wald" about the items to be included. But, on reflection, "at the time the itemized list seemed far more important than the generalized authorization to 'investigate everything appertaining to. . . .' How different experience has shown the case to be."[54] Indeed, in the years that followed, the Children's Bureau's vague mandate provided the flexibility needed to expand its efforts beyond research and dissemination in order to serve the "whole child." The drive to establish the bureau had provided child welfare activists with valuable political experience at the national level and mustered a powerful women's network that proved to be a formidable army of support for future Children's Bureau efforts.

Naming a Chief

Supporters now turned to the task of finding a Children's Bureau chief agreeable to all concerned. Taft asked the NCLC for advice, and the group responded by inviting Jane Addams and Lillian Wald to allow their names to be submitted as candidates. Both women immediately refused. It is not clear why they turned down the offer, but since neither woman ever accepted a government position, it might be safe to assume that even this job offered no appeal. NCLC executives then asked Samuel Lindsay, but he also turned down the opportunity with no written explanation.[55] It is interesting to note that the NCLC almost suggested a man as the Children's Bureau's first chief, despite the fact that women clearly claimed the agency as a department for which "a woman naturally fitted."[56] In addition, it is clear that Addams favored a woman as her first choice, but she did not limit the possibilities to females. Three days after the act's passage, Addams and businessman-philanthropist Julius Rosenwald sent a telegram to Wald urging her to nominate Julia C. Lathrop as the NCLC board's candidate. On the same day Addams wrote a personal letter to Wald suggesting, "It does seem a pity not to have a woman—and a very able one in this position, and so much of Miss Lathrop's experience has naturally prepared her for a place of this sort. . . . Let's try hard for a woman first. If that is impossible I feel that I have no distinct preference in regard to a man."[57]

Julia Clifford Lathrop was born on June 29, 1858, in Rockford, Illinois. She was the first of five children born to Sarah Adeline Potter and William Lathrop. Julia's father was a founding member of the Illinois Republican party and later served in the state legislature and as a representative to Congress. Lathrop's mother was the first valedictorian of Rockford Seminary (later renamed Rockford College) in

1854 and an enthusiastic women's suffrage advocate. Upon finishing high school, Julia attended Rockford Seminary for one year and then transferred to Vassar College, where she earned a degree in 1880. Over the next ten years Lathrop worked in her father's law office and made lucrative investments in two local manufacturing companies where she also worked as a secretary. In 1890 Julia moved to Chicago's Hull-House, where she remained with Rockford graduates Jane Addams and Ellen Gates Starr for the next twenty years. Firmly rooted in the settlement house movement, Julia worked as a county visiting agent, was appointed to the Illinois Board of Charities, traveled to Europe in order to observe institutions for the sick and dependent, became active in the juvenile court movement, was a founding member and trustee of the Illinois Immigrants Protective League, and helped Graham Taylor design and implement social work courses for the Chicago School of Civics and Philanthropy. After a trip around the world with her sister, Anna Lathrop Case, in 1911, Lathrop published a report on public schools in the Philippines which caught the attention of policymakers in Washington. As Addams maintained, Lathrop was qualified for the job of Children's Bureau chief, but few social workers outside of Illinois knew of her work.[58]

Wald gladly placed Lathrop's name before the NCLC board. Apparently the male members of the NCLC executive committee agreed that she was a well-suited candidate, because in an April 15 meeting with President Taft members of the NCLC reported Julia Lathrop as their first choice. Taft wrote Addams asking her if she believed Lathrop had "the special qualities, the special training, and the administrative ability which make her preeminently fitted for the building up of the Bureau on the right lines?" He then questioned Attorney General George Wickersham if any legal restrictions prohibited appointing a woman to the position. Wickersham assured Taft that there was "no limitation which would require the appointment of a man." So, on April 17, 1912, Taft named Lathrop Children's Bureau chief, making her the first woman to head a federal bureau. After Taft's announcement Lathrop telegraphed Wald, "I am still dazed by appointed [*sic*]. If Senate confirms I fly to consult you. Remember, hence forward I am your chief. Responsibility to the people who made the Bureau must now make me. I will try my best to make good." Her acceptance letter to Taft reveals worried anticipation: "No one can know as well as I do, my inability to accomplish all that this opportunity renders possible. I can only say that I shall do all that I can."[59]

Lathrop had not sought the appointment, and actually had little to do with the effort to establish the bureau, though she had supported the idea of a federal children's bureau and had attended the 1909 White House Conference on the Care of Dependent Children. But during the next three years Lathrop had little else to do with the fight for the agency.[60] Nonetheless, the *Survey* lauded her qualifications and praised her "political farsightedness." The editors agreed with the judgment of Addams and Rosenwald by quoting from their telegram urging Lathrop's nomination. "We cannot conceive of a more ideal appointment, considering executive ability, sympathy, deliberate, sane judgment combined with years of experience. In our opinion woman's ability could have no better demonstration that would result from her appointment."[61] Although practically unknown to most social workers and child welfare activists outside of Illinois, Julia Lathrop helped to define the role of women in public policy development. Children's Bureau supporters would have agreed with Linda Gordon's contention that "if the state were a family, it would be assumed that welfare is a woman's affair."[62] As the history of the effort to establish the bureau reveals, women played a significant part in formulating social welfare policy. But these women did not operate in a world separate from men. Male and female child welfare activists worked side by side to promote "a right to childhood." The child welfare movement provides an excellent example of Progressive Era ideology across gender lines. In the minds of Children's Bureau advocates, the effort to protect "a right to childhood" was now elevated from sentimentalized local charity work to national policy, studied by trained professionals, many of whom happened to be female, utilizing the most modern scientific techniques.

2

The Bureau Goes to Work, 1912-13

Under Julia Lathrop's direction the Children's Bureau's first efforts consisted of organizing and hiring a staff, selecting fields of work, and designing and implementing a program. Breaking new ground, the U.S. Children's Bureau was the first governmental agency in the world created solely to consider the problems of children.[1] Lathrop recognized that the act establishing the agency defined its general agenda, but initial budget and staff limitations made a broad-based program impossible. She would have to rely on volunteers as well as a small professional staff to accomplish even modest goals. In addition to this creative approach, Lathrop selected a noncontroversial issue, reducing infant mortality, as the agency's first project. The game plan advanced during the agency's first year hinged on protectionist legislation at the local and state level, "scientific" research, and reliance on the middle-class family ideal. Although she probably did not realize it at the time, this strategy set the pattern for federal children's health and social welfare policy for the next half-century.

In his presidential address at the National Conference of Charities and Correction (NCCC) 1912 meeting, Judge Julian Mack asserted that "the golden age of childhood [had] arrived." He urged those present to "rejoice in the establishment of the Children's Bureau and [the naming of] its first chief." To Mack, the agency's birth was "perhaps the most significant event for us during the past year . . . the final recognition by the federal government that it, too, has a duty towards the children of the nation, limited in its scope, it is true, but nevertheless of great importance." No doubt encouraged by such remarks, Julia Lathrop reported that she wanted the Children's Bureau to "be the nation's greatest aid in making effective the constantly richer terms in which the sense of justice toward all children is expressed." She hoped that "some day under someone [it would] become a great department."[2]

Indeed, the agency's potential seemed far-reaching. Although burdened by limited resources, it had a vast constituency. The 1910 census reported 29,499,136 persons fourteen and under (the years generally accepted at the time as those of childhood) or about 32

Table 1. Persons under Twenty Years of Age by Age Cohort Listed in 1910 Census

Age	Total in Age Cohort	Number of Girls	Number of Boys
15-19	9,063,603	4,536,321	4,527,282
10-14	9,107,140	4,505,387	4,601,753
5-9	9,760,632	4,836,509	4,924,123
Under 5	10,631,364	5,250,768	5,380,596
Total	38,562,739	19,128,985	19,433,754

Source: Statistics gathered from U.S. Children's Bureau, "Handbook of Federal Statistics of Children," part 1, Children's Bureau pub. no. 5 (Washington, D.C.: Government Printing Office, 1914), pp. 8-10, 12.

percent of the total U.S. population. Some child labor reformers and compulsory education advocates went even further by asserting that the need for protective legislation extended until at least age nineteen. Using this standard there were 38,562,739 children, approximately 42 percent of the total population (see table 1). For many child welfare reformers, the Children's Bureau Act opened the door to improving the lives of American children everywhere.

In the wider spectrum of public policy history, the 1912 Children's Bureau Act set the stage for a reversal of previous guidelines generally denying federal responsibility for social welfare. The 1819 Civilizing Act providing $10,000 to pay teachers assigned to Indian reservations was the first federal legislation specifically directed at children. However, besides land grants for schools and colleges (and occasionally for service institutions), veterans pensions, and epidemic research, for most of U.S. history the federal government had not been concerned with social welfare issues. Most Americans accepted existing policy that placed social welfare responsibility on the states and local communities. President Franklin Pierce had formalized this circumstance by vetoing a 1854 bill (advocated by Dorothea Dix) providing land grants to states for the construction and maintenance of mental hospitals. At the time Pierce argued that while he felt "deep sympathies . . . [for] the humane purposes sought to be accomplished by the bill . . . I cannot find any authority in the Constitution for making the Federal Government the great almoner of public charity throughout the States." In 1865, President Andrew Johnson vetoed a bill extending the life of the Freedmen's Bureau on similar grounds. Although Congress overrode this action, the Freedmen's Bureau was short-lived and woefully underfunded. The reform mood of the late nineteenth and early twentieth century again stimulated debate about government responsibility and social welfare.

Turn-of-the-century child labor reform efforts and the 1909 White House Conference on the Care of Dependent Children brought child welfare issues to the national stage. Nonetheless, as Julian Mack suggested, although limited to investigation and reporting, the Children's Bureau's establishment in 1912 served as the impetus for federal responsibility in child welfare.[3]

In fact, some Progressive Era reformers believed that the establishment of the Children's Bureau signaled a political atmosphere which might foster an expanding federal interest in many areas of social welfare policy. Few members of Congress had actually voted against the Children's Bureau bill (albeit 119 had not voted at all) and all four presidential candidates in 1912, Theodore Roosevelt, William Howard Taft, Woodrow Wilson, and Eugene V. Debs, supported the bureau. To many an acceptance of various Progressive social reforms looked imminent no matter which candidate was elected. "We will be able to get the things we want and at once make a start on our social and industrial program," one social worker wrote Lillian Wald. "The thought of it simply makes me feel like busting!"[4]

This confidence was also rooted in the belief of female suffrage advocates that women could serve as a powerful political influence for the common good. While not all child welfare reformers supported extending the vote to women, the Progressive Era produced a change in suffrage rationale, stressing "what enfranchised women could do for the government and their communities." Following this line of thought, suffrage advocates contended that women should have the vote in order to secure reforms because "municipal business . . . was large scale housekeeping." Such reasoning fueled women's participation in the child welfare movement. Julia Lathrop felt that women had "good reasons . . . to feel that they are concerned with the matters which the suffrage decides and that they can not in fairness to themselves, their husbands or their children, fail to take their share in the responsibility which can only be expressed by voting." What issue better fit the traditional female gender role than child welfare?[5]

Interestingly, at the same time antisuffragists argued that women's participation in politics threatened, rather than helped, children and their families. Furthermore, some maintained that the growing trend encouraging government responsibility for education, health care, and other children's issues weakened women's position in families by infringing upon family autonomy and women's traditional roles. But in general activist women, many of whom supported Lathrop and the Children's Bureau, dismissed such logic.[6]

Realizing this circumstance, the NCLC had effectively utilized the letter-writing skills and persuasive abilities of the General Federation of Women's Clubs, Daughters of the American Revolution, National Congress of Mothers, National Consumers' League, and other organizations dominated by middle-class white females to promote the Children's Bureau. Once the bureau was created, many such women applauded Taft's appointment of Julia Lathrop as its chief. The president's action seemed to symbolize a recognition of clubwomen's collective political influence and an acknowledgment of at least one woman's administrative competence. Lathrop's educational background, experience as a member of the Illinois State Board of Charities, work advocating the establishment of the Illinois Juvenile Court system, and position as a Vassar College trustee made her well qualified for the job. In an *American City* article, Lillian Wald described Lathrop as "the right woman in the right place." A resolution passed during the Daughters of the American Revolution's Twenty-first Congress "tendered a vote of thanks to the President of the United States in appreciation of his appointment of a woman to the position of Chief of the new Children's Bureau." Anna Garlin Spencer, president of the New York Women's Suffrage Association, wrote Taft expressing her group's "deep appreciation of your choice of a woman . . . as head of the newly created Children's Bureau. . . . The fitness of Miss Lathrop for the position is universally recognized and your progressive and wise use of competent womanhood in this connection marks your choice as exceptional and worthy of honour." Obviously some believed that Lathrop's gender as well as her administrative expertise suited her for the job. As another admirer wrote, "It is with a feeling of pride that not only I, but women generally, note a woman has been appointed . . . thus conferring a new honor upon women and at the same time placing the interests of the children in the hands of those who are by nature best fitted for this duty."[7] Indeed, Lathrop's appointment set a precedent followed until 1972, when Richard Nixon named Edward F. Zigler the first male U.S. Children's Bureau chief.[8] Child welfare was an area where stereotypical beliefs about women's innate qualities offered opportunities for female political power, even in an era before national female suffrage.

Appointed on April 17, 1912, Lathrop went to work almost immediately. Because the agency's operational funds would not be available until August 23, Lathrop traveled at her own expense gathering support and soliciting opinions from women's organizations, prominent child welfare reformers, and social workers. First, she consulted with Homer Folks, Lillian Wald, Edward Devine, and others in New

York concerning the direction the new bureau should pursue. She then moved on to Washington, D.C., for the swearing-in ceremony and a meeting with her new boss, Secretary of Commerce and Labor Charles Nagel. While in Washington Lathrop also visited Bureau of the Census statistician Cressy L. Wilbur. Although no account of this meeting has been located, the two most likely shared strategy ideas defining cooperative efforts between the two bureaus and possible personnel appointments. Following her trip to Washington, Lathrop traveled to Cleveland for the annual meeting of the NCCC and soon thereafter attended the biennial convention of the General Federation of Women's Clubs in San Francisco.[9] These excursions not only introduced the new chief to individuals unfamiliar with her but they also afforded Lathrop an opportunity to hear from many who had worked for the creation of the Children's Bureau and would continue to play an important role in its future.

In her address to the NCCC's June meeting, Lathrop argued that "the new bureau [had] an illimitable task," but there were "certain limitations which must be accepted at the outset."[10] The agency's appropriation of $25,640 was small when compared to that provided to other governmental research and reporting departments and also when contrasted with many nationally based private child welfare organizations. For example, the Department of Agriculture's Bureau of Animal Industry's budget and that of the NCLC each exceeded $1,000,000 annually.[11] Determined that financial obstacles should not hinder the bureau's beginnings, the new chief devised an ingenious strategy. First, in order to identify the Children's Bureau's constituency she planned to build on the statistical work already completed by the Bureau of the Census and other government agencies dealing with labor and education. In addition, Lathrop intended to supplement her staff by relying heavily on volunteers from the General Federation of Women's Clubs and other private organizations who could be enlisted to assist in the collection of new statistical and sociological research. Other federal agencies such as the Public Health Service (PHS) also relied on private organizations to enhance outreach and research capabilities, but the Children's Bureau's reliance on "lay" volunteer surpassed all such efforts. Women's associations had played a significant role in child welfare activism since before the American Civil War. Lathrop logically utilized this pool of dedicated reformers to expand the tiny bureau's capabilities. Optimistically she saw some advantages to the agency's small beginnings and maintained that "first work must necessarily be experimental and tentative."[12] In addition, her use of volunteers encouraged many women to feel that they had a personal stake in securing the new bureau's success. This tactic proved to be a valuable source of public support for the young agency and substantiated contemporaries' promotion of Lathrop's fine administrative skills. But it also illustrates her considerable political competence, a point often overlooked by her contemporaries as well as historians.

Lathrop's choice of infant mortality as the bureau's first subject of original investigation was also politically astute. As congressional debates concerning the agency's establishment had revealed, some individuals believed that the Children's Bureau might violate parental and states' rights as well as serve as a wasteful duplication of federal activities already undertaken by existing agencies. Sensitive to this criticism, Lathrop seized on infant mortality as the least controversial issue specified in the Children's Bureau's mandate. As a 1908 article published by the American Statistical Association argued, infant mortality rates (the number of babies under one year old who died per 1000 live births) revealed the general welfare "of the entire civilized world." The United States lagged far behind many other countries in the collection and analysis of such data. Only the state of Massachusetts uniformly required the registration of births and deaths necessary for the reliable computation of infant mortality rates. Eight other states (Connecticut, Maine, Michigan, New Hampshire, New Jersey, New York, Rhode Island, and Vermont) and the District of Columbia were part of the national death registration area. This made the estimation of infant mortality rates possible for these areas, but the lack of mandatory birth registration led officials to assume such estimates were less than accurate.[13]

Using Bureau of the Census estimates, Lathrop judged that of the 2,500,000 babies born in the United States each year at least 200,000 died before their first birthday. She deplored this "human waste," arguing that according to experts "one half of the deaths of these infants [were] preventable by known methods, already within the reach of [every] community."[14] She felt that the investigation of why and how babies died was a politically acceptable topic within the capabilities of the Children's Bureau's small staff and budget.

Furthermore, public interest in infant welfare already existed. Efforts to save babies' lives had their origins in the nineteenth-century public health movement and specifically in the establishment of urban milk stations and child health clinics. Dr. Abraham Jacobi, a founder of the American Pediatric Association, had opened the nation's first children's health clinic in New York City in 1862. Similar children's health centers in other cities followed. Many were connected with milk stations designed to distribute "certified" cow's milk, since contaminated milk, mainly in the nation's growing urban centers, led to the deaths of many children. At its worse during each year's hottest months, "Summer complaint" was an especially deadly disease among poor children. The need for regulation arose as commercial dairies proliferated. In 1892 Henry L. Coit, M.D., encouraged the Newark, New Jersey, doctors' medical association to establish a local Medical Milk Commission. In 1906 Cincinnati physicians established a similar milk commission which called for a national conference to be held on June 3, 1907, in Atlantic City. This meeting established the American Association of Medical Milk Commissions. According to the commission, certified milk had to be drawn from healthy cows, bottled immediately, its temperature maintained at not more than fifty degrees, and its bacterial content upon delivery not more than 10,000 per cubic centimeter. By 1908, pure milk stations operated in twenty-one American cities. But, despite this improvement in supply, the health problems caused by impure milk remained for many because certified milk cost approximately 60 percent more than substandard products. Some local reformers established community milk funds that distributed certified milk to poor children at lower or no cost. Women's organizations and pediatricians were the most significant contributors to this early effort to reduce infant and child mortality. But the American Medical Association (AMA) did not take the lead in this effort, perhaps, as James Burrows maintains, because the bulk of the AMA's public health work focused on the "white plague" (tuberculosis), the single greatest cause of death for most Americans. Whatever the reason for the AMA's disinterest, women became significant players in the development and implementation of infant mortality prevention programs.[15]

Furthering this role, in 1909 the National Congress of Mothers began to wage "better baby" campaigns designed to encourage good infant health care. That same year representatives from women's groups, physicians, social work professionals, and educators attended the AMA's first infant mortality conference held at Yale University. This meeting resulted in the creation of the American Association for the Study and Prevention of Infant Mortality (renamed the American Child Health Association in 1919). Also in 1909, the Metropolitan Life Insurance Company launched a campaign encouraging preventive infant health care for its policyholders.[16]

The PHS had recognized infant mortality as a serious problem as early as 1909 and conducted studies of the relationship between contaminated milk and infant mortality. But the PHS's work did not focus on the overall study of infant mortality; instead it centered on public sanitation and the elimination of contagious diseases such as tuberculosis and hookworm. Thus, despite the public attention brought to the issue by 1912, no branch of the federal government had done a comprehensive investigation of why babies died.[17] Lathrop grasped the opportunity for the Children's Bureau knowing that the work would not duplicate the efforts of any other federal agency. The fact that infant mortality was easily measurable and that simple preventive efforts could obtain relatively fast results also contributed to the subject's attractiveness. In addition, by embracing infant mortality as its first field of investigation the Children's Bureau avoided directly addressing the controversial topic of child labor. In May 1912, Homer Folks had advised Lathrop to chose a subject for the bureau's first area of investigation that would not closely identify the new agency with child labor reform: "As the NCLC was especially active in securing the establishment of the Children's Bureau . . . it would seem to me desirable to take special pains to obviate any possible criticism to the effect that the Federal Children's Bureau is simply an annex of the Child Labor Committee. I should incline, therefore, toward subordinating child labor for the first year or two, not making child labor the first or most important phase of its work."[18]

Folks suggested that infant mortality or "the mentally defective" might be good choices for the bureau's first subjects of original investigation. Understandably, Lathrop's experience on the Illinois Board of Charities and as a leading member of the Illinois Society for Mental Hygiene made her well acquainted with the problems of the mentally handicapped. But she also knew of the heated debates among "medical men" and "lay professionals" over strategies designed to improve the care and quality of life for mentally ill and handicapped individuals. Lathrop maintained that she did not "care to be drawn into either camp regarding the feeble-minded." With this in mind, infant mortality seemed to be a much safer subject, "fundamental to social welfare, [with] popular interest, and [serving] a real human need."[19]

Furthermore, although the prevention of infant deaths was closely tied with medical care and might be challenged as a duplication of PHS work, Lathrop argued that her agency would focus on the social and environmental aspects of the problem and therefore not poach on the territory of other federal departments. The chief told Congress that before deciding on the study of infant mortality as the bureau's primary project, she had "consulted very carefully with the Public Health Bureau [*sic*] . . . and with the Bureaus of Labor and the Census, and we all agreed . . . that no one else was undertaking it . . . and that it was within the province of the Children's Bureau."[20]

Naming a Staff and Organizing the Office

At the same time that Lathrop formulated the bureau's agenda, she began choosing its staff. The Children's Bureau Act provided for fifteen employees, but the full contingent was not reached until March 1913. A strong advocate of civil service, Lathrop had resigned in protest from the Illinois Board of Charities in 1901 because she felt the newly elected governor circumvented that organization's authority by making job appointments solely "for party ends." Lathrop believed that the success of the Children's Bureau rested on staffing it with experts capable beyond reproach. She illustrated her commitment to civil service in a somewhat testy letter to Lillian Wald:

> I may say that the whole crux of the matter seems to lie in . . . [the] good administration of the Civil Service. Nobody questions that children ought to have their chance in this world. But the question is whether that chance can be bestowed upon them by a Governmental agency without waste, fraud and pauperizing. . . . I take it, the sole question is whether we can get into public service, state or city or whatever, individuals of cultivation and sense and devotion. If we cannot, then it is not only goodby to government pensions, but it is, to speak lightly, goodby to the Republic. Please don't ever again say "however" to me when I am urging a steady responsible, skilled public service! I am still with only *slight* reservations! Yours with confidence and admiration . . .[21]

Lathrop patiently waited to make her staff selections until prospective employees qualified under the civil service system. Nagel assured Wald during the bureau's fourth week of operation that "so far every appointment has been made upon her [Lathrop's] suggestion. The same policy will be adopted in practically all cases." However, Nagel pointedly reminded Wald that he had ultimate authority. "There were perhaps two [positions] in which I have been a little disposed to insist upon my judgment. In other words, political influence will not interfere, but it is possible that my judgment may prevail." It is not clear whether Nagel was responding to accusations by Wald that he infringed upon Lathrop's freedom or if he was merely assuring her of his respect for Lathrop as Children's Bureau chief. Some reported that when she first arrived in Washington Lathrop "found the forces of practical politics all ready to gobble up the remaining fourteen positions in the Children's Bureau. Arrayed against her were not only the small fry, but the biggest fish in the political pool." But in the end Lathrop was pleased that she did not succumb to such political pressure and approved all appointments to her staff.[22]

Despite the fact that all bureau positions were not filled until more than six months after it began operation, as early as the 1912 NCCC meeting the new chief announced her choices for two important posts. Describing them as appointments "made not only under the Civil Service law governing promotions and transfers, but [also] under very searching requirements as to special fitness," Lathrop named Lewis Meriam as assistant chief and Ethelbert Stewart as chief statistician. Both men were distinguished civil servants who transferred to the new agency from the Bureau of the Census. Lathrop believed their selection guaranteed "that the statistical work of the Bureau will be sound, practical, and scientific."[23] Awareness of her own inexperience at the federal level might have influenced Lathrop to name men with such expertise. Furthermore, accepting her nomination to the Illinois Board of Charities in 1894, Lathrop had said that she did not believe women "solely because [they] were women . . . necessarily have any more light or inspiration . . . than men have" concerning social welfare issues. In fact, suggested Lathrop, "perhaps we need even more than men do to constantly guard against unfairness, and against the sentimentality to which, I think, women are peculiarly susceptible."[24] As Lathrop anticipated, Meriam's government experience proved useful in negotiating Washington's growing bureaucracy. Lathrop's choice of a man as assistant chief may have also been influenced by the fact that few women (or perhaps no women) had high level federal statistical and administrative experience because sexual discrimination had denied them such jobs. Meriam later noted that the Civil Service registry listed few women candidates for possible bureau positions. By March 1913, the bureau's staff, including Lathrop, consisted of three men (the third holding the position of messenger) and twelve women. This list included the job of librarian and translator, a civil service position limited to women candidates. The bureau's two field investigator openings were also limited to females because Lathrop and Meriam felt that the questioning of mothers concerning their reproductive history, family income, and other social circumstances was an area too sensitive for male investigators.[25]

Changes occurring in Washington made such practical considerations about the bureau's staff essential. The presidency changed hands from Taft to Woodrow Wilson and the Children's Bureau relocated to new headquarters. Lathrop also recognized that the incoming Democratic administration might replace her as chief. She hoped that at minimum her civil service appointments would remain unchanged.

> It has cost much effort and considerable ill-will to make these appointments, so that at the present time, while the staff is absolutely

> beyond fair criticism as far as I can judge, I think there is [little] doubt that there are certain disappointed applicants, who depended upon political friends rather than upon their records, who would be hostile. There are also, I am told, certain members of Congress who are hostile. . . . I think it is not unlikely that there will be an effort in very powerful Democratic quarters to secure my removal. Should such an effort be made, I should like, if it were possible, to feel that I might go frankly to the President and place at his disposal the actual facts concerning those appointments over which the struggle was sharpest.

The Children's Bureau chief asked her friend, Lillian Wald, to "please make clear [to Wilson] that *I* want nothing." Wald did have Wilson's ear and she assured Lathrop, "I will try to be your interpreter with the President-elect. . . . I will communicate with you after the visit with him, and let you know the symptoms, possibly the reaction!"[26]

Indeed, Lathrop's reappointment was in danger, as her position was coveted by many individuals, both male and female. A female Michigan Democrat urged that Lathrop be replaced because the Wilson administration "owes something to the Democratic Party and all things being equal, qualifications, etc., a woman of the Party should be given the post." In addition, she accused Lathrop of forgetting "the dignity of her position [by marching] in the parade to the Coliseum in Chicago to honor Theodore Roosevelt—*proof positive* that she is a *partisan*."[27] One member of Congress suggested the appointment of Lydia C. Wyckliffe, widow of Representative Robert G. Wyckliffe (D-La.) because "she is a mother and humanitarian." Widowed when her husband died after being hit by a train in Washington, D.C., Wyckliffe seems to have had few qualifications for the job except her Democratic party affiliation and motherhood. The suggestion that a mother was best qualified to "investigate and report" on child welfare later became an oft repeated criticism of the many childless female employees of the Children's Bureau. A more formidable threat, Katharine B. Davis, a penologist and social worker born in Buffalo, New York (1860), lobbied for the job by sending form letters to prominent businessmen and politicians asking for their endorsement. She also wrote Wilson arguing that her scientific training and work in the infant welfare movement qualified her for the job. She had headed the St. Mary's Street College Settlement in Philadelphia and had received a Ph.D. in political economy at the University of Chicago in 1900. At the time of her drive to win the position of Children's Bureau chief, Davis worked as superintendent of the Reformatory for Woman at Bedford Hills, New Jersey, a job she had held since 1901.[28]

At the same time, the army of clubwomen mobilized during the NCLC's efforts to establish the Children's Bureau resurfaced, this time urging Lathrop's retention. State branches of the General Federation of Women's Clubs, the Daughters of the American Revolution, and the National Congress of Mothers launched another letter-writing campaign. In a letter to Secretary of Labor William B. Wilson, the corresponding secretary of the General Federation of Women's Clubs expressed the concern many such women felt, "When I was in Washington during the inauguration, I heard that there was a possibility of Miss Lathrop meeting with opposition, because there were others that wanted the position and not because of any inefficiency on her part." As a loyal Democrat, she questioned the wisdom of replacing "Miss Lathrop, supported as she is by our Federation of a million women." Claiming to be "naturally much disturbed over the situation," she pleaded with Wilson, "I beg of you to consider our request to retain her."[29] Such sentiments successfully convinced President Wilson to keep Julia Lathrop as Children's Bureau chief. The Senate unanimously confirmed her reappointment.

The agency's transfer on March 4, 1913, to the newly created Department of Labor served as a second challenge faced by Lathrop and her staff.[30] The switch meant that the young bureau was placed under the authority of newly appointed administrators. The change, however, did not concern Lathrop. She believed that the move was done "although unexpectedly . . . neatly." Lillian Wald agreed, except for the possibility that the change might contain an "emphasis laid upon labor, from which I think the idea of the Children's Bureau has suffered somewhat. President Wilson warned us not to get it confused." Wald was referring to Wilson's acknowledgment of the Democratic party's "strong state's rights feeling . . . with regard to the Children's Bureau." On the subject of child labor, the president felt that "you would have to go much further than most interpretations of the Constitution would allow if you were to give to governmental [*sic*] general control over child labor throughout the country." Apparently the Children's Bureau's "purpose . . . to collect and coordinate information on the subject" did not contradict Wilson's stand on child labor. He even accepted an honorary membership in the NCLC, which at the time urged passage of state regulations concerning child labor. Lathrop understood Wald's caution. Most individuals who complained that a federal children's bureau violated states' rights also staunchly opposed child labor reform. Associating the Children's Bureau with labor might provide ammunition for the agency's critics. But criticisms had been few and Lathrop anticipated that "on the whole I am inclined to think [that the move is] not to the temporary or permanent disadvantage of the Bureau. If it does not work well, there is quite sure to come soon an opportunity to go into a partnership with some other great movement."[31]

Although Lathrop described the transfer as "neatly" accomplished, the move to the Department of Labor did initially hamper bureau work, but not for the reason Wald had anticipated. One bureau employee, Fannie Fisk, explained that although Secretary Wilson and his staff were "just as nice as they can be," they were inefficient because "they're not onto the tricks of their job. . . . they are *most* affable, and I think if we are seriously held up by them it is because they don't understand the situation." In addition, the staff "hung on the edge of our desks," for seven months, with boxes packed, in anticipation of the office's move, which finally took place in late October 1913. Fisk described the agency's new surroundings as "rather sad" with little sunlight. "But," she joked, "we have a fine view of ladies and gentlemen dressing at the windows in the [Willard] hotel and chambermaids shaking things." She also noted, "We are the only women in the building and the elevator man has learned to dump all the ladies at the fifth floor."[32] Fisk's last remark highlights the pioneering status of the bureau's largely female staff—not only because of their new role as federal social welfare advocates but also simply because they were there.

Lathrop's forced absence from Washington during part of 1913 likely contributed to the staff's difficult situation. Seriously ill with typhoid fever, she spent the entire month of October in bed at her sister's home in Rockford, Illinois. Anne Case frequently reported the boss's temperature to bureau employees. She also felt the need to deny that female weakness or inability to handle the responsibilities associated with heading a federal bureau had contributed to Lathrop's illness. On the contrary, "Miss Lathrop's illness is a straight case of infection called para-typhoid; . . . the Associated Press has announced the case as para-typhoid; not exhaustion due to overwork." The chief recovered in November and anxiously returned to Washington.

Putting the Proposals and Staff to Work

In a speech before the fortieth annual meeting of the NCCC in July 1913, Lewis Meriam described the three areas of child welfare work initiated during the Children's Bureau's first year. First, the agency established a child welfare library, headed by Laura A. Thompson, a "librarian-translator, a woman with excellent university training in economics, history, sociology, and the languages, with ten years' experience in the Library of Congress." Second, under Meriam's direction, the statistical staff began to correlate existing government data "showing how many children there are, and where they are, together with facts about their sex, race, nativity, parentage, and age." The agency intended this information to assist child welfare reformers in their local and national efforts to improve children's lives. The assistant chief hoped that the bureau would be able to produce five such volumes, each concentrating on a different aspect of child welfare including migration, school attendance and illiteracy, child labor, and "defective, dependent, and delinquent children." Third, the bureau began its "original investigative work" in the study of infant mortality and the advocacy of birth registration. Each aspect of the first year's program reflected Lathrop's intention to make the agency "a great national clearing house for information regarding the welfare of children."[33]

In accordance with this goal, Meriam maintained that there was "no single object . . . more immediately before us than to secure birth registration in every state in the Union."[34] The Children's Bureau defined birth registration (the issuing of birth certificates) as "the record in the public archives of the birth of children," necessary "to protect individual and property rights." Meriam explained the consequences of this definition. He held that a good registration system was "indispensible in the eradication of three great evils which affect the children of the country: . . . the reduction of infant mortality, the preservation of the child's right to education, and the abolishing of child labor." The Children's Bureau estimated that the U.S. infant mortality rate was even worse than had been anticipated. Of the 2,500,000 babies born each year, perhaps 300,000 or approximately one of every eight died before its first birthday. The agency also pointed out that unequal educational opportunities explained the 1910 census calculation that 5,516,163 children between five and under nine years of age were illiterate. And to the surprise of many, more than two-thirds of those children had been born in the United States.[35] Mandatory birth registration would help solve these problems by identifying newborns to public health officials, who could then promote good infant health care. In addition, birth certificates could be used as proof of age to enforce state compulsory school attendance and child labor laws.

Although the subject of birth registration included this broad child welfare agenda, Lathrop chose first to focus on obtaining an understanding of why and how babies died. An estimated infant mortality rate of approximately 132 deaths per 1000 live births placed the United States behind New Zealand (83), Norway (94), Ireland (99), Sweden (104), Australia (108), Bulgaria (120), and Scotland (123).[36]

The Children's Bureau argued that "the mere business of being a baby must be classified as an extra-hazardous occupation, since the perils which ever encompass human existence are never so bitterly emphasized as in the first year of life." Utilizing the limited data then available, the bureau estimated that death rates for children under one year of age were ten times higher than those of children one to four. Persons aged seventy-five to eighty-four had a better chance of seeing their next birthday than newborns (see table 2). Additionally, argued the bureau, "a necessary sequence to a high infant mortality rate is the larger number of children, who having weathered the storms of the first year, reach the haven of comparative safety of the other years of life in a battered, weakened, and crippled condition, such as forever handicaps them in becoming efficient social units." By requiring "adequate birth and death registration all over the country," the Children's Bureau predicted that "public health authorities can watch the infant mortality rate as the weatherman watches his barometer, and they can pick out the areas of social storm just as the weather man traces areas of ordinary storm." Reported births would be referred to local health departments which dispatched visiting nurses to instruct mothers in the proper care and feeding of their newborns. Such service, although not always welcome, was particularly effective in an era when most babies were delivered at home. Visiting nurses could also administer silver nitrate to babies' eyes, often threatened by gonorrheal infection. Although this preventive treatment had been available since 1881, in 1912 experts estimated that ophthalmia neonatorum (newborn blindness) was responsible for at least 25 percent of all child blindness.[37] Thus, the fight to reduce infant mortality involved improving social conditions and health care, as the Children's Bureau promoted the campaign for birth registration as the most important part in its effort to understand why and how babies died.

Lathrop's small staff and limited funds made a national study of infant mortality impractical. Even the investigation of infant deaths in a single city with a population over 100,000 went beyond the bureau's available resources. But with the cooperation of local authorities, an already existing birth and death registration program, and the volunteer efforts of local clubwomen, a thorough investigation of infant mortality in a town with a population between 50,000 and 100,000 seemed within the bureau's capabilities.

On January 15, 1913, four Children's Bureau "special" field agents —Emma Duke, Sophia Vogt, Emily Miladofsky, and Arthur V. Parsons—with a budget of $2,500 began an infant mortality investigation in Johnstown, Pennsylvania. The work took a total of 349 days and

Table 2. Estimated Death Rates by Age Cohort in 1910 Death Registration Area

Age	Rate per 1000 of Specified Age
Under 1 year	131.8[a]
1-4	14.0
Under 5	32.9[b]
5-9	3.1[b]
10-14	2.2[b]
15-24	4.5
25-34	6.5
35-44	9.0
45-54	13.7
55-64	26.2
65-74	55.6
75-84	122.2
85 and over	250.3

Sources: Compiled from U.S. Bureau of the Census, *Historical Statistics of the United States, Colonial Times to 1970, Bicentennial Edition, Part 1* (Washington, D.C.: Government Printing Office, 1976), p. 60; and George Mangold, *Problems of Child Welfare* (New York: Macmillan, 1922), p. 52.

a. George Mangold estimated the infant mortality rate as 112.9 in the 1911 U.S. death registration area. Bureau of the Census figures are quoted here.
b. 1911 estimates.

established a blueprint for future studies.[38] Lathrop explained that Johnstown was chosen because it was the "type of town in which there are no large factories employing women and because its size and its good birth registration permitted a study by a staff which the bureau could at first assign to this work." Results from the investigation could be combined with those of other "typical" communities and provide "in the course of a few years' study . . . a fairly adequate measure of the conditions under which American-born infants survive or perish, and of the possibilities of modifying these conditions by local action." As part of its strategy the bureau identified every child born in Johnstown during 1911 and if possible "scientifically" recorded the first year's history of each through interviews with the babies' mothers. The only male member of the Children's Bureau's contingent, Parsons took pictures of the town's environmental conditions and transferred the 1,763 Johnstown birth registrations to Children's Bureau schedules. The agency located another 168 babies through Serbian Church christening records or simply by accident.[39]

Children's Bureau agents, assisted by local female volunteers, successfully interviewed 1,551 mothers concerning the "family, social, industrial, and civic factors" pertaining to their baby's birth and in some cases death. Questions focused on income, ethnicity, the mother's maternal history and age, parentage, and environmental conditions. Agents recorded responses on standard forms supplied by the Children's Bureau. However, the interviews did not include two significant causes of infant mortality: venereal disease and alcoholism. Lathrop explained, "it is not fair or practicable to enter a home and ask questions regarding conditions which, if they exist, are considered personally humiliating."[40] Interpreters accompanied agents to non-English-speaking homes, contributing to the bureau's claim that the study was "entirely democratic." The only qualifying factor was that the birth of a baby had taken place in the household sometime during 1911, and the bureau was able to report "surprising co-operation of the people." This came as a surprise to some critics who claimed that such a study invaded family privacy. Instead, Meriam reported that "poor mothers whose infants had been born in 1912 or 1913 complained because we had to confine our activities to the 1911 babies." He added that "the richer mothers complained because we were not ready to furnish them with pamphlets on better ways of caring for the babies."[41] The histories of 380 infants born in Johnstown during 1911 were not included in the study because 220 had moved from the community, 149 could not be located, the mothers of 6 infants had died, three families could not be located at home after repeated calls, and two mothers refused to be interviewed.[42]

Not surprisingly, infant mortality rates were not so "democratic." The bureau calculated an infant mortality rate for the entire cohort at 134 deaths per 1,000 live births, slightly higher than the estimated national rate. But, the overall average did not reveal the great discrepancies existing within the town's socioeconomic and cultural structure. Children of native-born mothers had a much better chance of survival (104.3) than those of foreign-born women (171.3). The mother's literacy, age, length of recovery period, outside employment, marital status, and reproductive history also played significant roles in a newborn's chances for survival. Even amongst children of immigrant mothers, babies born to illiterate women died at a rate of 214 per 1,000 compared to 148 for those able to read. While literacy did not directly contribute to a baby's chances for survival, uneducated women most likely lived in the poorest households, under the most squalid conditions. Many of these women also reported long workdays, a history of multiple pregnancies, and the loss of numerous children.

One mother, age thirty, told of "11 pregnancies in 12 years; all live born; [but] 5 died [within their] first year." Perhaps most significantly, the Children's Bureau found that as family income levels fell the infant mortality rate rose. Babies whose fathers' earned the lowest wages were more than twice as likely to die as those in the most prosperous families. Infants of fathers earning under $625 annually had an infant mortality rate of 213.5 per 1,000, but babies whose fathers earned $900 or more died at a rate of 96.8. Children born to women without husbands (regardless of income) had infant mortality rates twice that of those whose mothers were married at the time of delivery—281.3 and 130.7 respectively.[43]

As Lathrop had told Congress, such findings focused on social conditions and neglected the medical causes of infant deaths. The Children's Bureau had no physician on its staff in 1913. With such emphasis on social and cultural aspects, the Johnstown results placed the heaviest responsibility for the prevention of infant deaths on mothers and their communities. It should also be noted that bureau standards identified "families" as those with fathers present. Overall infant mortality rates for Johnstown include thirty-four babies born to thirty-three unmarried mothers (one woman had twins), but excluded these women and their children from the income analysis. Clearly, the Children's Bureau wanted to encourage the establishment of families with a father as wage earner and mother as housewife. The Children's Bureau held employers and communities responsible for enabling families to engage in a middle-class lifestyle. Although the study found that "nearly one-fifth of the mothers did resort to some means of supplementing the earnings of their husbands," Duke argued that "when a mother of a young baby does not give her full time to her duties within the home but resorts to means of earning money, it generally indicates poverty." Lathrop concluded, "All this points toward the imperative need of ascertaining a standard of life for the American family, a standard which must rest upon such betterment of conditions of work and pay as will permit parents to safeguard infants within the household. . . . Clearly the law creating the Children's Bureau, framed by experts in child welfare, embodies the conviction that if the Government can 'investigate and report' upon infant mortality, the conscience and power of local communities can depended upon for necessary action."[44]

The Children's Bureau's instructional pamphlets, "Prenatal Care" and "Infant Care," were at the forefront of the agency's educational efforts. Written by Mary Mills West, "a mother of five," the pamphlets advocated social and health standards believed to offer babies the best chances for survival. Directed at mothers, they encouraged women to seek medical attention, eat properly, exercise moderately, and rest. In addition, the household income should permit a mother "to conserve her strength for her family." West instructed women to breast-feed, promote regular daily habits in their child, and keep the baby's surroundings spacious, clean, dry, and sunny. A nurse should be employed to assist the new mother for two to three weeks after delivery. Further, West judged that "tenements with dark rooms are not fit homes for children. Suburban homes, or those in the outskirts of cities or close to public parks, give to city children of the average family the best chance for proper growth and development."[45] While West surely believed such recommendations to be ideal, the bureau's own statistics showed that many parents could not provide such conditions. Mothers who worked outside of the home could not breast-feed and as the interviews in Johnstown had revealed, poverty and the heavy household responsibilities of some mothers made many of West's recommendations impractical.

But this fact did not seem to diminish the popularity of West's advice. Requests for the pamphlets far outpaced the bureau's ability to comply. Elizabeth Lowell Putnam, a member of the American Association for the Study and Prevention of Infant Mortality and founder of the Women's Municipal League of Boston's visiting nurse project, served as a reviewer of West's work. She praised the publications "as a remarkably clear and well balanced statement of all the circumstances, and I like to think what an era it will make—it makes me so proud of your bureau!"[46] Such praise underscored the bureau's rejection of nineteenth-century Social Darwinist attitudes accepting high infant death rates as inevitable.

The results of the bureau's first field investigation came as no surprise to infant mortality experts, but the endeavor was the first project of such magnitude. It was also the first time infant mortality rates had been calculated by combining birth and death records rather than simply counting the number of babies listed on death certificates in a given year. The Johnstown study substantiated many children's advocates' beliefs about the link between high infant mortality and poverty. It also revealed that good education and good sanitation could prevent many infant deaths. As a result the bureau encouraged communities to improve public sanitation and milk supplies. For example, in Johnstown city officials implemented improvements in the town's garbage disposal practices and sewer system, and tightened dairy inspection standards with the help of the Bureau of Animal Industry of the Department of Agriculture.[47] In general, the Children's Bureau's interest in infant mortality bolstered the national infant welfare movement, emphasized motherhood as an important job requiring training and full-time attention, and likely had the immediate effect of saving some children's lives.

The attention brought to the nation's high infant mortality rate further encouraged the growth of "Baby Saving" campaigns. The Children's Bureau's interest in reducing infant mortality built on such efforts. The most visible aspect of the infant welfare movement, the National Congress of Mothers' "well baby conferences" (first launched in 1909), provided free diagnostic evaluations conducted by health care professionals. The group expanded its efforts the following year by joining forces with the popular women's magazine, the *Delineator*. In 1912, the General Federation of Women's Clubs officially advocated education and community responsibility for sanitary conditions as an effective way to reduce infant deaths. Two Iowa clubwomen, Mary Watts and Margaret Clarke, M.D., took the lead in this effort by holding the nation's first "baby health contest" at the Iowa state fair in 1911. Arguing that competitive shows had greatly improved the quality of livestock, these women held that the same effect might result if the technique were applied to infants. Similarly, in 1913 the *Woman's Home Companion* initiated its own Better Baby Campaign and further popularized the idea by offering a prize of $100 and a gold cup to the top scoring rural and city babies at state fairs. Such contests, although highly commercialized and biased toward aesthetics over actual conditions of good health, helped to popularize the idea of preventive infant health care.[48]

In this atmosphere, Julia Lathrop sent letters to the mayors of 109 American cities with populations of 50,000 or more asking them to report on the "baby saving" work conducted by their municipal and state health departments. The results showed that, in general, "the principal impediment to efficient work in the health department of most cities is lack of adequate funds."[49] Immediate work in the area of infant mortality reduction necessitated cooperation in private and public efforts. Limited by its own resources and those of local health departments, the Children's Bureau continued to forge relationships with private child welfare organizations and women's clubs that vastly contributed to the agency's initial projects and future work. The General Federation of Women's Clubs was and would prove to be an especially reliable ally in the bureau's efforts to encourage birth registration and reduce infant mortality. Although grateful to its volunteer labor force and private contributors to its library, Meriam contended that this was "not the way the government should work. The United

States Government should not depend . . . on the kindness of private organizations."[50]

The AMA's Committee on Women's and Children's Welfare also cooperated with the Children's Bureau staff in its effort to reduce infant mortality by developing standards for "a successful baby saving campaign." With the advice of these physicians and the bureau's own experience in child welfare, the agency denounced the commercial and aesthetic aspects of baby contests and instead encouraged community-wide baby-saving campaigns emphasizing prenatal care, instruction of mothers in the benefits of breast-feeding, overall good infant health care, and public sanitation through attention to housing, sewage systems, and the eradication of flies. The bureau also advocated the development of dairy inspection, certified milk stations, infant health clinics, visiting nurse programs, and the formation of "Little Mothers' Leagues" where school-age girls could be taught modern methods of infant care. The Children's Bureau considered reaching these girls especially important because many were responsible for the care of their younger siblings and would likely eventually be mothers themselves. The agency incorporated its infant care recommendations in a child welfare demonstration included in the National Conservation Exposition held in Knoxville, Tennessee, in October and November 1913. Such demonstration exhibits became common practice throughout the country and generally replaced the more commercial and less "scientific" baby contest.[51]

Work undertaken by Lathrop and her staff from the bureau's founding until publication of its first annual report on January 17, 1914, illustrated the chief's commitment to the Progressive notion that information and education led to a better future for the nation's children. It also emphasized the importance of environment and other circumstances of social welfare as significant factors in the protection of children. But such advice most benefited middle-class families and offered little practical means for poor families or those that did not fit the bureau's ideal. The agency talked about the economic importance of local communities as well as fathers, but eliminating poverty was a much more difficult task than providing motherhood education.

By the time of its first annual report in January 1914, the Children's Bureau had issued a brief circular describing its establishment, a report advocating the importance of birth registration, and a bulletin on "baby saving campaigns." The agency had also published West's first pamphlet on prenatal care, begun work on her second concerning infant care, and issued Meriam's statistical handbook enumerating the age, gender, race nativity, parentage, and geographic distribution of children then living in the United States. But the chief and her staff were not content. In the first annual report, Lathrop proposed that the bureau's budget be increased to $164,640 and its staff expanded to seventy-six. She also wanted to organize five divisions within the agency—statistical, library, industrial, hygiene, and social service. The recommendation to add a hygiene division was especially significant because it brought the bureau into the field of children's health care, thereby uniting medicine and social work. But this path also opened the door to criticism claiming that the Children's Bureau trespassed on the PHS's jurisdiction.[52] Although Lathrop saw some advantages in the bureau's small beginnings, she had bigger plans for its future. As Lewis Meriam had complained in his 1913 speech to the NCCC: "The work of the first year has been, I must confess, a little disappointing in that it has brought us so quickly to the limits of our present appropriation and to the physical powers of fifteen persons; and in spite of the fact that we have been very modest in our program. . . . With a staff of fifteen persons and an appropriation, including our allowance for contingent expenses and printing, of less than $35,000, it was perfectly obvious that we could not attempt at the present time to cover any very considerable part of the [child welfare] field."[53] Using her political contacts and mobilizing her army of public support, Lathrop initiated an attack on Congress designed to expand the Children's Bureau's influence.

3

Expanding the Bureau through a Blueprint for Maternal and Child Health, 1914-20

In the agency's first annual report, Julia Lathrop described her plan to expand the Children's Bureau's work and influence. With the additional money, the chief intended to continue the agency's promotion of birth registration, conduct a series of infant mortality field studies in "typical communities," and produce numerous instructional pamphlets and analytical reports. More funding also meant that the bureau could expand its study of child labor laws, examine the topic of mothers' pensions, and investigate the circumstances of "dependent, defective, and delinquent" children. Bureau supporters argued that children were America's future and that their value went beyond economics. Indeed, as Viviana Zelizer has shown, by the second decade of the twentieth century, children's worth was increasingly based on sentimentality and the press promoted child welfare reform.

Amid the changing perception of children and the great attention afforded child welfare issues in the press, Lathrop and her supporters believed that the Children's Bureau had proven its value. The agency's Johnstown study, praised on both the national and local level, illustrated a high incidence of preventable infant mortality. The town's mothers and community leaders enthusiastically cooperated with the study and local interest in the project was so high that two Johnstown newspapers published the full Children's Bureau report. Baby-saving campaigns conducted throughout the United States refuted popular notions accepting the inevitability of high infant mortality rates. The outstanding cooperation of mothers and community leaders in the Johnstown study and the popularity of West's pamphlets showed that many American women wanted information about their children's health, believing that learning the most modern child care methods could save babies' lives. The Children's Bureau was strategically positioned to fill that need. In addition, Meriam's statistical handbook identified the agency's significant and disparate constituency. It seemed clear to Lathrop and her supporters that the young bureau should play a larger role in the growing effort to improve children's lives and health.[1]

However, despite the general popularity of its cause and early work, concerns over the Children's Bureau's constitutional legitimacy and economic efficiency persisted. In its April 2, 1914, report, the House Committee on Appropriations inexplicably denied Lathrop's request for increased funding.[2] The chief turned to her network of supporters for help.

Indeed, even before the House committee had released its report, Lathrop asked Lillian Wald to organize the kind of public pressure necessary to get additional funds for the Children's Bureau. Wald and Florence Kelley "put their heads together." On April 3, Wald described Lathrop's predicament to Jane Addams:

> She humorously says that they are down so flat that the only motion left is an upward one, but she and all of us believe that no publicity should be left undone that would draw attention to the problem. We have divided up tasks and assigned you the *Ladies Home Journal*. J.L. says you do not need facts, that you can work out any story in your head, but it is interesting that the same week that the Appropriation Committee allowed $25,000 for the Bureau below which even they could not go, according to the law, $165,000 was appropriated for free seeds and $400,000 for hog cholera. J.L. is taking the stand that she approves of $400,000 for hog cholera, as tending to higher standards of living, but it makes the $25,000 for the children impressive.[3]

Wald and Kelley devised a plan of action that centered on publicity and a national letter-writing campaign similar to the one undertaken during the fight to establish the bureau. They wired the NCLC's Owen R. Lovejoy that "immediate nation-wide protest [was] required. Urge your *[sic]* starting machinery. Only hope amendment from floor." Lovejoy mailed letters to each of the NCLC's over 4200 members and sent telegrams to the organization's twenty-five state child labor committees. He directed "each to write or telegraph their Representatives and Senators protesting against this report of the House Committee and . . . to use their influence to get the full appropriation." The NCLC's general secretary also contacted the General Federation of Women's Clubs and encouraged it to initiate an additional letter-writing campaign. Furthermore, Lovejoy instructed the NCLC's Washington lobbyist, Alexander McKelway, "to reach Congressmen [by] personal interviews" and to contact the American Federation of Labor.[4]

The federation responded through its journal in an editorial condemning the denial of increased funds for the Children's Bureau. Noting that the full appropriation asked for was less than the annual repair costs to two torpedo boats, "surely," suggested the *American*

Federationist, "we are too great and too just a nation to place so much higher value upon things pertaining to war and the taking of human life than we do upon protecting and developing the lives of the young." This "policy of parsimony will inevitably destroy child life. The future of the nation is wrapped up in the lives of the children."[5]

In another effort to gain public support, Lovejoy suggested that Lathrop give him a list of names of those who had requested copies of West's popular pamphlets. He argued that because the suggestion to protest the committee's action would come from the NCLC "no one would ever suspect that we wrote them because their name was on your list, and it would in no way involve the Children's Bureau." However, Lathrop believed this strategy unethical and scrawled "DECLINED" across the top of Lovejoy's letter.[6] Although designated as the nation's advocate for children, Lathrop believed that the bureau should not openly lobby in its own behalf. Instead, she self-righteously believed that an increase in the agency's funding would result from public pressure solicited by sources outside of the bureau. In her mind, cooperation between the Children's Bureau and private child welfare agencies did not include exchanging bureau mailing lists. Her action also suggests that although she valued the support and even the labor donated by members of private associations, Lathrop drew a sharp distinction between the acceptable boundaries of public and private child welfare work, a somewhat ironic belief because the Children's Bureau's initial survival depended upon the backing and labor provided by philanthropic groups. But, as Lathrop perhaps envisioned, over time an increased public role by government "professionals" in child protection overshadowed the influence of charity organizations in the development of public child welfare policy.[7]

Other Children's Bureau supporters also joined the effort to gain a larger appropriation for Lathrop's agency. Mary McDowell, then president of the National Federation of Settlements, got "the machinery of the settlements going." Juvenile court judges, members of the National Congress of Mothers, the YMCA, the Russell Sage Foundation, and the Archdiocese of Chicago also denounced the House committee's decision. Children's Bureau advocates deluged Congress with letters.[8]

Nevertheless, some members of Congress defended the committee's action and continued to object to any increase in the Children's Bureau's budget. As might be expected, such opponents were congressmen mainly from states that also resisted child labor regulation. They attempted to thwart the effort to increase the Children's Bureau's budget by focusing on economic efficiency and legal technicalities. For example, Representative Joseph T. Johnson (D-S.C.) contended that the wording of the original Children's Bureau Act forever limited the agency's annual appropriation to $25,640 and its staff to fifteen. But several other congressmen refuted this claim. Melville C. Kelly (R-Pa.) maintained that it was "inconceivable that Congress" intended for the Children's Bureau's budget and staff to be forever restricted to that set in the original act. In fact, he called the original appropriation "pitiful" and lamented that "the Children's Bureau is absolutely crippled" in the work it must do. After appealing to members' sentimentality, Kelly noted that the full appropriation was "less than 1 cent for every 12 children in this country under the age of 15 years. By this method of figuring a hog or cow or a bale of cotton is more valuable than a child." Such tactics worked. Members voted 64 to 42 to overrule Johnson's technical objection.[9]

Representative James William Good (R-Iowa) then introduced a compromise amendment increasing the Children's Bureau's appropriation by $50,000. After no action was taken on this amendment, Good replaced it with one approving Lathrop's entire request. In explanation Good praised the Children's Bureau's performance and argued that "the work in which Miss Lathrop is engaged is too great, the necessity of having her succeed is too important and the cause of sick infants . . . is too tremendous for this House to assume the responsibility of reducing her estimate." Johnson tried to stifle Good's proposal by attaching his own amendment specifying that Children's Bureau funds be limited to areas not under the jurisdiction of the PHS or Bureau of Education. This would have made any efforts by Lathrop's staff in children's health or infant mortality, as well as compulsory school laws, impossible. House members again defeated a Johnson proposal, this time 85 to 59.[10]

Although publicly avoiding any connection, Lathrop expertly exploited the influence of the "unofficial" child welfare lobby. After receiving a letter from the editor of the *New York Times* "inviting me to pour out my soul confidentially to him anytime," Lathrop wrote Kelley, I am "filled . . . with a sense of the power of yourself and L.D.W. and with much gratitude to you both." Indeed, by April 15 Lathrop felt confident that at least part of the additional appropriation she requested would pass. She wrote Lillian Wald, "I think publicity has turned the trick. The papers . . . show an unexpected lot of comment and we have wires and letters of inquiry, while a Senator's secretary accused the Bureau of having sent out a 'round-robin' because 'on the Hill' they had so many letters about it. We can proudly retort that we have not asked them for them; but . . . pen and persuasion are better than cannon. With affectionate appreciation in behalf of *Your Bureau*."[11]

The chief's prediction was correct. The House authorized her request on April 16, 1914, by a vote of 276 to 47.[12] But the skirmish had for the first time publicized opposition arguments concerning states' rights and economic efficiency. Earlier such accusations had remained within congressional committees. Now attention to opposition arguments stating that the Children's Bureau duplicated work that could be done by other federal agencies, especially the Bureau of Education and the PHS, intensified. Lathrop's supporters had successfully lobbied for her retention as chief and for a larger appropriation, but as the chief explained to Kelley, the political atmosphere in Washington had changed under the Wilson administration. "We may as well take notice that the Bureau of Education and the Public Health Service are endeavoring to destroy the Children's Bureau." Indeed, as the bureau's influence grew, it appeared that the potential for territorial disputes also expanded. Lathrop's concerns about the Bureau of Education never materialized, most likely because the Children's Bureau never embraced education as part of its responsibility. But the Wilson years marked the beginning of bitter "turf" struggles with the PHS. Noting that the PHS had just published a pamphlet entitled *Care of the Baby*, Lathrop complained that "it was most cheeky for the Public Health Service to publish this, more than a year after the creation of this Bureau and after [Surgeon General Rupert] Blue had assured me that they had no purpose to enter our field. Now to attack us and the strength of it is singularly like the attack of the Wolf on the Lamb for muddying the water." In addition, she cautioned that even though some members of Congress were not openly hostile to the bureau, many seemed "friendly to the Public Health Service." Nevertheless, Lathrop optimistically insisted, "this Lamb may grow into a real Bureau . . . ; instead of into a still sheep, if Fortune & the Public favor it."[13] It might be argued that Lathrop's concerns were more for "turf" than babies, but she felt that the Children's Bureau could only be successful if it served as the sole federal agency mandated to care for the "whole child."

Under Lathrop's leadership, the Children's Bureau's annual appropriation ranged from between $250,000 and $350,000 but constitutional and efficiency objections continued to plague its efforts. As Senator John D. Works (R-Calif.) explained during debates on the bureau's 1917 appropriation, "I voted against the bill establishing the Children's Bureau because, as I believed and understood, the very work that was expected to be done by the Children's Bureau was already being done by other departments and bureaus of the Government." Works further argued that "the Government of the United States ought in the first instance to keep itself within its own jurisdiction and not be doing the work that belongs to the States." Besides, Works complained, the federal government did not do enough for children living directly under its responsibility. By calling attention to the desperate situation of many children living in the District of Columbia, Works questioned what "the Children's Bureau or the Public Health Service [were doing] for these children?" He contradicted himself by stating, "I believe in doing something more than merely taking and publishing statistics, making an investigation, and dealing theoretically with these important questions."[14] However, Works offered no solutions and probably would have objected to larger federal expenditures for children. But his observations do point to the Children's Bureau's limited strategy of investigation and advocacy.

Arguments expressed by Works and those who agreed with him recognized the political propriety of supporting child welfare, but at the same time denied the necessity of a federal bureau for children. Bureau rhetoric was also somewhat ambiguous. Lathrop and her supporters stated that the practical child welfare work outlined by the Children's Bureau should be accomplished by a coalition of state welfare and health departments working with municipal agencies and charity organizations. However, unlike those who opposed the bureau on the grounds that it violated states' rights principles, Children's Bureau supporters believed that a only a federal body could "scientifically investigate" and recommend national standards for the "whole child." But anti-statism and concerns over growing federal bureaucracy limited the Children's Bureau's arsenal to investigation, instruction, and publicity throughout Lathrop's tenure and beyond.

Bigger and Better

With the bigger 1915 appropriation, Lathrop enlarged the bureau's staff from fifteen to seventy-six and instituted her proposed reorganization plan. She selected department heads and employees after each qualified under Civil Service. Arthur P. Perry, M.D., headed the Statistical Division; Laura A. Thompson remained as the bureau's librarian; Frank S. Drown was promoted to head of the Industrial Division; Grace L. Meigs, M.D., ran Child Hygiene; and Emma O. Lundberg supervised Social Service.[15]

This second wave of employees further points to Lathrop's commitment to acquiring a qualified staff including both men and women.

Arthur P. Perry had conducted a study of women and children workers in cotton textile mills for the Department of Labor. He replaced Ethelbert Stewart. Frank S. Drown, a 1903 Dartmouth College graduate, had extensive government work experience at the federal and state levels. The Children's Bureau's first staff physician, Grace L. Meigs, was graduated from Bryn Mawr College in 1903 and earned her medical degree from Rush Medical College at the University of Chicago in 1908. In 1902 Emma Octavia Lundberg published *Unto the Least of These,* a book urging a variety of children's reform efforts. Lundberg spent much of her childhood in Rockford, Illinois, the same hometown as Jane Addams and Julia Lathrop. She earned degrees from the University of Wisconsin and attended the New York School of Philanthropy and the Chicago School of Civics and Philanthropy. She also had government work experience at the federal and state levels.[16]

The Children's Bureau's new division heads cooperated with each other, but generally the industrial section focused on child labor, hygiene on child and maternal health, and social service on mothers' pensions, illegitimacy, and handicapped children or those without supporting parents. The Social Service Division also administered the bureau's infant mortality studies. The placement of the infant mortality studies reveals the bureau's continuing emphasis on social factors as the primary reasons for babies' deaths.[17]

Obviously the bureau did not hire exclusively women, but the agency's staff was overwhelmingly female at all levels. This resulted from several factors. First, college-educated and medically trained women professionals had few employment choices outside the public sector or service work in philanthropic agencies. Before the establishment of the Women's Bureau in 1920, the Children's Bureau offered some of the few employment opportunities for women professionals in the federal government. Furthermore, individuals who possessed the child welfare training and experience required by the Children's Bureau were generally part of the female-dominated settlement movement or educated at the newly developing institutes of social work education where female students predominated. Women physicians concentrated in the obstetric, pediatric, or family practice fields. Second, in an era glorifying motherhood, social work in general and the child welfare field in particular were socially acceptable occupations for women. An entry-level position with the Children's Bureau might lead to a better-paying job within the agency or elsewhere. At the same time, low salaries and cultural stigmas attached to social work discouraged most men from choosing it as a profession. But, for both men and women the Children's Bureau could be a step to a better job. A

1919 report shows that of twenty-two employees who left the bureau between 1912 and 1919, fifteen got higher paying positions (the new salaries of seven are unknown). Salary increases ranged from 10 percent to 212 percent. Other Children's Bureau employees advanced within the agency to higher paying jobs.[18] Third, Lathrop initiated hiring procedures that favored female applicants. In a memorandum to the Civil Service Bureau in July 1914, Lewis Meriam and statistical expert Helen L. Sumner explained that "after a careful examination of the [Civil Service] registers already available . . . it seems to us highly desireable, indeed essential to the highest efficiency of our work, that a special examination be given." Necessary, they argued, because "most of our agents must be women, and the number of women on the Special Agent register of the Bureau of Labor Statistics is not sufficient to fill our positions." As in the bureau's first infant mortality study conducted in Johnstown, Pennsylvania, Lathrop and her staff intended to continue to use women field agents for what they considered the sensitive job of interviewing mothers.[19]

In addition, even for positions open to male candidates, Meriam and Sumner explained that "an examination held for the Bureau of Labor Statistics does not bring out the kind of ability, education, and experience which we need in our work." They noted an example of "at least one man [who] did not take the Bureau of Labor Statistics' examination, because he is particularly interested in child labor and knew that [that agency] was no longer studying that question." Children's Bureau's topics were "subjects which have never before been studied by any Federal agency" and therefore necessitated the establishment of new qualifications and a completely new list of candidates.[20]

On July 22, 1914, Lathrop wrote Secretary of Labor Wilson that the Civil Service Commission listed only twenty women as certified for appointment as temporary special agents and research assistants. She asked Wilson to request that the commission make "a further certification of either males or females eligible for temporary appointment to the remaining positions." Lathrop counted Frank Drown as the only acceptable male candidate on the commission's roster. She argued that the other men certified by the commission "have done no child welfare work and we should hardly feel justified in making any appointments from this list." Therefore, she asked permission to make outside appointments until the remaining positions could be filled under Civil Service. Wilson forwarded the suggestion to John A. McIlhenny, president of the Civil Service Commission, who agreed to Lathrop's request.[21] In addition, McIlhenny approved the use of "nonassembled" examinations for some bureau openings. This procedure allowed applicants to mail letters of recommendation, along with statements describing their education, practical and theoretical experience (meaning child welfare work and/or completion of a thesis), and general fitness for the position. Each application received a numerical value score as specified by Lathrop and her staff. Over the next four years advertised annual salaries ranged from $1,200 for special agents and research assistants to $2,800 for sanitarian, a position requiring graduation from a "recognized" medical school and at least three years' specialization in hygiene and diseases of childhood or sanitary inspection work. The first round of Civil Service "examinations" took place in August 1914, from which "a sufficient number of eligibles [was] secured for some time to come." Several of these candidates qualified under the "nonassembled" examinations or transferred from other federal agencies. By November 20, 1918, the Children's Bureau had a staff of 196 (eighty-six in Washington, eighty-six in Chicago, eleven doing investigative fieldwork in child labor in several states, two in Alabama, six in Boston, and five in Providence, Rhode Island). In addition, the bureau paid seventy individuals a token annual salary of one dollar. Consistent with the bureau's employment pattern throughout its history, females overwhelmingly dominated the agency's staff, including the position of assistant chief after 1916. Contrary to popular beliefs about women's employment, a questionnaire distributed among Children's Bureau employees in 1918 showed that many of these women were the sole support for their families or aged parents.[22]

Male applicants were a distinct minority. For example, Children's Bureau records show that men constituted only seventeen of the seventy-six applicants for agency openings in 1918. Of twenty-six applicants for the position of Expert in the Prevention of Infant Mortality, only six were male, as Expert in Child Welfare only seven, and men made up only four of the nine applicants for the position of director of the Child Labor Division. The bureau reported that "in none of these did a man score the top score." The dearth of male applicants can be partially attributed to bureau qualification requirements and prejudices favoring female candidates, but is probably more directly due to the fact that women officials relied on the largely female social work network to fill agency openings.[23]

Building on their settlement experience and social work training, Lathrop and her mostly female staff designed and implemented a blueprint of preventive maternal, infant, and child health that united social and medical reform efforts. As noted earlier, this had three important consequences. It expanded the bureau's jurisdiction by uniting social welfare and public health strategies, suggested a permanent role for the Children's Bureau in the nation's growing social welfare policy, and inadvertently fueled criticism that the Children's Bureau encroached on areas also covered by the PHS.

Perfecting a Blueprint for Children's Health

From 1914 to 1920 the Children's Bureau expanded its birth registration campaign and completed nine more studies analyzing the causes of infant mortality. Lathrop and her staff considered life and health "the first right of the child."[24] The huge volunteer labor force, composed mainly of members of the General Federation of Women's Clubs, National Consumers' League, Congress of Mothers, Daughters of the American Revolution, and various other women's associations, continued to play a primary role in the bureau's birth registration effort. These women conducted door-to-door registration campaigns throughout the country and pressured state legislatures to pass compulsory birth registration laws. By 1915 the Children's Bureau reported that over 3,000 women volunteers had helped with the effort.[25] That same year, the U.S. Bureau of the Census established a national birth registration area consisting of ten states and the District of Columbia, each of which had implemented programs providing for the registration of at least 90 percent of all babies born within its boundaries. By 1921, the campaign had succeeded in drawing twenty-seven states into the federally recognized area.[26]

The bureau also made progress in its effort to understand "why babies died." Following the pilot field study completed in Johnstown, Pennsylvania ("a steel city"), the Children's Bureau undertook similar projects in other "typical" American cities: Manchester, New Hampshire, and New Bedford, Massachusetts, "two textile cities"; Waterbury, Connecticut, a brass manufacturing center; Saginaw, Michigan, a town with "no one predominating industry"; Akron, Ohio, "a rubber manufacturing city"; Gary, Indiana, "a war industries town"; and Baltimore, Maryland, "a large cosmopolitan city." Seven of these projects took place in moderately sized urban areas with substantial immigrant populations. The single exception was Saginaw, which, while industrial, did not have a large immigrant population. The bureau also published an infant mortality study of Montclair, New Jersey, "a residential suburb," conducted by local officials with assistance from the Children's Bureau, and one completed in Pittsburgh, Pennsylvania. Only the bureau's Baltimore study discussed the impact of race. The infant mortality rate for blacks, 219 per 1,000, was over twice that of the city's whites at 104 per 1,000.[27]

As noted in its first study, the Children's Bureau continued to find a correlation between fathers' earnings and infant mortality rates. Eighty-eight percent of the fathers in the agency's studies earned less than $1,250 per year and 27 percent less than $550. As income doubled the infant mortality rate dropped by more than half. Income alone did not save babies, but earnings were important for what they could buy. Babies whose parents rented their homes died at twice the rate of those living in homes owned by their parents. Using the presence of a bathtub as an index of "a good home . . . suitable from a sanitary standpoint, and a fairly comfortable income," the bureau found an infant mortality rate of 72.6 per 1,000 in such residences. But in those without the appliance babies died at more than twice that rate, 164.8 per 1,000. The agency also concluded that a father's low earnings contributed to high infant mortality rates by driving mothers into the work force. The bureau found that only 9.5 percent of women whose husbands made more than $1,250 a year worked for wages, compared with 65.7 percent of those whose husbands made less than $550 annually. Infants of mothers working outside the home died at a rate of 312.9 per 1,000 compared to 122.0 for that of babies whose mothers had "no employment save that of caring for their households."[28]

Understandably, employed mothers who spent long periods of time away from their infants found breast-feeding difficult if not impossible. But breast-fed babies had a much higher survival rate than those fed "artificially." As discussed previously, in an era before uniformly enforced milk pasteurization, bottle-fed babies in poor families often received inferior milk products or milk exposed to bacterial infection. Germany, England, and France used maternity insurance payments (benefits) as one method to encourage mothers of young children to remain at home. In the United States the American Association for Labor Legislation proposed a national health insurance act in 1917 that included a plan to provide weekly cash compensation for expectant women, payable for eight weeks and "equal to the regular sick benefit of the insured." The purpose of maternity insurance, according to Julia Lathrop, was "of course . . . to protect the low income section of the population." But she believed that the maternity benefit systems in Germany, England, and France were inadequate and ineffective. While open to a study of the issue, Lathrop stated that "no system of health insurance is complete which ignores maternity insurance, yet apparently no system of health insurance can independently furnish adequate funds and equipment." Faced with opposition from the private insurance industry and the AMA, and only lukewarm support from the Children's Bureau (and the general infant welfare movement), the proposal for national maternity benefits died.[29] The bureau's inflexible policy assumed that no woman with a baby would want to work outside of the home. This attitude left mothers who could not afford to stay at home in a no-win situation. According to the Children's Bureau's own studies, poverty was a significant factor contributing to high infant mortality rates, but mothers who could not afford to stay at home risked their babies' lives and good health.

Aside from this obvious lack of inventive solutions to the immediate needs of many families, the Children's Bureau's urban infant mortality studies encouraged a more sympathetic view of the poor and led to a better understanding of the reasons why babies died. Julia Lathrop summarized much of the Children's Bureau's findings in an address before the American Public Health Association's 1918 meeting in Chicago. She argued that high infant mortality among the urban poor was not a result of "hopelessly stupid, or incorrigibly lazy" parents. Instead, "poverty takes away the defenses by which the effects of ignorance may be evaded." She called for a "general recognition throughout the country that a decent income, self-respectingly earned by the father is the beginning of wisdom, the only fair division of labor between the father and the mother of young children, and the strongest safeguard against a high infant mortality rate." Lathrop asked, "Which is the more safe and sane conclusion! That 88 per cent of all these fathers were incorrigibly indolent or below normal mentally, or that sound public economy demands an irreducible minimum living standard to be sustained by a minimum wage and other such expedients as may be developed in a determined effort to give every child a fair chance?"[30] The fight to save babies' lives included the needs of the "whole child" and its family.

Accordingly, "the cure for poverty . . . was simply correction of unjust and degrading conditions of work and living," including protectionist legislative action to insure minimum wages and hours, basic housing standards, child labor regulation, unemployment compensation, accident and old age security insurance, recreation facilities, immigration restrictions, and public health improvements. But significantly, maternity benefits, which might have offered a more immediate solution, were absent from this menu of reform. Julia Lathrop's remarks seem to support Richard Meckel's contention that even though reformers viewed poverty as a reason why many mothers of young children worked for wages, American policy makers in part failed to endorse maternity insurance because it "meant accepting the necessity of married women working." This seemed inappropriate to reformers "committed to an ideal vision of the family as small and nurturing. . . . most middle-class social workers and social scientists saw employment of any family member but the father as deviant." Lathrop and her staff concluded that each of the bureau's infant mortality investigations reemphasized "the importance of family income and better domestic sanitation." They also indicated the need to teach "mothers how to take care of babies." The latter seemed to be more attainable in the immediate future.[31]

As reflected in the Johnstown study, the bureau's early infant mortality projects hinged on the belief that urban immigrant communities had the greatest problems. Children's Bureau data substantiated this assumption and the theory predominated in the general infant welfare movement. Many reformers believed that infant mortality would be reduced if immigrant mothers could be "Americanized" to accept middle-class standards of hygiene and infant care. Although many viewed African American mothers with even more skepticism than the new immigrants, the attention of the general infant welfare movement focused on the high infant mortality rates in urban immigrant neighborhoods. This circumstantial prejudice practically ignored the appallingly high rates among African American babies. In addition, blacks continued to live mostly in the rural South, where the infant welfare movement had little effect. Although they received minimal support or recognition for their work, Dorothy Salem has demonstrated that African American clubwomen launched their own public health campaigns during the second decade of the twentieth century in a number of cities, including Atlanta, New Orleans, and Richmond, Virginia. As noted, the Children's Bureau's Baltimore study is an exception to this general trend. In addition, the Children's Bureau's early studies reflect a regional bias and no study took place in areas with large Asian or Hispanic populations.[32] Perhaps it is too much to expect that Lathrop and her staff could implement a sweeping social and economic reform policy. The cultural and political hurdles were too high. Increasingly over time, the Children's Bureau diminished the importance of poverty eradication and instead embraced "Americanizing" standards for motherhood education as the best means to saving babies' lives. This formula for change augmented programs placing the primary responsibility on mothers and lessened community and/or business responsibility. In other words, despite the bureau's early recognition of poverty as the primary contributing factor to high infant mortality rates, after 1914 the Children's Bureau primarily implemented and advocated efforts directed at individual mothers rather than a broad program also addressing society's responsibility toward children.

Despite its weaknesses, the bureau's post-1914 approach, for the first time, recognized good prenatal care as a sure means of saving babies' lives. The general infant welfare movement had centered its focus on child hygiene, a safe milk supply, and a condemnation of poverty. The Children's Bureau's studies, the most comprehensive investigations into the causes of infant mortality undertaken to date, revealed a high correlation between good prenatal care and the survival of babies. According to the bureau's urban studies, over 36 percent of all the infants who died perished from conditions which were present very early in infancy and could therefore be attributed to poor prenatal care. One-fifth of the infant deaths reported for the U.S. death registration area in 1916 occurred less than forty-eight hours after birth. Further, more than two-fifths of the babies who died that year did so within their first month of life. The primary causes for many of these deaths—"premature birth, congenital debility, injuries at birth, malformations, and syphilis"—pointed to inadequate prenatal care as "the paramount [factor] in the vigor and resistance of . . . children." The Children's Bureau argued that its infant mortality studies provided "evidence . . . of the great numbers of mothers who come to childbirth without any advice or trained care during pregnancy and, too often, without care at confinement."[33]

The bureau's studies also suggested a "close connection between infant mortality and ill-health and death of mothers." As Lathrop told a meeting of the General Federation of Women's Clubs in June 1916, "maternal mortality is a part of the problem of infant mortality." Complications associated with pregnancy ranked second only to tuberculosis as the primary cause of death among women between the ages of fifteen and forty-four. The U.S. Census Bureau estimated that over 15,000 women died from complications associated with pregnancy in 1913. A Children's Bureau study published in 1917 reported that the United States' 1916 maternal mortality rate of 62 per 10,000 live births ranked fourteenth among sixteen "civilized" nations (see table 3). African American women died at a rate of 118 per 10,000 live births and white women had a maternal mortality rate of 60. The U.S. total death rate (number of deaths per 1,000 population) in 1900 was 17.2, but had fallen to 14.7 by 1910 and to 13.0 by 1920, translating to a 24 percent reduction since 1900. The combined rate of 118 for African American women and 60 for white women should likely be higher than 62 (approximately 65). This discrepancy is probably due to the incomplete registration area existing in 1916.[34]

Table 3. Maternal Mortality Rates in the United States and Certain Foreign Countries, 1915-21

	Maternal Deaths per 10,000 Live Births						
Country	1915	1916	1917	1918	1919	1920	1921
Australia	43	53	56	47	47	50	47
Belgium	—	—	—	—	72	60	57
Canada	—	—	—	—	—	—	51
Chile	66	73	72	82	88	75	79
Czechoslovakia	—	—	—	—	37	40	37
Denmark	—	—	—	—	—	—	16
England and Wales	42	41	39	38	44	43	39
Finland	—	36	38	44	40	36	33
Greece	—	—	—	—	—	—	73
Hungary	—	42	40	52	29	32	29
Irish Free State[a]	53	57	49	48	47	49	50
Italy	22	27	30	37	29	28	26
Japan	36	35	35	38	33	35	36
Netherlands	—	—	—	29	33	24	23
New Zealand	47	59	60	52	51	65	51
Northern Ireland	56	50	51	47	46	69	52
Norway	27	28	30	30	34	26	22
Salvador	—	—	—	—	—	57	57
Scotland	61	57	59	70	62	62	64
Sweden	29	27	25	26	32	27	27
Switzerland	—	54	56	51	57	56	55
United States	61	62	66	92	74	80	68
Uruguay	22	29	32	30	23	34	33

Source: Department of Labor, Children's Bureau, "Trend of Maternal Mortality in the United States and Certain Foreign Countries," RG 47 DLP, box 23, file "Sec. for Children, Lenroot and Eliot."

a. Identification as found in the Children's Bureau report.

Census data also suggested that women living in rural areas had a higher maternal mortality rate than those in urban settings. For the entire population, males had a higher death rate than females of comparable ages. But, in rural areas, women between the ages of twenty-five and thirty actually died at a higher rate than males of that cohort. High maternal mortality rates due primarily to inadequate prenatal and obstetrical care seemed to be the only explanation.[35] The Children's Bureau's effort to improve women's health focused solely on their role as mothers. Nevertheless, no other federal agency was interested in maternal mortality for any reason.

Such findings made it clear by 1916 that the problems of maternal mortality, infant death, and poor child health were most likely not restricted to urban communities. Between 1916 and 1921 the Children's Bureau also conducted maternal and infant mortality studies in rural counties in six states: Kansas, North Carolina, Montana, Wisconsin, Mississippi, and Georgia.[36] Generally, the bureau's suspicions were correct. These areas had lower infant mortality rates but much higher incidents of maternal mortality.[37] In addition, infant deaths within the first month of life compared to those in cities, therefore indicating insufficient prenatal care and medical services at the time of delivery in most rural areas. Poor roads, a lack of doctors, and little money for medical fees contributed to the problem in many rural districts. Midwives offered some help, but many were poorly trained. Housing and sanitary conditions often rivaled those in the poorest urban areas. Thousands of letters sent to the bureau from women living in remote sections of the country supported the agency's conclusions.

For many of these women the bureau's *Infant Care, Prenatal Care* and the later *The Child from 2-6* (published in 1915) were the sole source of "scientific" information concerning pregnancy and children's health care. As one woman from Burntfork, Wyoming, explained in a letter to Julia Lathrop,

> I should very much like all the Publications on the Care of myself, who am now pregnant, also the care of a baby. . . . I live sixty-five miles from a Dr. and my other babies (two) were very large at birth,—one 12 lbs., the other 10½ lbs. I have been *very* badly torn each time, through the rectum the last time. My youngest child is 7½ (and when I am delivered this [time] it will be 8½). I am 37 years old and I am so worried and filled with perfect horror at the prospects ahead. So many of my neighbors die at giving birth to their children. I have a baby 11 months old in my keeping now whose mother died—when I reached their cabin last Nov It was 22 below zero and I had to ride 7 miles horse back. She was nearly dead when I got there and died after giving birth to a 14 lb. boy. It seems awfull to me to think of giving up all my work and leaving my little ones, 2 of which are adopted—a girl 10 and this baby. Will you please send me all the information for the care of my self before and after and at the time of delivery. I am far from a Dr. and we have no means, only what we get on this rented ranch. I also want all the information on baby care especially right young new born ones. If there is *a[n]ything* what I can do to escape being torn again wont you let me know. I am just 4 months along now but I haven't quickened yet. I am very Resp.[38]

Mary West sent the requested pamphlets and asked the writer if the bureau might publish her letter to draw attention to the plight of women living in remote areas. Mrs. A. P. agreed and wrote the bureau about others that she knew. Julia Lathrop read the original letter with "most earnest attention and sympathy," acknowledging that "it is not the only letter of that kind which the Bureau has received." The absence of good medical care for women and children in remote areas was "an old need, but a new practical question." Here, Lathrop's efforts went beyond encouragement, but did not include "official" government intervention. She believed that "certainly [this woman] is too good to be wasted" and asked a Children's Bureau supporter and child welfare advocate working in Chicago, Mrs. W. F. Dummer, "to take a little flier at old-fashioned practical neighborliness at long range?" Lathrop and Mrs. Dummer became "financial partners" and paid the Wyoming mother's medical expenses and the seven-week boarding home bill so that the she could stay near the state hospital before and immediately after the baby's birth. Additionally, members of the Children's Bureau's staff contributed baby clothes. On June 5, 1917, the grateful mother wrote Lathrop. "Just a few words to you flat on my back. If it hadn't been for you, baby or I would not have been here today—for if I had to have stayed on the ranch he never would have been born. . . . Dr. Young and his nurses who assisted at the delivery were wonderful. I didn't know such things as was done could be done. . . . The baby weighed 8½ lbs., he has blue eyes and light hair and is a darling."[39]

While the degree of involvement by Lathrop and her staff in this case was exceptional, Mrs. A. P.'s plea for information does illustrate the feelings expressed by many women who wrote the bureau for help. Generally, correspondents received sympathetic responses from the bureau staff. The thousands of letters to the agency not only reveal the actions taken by women to improve their circumstances, they also influenced the Children's Bureau's developing maternal and child health strategies. Childbirth could be a lonely and frightening experience, and many of these women had few places to turn. Some letters to the bureau communicate confusion over conflicting advice from friends, relatives, doctors, and in the popular press about maternal and infant care. Others asked about very personal topics such as the propriety of having sexual relations while pregnant and abortion. The bureau recommended that during pregnancy, the "frequency [of sexual activity between couples] rests with the wife" and urged total abstinence during the last months. On the subject of abortion the bureau wrote that "it is not only dangerous to the mother . . . but also the taking of another life." But to a woman who feared that an earlier illegal abortion might prevent her from having children now that she wanted them, the bureau advised her to see a physician, and sympathetically assured that "nature is usually very kind and she does not always punish by depriving women of children when they have destroyed only one child." Some letters address basic questions such as how does a woman know if she is pregnant? Many of the writers were advised to contact their local or state child hygiene agency for help, and sometimes the bureau asked the state health department or social welfare organization to follow-up on the writer's request. Correspondents came from every region and socioeconomic group. Older children sometimes wrote the bureau for mothers who could not write or speak English. Most letters received a personal response, intended to reassure the writer that her feelings and concerns were normal, accompanied by the bureau's instructional pamphlets.[40] Bureau responses often helped women to help themselves, but at the same time they may have contributed to the agency's increasing emphasis on the individual education of mothers as a means to insure child welfare.

A letter from a pregnant twenty-two-year-old mother from Racine, Wisconsin, beautifully expresses the affection some women felt for the bureau. But Lathrop's response shows the agency's limited power to actually help individuals. The woman asked Lathrop to "be a Friend" and to "not think me rude for writing the things I am about to write. . . . I feel as if I could trust you." The writer explained that she was pregnant for the third time in three years. Her first baby died at six weeks of age and her second child would be 1½ years of age when the new baby was due. The woman lamented becoming "sick with blood poisoning" after her first delivery and had "never built up again and stayed thin." Her husband acted "disgusted and very cruel to her," she believed due to her poor health, sickly appearance, and new pregnancy. He blamed his wife for becoming pregnant again and told her that he wished he had "married a nice built woman in the first place." "Those words," wrote the young wife, "went through me like a stab, for he always seemed to think so much of me before we were married. I cannot tell you and express in writing . . . the sick feeling which overpowers me, that sometimes I think I will go insane." Afraid that her husband would leave her, she told him that "perhaps I will build up again after my baby is born, but he said [that] he would not wait that long." She feared that her "fretting and worrying [would] affect my unborn child."[41]

Lathrop responded "with great sympathy. . . . Nature makes great demands upon mothers and sometimes she seems to forget that they need a vigor and strength greater than she bestows." The chief noted that "sometimes men seem not to realize how little rough jokes may hurt if one is sick and nervous." Lathrop wrote that she could "not help but hope that this is the case with your husband and that at bottom he does know that you are the girl he married,—a very young girl to have had the burden of sickness and sadness involved in your history since you became his wife," and that she had seen "many a young wife grow thin and worn with the care of little children and the illness of pregnancy and childbirth, who in a few years as the strain lessened, came out rosy and strong and prettier than ever before." But the woman's young son received Lathrop's major concern. "Whatever comes," she counseled, "you have your little boy and *remember no one* can be as near to him or give him as happy a childhood as you can."[42] The Children's Bureau chief had offered sympathy, but little concrete advice. Underlying the women's words was a request for birth control information; a service the Children's Bureau did not provide. Various Comstock laws made the dissemination of birth control advice or materials through the mail illegal and a controversial political issue. The Children's Bureau generally answered letters directly requesting birth control advice with the comment that the agency had no such information available. In addition, the bureau perpetuated the idea that motherhood was the path to women's "true" fulfillment. Initially Lathrop seemed to be more open to birth control than might be expected. In a letter to a woman from Montana who wrote requesting birth control information, Lathrop responded that "the Bureau has published nothing upon the regulation of birth." But she recommended that the woman "write to Dr. Maria Dean, Helena, Montana, I believe she will give you the advice of a wise and conscientious physician." Despite this beginning, according to the policy that developed under the agency's second chief, Grace Abbott, during the next decade, the Children's Bureau denied any connection to the birth control movement and offered no such advice.[43] However limited the bureau's response was, many women relied on it as a friend they could turn to for answers to some of the most personal questions in their lives. The Children's Bureau's pamphlets and sympathetic replies were often used as "do-it-yourself" advice concerning childbirth and infant care. It may be argued that West's instructional pamphlets were superior to the bureau's later revised versions and to Dr. Benjamin Spock's *Baby and Child Care* because each imbued greater respect for the mother's ability and sympathy for her circumstance.[44]

Clearly many women welcomed the bureau's advice and there is evidence of a nationwide call for information concerning good infant care. Between 1911 and 1914 municipal health departments in cooperation with local child welfare organizations in New York, Pittsburgh, Philadelphia, Chicago, and Indianapolis had organized Baby Week campaigns to provide mothers with information concerning the "do's and don't's" of infant care and in some cases general child welfare. These local efforts encouraged mothers of all classes and socioeconomic groups to seek instruction. The Children's Bureau urged other communities to implement similar efforts in its 1915 publications, "Baby-Week Campaigns: Suggestions for Communities of Various Sizes" (pub. no. 15) and "Child-Welfare Exhibits, Types and Preparations," (pub. no. 14). In the spring of 1915, the Children's Bureau and the General Federation of Women's Clubs announced their intention to celebrate National Baby Week in March 1916. The effort involved a nationwide publicity campaign encouraging local promotion of mothers' education. The Children's Bureau's publications offered detailed instructions for constructing a demonstration. These included how to coordinate the effort with local officials, and the most effective color scheme for display materials. Publicity posters encouraged women to breast-feed at regular intervals and decried baby's foes: "Poverty, Ignorance and Bad Surroundings." Lathrop contended that the success of National Baby Week went "far beyond our most extravagant anticipation . . . to date, . . . observances took place in more than 4,700 communities." Happy with such results, the bureau repeated the program in May 1917.[45]

The entry of the United States into World War I had a positive effect on the Children's Bureau's developing maternal and child health program. Congress had created the National Council of Defense in 1916 as a preparedness measure for possible entry into the war. The council created a Woman's Committee in April 1917, after the United States declared war. This committee, headed by suffragist Anna Howard Shaw, had ten division directors and state chairpersons positioned to help with its various home front programs.[46] The Children's Bureau and the Woman's Committee of the National Council of Defense jointly sponsored Children's Year, beginning April 6, 1918, with the stated purpose of stimulating the "civil population [to do] all in its power to protect the children of this nation as a patriotic duty." As their primary goal, sponsors of Children's Year worked to save the lives of 100,000 of the estimated 300,000 children under five years of age who died each year in the United States. In a letter to the secretary of labor, President Wilson said, "Next to the duty of doing everything possible for the soldiers at the front, there could be, it seems to me, no more practical duty than that of protecting the children who constitute one third of our population. . . . The success of the efforts made in England on behalf of the children is evidenced by the fact that the infant death-rate in England for the second year of the war was the lowest in her history. . . . I am very glad that the same processes are being set afoot in this country."[47]

The war brought a variety of concerns for child welfare advocates. Some acted by promoting better children's health care in response to the poor physical condition of many military recruits. Almost one-third of draftees were found unfit for military service and many suffered from conditions which might have been corrected or prevented in childhood. Building on this data the Children's Bureau tried to bring attention to the potential threats which the United States' support of the allied effort and later actual entrance into the war brought to children. Milk was in short supply and excessively expensive as farmers slaughtered growing numbers of dairy cows to supply meat for the allied forces overseas. The Children's Bureau also worried that public health nurses, vital to the agency's plan to reduce infant mortality through education and diagnostic work, would be removed from child health duties and called into war work. Dora E. Thompson, superintendent of the Army Nurse Corps, assured Julia Lathrop that "every effort [had] been made by the American Red Cross not to deplete the public health nursing force." She insisted that Public Health nurses "are not encouraged to enter the service but to remain in their present positions."[48]

The Children's Bureau also feared that high wages and increased demands for women's labor might encourage mothers of young children to take jobs in booming war industries. In May 1917, at the Conference on Infant and Maternal Welfare in War Time sponsored by the American Association for the Study and Prevention of Infant Mortality and the Medical Section of the Council of National Defense, Grace Meigs, a member of the executive committee responsible for the constructing the group's final report, objected to a recommendation urging "that adequately supervised care [for children of working mothers] be furnished at the place of employment." Meigs wrote in a memorandum that she was "aware of no examples of such care" in the United States and believed that "some other system, such as that of mothers' pensions and family allowances . . . [should] be devised for the support of women with nursing infants." Although the three other members of the executive committee agreed and felt that "*everything possible* should be done to enable the mother and the very young children to be cared for in their own homes," they concluded that the recommendation for on-site day care should be maintained despite

Meigs's objection. The committee offered to remove her name from the final report, but she declined.[49] Instead, the Children's Bureau contended that "the employment of women with young children may be avoided by local patriotic effort." Indeed, the Children's Bureau relied on patriotism in its entire endeavor to save children's lives immediately before and after U.S. entrance into the war. "Victory in arms," declared the bureau, "will be settled in this war by the stamina of our fighting men. Ultimate victory can come only to the Nation that defends the future of the race."[50]

In addition to his verbal support, Wilson provided the Children's Bureau with $150,000 from a special wartime defense fund to implement Children's Year. The bureau's program included three distinct "drives": a back-to-school drive designed to remove children from the work force, a recreation drive intended to increase "physical vigor" among children, and a children's hygiene drive urging education in health care and proper nutrition. The Children's Bureau distributed more than 6,500,000 weighing and measuring cards used to record the weight and measurements of children under six years of age. The agency believed that the presence or absence of proper nutrition or disease could be determined by comparing a child's size with established standards set by the bureau. If there seemed to be a problem, the child could then be referred to a local physician for treatment. Many communities held child health demonstrations which included free physical examinations incorporating the bureau's weight and measurement standards. Marches and parades also promoted child welfare. Children's Year efforts urged local communities to establish public nursing programs operated in conjunction with children's health clinics and encouraged mothers to educate themselves about proper child nutrition and health care. The bureau also instructed state agencies to develop traveling child welfare exhibits and health demonstrations designed to reach mothers and children living in rural areas.[51]

Children's Year brought increased public attention to the Children's Bureau's efforts to improve maternal and child health. In 1912, Louisiana (an unlikely leader) became the first state to establish a child hygiene division within its department of health. By the close of 1920, largely due to the bureau's Children's Year campaign, thirty-five states had done so.[52] The major result of the crusade, judged Children's Bureau physician Anna E. Rude, was the "establishment of standards of prenatal, obstetrical and postnatal care, infant care, examination and supervision through the preschool period, [and] standardized periodic physical examinations throughout school life."[53] However, such standards left little room for individual variation and made conformity one of the primary goals of the bureau's infant and child health work from 1914 to 1920.

As another part of the effort to encourage the development of minimum standards for children, Wilson and the Children's Bureau called the Second White House Conference on Children, to be held in Washington, D.C., May 5-8, 1919. Lathrop described the meeting as a "small working conference" of U.S. and foreign child welfare experts. The Children's Bureau had joined the international child welfare effort during World War I by sending staff volunteers to work with the International Red Cross. These ties, coupled with Wilson's peace effort, encouraged the Children's Bureau to invite representatives from the allied nations of Belgium, France, Great Britain, Japan, and Serbia to the second White House conference. From late December 1918 to mid-February 1919, Julia Lathrop and Grace Abbott visited France, England, and Belgium interviewing potential conference participants and examining the plight of children in wartorn Europe. Abbott also visited Italy for the same purpose. A close associate of Jane Addams, Abbott, a resident of Hull-House from 1912 to 1917, had a master's degree in political science from the University of Chicago. She had also worked with Lathrop at the Chicago Juvenile Protection Association. Her trip with Lathrop further opened the door to future employment with the Children's Bureau. White House conference participants also included representatives of the PHS, juvenile court judges, various state health officials, and others involved in professional child welfare work. President Wilson, then attending the Paris Peace Conference, sent his support, stating that he hoped the effort would result in the development of certain irreducible minimum standards for children. By the end of the second decade of the twentieth century, the U.S. Children's Bureau was viewed as a world leader in the child welfare movement.[54]

From 1914 to 1920 the Children's Bureau dramatically increased its funding, developed a blueprint for future programs, and moved toward professionalization of child welfare advocacy. Although somewhat hindered in its efforts to serve the "whole child" by its sole reliance on motherhood education, middle-class ideals, and protectionist legislation, the Children's Bureau's efforts drew attention to the desperate circumstances of many children in the United States. In addition, the agency made an important contribution to the development of state maternal and child health policy by uniting social welfare issues with preventive health care strategies.

Ever the astute politician, Lathrop used the popularity of Children's Year to generate support for a new federal plan advocating infant and maternal health care education. The money provided for the wartime campaign previewed what the bureau could do with funds to champion good maternal and children's health practices in the states. Lathrop suggested that the federal government provide the states with grants-in-aid for the development of educational programs intended to reduce infant and maternal mortality and increase health care opportunities for children. Her plan was built on the bureau's blueprint developed since implementation of its first infant mortality studies.[55]

4

Saving Mothers and Babies: Designing and Implementing a National Maternity and Infancy Act, 1918–30

Building on the momentum established during the war, Lathrop envisioned a national program to save the lives of mothers and babies funded jointly by the federal government and the states. Her idea emphasized standardization, maternal education, community cooperation, and a recognition of the combined influences of social and medical factors in preserving the health of children. The resulting program was a bittersweet success for the Children's Bureau, mainly because the effort fueled old arguments threatening the agency's future. Such criticism undermined the bureau's fundamental philosophy that a single federal agency should advocate the needs of the "whole child." Nevertheless, the 1921 Maternity and Infancy Act, better known as Sheppard-Towner, set an important precedent illustrating that even limited government intervention could contribute to improving the lives of mothers and children living in the United States.[1]

The plan also reflected women's growing political influence. The first woman elected to Congress and a legislator whose name was synonymous with Progressive reform, Jeannette Pickering Rankin (R-Mont.), helped design and set strategy for the program Lathrop and her supporters hoped to implement. Lathrop had enthusiastically welcomed Rankin to Washington and hoped "to count upon [Rankin's] special interest for the Children's Bureau."[2] In August 1917, Rankin joined Lathrop, Lillian Wald, Florence Kelley, and several members of the Children's Bureau staff, including Dorothy Reed Mendenhall, M.D., in drafting a plan to promote better care for mothers and babies at the federal level. The group originated a proposal similar to maternity and infancy programs already instituted in Great Britain and New Zealand and incorporated many of the insights derived from the Children's Bureau's infant mortality studies. However, unlike the programs in Great Britain and New Zealand, the plan did not include maternity benefits. This is not a surprise considering Lathrop's attitude about such matters.

The group's proposal relied most heavily upon the existing model designed and implemented by S. Josephine Baker, M.D., for the New York City Health Department. The New York program included visiting nurses used to provide mothers with instruction in good maternal and child hygiene; the advocacy of improved access to prenatal, obstetric, and postnatal care; and routine physical examinations of young children in state-sponsored demonstration clinics. As head of the New York City Health Department's Division of Child Hygiene, Baker dramatically reduced the city's infant mortality rate. Lathrop and her group knew of Baker's accomplishments and hoped for the same kind of success at the national level.[3]

However, as shown earlier, many of the women writing the Children's Bureau described the lack of good medical care in the nation's countryside as well as its cities. The agency's own infant and maternal mortality studies corroborated these complaints and led the bureau to conclude that as many as 80 percent of American mothers received little or no prenatal or postnatal care. Therefore, the bureau's strategists concluded that the greatest need for combined federal and state funding existed outside of cities because rural districts suffered the most from a lack of public and private funds spent for preventive obstetric and pediatric medicine. It appeared that urban areas had the potential to develop programs of their own, since metropolitan centers had greater public resources and philanthropic efforts seemed more predominant. Further, as Children's Bureau physician Dorothy Reed Mendenhall explained, "The rural districts are less able to speak for themselves. I should be a little afraid of some of our big cities with their powerful organizations; if there were any funds to be obtained, they might obtain them and leave little for the country."[4]

Mendenhall was well qualified to discuss the subject. A Smith College graduate, she earned her medical degree from Johns Hopkins Medical School in 1895 and gained international recognition as a researcher by discovering the cell that causes Hodgkin's disease. Unlike many other women of her generation, Mendenhall combined a professional career, marriage, and motherhood. She had four children, the first of whom, Margaret (b. 1907), died only a few hours after birth, largely due to botched obstetrics. Her second child, Richard (b. 1908), died in 1910 from injuries received in a fall. Beginning in 1915 Mendenhall worked with the U.S. Department of Agriculture and a variety of women's organizations to establish Wisconsin's first infant welfare clinic. Concerned that mothers living in rural areas lacked access to good prenatal and maternal care, Mendenhall developed a correspondence course for the Department of Agriculture entitled

"Nutrition Series for Mothers." She joined the Children's Bureau staff in 1917 and throughout her professional career advocated that pregnancy and delivery were natural conditions, usually progressing without invasive medical and surgical procedures. In addition, unlike the AMA, Mendenhall advocated the use of well-trained midwives as a solution to the lack of good medical care available to many American women living in rural areas.[5]

Mendenhall's somewhat radical opinions are evident in the Children's Bureau's proposed program to reduce the nation's infant and maternal mortality rates. Increasingly bureau policies suggested that *all* mothers, not just immigrant women in urban areas, needed motherhood training and good medical care in order to best guarantee the first "right" of childhood: good health. Lathrop argued that the federal government already recognized the need of rural areas for economic aid under the Department of Agriculture's assistance programs. She cited the 1914 Smith-Lever Act as a precedent for funding state grant-in-aid programs. That act provided federal matching funds to states for use by county agricultural agents. Through individual visits and group demonstrations these agents taught agricultural and home economics skills to people living in rural areas.[6] Lathrop and other child welfare advocates believed that a program based on this model could also be instituted to save mothers and babies.

The effort to gain passage of what eventually became the 1921 Sheppard-Towner Maternity and Infancy Act began with the introduction of identical bills by Rankin and Senator Joseph T. Robinson (D-Ark.) on July 1, 1918 (H.R. 12634 and S. 4782). The House Committee on Labor received Rankin's bill and Robinson's version was sent to the Senate Committee on Education and Labor. The Robinson proposal never reached hearings, but Rankin's bill was more successful. On January 15 and 28, 1919, the House Committee on Labor held hearings on Rankin's "Bill to Encourage Instruction in the Hygiene of Maternity and Infancy."[7] It called for (1) an annual outright appropriation of $480,000 ($10,000 for each of the forty-eight states), and (2) a yearly allotment of $1,000,000 apportioned according to the percentage of U.S. rural population living in each state contingent on state legislatures appropriating matching funds. Over the next five years, the supplemental allotment was to increase annually by $200,000 until it reached $2,000,000. In order to qualify for federal money, states were also required to establish a state board of maternity and infant hygiene including the governor and a state board composed of the state health physician, a registered nurse, and an educator from the state university. Federal funds were to be administered through the Children's Bureau in cooperation with each state board. However, the bill included no specifics about what the money should be spent on, except to note that this legislation was designed solely to encourage instruction in hygiene and maternity, not provide actual medical care.[8]

Lathrop and her supporters believed that the bureau's infant and maternal mortality studies as well as its experience during the Children's Year campaign revealed the positive benefits of educating mothers on how best to care for their children. They also showed the importance of good prenatal and infant health practices promoted with the assistance of local physicians and nurses. The agency's later studies revealed an overwhelming need for medical care and hygiene information in rural areas where few physicians and public health nurses practiced, and no hospitals or clinics were located. According to Lathrop, the proposal's highlighting of children and mothers living in isolated regions did not deviate from the bureau's mandate to serve "all classes" of American children because the legislation would draw attention to the need for state governments to take responsibility for preventing the unnecessary deaths and suffering of many American women and children. Further, Lathrop and her allies carefully constructed the bill's language to insure voluntary cooperation and to avoid the plan's being labeled as charity intended only for the poor.[9]

Representatives from the Children's Bureau, the American Federation of Labor, and the National Consumers' League and individuals active in maternity and infant welfare work testified in support of the proposed legislation. No one appeared before the House committee in direct opposition to the bill. As a result, the committee agreed with the Children's Bureau's contention that rural areas were in the greatest need of federal assistance and reported favorably on the proposal. However, the Rankin bill did not reach the floor during the Sixty-fifth Congress.[10] Senator Robinson introduced another maternity and infancy bill (S. 233) in May 1919, which again went no further than the Senate Committee on Education and Labor. In the same month Representative Asbury F. Levy introduced a maternity and infancy bill drafted by the PHS (H.R. 2845), but it died in the House Committee on Agriculture.[11]

During the balance of 1919, confusion surrounded further efforts to gain a federal maternity and infancy act. Apparently without contacting the Children's Bureau, Senator Morris Sheppard (D-Tex.) introduced two slightly altered versions of the Rankin bill (S. 3162 and S. 3259). Sheppard was a women's suffrage supporter, prohibitionist, child labor reform activist, and Children's Bureau advocate. He had voted in favor of past bureau appropriations and spoke emotionally in Congress on the problem of infant and maternal mortality.[12] Both measures were referred to the Senate Committee on Public Health and Quarantine, which reported favorably on S. 3259 on June 2, 1920. Agreeing with the Children's Bureau, the committee report stated that isolation, civic neglect, poverty, and ignorance were among the chief reasons for the high infant mortality rate in the United States. Members contended that practices promoted by the bill might help to reduce such deaths by one-half or more.[13]

Approximately seven months earlier, on December 5, 1919, Representative Horace Mann Towner (R-Iowa) had introduced an identical House version (H.R. 10925) of Senator Sheppard's bill. He too apparently acted without the prior knowledge of the Children's Bureau. A Republican, Towner represented a farming district and was a supporter of grant-in-aid legislation. The bipartisan alliance between Sheppard, a progressive southern Democrat, and Towner, a Republican from a farm state, was not an unusual circumstance. But this first attempt failed and neither bill came to a vote. One reason for this lack of attention may have been Wilson's failure to endorse the idea. Woodrow Wilson had stated his support for "irreducible minimum standards" for children in his message to the 1919 White House conference on children, but he did not specifically urge passage of the maternity and infancy bill. It is not clear why Wilson was so reluctant to support the proposal, but perhaps his southern background and that region's lack of enthusiasm for federal child labor reform led him to avoid endorsing any federal program involving children.[14]

Following consultation with Sheppard and Towner, the usual army of Children's Bureau supporters drew national attention to the legislators' efforts just in time for the fall presidential election. The women's organizations assembled to implement Children's Year formed a permanent Children's Bureau advisory group composed of the chairs of the state child welfare committees organized during wartime as local branches of the Women's Committee of the Council of National Defense. As a result middle-class women reformers were better organized than ever before. From the viewpoint of many politicians, backing the Sheppard-Towner idea appeared to be a politically popular and safe thing to do. In addition, as Julia Lathrop had suggested, the precedent for federal grant-in-aid programs was well established by 1920. Besides the previously noted Smith-Lever Act, Congress had also enacted the 1916 Federal Aid Road Act (highway construction), the 1917 Smith-Hughes Act (vocational education), and the 1918 Chamberlain-Kahn Act (to fight venereal disease). But the most potent political argument drawing support for the idea from politicians and their parties came from strategists who noted that the largest group of Sheppard-Towner advocates were women, recently enfranchised under the Nineteenth Amendment.[15]

The unknown power of women voters was an important political concern during the 1920 presidential election. Herbert Hoover, then president of the American Child Health Association, commenting on the issues of child care and the effort to save the lives of mothers and children, predicted that "future political parties will need to advance these issues to the forefront if they [are going to] secure the adherence of the women." He concluded that passage of the Sheppard-Towner proposal would constitute "a demonstration of . . . the political power of American women . . . [and would provide] a concrete example of why this power is valuable to them as women."[16]

Attempting to court women's votes, the Democratic, Socialist, Prohibition, and Farmer-Labor parties each endorsed the maternity and infancy bill in their platforms. However, the Democratic nominee, James M. Cox, did not raise the issue in the campaign. On the other hand, although the Republican document did not formally endorse Sheppard-Towner, Republican presidential candidate Warren G. Harding spoke in favor of the bill in a well-publicized speech delivered one month before the November election.[17]

Harding's action may have been a response to the increased attention given the maternity and infancy bill by women's organizations. The recently organized National League of Women Voters (NLWV) made the issue a top priority. One NLWV member suggested to the group's president that the relationship between the NLWV and the Children's Bureau could be especially strong concerning "the necessity of adequate provision for maternity and infancy." She contended that women should support this effort because "it is a task which I believe will be better done by women than by men" and its success would contribute to the prestige of all women. Those involved in the NLWV and other female-dominated organizations made the promotion of maternal and infant care a national issue which they believed the responsibility of women.[18]

The Women's Joint Congressional Committee (WJCC), formed in 1920, served as the clearinghouse for groups supporting women's and children's issues.[19] Soon after its formation, the WJCC made passage of the Sheppard-Towner proposal a primary goal and established a subcommittee, headed by Florence Kelley, to organize the effort. Kelley and the WJCC successfully organized what one male observer called "the most powerful lobby in Washington."[20] In accordance with her philosophy that the bureau should not openly lobby in its own behalf, Lathrop happily relied on the WJCC and the NLWV to do the job.

As the postelection lame duck session reconsidered the bills, debate again focused on many of the issues somewhat familiar to Children's Bureau supporters. One question centered on whether responsibility for the program should be given to the Children's Bureau or the PHS. Another reflected economic concerns and suggested cutting the program's entire appropriation by 75 percent to $480,000. However, after three days of debate, on December 18, 1920, the Senate passed the bill (S. 3259) over all objections by a voice vote. The Senate immediately sent the approved bill to the House, where it was referred to the Interstate and Foreign Commerce Committee. The committee quickly held hearings on the issue December 20-23 and 28-29, 1920.[21]

Florence Kelley organized members of the WJCC and other bureau supporters to testify before the House committee, conduct personal interviews with various members of Congress, encourage prominent newspapers and magazines to publicize support for the bill, and inundate legislators with letters advocating passage of Sheppard-Towner. Kelley used emotional ploys as well as statistics. She threatened that if the act were not passed, members of Congress would be condemning many American infants to death. She asked, "What answer can be given to the women in a myriad of organizations, who are marveling and asking, 'Why does Congress wish women and children to die?'" For the first time, a small number of opponents also testified before the committee, using many of the same arguments which had been suggested by Senators in the debate over S. 3259. Opponents included representatives of the American Medicine Liberty League, Citizens Medical Reference Bureau, the Maryland Association Opposed to Woman Suffrage, the New York Antivivisection Society, and the National Society for Human Regulation of Vivisection. Surgeon General Rupert Blue testified in favor of the idea of a federal program designed to promote maternity and infancy hygiene, but he contended that the act's administration should be placed with his agency. Other members of the PHS also spoke in favor of this revision. House committee members, however, found Kelley's group of advocates most convincing. The committee's report stated that actually "very little opposition was developed against the general purposes of the bill" and therefore members recommended its passage. But Sheppard-Towner did not come to a vote before the close of the Sixty-sixth Congress. Despite this disappointment, it appeared to the bill's supporters that the proposal would pass during 1921. After taking office, Harding again backed the idea in his first annual message: "I must assume the maternity bill, already strongly approved, will be enacted promptly." With the presidential endorsement, Sheppard and Towner reintroduced their bills in April 1921 (S. 1039 and H.R. 2366).[22]

National magazines such as *Ladies' Home Journal, Women's Home Companion, McCall's,* and *Good Housekeeping* urged senators and representatives to vote in favor of the Sheppard-Towner bill. The WJCC "directed the strongest of pressures against the home folks and used every recognized means for passing a bill in which the womanhood of the country was interested." Harriett Taylor Upton, vice-chairwoman of the Republican National Committee, warned Harding that the delay in the bill's passage by Congress was alienating women. In response, Harding also exerted new pressure for quick passage.[23] By the summer of 1921 supporters of the Sheppard-Towner bill were well organized and optimistic.

Thwarting Any Opposition

While the WJCC and the Children's Bureau refined the proposal, opponents also strengthened their efforts, but most came late in the debate. As indicated by the lack of opposition during the initial congressional hearings, potential opponents showed little interest until 1920. However, a strong resistance did manifest from the recently organized Woman Patriot Corporation, which was supported by the Sentinels of the Republic, a conservative men's anticommunist group. Prior to 1920 the Woman Patriots had been known as the National Association Opposed to Woman Suffrage. Although a distinct minority, this group demonstrated that not all women supported the Children's Bureau. The Woman Patriots attacked the maternity and infancy proposal as communist-inspired legislation designed to undermine the American family. Antisuffragist and former president of the National Association Opposed to Woman Suffrage Mary G. Kilbreth wrote Harding in protest that there were "many loyal American men and women who [believe] that this bill, inspired by foreign experiments in Communism and backed by the radical forces of this country, strikes at the very heart of our American civilization." The Woman Patriots generally opposed any measure supported by woman suffragists, many of whom were members of the WJCC and other organizations supporting the Children's Bureau. Throughout the 1920s, this conservative group of women used their publication, the *Woman Patriot,* to denounce the bureau as a "Bolshevik" plot and part of the infamous

"Spider Web" of female-led subversive organizations. Julia Lathrop was called "unAmerican" and the paper often pointed to Florence Kelley and Jane Addams as examples of "Bolshevik" influence on the agency. Bitter opposition to the suffragists remained strong in the remnants of the antisuffrage ranks.[24]

By 1920, some women active in the broader infant welfare movement also opposed the bureau. Elizabeth Lowell Putnam renounced her earlier support of the Children's Bureau and was instead a vocal opponent of its work, especially Sheppard-Towner. Putnam was an ardent antisuffragist, but had agreed to be named a member of the Massachusetts Republican State Executive Committee upon enactment of the Nineteenth Amendment. She explained that despite her belief that women should not possess the vote, she "believed that the right of suffrage carried with it the duty to use it . . . [and] put her heart into this work." Her activities also included serving as chair of the Women's Municipal League of Boston; vice president of the Household Nursing Association; a member of the National Child Welfare Association, the Massachusetts Social Hygiene Association, and the Massachusetts Anti-Suffrage Association; and the American Red Cross. In 1918 she became the first woman president of the American Child Health Association. She spent the bulk of her time with the Boston Women's Municipal League, an organization that operated one of the country's first prenatal and maternity clinics open to poor women. Putnam, describing herself as "a laywoman who has herself borne children," contended that "the care of maternity and infancy is a very vital need, and it should be administered by those who are expert in it." Therefore, she maintained, "the United States Public Health Service should . . . have jurisdiction [over] a federal maternity and infancy bill." Putnam condemned the Children's Bureau for dealing with the issue of maternal and infant mortality "as if it were a social question." Instead, she asserted, "it is a medical question, pure and simple."[25] This makes it sound as if Putnam's opposition was purely a professional bias toward the AMA and the PHS. But, as noted earlier, the Children's Bureau had already made moves deemphasizing social conditions as the primary reasons why babies died. Much of Putnam's disdain was directed at the "feminist" (suffragist) supporters and employees of the Children's Bureau. She discounted the attitude held by Lathrop and other Children's Bureau advocates that there were certain issues women should be especially concerned with. "These League of Women Voters women drive me wild," she complained. "I never have been able to see why because women have the vote, they should consider that their job is only to devote themselves to bills which they consider to be solely for the benefit of women and children. I suppose they are likely to draw benefit from these bills themselves, perhaps, but in our households and daily life we consider that women have something to do with the welfare of men also."[26]

Some members of Congress shared the viewpoint of angry antisuffragists such as Putnam and the Woman Patriots. Representative Samuel Winslow (R-Mass.) disliked Julia Lathrop and as chair of the House Committee on Interstate and Foreign Commerce had successfully stalled the Sheppard-Towner bill during 1920.[27] Another opponent, Senator James A. Reed (D-Mo.), ridiculed the women officials of the Children's Bureau on the Senate floor, using personal attacks which questioned the "womanhood" of bureau employees. Reed observed that "the entire bureau is composed of unmarried women, except Mrs. Helen Woodbury and her husband, who both hold jobs in the same department." He asked, "When we employ female celibates to instruct mothers how to raise babies they have brought into the earth, do we not indulge in a rare bit of irony?" Furthermore, the senator passionately argued that "official meddling cannot take the place of mother love": "Mother Love! The golden cord that stretches from the throne of God, uniting all creation to divinity. Its light gleams down the path of time from barbarous ages, when savage women held their babies to almost famished breasts and died that they might live. Its gold flame glows as bright in hovels where poverty breaks a meager crust as in palaces where wealth holds Lucullian feasts. It is the one great universal passion—the sinless passion of sacrifice. Incomparable in its sublimity, interference is sacrilege, regulation is mockery." Reed concluded, "I care not how inestimable the office-holding spinster may be, nor how her heart may throb for the dream children she may not possess, her yearnings cannot be substituted for a mother's experience." Senator William S. Kenyon (R-Iowa) responded jokingly that he hoped "the old maid brigade in Missouri will not be a large one at election time."[28] Despite support for the women of the bureau from congressmen such as Kenyon, it seems that after passage of the Nineteenth Amendment the gender-based attacks on the bureau became sharper and more frequent. Nevertheless such sensational charges backfired by drawing attention away from some of the more rational objections expressed by the Sheppard-Towner bill's other major opponent, organized medicine.[29]

James Burrow has shown that AMA opposition to a federal maternal and infant hygiene plan was negligible until 1920. Earlier the AMA had focused its lobbying efforts on defeating national health insurance, but after 1920 AMA physicians, mostly general practitioners, proved to be the most serious threat to Sheppard-Towner. Editorials in the AMA's professional publication, the *Journal of the American Medical Association (JAMA),* expressed special concern that Sheppard-Towner gave too much control of health care to the federal government and was therefore a first step toward "socialized" medicine. For example, one article contended that the "care of the mother and child is a state and local, not a federal function." In another vein, *JAMA* claimed that the limited funds available for the program could not produce any significant results and discounted Children's Bureau conclusions that its studies showed an emergency situation with regard to maternal and child health.[30]

By late 1920 it appeared that the proposal would pass despite the AMA's objections. Now the doctors' organization faced the inevitable and, as Elizabeth Putnam had argued earlier, began to contend that the Children's Bureau was not qualified to administer the bill. The AMA claimed that only the PHS under its newly appointed surgeon general, Hugh S. Cumming (1920-36), had the skills to handle a "medical" program.[31] Like those who supported the Sheppard-Towner bill, the lobbying efforts of the AMA included interviews with members of Congress and promotion of public opposition through editorials in its professional and "lay" journals, *JAMA* and *Hygeia.* Affiliated state organizations also joined the fight, and in Illinois, Ohio, Massachusetts, and New York led the battle against Sheppard-Towner.

Many doctors outside of the mainstream medical community, such as osteopaths and other anti-vaccinationists, also denounced the Sheppard-Towner bill. These individuals feared that the legislation encouraged medical practices that they ideologically opposed, such as vaccination against diphtheria and smallpox. These doctors argued that better sanitary conditions and "natural remedies" were the way to reduce maternal and infant mortality as well as to improve children's general health.[32] While not expressed openly, these doctors may have also felt that a program advocating maternal and infant hygiene might further lessen their influence. Despite the AMA's condemnation of the Children's Bureau, Lathrop's agency urged mothers to "see their physician," a phrase most likely interpreted as a doctor trained in a mainstream medical school and licensed by an AMA-controlled state medical board.

Doctors outside of the AMA's mainstream influence had good reason to believe that the Children's Bureau's efforts could hurt their practices. Bureau pediatrician Ella Oppenheimer, M.D., suggested that AMA physicians should support the maternity and infancy bill because it encouraged "the intelligent use of medical care." She explained that "a public health nurse and a consultation center in a county can do no other than provide the overworked country doctor with aid and equipment with which to work." Furthermore, the public health nurse paid with Sheppard-Towner funds would serve as an educational and interpretive link between the doctor and patient. But the AMA did not see Sheppard-Towner's potential in this way.[33] Instead, some general practitioners may have feared that the program's preventive health care emphasis advocated the use of obstetric and pediatric specialists.

This point is made clear by the Pediatric Section's support for Sheppard-Towner. Although members of the AMA, obstetric and pediatric specialists led the move toward preventive maternal and child health care, a rising trend during the late 1910s and 1920s. Many obstetric and pediatric physicians promoted regular health examinations, not only for altruistic reasons but also because it was difficult for a doctor to make a living by depending solely on delivering babies or caring for sick children. This disagreement with AMA official policy led to the formation of the independent American Academy of Pediatrics in 1922. It is also significant that although women constituted a minority in the obstetric and pediatric fields, female physicians were most commonly found in those specialties.[34]

Gender-based interest in Sheppard-Towner is evident by support for the program offered by the Medical Women's National Association. This organization had advocated federal funding for maternal and infant health programs as early as 1917. Often faced with discrimination, women physicians benefited by more equal opportunities in Children's Bureau and state-sponsored child hygiene programs.[35]

The American Child Health Association also supported the Sheppard-Towner bill. This endorsement was not popular with all of the group's members, for example, Elizabeth Lowell Putnam resigned from the organization in 1922 because she felt "out of sympathy with its . . . tendencies." But the general membership, consisting of obstetric and pediatric physicians, nurses, social workers, public administrators, and philanthropists, generally accepted the Children's Bureau's argument that good maternal and infant health involved more than professional medical care. Richard A. Bolt, M.D., then president of the association and a resident of Cleveland, Ohio (a state in which the AMA's affiliate strongly opposed the plan), testified in favor of the Sheppard-Towner bill before the House committee.[36]

Similarly, the National Organization of Public Health Nursing, the American Association of Hospital Social Workers, the Women's

Health Foundation, the Life Insurance Institute of New York, and the Association of Women in Public Health endorsed the bill. These groups were part of the powerful lobby organized by Kelley and the WJCC. By the fall of 1921 pressure to pass the Sheppard-Towner bill had intensified and criticism from "super patriots" and the AMA seemed weak in comparison. A 1921 letter to the editor published in the *Survey* explained that antisuffragists belatedly opposed the bill due to a lack of understanding of its "true" nature.[37] Other opponents may have been similarly confused. Still, despite its comparatively long legislative history, the Children's Bureau's maternity and infancy bill actually faced little organized opposition.

In a last ditch effort to challenge the bill, Senator George H. Moses (R-N.H.) introduced an amendment to transfer the administration of Sheppard-Towner to the PHS. His proposal failed. Another opponent argued that the bill was fiscally irresponsible and should at least be drastically cut if not shelved, but the majority also rejected this suggestion. On July 22, 1921, the Senate voted in favor of Sheppard-Towner (63H7). Defeated, James Reed bitterly quipped that its title should read "A Bill to Organize a Board of Spinsters to Teach Mothers How to Raise Babies."[38] The approved legislation was then referred to the House Committee on Interstate and Foreign Commerce, which made some final changes illustrating the effect of opposition arguments.

First, to appease those who contended that the requirement for a separate state board of maternity and infant hygiene was wasteful and cumbersome, the new Sheppard-Towner bill allowed already existing state boards of health to administer federal funds. However, the proposed legislation did require that in states which chose to use this organizational structure, a distinct division of child hygiene or child welfare must exist within the health department, thereby leaving intact the Children's Bureau's assertion that children should be treated distinctly from adults.[39]

Second, at the federal level, the Sheppard-Towner bill required the organization of a federal Board of Maternity and Infant Hygiene composed of the surgeon general, the commissioner of education, and the chief of the Children's Bureau. This body approved state maternity and infancy programs utilizing Sheppard-Towner funds and the Children's Bureau administered the federal money.[40] The change was intended to quell criticism from the AMA and women's suffrage opponents that Rankin's original bill had placed too much power with the Children's Bureau, whose officials were mainly female social workers, not (male) physicians, and therefore not qualified to direct a federal maternity and infant health care program. This change did weaken the Children's Bureau's role. But, as already noted, the establishment of the Children's Bureau's Child Hygiene Division moved the bureau from strictly social and environmental factors to a consideration of medical causes for infant death and morbidity. As the AMA continued its effort to become the primary professional group for American physicians, it increasingly gained control of the PHS and other branches of the government involved in health issues. This, however, was not true of the Children's Bureau's mainly female staff of doctors. Some were members of the AMA, but women generally had little power within that organization, and no woman would become president of an AMA-affiliated state medical society until 1948.[41]

Lathrop had discussed the establishment of a federal board with Surgeon General Rupert Blue as early as 1919, though she reported that he was not interested in the specifics of the proposal. Instead, maintained Lathrop, Blue felt that the creation of a federal department of health was imminent and that "the Children's Bureau would be brought over to it." Lathrop adamantly argued that her agency should remain in the Department of Labor because its efforts there could better be directed at the "whole child." Blue's successor, Hugh S. Cumming, went even further. As noted earlier, he did not oppose the creation of a federal maternity and infancy act but he believed that it should be administrated by the PHS.[42]

Third, the final Sheppard-Towner proposal reduced the annual $4,000,000 appropriation advocated by Sheppard and Towner to $1,240,000 with an outright annual grant of $5,000 to each state and another $5,000 available to state legislatures approving matching funds. Under the final plan the Children's Bureau was given $50,000 for administration with the bulk of the money to be divided among the states on a general, not just rural, population basis. This resulted in a maternity and infancy bill emphasizing promotion over actual protection (in other words, prohibiting the actual administration of medical care), stipulated the Children's Bureau role as solely administrative, limited the act's funding to five years (1922-27), and specifically guarded against the payment of maternity benefits or stipends by the federal government.[43]

On November 19, 1921, at Harding's request, presidential secretary George B. Christian, Jr., sent a letter to the House again offering the president's support for the proposal. The House voted in favor of the bill on November 21, 1921 (279H39). The Senate then passed the amended act and President Harding signed the measure into law on November 23, 1921.[44] The only female member of Congress at the time, Alice Mary Robertson (R-Okla.) voted against the bill. Robertson, an antisuffragist and friend of Elizabeth Lowell Putnam, likewise differed ideologically with the Children's Bureau staff and its army of female lobbyists. She was elected to the House of Representatives in 1920 on the campaign principles of "Christianity, Americanism and Standpattism." The *New York Times,* commenting on Robertson's opposition to Sheppard-Towner during the House debate, reported that she "took a fling at clubwomen, who she said, sit at ease in comfortable homes, worrying about other people's children, and get a thrill over teacups by passing resolutions designed to bring about a new order in governmental affairs."[45] Robertson also suggested that Sheppard-Towner might encourage the use of birth control. However, it seems that at least in 1921, few accepted this argument. The Catholic hierarchy did not take a stand on Sheppard-Towner, but the Jesuit periodical *America* opposed the legislation. Social welfare activist Msgr. John A. Ryan testified in favor of Sheppard-Towner, and the National Council of Catholic Women and the National Catholic Welfare Council "unreservedly endorsed the bill."[46]

J. Stanley Lemons calls the passage of the Sheppard-Towner Maternity and Infancy Act "the first major dividend of the full enfranchisement of women . . . [and] a product of progressivism." It was also a product of Julia Lathrop's vision of the educational and research role the Children's Bureau should play in the effort to save the lives of mothers and babies. The purpose of the bureau, according to Lathrop, was to collect and distribute information. Under the Sheppard-Towner Act the Children's Bureau would not provide health care or trespass on the jurisdiction of state health and child welfare authorities.[47]

The push for a federal maternity and infancy act had met some obstacles. But perhaps more significantly, as Florence Kelley estimated, during the four years it took to gain the legislation, "625,000 babies died of largely preventable causes related to prenatal care, childbirth and early infancy."[48] The Children's Bureau and child welfare advocates needed patience and persistence in their efforts to improve children's lives.

As part of her desire to maintain consistency for the bureau, in June 1921 Lathrop wrote former Children's Bureau employee Grace Abbott about coming back to the agency, this time as chief.[49] It is not clear why Lathrop wanted to leave the agency, but her tenure had been longer than most Washington bureaucrats and she would celebrate her sixty-third birthday on June 29. It is logical that she might want to leave Washington after eight taxing years. It is also understandable that she looked to her friend, Grace Abbott, to carry on the fight. By

1921 Abbott was a well-respected scholar and articulate champion for progressive reform. Born in Grand Island, Nebraska, on November 17, 1878, Abbott graduated from Grand Island College in 1898 and immediately began teaching school in her home state. Finding such work unsatisfying, she earned a master's degree in political science from the University of Chicago in 1907. While attending school Abbott accepted a position with the Chicago Juvenile Protection Association, where she worked with Julia Lathrop for the first time. In late summer of 1908, the newly formed Immigrants' Protective League named Abbott as head. Furthering her ties to the settlement house movement, from 1912 to 1917 Abbott resided at Jane Addams's Hull-House. During those years Julia Lathrop asked Abbott to join the Children's Bureau staff in Washington several times, but each time Abbott refused. Passage of the Keating-Owen Child Labor Reform Act on September 1, 1916, finally enticed Abbott to take on the job of director of the Children's Bureau's Child Labor Division. Disappointed when the Supreme Court declared the law unconstitutional on June 2, 1918, Abbott agreed to remain with the Children's Bureau through the 1919 White House Child Welfare Conference. Abbott returned to Chicago for a teaching position at the Chicago School of Civics and Philanthropy immediately following the conference.[50]

According to her biographer Abbott was not sure she wanted to accept the job of Children's Bureau chief. She enjoyed her position at the School of Civics and Philanthropy and had earlier considered running for Congress. But the "women's network" placed considerable pressure on her to accept the job.[51] Lathrop felt sure that Abbott was the most qualified and best suited candidate, and support for Abbott's appointment came from a variety of sources. Besides the usual female reformers, backers included Julius Rosenwald, Wisconsin senator Robert M. La Follette (R), and former Illinois governor Frank O. Lowden, an influential and generally conservative Republican. Such support was somewhat surprising since many suspected Abbott of having Democratic party sympathies. As with Lathrop's retention in 1912, there was some concern by at least one partisan female Republican that the Children's Bureau chief should be "true to the . . . Party." But Harriet Taylor Upton liked Abbott and approved of the appointment. Lathrop was determined that her retirement announcement not threaten passage of Sheppard-Towner. On August 18 Lathrop requested that Secretary of Labor James J. Davis send a memo to President Harding announcing her intention to retire and making a recommendation that Abbott be appointed as Children's Bureau chief. Harding then forwarded Abbott's nomination to the Senate, which gave unanimous approval. Apparently the Senate agreed with Frank Lowden's assessment that "it would be difficult to find anyone anywhere in the country so peculiarly fitted to become Miss Lathrop's successor as Miss Abbott."[52]

The *Nation* also expressed its approval of the selection. "Higher praise we cannot give," lauded the editorial. Abbott "possesses the same scientific training, non-bureaucratic temperament, and plain love of folks" as Julia Lathrop. Furthermore, contended the editor, "such women as Miss Lathrop and her successor tend to raise the whole conception of what government may be made to mean in terms of human values."[53]

Lathrop had successfully chosen an heir who she believed would continue her vision for the bureau. In a letter to her friend Graham Taylor, editor of the *Survey,* Julia Lathrop wrote, "I cannot tell you how delighted I am that Miss Abbott was appointed." Lathrop was principally pleased that she kept the job from becoming open to political patronage. "In view of all the circumstances," prophetically noted Lathrop, "it is a genuine triumph for the principle of keeping the scientific services of the government out of the political field. Only the public back of us made this success possible."[54] The chief always believed that she had the public's support for the Children's Bureau's efforts. In Abbott, Lathrop felt that she had chosen someone possessing the skills and ideology to continue her program. Indeed, it appeared that the bureau's infant and maternity agenda, as well as its other efforts, would continue without skipping a beat.

Putting the Sheppard-Towner Law into Action

It was now up to Grace Abbott to put Sheppard-Towner into action. The debate moved to state legislatures considering the passage of required matching funds. Powerful lobbying efforts led by the state Leagues of Women Voters and officials working with state Departments of Health eventually secured approval sometime during the program's duration in every state except Connecticut, Illinois, and Massachusetts. Utilizing the same network as her predecessor, Abbott encouraged women's organizations sympathetic to the bureau and its work to pressure legislators to take full advantage of the act. Abbott also offered her staff's expertise to assist the drafting of laws necessary to implement the federal program.[55]

It is significant that each of the states that chose never to participate in the Sheppard-Towner program contained a large Catholic population. Catholic opposition to any form of government "intervention" in family life intensified during the 1920s as anti-Catholic sentiment also spread. By the time state legislatures began to debate Sheppard-Towner, some members of the Catholic hierarchy feared that such legislation might lead to further religious discrimination and the dissemination of birth control information. It is not clear whether members of local parishes felt the same way.

Funds provided under Sheppard-Towner became available to the states on March 20, 1922. However, although many were anxious to do so, few states were sufficiently prepared to immediately accept the matching funds. Anticipating congressional appropriation, the Delaware, Minnesota, New Hampshire, and New Mexico legislatures were the first to comply in December 1921. By June 30, 1922, seven more states had qualified and thirty-one others (through the governor or other state provision pending the next regular session of the state legislature) were in the process of compliance.[56]

But not all legislatures had great enthusiasm for the act and some states rejected federal funds despite gubernatorial acceptance. Connecticut legislators refused to sustain the governor's provisional approval of federal monies on the grounds that Sheppard-Towner infringed upon states' rights. In addition, Connecticut representatives opposing the act declared that such legislation expanded the federal government beyond its means and therefore it was time to stop the federal aid process. This claim seemed hollow to Sheppard-Towner advocates when the Connecticut legislature later agreed to accept federal funds for an "airplane squadron program."[57]

Citing similar reasons, California, Illinois, and Vermont returned their 1922 funds to the U.S. Treasury unspent. California and Vermont legislators later changed their minds. Retired Children's Bureau chief Julia Lathrop got involved in the drive to encourage acceptance of Sheppard-Towner in Illinois. However, her advocacy was not enough to thwart the opposition, which expressed many of the same objections expressed during congressional debate on the bill's passage. Lathrop enjoyed lobbying and called it "an alluring indoor sport if properly played," but she wrote Florence Kelley of her surprise at "the amount of mis-statement . . . especially among the ladies of high standing" concerning the Children's Bureau and Sheppard-Towner. Lathrop judged that the AMA clearly ran the politicians and carried the greatest influence in Illinois.[58]

The animosity of female antisuffragists toward the Children's Bureau may have also been an unrecognized but important part of this opposition. For example, Massachusetts and one of its citizens, Harriet A. Frothingham, a member of the Woman Patriots, brought separate suits against the Sheppard-Towner Act on constitutional grounds. The combined cases reached the U.S. Supreme Court, which judged that Frothingham's claim of unfair taxation was so minor that the Court had no jurisdiction. However, "the Court held that a state could not, in its role of 'parens patriate,' institute judicial proceedings to protect its citizens from operation of otherwise valid federal laws." This seems to suggest that the Court accepted the constitutionality of Sheppard-Towner although it avoided ruling directly on this issue.[59]

In New York, Governor Nathan Miller (R) encouraged the state legislature to refuse Sheppard-Towner funds, promising that he would veto any bill accepting the program. Twenty-eight New York women's organizations, led by the state's League of Women Voters, attacked Miller's position and circulated petitions showing public support for the measure, but the governor's influence proved too powerful and the legislature failed to appropriate matching funds for fiscal 1922. Florence Kelley had warned Miller in February 1923, after he had approved $125,000 to build a hog barn on the state fairgrounds, that his actions did "not improve the outlook of a candidate for the governorship of New York . . . [to] know that swine shelters appeal to him more strongly than dying mothers and babies." Kelley and members of the League of Women Voters likely felt some satisfaction when Alfred E. Smith (D) defeated Miller in the fall election. Smith, the country's most prominent Catholic politician, advocated acceptance of Sheppard-Towner as part of his campaign and gained approval for state matching funds in 1923. By June 30, 1923, forty-one states (including California and Vermont, which had returned their 1922 appropriations) had accepted Sheppard-Towner funds.[60]

Overall, passage of the federal Maternity and Infancy Act led to the initiation of increased state expenditures for maternal and infant care. Within three years, wrote Grace Abbott, "all the states excepting two [New Jersey and California] are appropriating either considerably more than or the same amount that they were . . . before the passage of the Maternity and Infancy Act." In addition, argued Abbott, most states had more money because those accepting the program "now have both State and Federal funds to spend for maternity and infancy." Even the three states continuing to refuse federal funds (Connecticut, Illinois, and Massachusetts), expanded state-sponsored efforts to reduce infant and maternal mortality. For example, Connecticut appropriated $55,000 for a new program intended to improve health care for pregnant women and young children. This amount was $12,000 less than that available to Connecticut through the combined federal and state Sheppard-Towner funds and was intended to offset a

$30,720 budget cut absorbed by the state's already established Bureau of Child Welfare.[61] But Connecticut's example illustrates that even a state which rejected Sheppard-Towner funds enacted programs to promote health care for mothers and babies.

The federal Board of Maternity and Infant Hygiene approved state plans for federally appropriated Sheppard-Towner funds. In early 1922, the Children's Bureau established a Division of Maternal and Infant Hygiene to administer board-approved monies. The bureau's already existing Division of Child Hygiene continued to conduct research in the general field of child health but had no direct responsibility for the administration of the Sheppard-Towner program. As another part of the plan, the Children's Bureau sponsored five annual conferences in Washington for directors, assistant directors, supervising nurses, and other staff officers of the state agencies administering Sheppard-Towner funds. These meetings offered the opportunity for those involved to exchange ideas and formulate new strategies.[62]

Each state determined the degree of Children's Bureau involvement in actual maternal and infant welfare work. Those states cooperating in the Sheppard-Towner program requested either direct supervision or various amounts of consultation from the bureau's Division of Maternal and Infant Hygiene. Anna E. Rude, M.D., headed the division and another women doctor served as assistant director. Women also worked as office staff: an accountant, a secretary, two clerks, and a social worker. Generally, the field staff included twelve doctors and two or more nurses. As might be expected, most physicians working for the bureau were women and the nurses were all female.[63]

Women also played the primary role in implementing the Sheppard-Towner program on the state level. Utilizing Children's Bureau records, Robyn Muncy estimates that at least 75 percent of these administrators were women and the more than 800 state board of health nurses, whose salaries were supplemented by Sheppard-Towner funds, were female. Women also composed approximately half of the state programs' full-time doctors and held the majority of other paid and volunteer positions in the Sheppard-Towner program.[64] However, it should also be noted that even under Sheppard-Towner no woman served as head of any state board of health responsible for administering the program. Further, state maternity and infancy advisory committees which developed the plans for spending Sheppard-Towner funds followed the pattern established in Ohio, where at least eighteen of the committee's twenty-six members were male.[65] Many Americans accepted maternal and infant child care as a women's issue but men still held most policy-making positions outside of the

Children's Bureau. In addition, over the duration of the program the proportion of women in positions of authority declined.[66]

But at the federal level women held the most important positions, For example, Dorothy Reed Mendenhall's influence may be seen in Sheppard-Towner's efforts to reduce infant and maternal mortality through midwife training. Although they had virtually disappeared from most native-born white communities, in many urban immigrant neighborhoods and rural areas midwives attended more than half of all births. Midwives were generally foreign born or African American and many working-class mothers chose them because they were less expensive than doctors or because there were few or no physicians practicing in their neighborhoods. Tradition and female modesty also contributed to the preference of some women for midwives rather than male doctors.[67] While head of the Chicago Immigrants' Protective League, Grace Abbott concluded that it was, at least for the time being, inevitable that some women would use midwives. Therefore, under Sheppard-Towner the Children's Bureau encouraged states to develop midwife training programs and enforce (or establish) state licensing. Abbott agreed with medical organizations such as the AMA that there were some "careless, dirty, and dangerous" midwives who were partly responsible for the higher death rates of immigrant and black mothers and babies. She felt that medical doctors could offer superior care in all cases. But Abbott argued that ignoring the country's estimated 45,000 midwives, or putting them out of business before physicians were readily available to all women, was not in the immediate best interest of mothers and babies. Contrary to what many reformers believed at the time, scholars have demonstrated that mortality and morbidity rates were not necessarily higher among births attended by midwives. Only six states had no laws regulating midwives by 1921.[68]

The Children's Bureau primarily directed its midwife training and licensing program in areas where few white physicians worked. In Georgia, Tennessee, Texas, Delaware, and Virginia the Children's Bureau's only African American staff physician, Ionia Whipper, M.D., conducted special classes for "granny" midwives. Some were anxious to earn the legitimacy that instruction and licensing afforded but many reluctantly gave up traditional practices. Molly Ladd-Taylor shows that some "granny" midwives felt their experience gave them the right to challenge the authority of Children's Bureau's "professional" representatives. All were told to register births and were instructed in the bureau's infant and maternal care standards. New Mexico instituted a similar program taught by an unidentified "Spanish-speaking" Children's Bureau staff nurse. The bureau reported no specific program for Native American women and children, although some western states established health care centers near Indian reservations with Sheppard-Towner funds.[69] Although the Children's Bureau's midwife training program recognized the important contribution of midwives, most states simply intensified efforts to license and control them.

Other activities undertaken with Sheppard-Towner funds also varied by state, but each generally "sought to teach the public how better care of mothers and babies [would] save lives and improve health." All relied on the combined efforts of physicians, nurses, and women volunteers who encouraged use of state-controlled diagnostic clinics. Education was the fundamental strategy and programs fell into four general categories: individual instruction, group education, distribution of literature, and standardization.[70]

The first tactic emphasized individual instruction. Traveling health demonstrations conducted by physicians and nurses under state auspices constituted the most visible part of this strategy. In addition, many states used Sheppard-Towner funds to establish permanent health diagnostic centers offering the same kinds of individual instruction. The latter were conducted by local health authorities and financed at least in part by community funds. In addition, public health nurses offered individual instruction through home visits. Although Sheppard-Towner specified that funds must be used solely for the promotion of good maternal and infant health practices, in many cases other family members also benefited from a visit by the Sheppard-Towner nurse. Anna Rude explained that while "a general health program would absolutely defeat the purpose of the . . . Federal Act . . . it is not possible in rural areas to do specialized public health nursing," so consequently many states used Sheppard-Towner funds to pay "from one-sixth to one-half of a nurse's time."[71] Individual instruction translated to direct contact with a health care professional, not accessible to many through any other resource.

Second, states organized group instruction efforts. Sheppard-Towner funding paid for classes in proper prenatal and infant care for midwives, mothers, and teachers. Adolescent girls received tutelage in clubs called Little Mothers' Leagues. Group instruction strategy also involved exhibits, "healthmobiles," and demonstration clinics. The Children's Bureau produced its own collection of silent movies and filmstrips that could be rented by state and local health departments. "The Best Fed Baby" is a film advocating breast-feeding and good postnatal care. "Motherhood," contends the introduction, is "the most beautiful thing in the world." But, cautioned the film, it is not something every mother is able to do without help. The film's opening scenes show a new mother who is unable to produce enough milk to feed her baby and must rely on formula. She is irritable and nervous, and while she prepares the infant's milk the father uncomfortably holds the child. A neighbor, described as a "good mother," tells the new mother how to relax so that she can produce enough milk to feed her baby. The attractive, calm neighbor also shows how to burp the child. A male doctor is called to help. Later, the film compares new mothers with farm animals to make the point that women should eat well, sleep eight hours per night, and nap for one hour each day so that they might have "the best fed baby." Both women in the film are white, middle-class, have only one child, and do not work outside the home. Another bureau production, "Our Children," filmed in Gadsen, Alabama, and first produced for Children's Year, shows how child health demonstrations could be organized by local women's clubs working in conjunction with the health department and the Children's Bureau. "Sun Babies," filmed in New Haven, Connecticut, has subtitles in both English and Spanish and concerns the prevention of rickets. Unlike the previously mentioned examples, this film features black and white children. The children have obviously bowed legs resulting from vitamin D deficiency. Such films and slide shows helped to make demonstration clinics and health conferences very popular. Movies and slide shows were novelties for many audiences. One state public health physician reported that many who attended his talks were "starved for a bit of amusement and thirsty for health knowledge." Probably more for the first than the second, as his next statement reveals, children sat with "mouths agape and . . . eyes shining." Some states also spent Sheppard-Towner funds on graduate courses for nurses and on instructive conferences and institutes for physicians.[72]

The third strategy, and the most widely spread, involved the distribution of literature on maternal and infant care, child care and management, and related subjects prepared by state boards of health and the Children's Bureau. Aware that non-English-speaking mothers could not be "Americanized" if unable to read the agency's literature, the Children's Bureau funded the translation of some of its instructional pamphlets into Yiddish, Italian, Spanish, Serbo-Croatian, and other languages.[73] Pamphlets produced by the bureau included its previous best sellers and some new additions such as "What Builds Babies?" (1925). This publication prescribed a diet for pregnant and nursing mothers with suggested menus. The daily diet included at least one quart of milk, one raw-vegetable salad, an egg, a citrus fruit or tomato, one cooked green leafy vegetable, and a serving of whole-grain cereal or bread. Another pamphlet, "Minimum Standards of Prenatal Care," told "the least a mother should do before her baby is born." As with other bureau advice, this pamphlet emphasized diet, sleep, and exercise. But it also included specific instructions concerning "elimination of waste products" (kidneys, bowels, skin, and lungs), care of the teeth, breasts, weight control, clothing, and "mental hygiene." "Remember," stated the pamphlet, "Pregnancy is a natural process. Simple, regular, normal living during this period makes for Good Health in both Mother and Baby. 'EVERY CHILD HAS A RIGHT TO BE WELL BORN.'" Such statements seem to contradict the agency's notion that all mothers had to be trained. Careful reading reveals that the bureau preached that pregnancy was "natural," but that the process should be supervised by medical professionals. It is important to note that the agency was trying to counter what it believed were dangerous myths surrounding pregnancy and the care of newborns. Beginning in 1921, Children's Bureau's physicians and the National Advisory Committee (composed of leading pediatricians and obstetricians) regularly revised and reissued the agency's pamphlets.[74]

Fourth, state bureaus responsible for administering the Sheppard-Towner Act established standards and licensing procedures for maternity homes and gathered data on maternal and infant mortality and morbidity. Following a strategy similar to that undertaken by the Children's Bureau in its earliest efforts, Sheppard-Towner advocates believed that the collection of accurate morbidity and mortality statistics in the states would provide a sound "scientific" basis for planning future needs and evaluating current programs. Even more importantly, many maintained that such knowledge encouraged the development of good health care for mothers and children on the private and public level. The Children's Bureau in cooperation with state and local public health officials conducted and published results from numerous maternal and infant mortality and morbidity studies.[75]

When the Sheppard-Towner appropriation act passed in 1922 its funding was authorized for only five years, to June 30, 1927. A December 25, 1925, letter from Secretary of Labor James J. Davis to Representative James S. Parker (R-N.Y.) suggested that a bill to extend the act would be introduced during the first session of the Sixty-ninth Congress and that President Calvin Coolidge said that the renewal of Sheppard-Towner was "not contrary to his fiscal policy." The *Woman Patriot* charged that Davis had merely signed the letter, and that Grace Abbott was its actual author. This would be the usual procedure for the secretary to follow and shows the assumption by

Abbott and Children's Bureau's supporters that Congress would extend the Sheppard-Towner Maternity and Infancy Act without much difficulty.[76]

The Beginning of the End

However, amid an increasingly conservative political climate and a better-organized opposition led by the AMA, Sheppard-Towner's future was not so certain. President Coolidge supported only a two-year extension of the program's appropriation and gave this "with the understanding and hope that the administration of the funds to be provided would be with a view to the gradual withdrawal of the Federal Government from this field." Again the stage was set and the bureau's usual supporters and critics lined up for a bitter struggle. But this time they faced an opposition encouraged by an administration that did not support federal intervention in social welfare. In addition, it was now clear that politicians had little to fear from the "women's bloc."[77]

Sheppard-Towner supporters argued that although much had been accomplished under the first years of the act, a great deal more needed to be done. They showed that while the United States had succeeded in reducing its infant mortality rate, it still ranked seventh behind Australia, Norway, Sweden, the Netherlands, the Irish Free State, and New Zealand. New Zealand had the lowest rate of 36 per 1,000 live births and not even an individual state in the United States met this figure. The 1925 U.S. infant mortality rate was 73.6 per 1,000 live births, and only four states in the birth registration area had a rate of less than 55.0. State administrators sent letters and testimonials in support of the Maternity and Infancy Act to Congress. Many health officials argued further that maternal and infant health programs designed to save the lives of mothers and babies could not be fully implemented during the proposed two-year extension period, but they were willing to take whatever they could get.[78]

Florence Kelley and the NLWV again came to the Children's Bureau's rescue. Kelley and Maud Wood Parks, former president of the NLWV, organized the Women's Committee for the Extension of the Maternity and Infancy Act, a coalition of eleven national women's groups from the WJCC. The Daughters of the American Revolution, which had withdrawn from the WJCC in 1921, was conspicuously absent.[79]

Julia Lathrop wrote an article for the December 1926 issue of the NLWV's publication, the *Woman Citizen,* praising the work accomplished under Sheppard-Towner but carefully noting that the job was not finished. She assumed passage of the extension and called the program evidence of the "finest proof of the sanity of women's new voting power." But Coolidge's attitude of fiscal conservatism provides a better reflection of the times.[80]

Opponents of Sheppard-Towner's extension argued that Coolidge's political philosophy opposed such "paternalistic and bureaucratic legislation," and that the claim by the program's advocates that the president supported such legislation overstated his position.[81] Conservative ideals seemed increasingly popular as the 1920s progressed. This trend combined with the growing strength of the AMA to condemn Sheppard-Towner and the Children's Bureau in general. Since the act's passage, the AMA and its state affiliates had criticized the Children's Bureau's Maternity and Infancy Act as a form of state medicine as defined in the organization's May 1922 resolution against Sheppard-Towner:

> "State Medicine" is hereby defined for the purpose of this resolution to be any form of medical treatment provided, conducted, controlled, or subsidized by the federal or any state government, or municipality, excepting such service as is provided by the Army, Navy, and the Public Health Service, and that which is necessary for the control of communicable diseases, the treatment of indigent sick, and such other services as may be approved by and administered under the direction of or by a local county medical society, and are not disapproved by the state medical society of which it is a component part.[82]

In keeping with this policy some *JAMA* editorials advocated coordination of federal health care programs, but most asked for physicians and others "to join in the movement to check the continuance of 'Sheppard-Townerism.'"[83]

Criticism from other groups included more than the Sheppard-Towner program. During a White House dinner, antisuffragist and maternal/infant-health-care-reformer Elizabeth Lowell Putnam told President Coolidge, "I am longing to do one more piece of work for [the] country before I die, and that is to be Chief of the Children's Bureau in order that I might secure its abolishment." Similarly, the Woman Patriots and the Sentinels of the Republic intensified their criticism of the Children's Bureau and its mandate. During the summer of 1926, seven issues of the *Woman Patriot* included the text of a thirty-six-page petition to the Senate dedicated to the defeat of the Sheppard-Towner program. It asked, "Can it be denied that the Maternity and Infancy Act is on the 'camel's-nose-under-the-tent' measure of a Marxian Communist and of a radical Children's Bureau seeking arbitrary, unlimited 'full grant of power' to standardize and socialize 'the whole field of child welfare and childcare?'" Further, the paper argued that the staff of the Children's Bureau was communist, unqualified, and "absolutely unnecessary." Such criticism encouraged the introduction of three bills in Congress to abolish the Children's Bureau but none were successful.[84]

Apprehension by some critics that federal maternal and infant legislation would usurp parental rights had been an argument against the Sheppard-Towner's original passage, but the opposition more effectively used this reasoning against the program's extension. Opponents complained that the "purpose of this maternity act . . . is not for the benefits of babies and of mothers of the country. It is for the conscious purpose of setting up State control of maternity and childhood." As noted earlier, some members of the Catholic hierarchy and its lay leadership continued to fear that such legislation would infringe upon religious freedom and advocate birth control. Even some "old friends" seemed swayed. Mrs. Frances E. Slattery, president of the Massachusetts League of Catholic Women, testified before the House committee holding hearings on the Sheppard-Towner extension that the women in her organization were "very proud to protect the health of our mothers and our babies, and we do not need any instruction from Washington as to the standardization of our children and mothers in Massachusetts." Mrs. Slattery stated that her organization's 400,000 members opposed renewal of the Maternity and Infancy Act and urged Congress to beware of women lobbyists who claimed to represent the desires of all women voters.[85]

The congressional committee report on Sheppard-Towner's extension (H.R. 7555) also reflected the more conservative fiscal trend toward social welfare. Although given a favorable report by the majority, the committee concluded that eventually the states ought to assume the full responsibility for the promotion of maternal and infant health care. The Senate committee considering the bill made a similar recommendation and reduced the program's extension period to one year. On the Senate floor, Morris Sheppard led the debate calling for extension of the program and James Reed again spoke for the act's opponents. Sheppard maintained that he "was the author of the measure" and that neither he nor Congress had intended for the bill to be limited to a five-year test and that a two-year extension was too short. Reed wanted no continuation of the Sheppard-Towner program in any form. Action was delayed and no vote was taken.[86]

During the second session of Congress, Sheppard submitted a compromise reappropriation bill with a significant change. The new bill provided funds for two years, and terminated the maternity and infancy program on June 30, 1929. This proposal passed the Senate on January 13, 1927. Twenty-one senators, twelve more than had opposed the original bill in 1921, voted against the measure.[87]

Although this was not a complete victory for the opposition, the Children's Bureau and their allies misjudged the compromise appropriation act as only a temporary difficulty. Grace Abbott wrote that "under the circumstances we yielded very little." Abbott and Kelley looked forward to a new bill which would reestablish a permanent federal maternal and infant program.[88] Abbott calculated that passage of such legislation would only be possible with the cooperation of organized medicine. The next major Children's Bureau study, an extensive examination of maternal mortality in fifteen states, was Abbott's effort to "show the doctors what they are doing by opposing maternity and infancy legislation."[89]

This strategy of courting the AMA did not work. Attempts to pass a renewal or new legislation providing for federal funds to promote maternal and infant care before the cutoff date of June 30, 1929, were unsuccessful. Even an effort to pass a federal maternity and infancy program administered by the PHS, the Jones-Cooper bill, introduced in April 1929 by Senator Wesley L. Jones (D-Wash.) and Representative James G. Cooper (R-Ohio), failed (H.R. 1195, S. 255). Cooper had been a supporter of the original Sheppard-Towner bill[90] and had said in 1920 that maternity and infancy protection was "not the work of a practicing physician; it must be done by a woman, a visiting nurse, or some woman of character." Apparently by 1929 he had changed his mind. Children's Bureau supporters opposed the Jones-Cooper bill and felt betrayed by Herbert Hoover, who many had believed was an advocate for children's welfare and therefore a supporter of the Children's Bureau. The Jones-Cooper bill had originally placed responsibility for the administration of the program in the Children's Bureau, but under pressure from the Hoover administration authority moved to the PHS. Hoover was likely influenced by Ray Lyman Wilbur, M.D., a former president of the AMA and Hoover's secretary of the interior.[91]

Sheppard-Towner Accomplishments and Failures, 1922-29

The Children's Bureau evaluated the four general types of programs instituted under Sheppard-Towner in a 1931 summary of seven years' work in the cooperating states and the Territory of Hawaii. It concluded correctly that only "approximate results can be shown by figures reported by the States, as the figures available fall short of actual accomplishments." Sheppard-Towner funds supported a total of 183,252 health conferences for mothers and babies and helped fund the establishment of 2,978 permanent child health and/or prenatal diagnostic clinics. From 1924 to 1929, 19,723 classes were held and 21,030,489 pieces of literature distributed. The state reports for the last four years of the act showed that some form of Sheppard-Towner maternity and infancy work reached more than 4,000,000 infants and preschool children and approximately 700,000 pregnant women. While these numbers are significant, the pregnant mothers reached by the Sheppard-Towner Act delivered only a minor fraction of the 10.9 million babies born in the United States from 1926 through 1929.[92]

As the Children's Bureau acknowledged, it is difficult to evaluate the direct effect of the program. However, it is likely that the Sheppard-Towner Act contributed to the nation's decreasing infant mortality rate. From 1921 to 1929 the birth registration area grew from twenty-seven states and Washington, D.C., to a birth and death registration area of forty-five states and Washington, D.C. The infant mortality rate for the birth registration area in 1921 was 75.6 per 1,000 live births. In 1929, the rate had declined to 67.9, even with the addition of many states with higher than average infant mortality rates.[93] Nevertheless, while the infant mortality rate declined, there was no significant change in maternal death trends. In 1921, 68.2 women per 10,000 live births died from causes associated with pregnancy and childbirth. In 1929, the rate had actually increased to 69.5.

Some voiced concerns about the country's high maternal mortality rate at the 1926 annual convention of state directors. As noted, Abbott believed that the great number of mothers dying as a result of pregnancy and childbirth presented clear evidence of the need for a national maternity program. Those attending the meeting agreed to undertake a study to determine why so many mothers were dying. Any state participating in the Sheppard-Towner program was also eligible to take part in the new study if the state department of health and the state medical society requested inclusion. Thirteen states participated for two years (1927-28) and two states (California and Oklahoma) for one year (1928).[94] Children's Bureau physicians conducted the two-year study in nine states, state authorities completed the remaining six. The two-year study combined interviews conducted with doctors, midwives, other birth attendants, and family members with data collected from birth and death certificates to ascertain the causes of maternal mortality for 7,380 women. When the cause of death could be ascertained, investigators categorized the quality of prenatal care these women had received. Only forty-two women were judged to have received excellent care, 2,611 had some prenatal care, and 3,025 had gotten no medical attention prior to delivery. The survey concluded that prenatal care was not only an important factor in saving the lives of babies but also in preventing the deaths of mothers.[95]

As this study indicated, pregnancy, childbirth, and the postnatal period were dangerous times for many American women. Approximately 40 percent (2,948) of the women in the study died from puerperal septis infection and about 25 percent (1,825) of all maternal deaths followed abortion. Of the abortion cases, 73 percent (1,324) died from infection. Investigators determined the type of abortion for 1,588 of the total abortion-related deaths, finding 50 percent (794) induced for other than "therapeutic" (medical) reasons, 37 percent (589) spontaneous, and 13 percent (205) classified as medically necessary. The report suggested that the 237 undetermined cases were probably induced, because "they were almost certainly not therapeutic." In addition, the study's advisory committee surmised that probably many of the "so-called spontaneous abortions were really induced" and highlighted the "seriousness" of abortion for unmarried women. The study found that botched abortions were responsible for the deaths of more than one-third of the unmarried pregnant women. Hence, argues the report, the "management of an abortion calls for the best medical care that can be given" and the "abortion problem is a widespread sociological and economic problem, which the medical profession must have help in solving."[96]

However, the Children's Bureau did not consider legalizing abortion and continued to ignore the promotion of safe birth control as a way to help save mothers' lives. This was true despite the growing influence of the national birth control movement, which is probably best evidenced by the fact that in 1929 the national birthrate fell below the replacement level for the first time since such data began to be collected. By 1929 birth control clinics operated in only twelve American cities, but this number dramatically increased over the next seven years. By 1936 activists had established an additional 240 birth control clinics throughout the United States.[97] Instead of advocating that women obtain the means to control their reproduction, under Grace Abbott's leadership the Children's Bureau tightened its policy of ignoring birth control as a health care option. In response to accusations by some Catholics and conservatives that the Children's Bureau promoted birth control, Abbott wrote, "the Children's Bureau has at no time urged birth control, nor are any of the State agencies which are in charge of the local administration of the Maternity and Infancy Act doing so." The chief believed that the

Children's Bureau's role was to educate the public about how to have healthy babies, not encourage the use of birth control. The ultimate goal of the bureau was to reduce the infant mortality rate and improve children's health. Preserving the health of American women was only important to the Children's Bureau because most women were mothers. Accessibility to safe and effective birth control might have helped some children achieve their "right to childhood" and preserved the health of their mothers, but for the Children's Bureau increasing public awareness of the need for prenatal and postnatal care was the most important means of reducing maternal and infant mortality. Obviously Grace Abbott felt that birth control was a controversial issue the agency should avoid, but ironically, as noted earlier, Children's Bureau critics continued to accuse the agency of advocating the use of birth control despite its actual policy.

Significantly, contrary to the AMA's fears, another effect of Sheppard-Towner was an increasing emphasis on public health measures and medical care provided by private physicians. This trend overshadowed the role played by poverty and inaccessibility to good medical care as significant causes of maternal and infant deaths. It is difficult to determine exactly what programs were part of the Sheppard-Towner efforts in each state, but most likely many followed the same pattern as Ohio, which limited its Sheppard-Towner work to education and diagnosis, advocating that women and children in need of medical care visit a private physician or a local public or private health clinic. Such policy placed physicians in the role of primary providers for women's and children's health care. But as Ohio's experience indicated, doctors were simply not available in many rural areas.[98]

The cost of its recommended physician-provided care was another problem not addressed directly by the Sheppard-Towner program. In 1927, the AMA, the PHS, and the Metropolitan Life Insurance Company formed the Committee on the Cost of Medical Care. This group conducted a five-year study examining "the one great outstanding problem before the medical profession . . . the delivery of adequate, scientific medical service to all the people, rich and poor, at a cost which can be reasonably met by them in their respective stations in life." The committee found "much complaint among the people because of the high cost of medical care [and] dissatisfaction among physicians and other personnel because of insufficient income." This two-edged sword revealed that even the AMA was aware that many Americans could not afford medical care.[99] The Children's Bureau felt that its advocacy of state- and community-funded clinics helped to make good health care accessible. However, as designed by the Children's Bureau, Sheppard-Towner funds were limited to diagnosis and education. Therefore, it was up to the states and local communities to provide affordable health care to mothers and babies. The AMA generally controlled state and local health departments, which, although often well intentioned, emphasized professionalization, cure, and the ability of physicians to make an "adequate" income over preventive and affordable health care.

Even though the Children's Bureau failed to address some fundamental issues concerning infant and maternal health, it is probably true that, as the agency claimed, a greater "interest on the part of the public was aroused in the welfare and hygiene of maternity and infancy as a result of the passage of the maternity and infancy act." States did give more attention to the effort. The bureau argued that "in 1921 it was still a moot question whether child hygiene and maternal mortality were necessary divisions in a good State public-health program. . . . Now, however, the general public as well as official State agencies, recognize the necessity of including in public-health programs the prevention of morbidity and mortality of mothers and babies."[100]

Sheppard-Towner implemented a Children's Bureau plan emphasizing standardization, maternal education, and medical care distributed by physicians. As Richard Meckel has argued, Sheppard-Towner was "a defeat in victory." Awareness was raised, but the program itself had limited application and defined the government's role in maternal and infant care as mainly promotion.[101] The primary responsibility for protecting the lives of mothers and babies rested with the states. Furthermore, Sheppard-Towner's reliance on the medical reasons why babies and mothers died ignored the social and economic issues contributing to why many were unable to maintain a lifestyle conducive to good health. In addition, the debate over the reappropriation of Sheppard-Towner funds legitimized criticism of the Children's Bureau's "whole child" philosophy, therefore undermining its very existence. Supporters of the PHS and the AMA clearly did not accept the notion that a single agency could best deal with the needs of the "whole child."

5

The Children's Bureau and Child Labor Reform, 1912-32

If Sheppard-Towner was a "defeat in victory," the Children's Bureau's contemporary effort to abolish child labor was simply a defeat. The agency's work in child labor reform temporarily took the Children's Bureau further than simply investigation, reporting, and persuasion. However, although the bureau's attention to this issue fostered discussion about creative alternatives, in the end the Children's Bureau's adherence to a middle-class family ideal hindered efforts to protect children from exploitive labor. The agency endorsed federal standardization of minimum-age work requirements and advocated state enforcement of compulsory school attendance laws. But these policies did not deal directly with the underlying causes that perpetuated child labor.

The definition of what constitutes exploitive child labor has changed over time. During the early nineteenth century, most people in the United States accepted the appenticeship or employment of children as young as eight as normal and even desirable in the case of orphans, those with no father in the household, or those from poor families. Tradition inherited from the Elizabethan Poor Law of 1598 provided that children dependent upon the community for financial assistance should contribute to their own support through appenticeship or some form of indentured labor. Adolescent boys often obtained job skills by working as apprentices or as farm laborers in exchange for room and board. Older girls frequently worked as live-in domestics or provided child care. But most jobs were not the kind associated with modern manufacturing or agribusiness. As some historians have suggested, before the Civil War only a minority of manufacturers hired children as factory workers due to discipline problems and the abundance of cheap adult labor. Although likely more myth than reality, in the Gilded Age and Progressive Era many held a romantic view of child labor in antebellum America. The forced labor of African American slave children is one obvious contradiction to this belief, but few post-Civil War reformers concerned themselves with this exception to the history of child labor. Instead they focused on the fact that throughout American history most white children had performed chores on the family farm, assisted with the care of younger siblings, or worked at other domestic tasks.[1]

These practices certainly provided the opportunity for exploitation, but many adults wrongly believed that emotional attachments fostered by such circumstances protected most children from abuse. However, by the mid-nineteenth century it appeared to some reformers that modernization and technology had altered working conditions for children. A growing number no longer labored on the family farm or in private homes or shops. Instead, many children toiled long hours for very low wages as migrant agricultural workers, in the nation's mines and factories, doing piecework in tenements, or on city streets as vendors, messengers, or "newsies," selling newspapers and magazines early in the morning or until late at night. The NCLC defined child labor as "*any* work done by children that interferes with their full physical development, their opportunity for a desirable minimum of education, or their needed recreation." Child labor, explained the NCLC, "is the employment of children *in any occupation* at unfit ages, . . . for unreasonable hours, . . . under unhealthful or hazardous conditions, or while the schools which they should attend are in session."[2] In general the NCLC viewed the wage employment of persons under fourteen years of age as an abusive child labor practice. By 1930 the organization would call for the prohibition of wage labor for persons under sixteen and for protective legislation applied to workers sixteen and seventeen years of age. Supported by the NCLC, during its first two decades of work the Children's Bureau served as the chief federal lobbyist attempting to initiate such change.

Children's Bureau Supporters and Child Labor Reform

Clarke Chambers concludes that "probably no segment of the progressive crusade engaged more fully the moral energies of reformers than the battle against the exploitation of children in mine, factory, street, and field." Progressive Era activist Samuel McCune Lindsay reported that the child labor reform movement was "planned with greater skill, prosecuted on a more truly national scale, and supported with greater generosity [than any other] organized effort for social welfare."[3] In this atmosphere the founders, supporters, and even opponents of the Children's Bureau believed that child labor reform was an inevitable part of the agency's responsibility. Indeed, the 1912 act establishing the bureau mandated that the agency investigate and report on "child labor" and the circumstance of children employed in what were vaguely defined as "dangerous occupations." The bureau's primary architect, Florence Kelley, had complained in a 1906 speech that child labor was a "national evil" and could only be eliminated through compulsory school attendance laws, diligent enforcement, and public condemnation. Arguing that legislation alone was not enough, she insisted that "ultimately the attitude of mind of the nation . . . decides whether child labor laws shall be enforced after they are enacted." On another occasion Kelley argued that attitudes could be changed through the "consecutive" publication of state child labor laws "in popular form" by a federal agency such as the Children's Bureau.[4]

Child labor critics did not solely rely on humanitarian arguments to promote their ideas. Using reasoning familiar to those involved in the infant welfare movement and the conservation efforts of the Progressive Era, child labor reformers contended that working children long hours or under dangerous conditions wasted human resources and had immediate as well as long-term economic consequences for everyone. Child labor robbed the nation of an "intelligent citizenship" for the future. Modern employment practices were an "evil" fostered by industrialization and greed. The United States needed an educated work force trained in "democratic" ideals. "Child labor," argued muckraking journalist John Spargo, "is not educative or wholesome, but blighting to body, mind, and spirit." In 1905, Florence Kelley wrote that "child labor and child illiteracy are twin problems [that] demand for their solution no mere sectional effort, but the vigorous determination of the whole people." She predicted that in the future "the years of childhood shall be held sacred to the work of education, free from the burden of wage-earning." Consequently, child welfare reformers warned that young persons who spent their hours working for wages were denied "a right to childhood" and grew to be unproductive adults with criminal personalities. Reformers often linked child labor, illiteracy, and criminal behavior. Kelley noted that at the turn of the century states with the highest percentages of children laboring in agricultural and industrial jobs also reported literacy rates below 80 percent for persons from age ten to fourteen: Louisiana (67.12 percent), South Carolina (70.44 percent), Alabama (71.11 percent), Georgia (77.21 percent), Mississippi (77.62 percent), and North Carolina (78.25 percent).[5] The popular press generally depicted children who worked for wages as poor waifs exploited by selfish parents and monopolistic industrialists. But the media also suggested that many of these children had the potential to be deviant and dependent adults. To child welfare advocates greedy parents, poverty, children anxious to leave school, exploitive employers, and an indifferent public were the causes of modern child labor practices.[6]

For these reformers the existence of child labor constituted a national crisis. From 1870 to 1910 the number and percentage of children working for wages had increased. Activists noted that this was true despite the increasingly popular recognition of childhood as a special period of life, separate from adult responsibilities. In 1870 approximately 740,000 children age ten through fifteen worked for wages in the United States (13.2 percent of that age cohort). By 1900 there were over 1,750,000 (18.2 percent) at work and in 1910 1,990,225 (18.4 percent).[7] The actual number of working children was probably much higher. This count did not include those under ten years of age, most who performed piecework at home, were illegally employed, or worked as "independent merchants." In addition, the data did not reflect the fact that some parents and employers lied about the age of young workers, a circumstance especially true in states which had already enacted compulsory school attendance and child labor laws.[8]

Some parents reluctantly sent their children to work. Many working-class adults' salaries fell below the amount needed to support a family, and although meager, a youngster's earnings were often crucial to a family's survival. The desperate circumstances of poor farmers in the South made the employment of children in the local mill a way to improve a family's immediate condition. Some urban immigrant families migrated to rural areas during the planting and harvest seasons to labor as pickers or to work in canneries. Others traveled a similar path seeking employment in oyster-, fish-, or shrimp-processing factories. In such cases entire families labored in order to improve their lot. Other parents sent their children to work because they believed that it built character and offered job training necessary for the future. For some, education beyond the lowest grades seemed a waste of time, and many children were anxious to leave school. The persistent romantic notion that farm labor, even migratory farm labor, was healthy for young bodies further fueled the acceptance of child labor among some Americans. The issue of parental rights was another factor complicating the issue. Although Massachusetts and Connecticut had passed the nation's first laws restricting child labor in 1842 (limiting the workday to ten hours for children under twelve and fourteen respectively), many still believed that only parents had the right to regulate the work patterns of their children.

Boys were more likely to work for wages than girls, although it should be noted that girls' labor often consisted of unpaid domestic and child care duties performed at home or for relatives. Neither child labor reformers nor the Bureau of the Census recognized the domestic contributions of "little mothers" as "gainful employment." But like labor engaged in by boys, such responsibilities often kept girls from attending school. Interestingly, black children living in urban areas during the late nineteenth and early twentieth century tended to remain in school longer than children from immigrant families, probably because few industrial jobs in cities were open to blacks. But many black children in rural areas of the South labored long hours in agriculture and few attended even the poor schools available to them beyond the eighth grade. Circumstances had changed surrounding children's labor, but attitudes had not transformed as quickly.[9] Technology and industrialization appeared to be the enemy rather than the friend of working-class children.

Most people in the United States were very familiar with child labor reform issues by the time the Children's Bureau was established in 1912. During the first decade of the twentieth century the popular press had highlighted numerous instances of exploitive child labor practices. For example, the exposure of what child welfare reformers cited as the worst effects of child labor surfaced as part of the highly publicized 1902 Pennsylvania coal strike. Young boys working in the coal industry were generally illiterate, malnourished, anemic, and had permanent physical deformities. The press coverage surrounding the strike showed that although Pennsylvania had a minimum age requirement of fourteen for such employment, the law was simply not enforced. Some of the boys were only ten or eleven years old. A few worked deep in the mine, but most toiled aboveground as breakers, where they sat stooped for ten or eleven hours a day picking slate, stone, and other waste materials from mined coal passing on conveyor belts below their feet. Their hands were often cut, sore, and infected. Experienced workers nicknamed new recruits "red tops" until the skin on the inexperienced workers' fingers hardened and no longer bled. Working conditions were unhealthy at best and dangerous at worst; and boys were often injured or killed on the job. For adult miners, the presence of children on the job site had the negative effect of keeping adult wages low. Articles in popular magazines such as *McClures,* the *Independent,* the *Outlook, Cosmopolitan,* and *Saturday Evening Post* agreed that child labor was bad for everyone involved and contended that the practice resulted in crime, poverty, poor health, and ignorance. The NCLC saw a contradiction in the simultaneous existence of child labor and the popular environmental conservation movement.

In a NCLC publication, Owen Lovejoy asked, "Why conserve our natural resources and not the generations that are to use them?"[10]

Congress also drew public attention to the issue of child labor reform. In 1907 it allocated $300,000 to the Bureau of Labor Statistics to conduct what it called an "Investigation of Woman and Child Wage-Earners in the United States." Congress published the results from 1910 to 1914 in nineteen volumes. The study revealed that almost three-fourths of working children labored in agriculture. Nevertheless, persistent stereotypes about the positive nature of farm work led the attention of reformers to the more than 500,000 children engaged in nonagricultural jobs. Over half of these children labored in the nation's coal mines (15,000), textile mills (78,000), clothing industry (19,000), iron and steel works (14,000), furniture and lumber factories (18,000), glass factories (5,000), as domestic servants (89,000), and as messengers, "newsboys," bundle, and office boys and girls (52,000).[11] Volume one of the investigation reported on the cotton textile industry in five southern states: Mississippi, South Carolina, Georgia, Virginia, and North Carolina. At the time of the investigation Mississippi had no child labor law. The other four states prohibited the employment of children under twelve, with the exception of orphans, children of widows, and those over ten years of age whose fathers were disabled. South Carolina went even further by permitting the employment of such children at any age. Bureau of Labor Statistics investigators found that "age-limit laws in effect at the time . . . were openly and freely violated in every State visited." Only two of thirty-two agents working on the project failed to find underage children working in the mills they inspected.[12]

The NCLC's widely distributed publications also acted as visible tools for reform. These effective pieces of propaganda included photographs (staged and spontaneous) taken by Lewis Hine during the first two decades of the NCLC's existence. Hine pictured disheveled, innocent-looking children working in mines, factories, city streets, and cotton and vegetable fields. He featured images of children such as that taken in 1907 of young spinner Sadie Pfeifer, described as "48 inches tall, (age not known) working in a Lancaster South Carolina textile mill," or that of "Luther Watson of Kentucky [who] is fourteen years old [with] his arm cut off by a veneering saw in a factory in Cincinnati a month ago." Such pictures effectively stirred the emotions of many middle-class adults.[13]

The Children's Bureau, according to child welfare advocates, should investigate and report on the condition of child workers.

Supporters believed that information distributed by the bureau would lead to the elimination of the "anxious problem of child labor." The most prominent reform organizations leading the effort to guarantee "the child's right to exemption from work" were also the Children's Bureau's most vocal supporters: the General Federation of Women's Clubs, the NCLC, and the National Consumers' League. The American Federation of Labor, another actor in the increasingly visible reform movement, endorsed the Children's Bureau and its work. As in their efforts in the infant welfare movement, these groups viewed the Children's Bureau as a clearinghouse for information and the standard-bearer for their cause. But bureau critics who had surfaced during the appropriation and infant mortality program debates believed the Children's Bureau's link with these organizations was one of the primary reasons to condemn the agency and its work.[14]

State child labor restrictions were discrete and the percentage of children working for wages differed greatly by region (see table 4). More northern children worked for wages, but certain southern industries had the highest concentration of child labor. In addition, organized resistance to child labor reform was strongest in the South. By 1912, every state had some form of protective child labor legislation and forty states set the minimum age for factory employment at fourteen. But five of the eight states (North Carolina, South Carolina, Georgia, Alabama, Mississippi, New Mexico, Nevada, and Vermont) which permitted children under fourteen to engage in industrial work were located in the South. Even in states with what contemporaries judged as "progressive" child labor restrictions, laws and enforcement varied widely.[15] The only answer appeared to be a federal child labor law that would standardize reform. As Children's Bureau opponents charged, this was a much more invasive and protectionist strategy than that undertaken to reduce infant mortality.

Getting a Federal Child Labor Law

As was the case during the struggles concerning the Children's Bureau's founding, subsequent annual appropriations, and its infant and maternal welfare program, some of the agency's most powerful opponents also objected to child labor legislation. The first attempt to gain passage of a federal child labor bill had taken place six years before the establishment of the Children's Bureau. In 1906 Senator Albert J. Beveridge (R-Ind.) and Representative Herbert A. Parsons (R-N.Y.) had introduced identical bills to prevent the employment of children in industry. The proposals stated that "no carrier of interstate com-

Table 4. Children Ten to Seventeen Years Old Gainfully Employed, by Region, 1910, 1920, 1930

	Ages 10-13			Ages 14-15			Ages 16-17	
Region	1910	1920	1930	1910	1920	1930	1920	1930
New England	4,390	2,999	1,297	59,549	56,240	18,990	135,633	106,997
Middle Atlantic	21,805	8,896	3,555	165,976	122,645	51,261	433,397	351,673
East North Central	36,255	14,562	7,778	139,985	86,239	29,408	327,774	231,245
West North Central	47,642	12,859	7,711	94,404	45,047	30,946	153,741	132,536
South Atlantic	308,347	123,547	73,258	254,899	150,434	124,427	257,391	264,993
East South Central	253,490	115,132	84,398	188,400	106,210	91,225	160,070	164,031
West South Central	211,694	91,113	50,949	160,979	93,154	69,699	156,212	153,665
Mountain	8,201	5,006	3,279	13,987	10,606	8,308	32,722	31,359
Pacific	4,152	3,949	3,103	16,070	12,220	7,526	55,708	42,342
Total	895,976	378,063	235,328	1,094,249	682,795	431,790	1,712,648	1,478,841
Rate per 1,000								
New England	10	6	2	268	235	64	570	369
Middle Atlantic	16	5	2	246	167	54	583	374
East North Central	27	9	4	206	119	32	451	258
West North Central	51	13	7	204	96	61	426	378
South Atlantic	277	94	52	475	251	183	451	387
East South Central	329	132	97	500	267	214	426	378
West South Central	261	92	49	409	204	138	361	297
Mountain	43	18	11	152	88	57	286	220
Pacific	16	11	6	121	75	30	344	166
Total	123	44	24	307	175	92	447	317

Source: Children's Bureau, "Child Labor Facts and Figures," Children's Bureau pub. no. 197 (Washington, D.C.: Government Printing Office, 1933), p. 5.

merce shall transport or accept for transportation the products of any factory or mine in which children under fourteen years of age are employed or permitted to work" (S. 6562 and H.R. 21404). During the same congressional session, Senator Henry Cabot Lodge (R-Mass.) introduced a similar bill designed to "prohibit the employment of children in the manufacture or production of articles intended for interstate commerce" (S. 6730). Beveridge gained a lot of attention for the issue when he gave a four-day speech on the Senate floor concerning the "crime of child labor."[16]

Florence Kelley and the National Consumers' League had aggressively supported the Beveridge measure, but the NCLC only reluctantly endorsed the bill. Preferring a state-by-state strategy the NCLC found federal legislation too hot to handle. Some NCLC members felt congressional action usurped states' rights and on November 26, 1907, the organization passed a resolution stating that the "National Child Labor Committee will for the present take no other action with reference to National legislation." Others feared that advocacy of a federal bill might provide the opposition with ammunition to kill the then-proposed federal children's bureau. Some members of the NCLC such as Florence Kelley, Samuel McCune Lindsay, Homer Folks, Jane Addams, and Owen Lovejoy were angry with the NCLC's state-by-state policy and continued to push for change at the federal level.[17]

Indeed, a federal amendment would bring the government into a field many considered the domain of the states. As noted earlier, Julia Lathrop also realized the controversial nature of child labor reform and instead chose the more benign topic of infant mortality as the Children's Bureau's first area of work.[18] This did not mean that Lathrop intended to neglect the issue. Instead, during the bureau's first year's work she simply relied on the NCLC and the National Consumers' League to draw the public's attention to the problem. Meanwhile, the Children's Bureau focused the bulk of its tiny budget and limited staff on the subject of infant mortality. But after its initial months of work the issue of child labor became a part of the Children's Bureau's public program. In her first annual report, Lathrop suggested that under the circumstances the agency should compile a summary of existing state child labor laws and study the enforcement of such regulations.[19]

The bureau's birth registration drive, part of its effort to reduce the nation's infant mortality rate, also contributed to child labor reform efforts. Lewis Meriam noted the connection between birth registration and child labor reform in his address before the 1913 National Conference of Charities and Corrections. Meriam explained that one of the motivations behind the bureau's registration drive was the belief that birth certificates provided a standardized age verification record, thus enabling efficient enforcement of local child labor and compulsory school attendance laws. By 1900 thirty-two states had enacted compulsory school attendance laws. Mississippi was the last state to do so in 1918. The Children's Bureau also advertised birth registration as a means to prove citizenship and claim accompanying civil rights. Nevertheless, despite its benefits for child labor reform and civil rights, the Children's Bureau primarily advocated birth registration as a means to reduce the nation's infant mortality rate. This strategy allowed the bureau to avoid directly confronting the controversial issue of child labor, but at the same time permitted Lathrop and her staff to design a program that they hoped would facilitate national reform.[20]

The bureau's work on child labor materialized in two 1915 publications. The first was a massive 1131-page study summarizing the child labor laws of every state. The second examined the enforcement and restriction of child labor in Connecticut. These publications pointed to the widely disparate circumstances and enforcement of child labor regulations in the United States. Certainly, child protection and opportunity was not equal in all regions of the country. As she had suggested in her first annual report, Lathrop intended that the bureau conduct other studies similar to the one completed in Connecticut. These would help the Children's Bureau to determine a recommended standard of child labor regulation and enforcement.[21]

Lathrop knew that the enactment of federal child labor legislation was a controversial solution even among child welfare advocates. But, by late 1913 many child labor reformers realized that there had been little progress in the effort to gain uniform legislation and enforcement. It appeared that any future efforts to regulate the employment of children in the South would continue to be thwarted by an opposition led and organized by the textile industry. This convinced Lathrop and other activists that child labor standards must be made uniform at the federal level. In addition, the Children's Bureau Act in 1912 removed the argument that advocacy for a federal child labor law would hinder the agency's establishment. In view of these circumstances, the NCLC changed its strategy. On January 6, 1914, the organization combined its state lobbying activities with a new policy calling for the passage of a federal child labor bill to be administered by the Children's Bureau.[22]

Twenty days later, Representative A. Mitchell Palmer (D-Pa.) and Senator Robert L. Owen (D-Okla.) introduced the NCLC's child labor proposal in Congress (H.R. 12292 and S. 4571).[23] Alexander

McKelway led the NCLC's Washington lobbying effort. The bill was reported favorably out of committee and passed overwhelmingly by the House (232H44). But it did not come to a vote in the Senate and failed to gain President Woodrow Wilson's endorsement. As noted earlier, Wilson, a southerner, said that he did not oppose the idea, but believed the proposal unconstitutional because it violated states' rights.[24] Senator Owen and Representative Edward Keating (D-Colo.) reintroduced the proposal during the next congressional session in January 1916. Despite the fact that hearings on the proposal were dominated by those opposing the measure, it passed the House on February 2, 1916 (337H46), and the Senate on August 8, 1916 (52H12). President Wilson, persuaded by McKelway and the fact that both the Democratic and Republican party platforms endorsed the bill, overlooked his constitutional misgivings about the proposed legislation's legality and supported its passage as part of his presidential reelection campaign. Wilson signed the bill into law on September 1, 1916, a very practical move in light of the fact that the Republican platform endorsed the bill's passage. Seizing the political spotlight, the Democratic party distributed placards with the slogan, "Abraham Lincoln freed the slaves; Woodrow Wilson freed the children."[25]

Like the 1906 Beveridge bill, the Keating-Owen Act did not outlaw child labor but instead used the interstate commerce clause to discourage its practice. Supporters believed that the federal government might not have the authority to outlaw child labor, but Congress did have the power to regulate interstate commerce. The measure prohibited the interstate or export shipment of materials produced in mines or quarries which employed children under sixteen years of age, products manufactured in facilities employing children under fourteen, or where children between the ages of fourteen and sixteen inclusive worked more than eight hours a day, six days a week, or at night (before 6:00 A.M. or after 7:00 P.M.). The act established a federal board, composed of the attorney general, the secretary of labor, and the secretary of commerce, to devise the law's administrative rules and regulations. The secretary of labor was ordered to secure the law's enforcement and the effective date was delayed for one year in order to allow employers time to comply with the act's provisions.

Fulfilling his responsibility, Secretary of Labor William B. Wilson designated the Children's Bureau to administer the law and Congress appropriated $150,000 for its enforcement (40 Stat., 24).[26] During the debate on the bill, Lathrop limited the Children's Bureau's role to testifying on behalf of the proposal before congressional committees. The chief did not want the Children's Bureau open to attack.

She intended to diminish debate about the Children's Bureau's role as enforcer and instead emphasized its educational and persuasive capacity.[27]

Grace Abbott became head of the bureau's newly created Child Labor Division on May 1, 1917. Although she was clearly capable, Abbott's appointment was not without controversy. As she explained in a letter to her sister Edith, "it seems the Child Labor people here [likely Owen Lovejoy and other members of the NCLC] and the Government Reference bureau had picked a young [male] lawyer for my job who had experience in drafting legislation and who worked on the Child Labor Bill . . . [this] made [my appointment] a little uncomfortable for Miss Lathrop."[28] But Lathrop resisted any interference from the NCLC. True to her beliefs concerning organization and professionalism, she explained that "the staff of the Child-Labor Division was selected with great care under the rules of the Civil Service Commission. . . . including several persons . . . who had previous experience in issuing [work] certificates or in the enforcement of State laws." In addition, Abbott shared Lathrop's outlook on child welfare and the role of the Children's Bureau, as well as the Hull-House network.[29]

The bureau's Child Labor Division was composed of a director (at a salary of $3,000), an assistant director ($2,500), law clerk ($2,500), eight inspectors ($1,800 to $2,100), thirty-one assistant inspectors ($1,260 to $1,680), seven clerks ($1,000 to $1,440), and a messenger ($480). Salaries for an additional nineteen persons came from the child labor appropriation for work related to the enforcement of the act, but none of these individuals worked directly under Abbott's supervision. Lathrop recognized that the Keating-Owen Act moved the Children's Bureau into an area of "administration," beyond its "previous activities . . . solely in the field of research."[30] This new status caused tension between the Children's Bureau and the NCLC. Lathrop resented the NCLC's paternalistic attitude and resisted Alexander McKelway's reminders that the bureau's existence and increased appropriations were due largely to efforts led by the NCLC. The ethical issue of a public body versus a private group may have also played a part. While gender may have been another element in this controversy, it is also understandable that Lathrop wanted to gain independence for the Children's Bureau at the same time that the NCLC resisted such autonomy for its "offspring." In addition, McKelway's attitude excluded the importance of the support afforded the bureau by the General Federation of Women's Clubs and other female organizations. McKelway may have resented the fact that Lathrop relied directly on Wald and Kelley, instead of going first to the NCLC, when the chief felt the Children's Bureau needed an organized drive for public support. Grace Abbott's biographer, Lela Costin, suggests that part of the problem was due to McKelway's lack of confidence in the administrative ability of women. In addition, she contends that Lathrop did not respect McKelway because of his racist attitudes. Whatever the reasons, tensions between Lathrop and McKelway intensified after passage of the Keating-Owen Act.[31]

Although the Keating-Owen Act moved the agency beyond its original role, Lathrop emphasized that states still held the primary responsibility for child labor regulation. It is also likely that she was well aware that the Children's Bureau's small staff could not adequately enforce a federal labor law without state cooperation. Lathrop contended that "the full value of a national minimum for the protection of children would never be secured except through a genuine working relationship between . . . Federal and State officials." Grace Abbott also adhered to this philosophy. With this in mind, on July 27, 1917, Secretary Wilson called a Washington conference of officials who would be responsible for enforcing the Keating-Owen Act within their states. The willing conferees, from the District of Columbia and twenty-eight states, voted that they wanted the federal government to grant the states full enforcement authority. This action made cooperation between the Children's Bureau and the states vital to the uniform application of the law. As Owen Lovejoy told his readers, "Congress has not abolished child labor but only made it possible for you to do so. Responsibility is laid on you, on every citizen to see that this law is enforced in your community."[32]

Such rhetoric had practical applications but the action also attempted to camouflage the new administrative and enforcement role assigned to the Children's Bureau under the Keating-Owen law. The act authorized Abbott and the Child Labor Division staff, in cooperation with state officials, to enforce fines and/or imprisonment against employers and shippers who *knowingly* violated the law. In addition, the Children's Bureau issued 19,969 work "certificates" (permits) to children from fourteen to sixteen years of age (inclusive) in the five states (North Carolina, South Carolina, Georgia, Mississippi, and Virginia) whose existing child labor standards fell below the federal level legislated by the act. In North Carolina there were 12,345 applicants and 9,377 work certificates issued; in South Carolina 6,727 applicants and 5,874 were given certificates; in Georgia 3,849 requests with 2,897 receiving certificates; in Mississippi 474 requests with 338 certificates issued; and in Virginia 1,935 applicants and

1,210 certified. The bureau also inspected facilities where resistance to enforcement was strong or where state officials requested assistance. From September 1, 1917, to June 3, 1918, Children's Bureau agents helped inspect 689 factories in twenty-four states and the District of Columbia engaged in producing textiles, clothing, glass, confections, tobacco, shoes and boots, furniture, and canned goods. Children's Bureau staff also investigated twenty-eight mines located in four states.[33]

The successful enforcement of the law depended on a "well administered certificating system." As a result, the Children's Bureau's experience under the Keating-Owen Act reinforced the agency's demand for uniform birth registration. The bureau found that birth certificates had been issued to almost none of the children applying for work permits in the five states directly under its jurisdiction: North Carolina (0.2 percent), South Carolina (0.3 percent), Georgia (1.4 percent), Mississippi (1.8 percent), and Virginia (6 percent). For the time being, Abbott and her staff devised an alternative age verification system. They judged baptismal records the most reliable, followed by information recorded in family Bibles, passport and immigration records, life insurance policies, and school records. The least credible, according to the Children's Bureau, were parent or guardian affidavits or similar statements. A physician's statement estimating a child's age was acceptable if none of the preferred records were available or if those presented needed corroboration. However, this was agreeable only if the child's physical condition met the agency's recommended weight and height standards, which were initially formulated with the advice of a temporary outside committee. The permanent Committee on Standards of Physical Fitness for Children Entering Employment was appointed by the Children's Bureau as a result of the 1919 White House Conference. This committee devised recommendations which it hoped state certification officers would follow because the Keating-Owen Act itself did not require that children applying for employment certificates meet physical standards. Members of the committee included physicians, state child labor enforcement administrators, Taliaferro Clark representing the PHS, and E. Nathalie Matthews from the Children's Bureau.[34]

The Children's Bureau advised enforcement agents to be skeptical of age records other than birth certificates. However, the lack of birth registration forced officials to rely on other forms of age verification. Bible records served as the most commonly accepted evidence of a child's age in North Carolina, South Carolina, and Georgia. Insurance policies were accepted for approximately half of all applicants in

Virginia and Mississippi. Such records were often "obviously changed" and therefore unreliable. At first, physician certificates were "very popular with parents and mill authorities," but the delays involved soon discouraged others. This was initially the case, according to the Children's Bureau, because "the impression . . . spread that any child who could pass the physical test could work." But the Children's Bureau often required corroborating evidence of an applicant's age, because a physician's statement supported only by school records or a parent's affidavit acted as a poor verification of age. "Unfortunately," noted the bureau's report, such proof "was for a discouragingly large per cent of the children the only evidence . . . obtained." This was true for 4,834 of the 19,696 children issued work certificates by the federal agency.[35]

The Children's Bureau cited several individuals for whom age verification records other than a birth certificate had proven to be unreliable. One North Carolina girl, whose work permit was initially refused because of an age claim based solely on a questionable Bible record, later received a work certificate after obtaining a physician's statement. The girl and her parents claimed that she was fourteen years old. At four feet eight and one-half inches tall, and weighing only eighty-four pounds (four pounds over the established standard) her physical recommendations for age verification were minimal at best. Soon thereafter, a check of school records for another child revealed that the girl already granted a certificate was actually younger than fourteen and the Children's Bureau revoked her permit.

Physical standards left little room for individual differences, but in the absence of other proof of age may have helped protect some young, ill, or physically impaired children from exploitive labor. As this example shows, parents, mill operators, and the children themselves often defied age restrictions. The parents of some children refused work certificates because they fell below the bureau's weight standard fed the youngsters a more wholesome diet in order to "fatten them up" before reapplying. Mill owners urged other parents to send their underweight youngsters to a mill-operated farm in the hope that they would gain weight. Sometimes this worked. For example, one boy gained eight pounds "by a regime that excluded tobacco in all forms and included regular school attendance." But despite his successful weight gain, the Children's Bureau still denied the boy a work certificate because an insurance policy revealed that he was under fourteen.[36] Keeping underage children and those in poor health out of the mills did not eliminate the poverty which led many families to try to circumvent the new law.

Although the Keating-Owen Act had obvious limitations, Lathrop believed that the enforcement system provided "a wholesome decentralization, stimulated other States to reach a [point] which allowed them to issue working certificates and inspect with Government sanction, rendered the central administration more economical and effective, and created a sound working understanding between all those trying in good faith to obey the law and those charged with its administration."[37] As in the field of children's health care, persuasion and education served as the major weapons in the Children's Bureau's arsenal to protect "a right to childhood" against underage and dangerous child labor. Lathrop hoped that the Children's Bureau's example would encourage every state to tighten its child labor restrictions beyond those established under the Keating-Owen Act.

But even before the act went into effect, opponents of child labor reform prepared for its repeal. On August 11, 1917, Roland H. Dagenhart filed suit in a North Carolina district court enjoining the Charlotte district attorney, William C. Hammer, from enforcing the child labor law set to go into effect on September 1. Dagenhart contended that the law violated the constitutional rights of his two sons, Ruben (age fourteen) and John (age twelve). David Clark, editor of the notorious North Carolina based anti-child labor reform journal the *Southern Textile Bulletin*, was the one who had suggested that Dagenhart bring the suit. Clark explained the history behind the case in a 1918 editorial: "The task of getting a man to apply for an injunction and a mill to permit the case to be brought against them, was placed upon David Clark, and after considerable work he found Ruben H. Dagenhart at the Fidelity Manufacturing Company of Charlotte, whose family offered an ideal case, and he induced Dagenhart to permit his name to be used. It can be stated now that Dagenhart never had an idea of making a test until approached by David Clark, and was only a figurehead."[38]

On August 31, 1917, one day before the law went into effect, a North Carolina judge ruled the Keating-Owen Act unconstitutional on the grounds that it deprived the Dagenhart boys' father of his "right of property," in this case his sons' labor. The judgment immediately prohibited the enforcement of the act in the western district of North Carolina.[39]

Julia Lathrop had asked Roscoe Pound, dean of the Harvard Law School, to work in behalf of the law's defense. At the same time, without consulting Lathrop, McKelway secured the services of Thomas I. Parkinson, a prominent Columbia University Law School professor, for the same purpose. Lathrop asked McKelway to request that Parkinson allow

Pound "to take the lead," but McKelway refused. Lathrop interpreted the rebuff as a personal insult, increasing tension between the two. Both stubbornly held their ground, and the Justice Department worked out a compromise in which Parkinson wrote the government's brief and Pound submitted a supplemental brief. The unexpected death of McKelway on April 16, 1918, ended the quarrel.[40]

Just short of two months later, on June 3, 1918, in a five-to-four decision, the Supreme Court held the Keating-Owen Act unconstitutional on the grounds that Congress could not invoke the interstate commerce clause to prevent child labor in the states. Child labor regulation, declared the court, was "purely a local matter to which the federal authority [does] not extend." However, the Court unanimously agreed that child labor was an "evil," stating that "there should be limitations upon the right to employ children in mines and factories in the interest of their own and the public welfare."[41]

Lathrop was disappointed but at the same time encouraged by the decision. The court had agreed that there was a need for child labor regulation. Furthermore, the close division of the Court's members indicated that another approach might be successful. Justice Oliver Wendell Holmes Jr. had denied in his angry dissent that Congress had wrongly invoked the interstate commerce clause. Justices Louis D. Brandeis, John H. Clarke, and Joseph McKenna concurred with Holmes's judgment that "this statute is clearly within the Congress's constitutional power." It was not the Court's place, the justices argued, to "pronounce when prohibition is necessary to regulation if it ever may be necessary—to say that it is permissible as against strong drink but not as against the product of ruined lives."[42] Furthermore, the NCLC prepared to reorganize its forces and continue the fight. Remaining optimistic, the day after the decision came down Grace Abbott sent a postcard to her mother saying, "Don't worry about the Supreme Court Decision. We are bearing up." Lathrop called the decision "only a stimulating setback." The Treasury Department told the chief that "certain conditions of the Child Labor Law had not been declared unconstitutional and that the appropriation [for its administration] should be available to carry on these activities." The Children's Bureau judged that "in view of the decision of the Supreme Court, it remains only to find a method of national limitation not repugnant to the Constitution."[43]

Lathrop's aplomb was also buoyed by her success in July 1918 to convince the War Labor Policies Board to instruct the federal government's production and purchasing departments to incorporate the major provisions of the then defunct Keating-Owen Act into all war materials contracts. Furthermore, the board and President Wilson agreed that the Division of Child Labor "should be utilized by all departments of the Government in administering" this policy. As a result the secretaries of the Navy and Army agreed to observe the standards established by the Keating-Owen Act in laundries, restaurants, and other facilities located on military installations. But in reality this success produced few positive results for child workers. Violations were rampant and the American Cotton Manufacturers' Association openly denounced the policy. Furthermore, soon after the rules went into effect, the German government began to make overtures toward peace, thereby diminishing the federal government's purchasing power and influence over industry.[44] Apparently Lathrop and her staff did not recognize the failures of the War Policies Board's measures.

Fearing that rising production rates accompanied by an increase in jobs and wages might entice children (adolescents) to drop out of school in order to take jobs in industry and agriculture, the Children's Bureau also initiated a "Back to School Drive" or "Stay in School Drive" as part of its wartime Children's Year campaign. Indeed, even before the United States entered the war, state legislatures felt increasing pressure from employers and "patriotic citizens" to relax child labor restrictions. The Baltimore *News* labeled Owen Lovejoy a "pro-German traitor" after he gave a speech calling on officials in Maryland to keep the schools open and to enforce existing child labor laws.[45] Clearly, some Americans felt that the circumstances demanded a loosening of child labor and compulsory school attendance regulations. Lovejoy recognized that some people believed young persons must also "make their share of the sacrifice." In addition, many working-class children and their parents were probably anxious to receive the immediate benefits of higher wages and job opportunities resulting from the wartime rise in production.

To counter such desires the Children's Bureau argued that "experience has shown that boys and girls who are restless and dissatisfied with school and even those who feel that they can ill-afford further training are often ready to make sacrifices to remain in school, once they realize the value of an education." The bureau needed "to show both children and parents that school may mean the difference between a position with a future at steadily increasing wages, and a life of unskilled labor and low pay." Lathrop and her staff used practical and patriotic arguments to accomplish this goal. Boys who stayed in school until they were eighteen, argued the Children's Bureau, made almost two and one-half times as much money at age twenty-five as those who quit school at fourteen. "Send your children back to school and keep them in school" instructed the bureau. Doing so "will release jobs for the soldiers, and the education will mean future better jobs and wages for the children." There were other practical advantages. "Few boys and girls of 14," argued the bureau, "are well enough developed physically to stand the strain of continuous work. . . . School combined with wholesome exercises are worth far more than the little child can earn at 14 years of age." The time a child spends in school "may mean the difference between a happy, useful life and a life of sickness and inefficiency."[46]

As with the other aspects of the Children's Year campaign, the Children's Bureau conducted the "Back to School" and "Stay in School" drives with the help of "millions of women in the Child Welfare Committees of the Council of National Defense." Women organized supporting committees in an estimated 281,000 schools in the United States. They studied local child labor and school attendance laws and called on the parents of children who had dropped out of school. The Children's Bureau launched its school campaigns in forty-five states, the District of Columbia, and Hawaii. Lathrop and her staff judged "scholarships for children, visiting teachers, continuation and part-time schools, vocational training courses, and vocational guidance bureaus or placement committees" the program's most useful aspects.[47] Such efforts had real potential for directly helping children and their families. But, as with state child labor laws, the opportunities available and the enforcement of compulsory school attendance laws varied widely. Nevertheless, an examination of school attendance records suggests a change in attitude by parents and children concerning the value of education. Although it is difficult to determine the direct effect of the Children's Bureau's efforts, by 1920, the number of students in the nation's high schools had increased approximately 2.5 times since 1910, a number six times higher than in 1890.[48]

Encouraged by its wartime campaigns, the nearly successful passage of the Keating-Owen Act, and the Supreme Court's close decision in *Hammer v. Dagenhart,* the Children's Bureau and the NCLC decided to make a second attempt at federal child labor regulation. George Alger, an attorney and member of the New York Child Labor Committee, encouraged Lathrop and the NCLC to use the federal government's taxing power to eliminate child labor. Lathrop, Abbott, and Florence Kelley had little confidence in this strategy. Nevertheless, believing that the timing was right and seeing no other acceptable alternative, they agreed to go ahead with the suggestion. Using this strategy they made several unsuccessful attempts to reenact a federal child labor law in the months immediately following the *Hammer v. Dagenhart* decision.[49]

On November 15, 1918, while Lathrop and Abbott prepared for their trip to Europe, an amendment to the annual revenue bill introduced in the House of Representatives provided for a 10 percent tax on the profits of goods manufactured in facilities or produced in mines or quarries employing children that violated terms similar to those in the defunct Keating-Owen Act. The amendment included a new strategy giving responsibility for the act's enforcement to the Treasury Department. The NCLC endorsed the act at its December meeting. Lathrop and Abbott, by then in Europe, would not have approved. With the two houses virtually unanimous, President Wilson signed the bill into law on February 24, 1919 (40 Stat., 1138), effective April 17, 1919. An abandonment of the Children's Bureau's "whole child" philosophy, the NCLC's approval of the plan greatly disappointed Lathrop and Abbott, though Lathrop hoped that her agency's experience under the first child labor law would drive the Treasury Department's Internal Revenue Service to seek the Children's Bureau's assistance. Nevertheless, in the two months following the act's passage, it became clear that the Internal Revenue Service would not seek the help of the Children's Bureau. Lathrop dismantled the Child Labor Division and Grace Abbott returned to Chicago after helping to plan and implement the 1919 White House conference.[50]

Despite the effort to avoid a constitutional problem, the Supreme Court declared the nation's second child labor law unconstitutional by a vote of eight to one. In its May 15, 1922, decision, *Bailey vs. Drexel Furniture Co.,* the Court again ruled that federal taxing power could not be used for the indirect purpose of regulating child labor. Although on the surface the court's decision seemed a defeat for child labor reform, the law had been ineffective and contrary to the Children's Bureau's fundamental philosophy. Even the NCLC's Owen Lovejoy called the law a "farce." However, Congress's support for the measure and the publicity surrounding the second child labor act did seem to sway public attitudes against the evils of child labor. A constitutional amendment seemed the best solution. On May 17, 1922, Representative Roy G. Fitzgerald (R-Ohio) introduced a constitutional amendment empowering Congress to regulate the employment of individuals under eighteen years of age. He was followed two days later by Senator Hiram W. Johnson (R-Calif.). Congress did not act immediately on the measure, but public pressure was growing in favor of such action.[51]

In the meantime there had been some changes at the Children's Bureau. Julia Lathrop resigned, and Grace Abbott accepted the position of chief.[52] In addition, the successful passage of the Sheppard-Towner Maternity and Infancy Act in 1921 freed the bureau to direct its legislative efforts solely to the promotion of child labor legislation. In 1922, the American Federation of Labor established a Permanent Conference for the Abolition of Child Labor as a result of a June 1 meeting on child labor reform. Grace Abbott represented the Children's Bureau at the gathering. Those present welcomed the idea of a constitutional amendment and support came from a wide variety of sources. Abbott quickly placed the Children's Bureau at the head of the endorsement parade. As with most Children's Bureau efforts, women's organizations were among the child labor amendment's most enthusiastic advocates. Florence Kelley urged Abbott to get "ammunition for us [the WJCC and other women's groups] about the return of the children to the mills and workshops." She contended that "it is Mrs. Park [Maud Wood Park, president of the NLWV] and the W.J. Cong. Committee [WJCC] that will have to pass the Amendment!"[53] The Children's Bureau's supporters again went to work.

But not everyone agreed on what path to take. Julia Lathrop believed that after two defeats on the federal level, the time was not right for successful ratification of a child labor amendment and instead urged state regulation. She felt that the fight for the Sheppard-Towner Act had revealed the existence of a strong conservative opposition to the Children's Bureau and its association with child labor reform. Further complicating matters, the NCLC had only reluctantly endorsed the idea of a federal amendment. It argued that such a measure should strongly emphasize the importance of state power to regulate child labor. Such statements led Florence Kelley to turn a suspicious eye toward the NCLC and she warned Abbott that Jane Addams and Lillian Wald were too "gullible in their dealings with Owen Lovejoy." In fact, Kelley eventually resigned from the NCLC board of trustees and would write Abbott in 1926 that the NCLC "Board [was] so *rotten*" that she could no longer trust them. Kelley also became disgusted with the permanent conference and worked for the child labor amendment's passage and ratification solely through the WJCC and the National Consumers' League.[54]

Nevertheless, by December 1923 members of the permanent conference, including the NCLC, reached a compromise and endorsed the proposed constitutional amendment. On April 26, 1924, the House enthusiastically passed the amendment (297 to 69) and the Senate concurred on June 2 (61 to 23).[55]

> Sec. 1. The Congress shall have power to limit, regulate, and prohibit the labor of persons under 18 years of age.
>
> Sec. 2. The power of the several States is unimpaired by this article except that the operation of State laws shall be suspended to the extent necessary to give effect to legislation enacted by Congress.[56]

Senator Robert M. La Follette, the 1924 Progressive party presidential nominee, also supported the amendment and was one of its primary proponents in the Senate. Both the Republican and Democratic parties took credit for the proposal's passage and urged its ratification by the states. In addition, President Calvin Coolidge offered his personal approval. The Children's Bureau and the its supporters optimistically felt that the amendment would soon be ratified by the required thirty-eight states. But Lathrop's earlier suspicions were closer to the mark. Congressional debate about the measure filled over one hundred pages of the *Congressional Record*,[57] and time revealed the validity of Julia Lathrop's prediction that substantial opposition to the Children's Bureau and its work centered on the child labor issue.

Opposition to the Amendment

David Clark, supported by the American Cotton Manufacturers Association, continued to offer the most formidable opposition to the effort to gain federal child labor regulation. After 1924 others familiar to the Children's Bureau joined Clark and his supporters: the Woman Patriots, the Sentinels of the Republic, and the American Catholic Church. The National Association of Manufacturers also worked for the opposition and new organizations formed solely for the purpose of defeating the child labor amendment. The *New Republic* noted that "the friends of the amendment were totally unprepared to combat the flood of distorted propaganda which was let loose upon them. They had been accustomed to argue their case before reasonable and attentive human beings . . . [but] suddenly found themselves compelled to discuss a matter of public policy with a monstrous jazz band."[58]

A 1924 article from the *Manufacturers' Record* summarized anti-child labor amendment arguments. It identified the child labor amendment as "perhaps the most dangerous movement ever proposed . . . to our Constitution." Furthermore, if ratified, contended the editors, the amendment "would give to the Federal government the absolute right to dictate as to the employment of all children, white and black, male and female under 18 years of age." The article charged that under the law, "some bureaucratic power in Washington would have the authority to say that no child under 18 years of age should be allowed to work on a farm or to engage in any other work of any kind." The article also recognized some of the class tensions which might be caused by the proposal. If ratified, claimed the editors, "millions of children from 15 to 18 years of age who should be at work in some gainful occupation, would be denied that privilege. . . . Where parents are abundantly able to send their children to college, and where children are eager for an education, employment may not be necessary. But there are millions of boys who will not benefit from college training one half so much as by training which they would get through profitable employment leading them on to success in business life." The amendment, contended the editors, "would limit the right of all parents, regardless of their business, regardless of their race or color, to permit their children under 18 years of age to engage in any gainful employment." While all of these arguments distort the intent and effect of the child labor amendment, the most outrageous claim was the contention that the farmer could no longer have his children help with farm work or that girls would not be permitted to do housework.[59]

David Clark's *Southern Textile Bulletin* published a special edition in 1919 entitled the "Health and Happiness Number" summarizing the textile mill owners' interests in defeating any effort to gain federal regulation of child labor. The *Bulletin* featured photographs of factories, housing, children at play, and mill-organized club meetings in an effort to refute claims by the Children's Bureau and the NCLC that child laborers were unhealthy and denied their right to childhood. The issue maintained that "for a number of years it has been profitable to certain individuals and organizations to create the impression that the Southern cotton mill operatives were oppressed and downtrodden and that mill owners cared nothing for the welfare of the employees." Clark claimed that the "Health and Happiness Number" showed "a true picture of a great industry and of its living and working conditions." Child labor, according to Clark, provided children the opportunity to learn a trade and earn a living. In addition, Clark and southern cotton mill owners used half-page newspaper advertisements in western states then debating the amendment's ratification to convince farmers that the child labor amendment ran contrary to their best interests. The advertisements were purchased under the name of the "Farmers' State Rights League." Each denounced the proposed child labor amendment on the grounds that it would prohibit farmers' children from working on the family farm. A reporter for the railroad brotherhood journal, *Labor,* discovered that the Farmers' State Rights League's president was cashier for a cotton mill bank and its vice president an employee at a cotton mill store. The chief agent for the group worked for David Clark's publishing company.[60]

Likewise, Clark accused the Children's Bureau of circulating false propaganda. He claimed that there was "no good reason why a Federal Child Labor Law should be enacted." Furthermore, he said that he "knew of no set of men nor manufacturers who today seek or desire child labor." According to one of Clark's admirers, "child labor [was] a thing which does not exist in any industry except" in the "wild and distorted imagination" of the Children's Bureau and its supporters. The benefits of a child labor amendment, Clark maintained, would be manifested exclusively by the employees of the Children's Bureau "who have more interest in the patronage they will secure than in the welfare of the child."[61]

Opponents also argued that a child labor amendment violated religious traditions and invited state regulation of children. In another *Manufacturers' Record* article a congressional representative called the proposal a "radical phase of obnoxious paternalism [and a] baneful socialistic suggestion . . . out of Russia to pester American people." He argued that during the Civil War, 850,000 of the Union army's soldiers were under eighteen years of age. Therefore, he concluded, "if they were old enough to fight for their country, they ought to be old enough to regulate the matter of their own employment." The congressman failed to point out that these boys were also old enough to die or suffer permanent injury. In a similar vein, the Missouri *Republican Record* asserted emotionally that contrary to "God's law," the child labor amendment would close "the Door of Hope to the Youth of America and Open the Gates to Hell."[62]

Catholic opposition to the proposed amendment, like that directed by some members of the church against the Sheppard-Towner Act, focused on parental rights. Some members of the Catholic hierarchy also feared that such laws might lead to the abolition of parochial schools. Catholic opponents pointed to the inclusion of the word "labor" rather than "work" in the amendment. This wording was dangerous, such critics argued, because the dictionary definition of "labor" was "physical or mental toil." Therefore the law might open a Pandora's box of possible interpretations. But Grace Abbott wanted to retain the word "labor" rather than "work" in the bill so that employers might not circumvent the law by contending that only children paid directly by their companies were workers. Such tactics had been used by newspapers and other industries to avoid child labor regulations for "independent merchants" or "helpers."[63]

As might be expected, the newspaper industry also proved to be a powerful source of opposition. Being a "newsie" encouraged responsibility and gave boys self-confidence. Besides, argued the newspaper owners, boys who sold papers part-time could still go to school. Whether their claims were substantiated or not, many newspapers denounced ratification of the child labor amendment.[64]

As noted in the effort to gain passage of Sheppard-Towner, former antisuffragists also continued to oppose the Children's Bureau. The *Woman Patriot* not only criticized the child labor amendment and other bureau programs but also directly attacked the women of the Children's Bureau and its supporters. Mary G. Kilbreth, president of the Woman Patriot Publishing Company, identified advocates of the measure as "communists" and called the amendment "a straight socialist measure . . . promoted under direct orders from Moscow." Elizabeth Lowell Putnam, antisuffragist and aforementioned vocal opponent of the Sheppard-Towner Act, also opposed the child labor amendment. Putnam condemned the proposed amendment as a measure to take away the "inherent rights" of young people, "the right to earn a living, the right to take their share of the family burdens, the right to help in the work world."[65]

The Children's Bureau and Child Laborers

"The problem" of child labor, stated the Children's Bureau, "must be visualized as a changing one, which lessens as higher standards are adopted, regulations improved, and employment restricted, but which increases as new light is shed upon the effects of industrial work on growing boys and girls."[66] From 1915 to 1930 the Children's Bureau published thirty-one studies exposing the negative consequences of child labor. Children's Bureau agents visited coal-mining areas in Pennsylvania and West Virginia and canneries on the Gulf Coast and in Washington State. They also examined the circumstances of youngsters who worked in their homes in Rhode Island and did studies of employed children in the street trades in four cities—Wilkes-Barre, Pennsylvania; Columbus, Ohio; Atlanta, Georgia; and Omaha, Nebraska. Other inquiries looked at the situations of children working on tobacco farms in Kentucky, South Carolina, Virginia, Massachusetts, and Connecticut. The Children's Bureau investigated child laborers in the sugar beet industry in Michigan and Colorado, as well as those picking cotton, growing hops, or harvesting fruit in Texas, Maryland, Virginia, New Jersey, North Dakota, and Illinois. These along with bureau reports on industrial accidents involving minors refuted opponents' claims that there was no need for a federal amendment.

As might be expected, the Children's Bureau found that the children of immigrant parents or those living in the South labored the longest and under the worst conditions. In the five states where the Children's Bureau issued work permits during its administration of the first child labor law, approximately 90 percent of all white children given work certificates took jobs in the textile mills. In addition, contrary to popular belief, more girls than boys received certificates to work in the mills. Most textile mill jobs were not open to blacks; instead, the bureau found that 56 percent of all black children with work permits held jobs in tobacco factories and the majority of those were girls. Racism as well as gender stereotyping played a part in this circumstance. The Children's Bureau judged the tobacco steamery to be one of the most hazardous and distasteful places to work. As expected, most individuals receiving work permits had very little schooling and many were unable to sign their names. They worked in jobs with little opportunity for advancement or self-improvement.[67] Clearly such results refuted employers' claims that working in industrial jobs served as vocational training and could be considered steps to a brighter future.

The Children's Bureau's studies also discredited claims by opponents that working in street trades offered children the opportunity to avoid poverty and obtain useful business training. Children's Bureau agents interviewed 6,347 boys and seventy-two girls over a two-month period during the winter and spring of 1922-23 in Newark and Paterson, New Jersey; Washington, D.C.; and Troy, New York. The report did not include an analysis of the data on girls, perhaps because the sample was so small. It is not surprising that the Children's Bureau's studies concerning street work involved mostly boys, because boys made up the overwhelming majority of children involved in selling newspapers and magazines or working as vendors, bootblacks, messengers, or in other types of street work. But, as David Nasaw has shown, a small number of girls did engage in such work. Reformers considered such employment "dangerous" and harmful for boys and even more so for girls.[68] The Children's Bureau conducted the studies in each city except Troy, where the New York Child Labor Committee did the work. Investigators revisited each location in 1926 or 1927 to gather follow-up data, and the Children's Bureau staff summarized its findings in a 1928 report, "Children in Street Work."

The young people studied worked as newspaper and magazine sellers and carriers (over 50 percent), as peddlers, bootblacks, and at variety of other miscellaneous jobs. The bureau found that boys as young as six sold newspapers on the streets and from 11 to 21 percent of these children were under ten years of age. Local regulations had little effect. Those selling evening papers worked after school until about seven o'clock and on Saturdays until two or three the next morning (because of Sunday morning editions). Few boys sold morning papers on weekdays. The Children's Bureau was particularly concerned about "dangers" in the street work environment—gambling, drinking, contact with "bums" and other "disreputable" characters. Adults who came in contact with the boys in the papers' distribution rooms presented a special problem. Many, reported the Children's Bureau, kept the boys in the distribution rooms "all night gambling and playing cards, cheating them and talking away their money, and they urged the newsboys to steal and bought stolen goods from them." Investigators found that the boys "boast[ed] of the tricks they had resorted to in selling their papers [and] relat[ed] adventures of a questionable nature, [while] indulging in indecent conversation." The Children's Bureau's analysts believed that these circumstances contributed to juvenile delinquency. In addition, they suggested that "the professional newsboy's work sets up a rival claim to his school work; and the fact that it brings in money, however small the amount may be, gives it an importance both in the boy's eyes and in the eyes of his poor and often ignorant parents that sanctions divided interest." Instead, the work of children should be school, while selling newspapers could hardly be considered business training. Besides, "the great majority of the boys were in normal homes; that is, homes in which both [of the boy's] own parents were present and in which the [boy's] own father was the chief breadwinner." Such findings, contended the bureau, denied arguments claiming that these children needed to work to relieve their family's poverty. In addition, the bureau found that the boys earned very little, somewhere between $1 and $5 per week. Most said they took up the trade because "all boys do it" or "there's nothing else to do." The bureau concluded that school and recreational activities should be the desirable alternatives offered these boys. Though this was perhaps a good idea, the child labor amendment alone did not provide for such options. Furthermore, the agency did not deal with the fact that children and their families lived in a rising consumer-based economy where even meager earnings gained through the street trades helped satisfied the desires of children living with parents of little means.[69]

Since the turn of the century, child labor reformers had focused most of their energy on the plight of working children in industry and in street trades. But by 1920, the Children's Bureau (and the NCLC) became increasingly aware of the difficult circumstances of many young Americans working in agriculture or industries connected with food production. This attention to rural communities for the first time also highlighted the conditions of youngsters employed in food production facilities. About half of the Children's Bureau's studies focused on rural employment, thereby exposing some of the worst consequences of child labor. The bureau summarized its findings in its 1929 publication "Children in Agriculture."[70]

The average American farmer depended on his children to supply part of the labor for the family farm. The majority of child workers listed by the Bureau of the Census in 1920 as engaged in agriculture lived on "home farms" (569,824 of 647,309), but the agency also reported that many thousands worked as hired agricultural laborers. The actual numbers were probably even higher since the census, taken in midwinter, was likely to have overlooked the children of many migrant workers. Eighty-four percent of all children reported as engaged in agricultural labor worked in twelve states: Arkansas, Florida, Georgia, Indiana, Kentucky, Louisiana, Mississippi, North Carolina, Oklahoma, South Carolina, Tennessee, and Texas. These states contained 45 percent of the nation's farms and 62 percent of the country's tenant farmers. The Children's Bureau's surveys involved 13,500 children doing farm work in fourteen states. The investigations did not include children whose work consisted only of "chores" or those whose labor lasted less than twelve days a year.[71]

Both boys and girls worked in agriculture. Even more than children involved in the street trades, youngsters employed in food production spent little time in school. The bureau reported the story of one typical twelve-year-old. The son of a white tenant farmer cultivating fifty acres, the boy worked at plowing, harrowing, planting, cultivating, and chopping cotton from February to May. During the summer he cut, raked, and did loading and hauling. Beginning in September he picked cotton for about six weeks. Though enrolled in school, he had only completed the first grade. The bureau's report summarizes in detail the work undertaken by such children on cotton, tobacco, beet, wheat, corn, vegetable, and fruit farms. In some districts nearly half of all the children ten and over who were enrolled in local schools worked in the fields. The labor was seasonal, but most children missed so much school due to their work responsibilities that they fell far behind. Workdays lasted from nine to fourteen hours and some young workers migrated along with their families from nearby cities for seasonal work. Housing for these migrant families was "only too often

. . . makeshift, violating every standard of decency as well as comfort" and wages were poor, $1.50 per ten-hour workday. The bureau concluded that, as was the case in industrial and street work, such labor did not offer children "valuable training." Instead those for whom "farm work cuts short their school days are not being given a fair chance in life." But the bureau carefully acknowledged that the farmer who had his children "help" with the chores while still allowing time for school was not an agency concern. "Children who do a reasonable amount of farm work, suited to their years and under the supervision of their parents, are fortunate. Such work inculcates habits of industry and develops family solidarity, both desirable objectives in any system of child training." However, according to the bureau, even farm parents must be "educated in regard to the importance of training and recreation." As with child health care, farm parents needed to be taught the "proper" ways to rear children.[72]

Further, although the abuses of migratory child labor were evident, the agency advocated federal regulation of child labor only for children working in industry and urban street trades. Bureau reports pushed for states to provide better educational opportunities for rural and migratory child laborers. But as in the case of young urban and industrial workers, the Children's Bureau did not offer a federal program designed to help ease the circumstances of these children and their families. The typical school year in rural areas and mill towns lasted only three to six months. The quality of school facilities also differed greatly for blacks and whites. Furthermore, in many rural areas even white children found it almost impossible to attend school beyond the eighth grade. Typical of the times was the case of Tilda Kemplen living in rural eastern Tennessee during the 1920s and 1930s. Kemplen remembered that she wanted to go to high school, but "we lived so far back in the mountains I couldn't go to high school. There was no transportation, and the nearest high school was twenty-five miles away. I had to walk three miles to get to a country road, which was no more than a wagon road, and then there wasn't any school bus service, even on the country road. So there was no way I could go to high school." Motivation was not the problem. Kemplen was a star student and went through the eighth grade twice "because I wanted to attend school so badly that I repeated the eighth grade to get to go another year." Federal funding for education may have helped children like Kemplen, but the Children's Bureau offered no such plan.[73]

Extensive domestic duties and farm labor also kept many rural children out of school. Partially attributable to the Children's Bureau's lack of leadership, only six states (Maine, Nebraska, New York, Ohio, Pennsylvania, and Wisconsin) provided any regulations affecting the employment of children in agricultural labor.[74]

Overall, despite the efforts of the Children's Bureau and other child labor reform organizations during the 1920s and early 1930s on behalf of the child labor amendment, only fifteen states had ratified by August 1933. Furthermore, the 1930 census reported that 2,145,919 boys and girls under sixteen years of age were "gainfully employed" in the United States.[75] Child labor remained a prominent part of American life.

Conclusion

In a 1922 article in the *North American Review,* Grace Abbott contended that the Supreme Court's decisions in *Hammer vs. Dagenhart* and *Bailey vs. Drexel Furniture Company* "clearly established that either the policy of Federal assistance in eliminating child labor must be abandoned, or the Constitution must be amended." She believed that a federal amendment would force even the most backward states to accept at least what the Children's Bureau and its supporters judged as minimum standards for child labor regulation.[76] However, the bureau failed to convince the majority of state legislatures of its viewpoint. Organized opposition to the idea remained strong and the conservative political atmosphere of the 1920s diminished the desires of many for reform.

The Children's Bureau's failure to gain federal regulation of child labor during its first two decades of work left the agency with only the power to investigate and report on the circumstances of working children. In a 1923 interview, Ruben Dagenhart (then twenty years old), expressed the reality for many laboring children in the United States. When asked, "what benefit" he received from the suit won in his name before the Supreme Court, Dagenhart reportedly answered, "I don't see that I got any benefit. I guess I'd been a lot better off if they hadn't won it." He continued, "Look at me! A hundred and five pounds, a grown man and no education. I may be mistaken, but I think the years I've put in the cotton mills have stunted my growth. . . . I don't know—the dust and the lint, maybe. But, from 12 years old on, I was working 12 hours a day—from 6 in the morning until 7 at night, with time out for meals. And sometimes I worked nights besides. . . . It would have been a good thing for all the kids in this state if that law they passed had been kept." Furthermore, Dagenhart said that while he could do nothing to change his own past he wasn't "going to let them [his parents] put my kid sister in the mill. . . . She's only 15 and she's crippled and I bet I stop that!"[77]

Abbott and her staff would have agreed with Dagenhart that greedy parents and employers perpetuated child labor. Nevertheless, hindered by opponents' shouts of states' rights, business and manufacturing interests, and fears about the undermining of parental authority, the Children's Bureau tried to change American attitudes about the role of children in family and society. Some children likely benefited from this effort, but even the Children's Bureau seemed to ignore the realities of its own findings. Bureau reports condemned the circumstances of children laboring in agriculture, industry, at homework, and in the streets, but the agency offered few alternatives to families who believed that putting their children to work was a legitimate means to obtaining the American dream. Lathrop and her successor abandoned the family wage idea. Similarly the agency suggested that privately funded scholarships for those who stayed in school might be a way to discourage needy children from seeking employment. But the idea got little attention, received limited enthusiasm from either those in the Children's Bureau or the general public, and was quickly abandoned.[78] The federal government did not offer relief or vocational training to young people until the New Deal's Civilian Conservation Corps (1933) and the National Youth Administration (1935) programs. These did not develop as Children's Bureau programs and served only those of high school and college age, and the Civilian Conservation Corps restricted employment to males. A rejection of nineteenth-century romantic attitudes about agricultural labor, cooperative education programs, a greater emphasis on apprenticeship and vocational training, after-school care for children of working mothers, gender pay equity, scholarships for children who remained in school, federally mandated minimum wages for adults, and unemployment compensation might have served as more effective and creative alternatives for reducing child labor throughout the United States.

6

When Families Fail: Defining Social Policy for Children with "Special Needs," 1912-30

As the previous chapters have shown, most of the Children's Bureau's work during its first two decades centered on investigating, reporting, and promoting preventive health care and child labor reform. During the same period, but on a smaller scale, the bureau also conducted forty-nine studies concerning the social welfare of children "in need of special care—the dependent, the delinquent, and the mentally or physically handicapped." Or more specifically, "one who is (1) destitute, (2) homeless, (3) abandoned, (4) dependent upon the public for support, (5) without proper prenatal care or guardianship, (6) begging or receiving alms, (7) found living in a house of ill fame or with a vicious or disreputable person, (8) in a home unfit because of neglect, cruelty, or depravity on the part of the parents, (9) peddling or playing a musical instrument or singing in a public place, (10) in surroundings dangerous to morals, health, or general welfare or such as to warrant the State in assuming guardianship." The Children's Bureau's Social Service Division, headed by Emma O. Lundberg, defined the scope and direction of bureau efforts in behalf of children with special needs.[1]

The 1909 White House Conference on Dependent Children explicated most of the bureau's criteria concerning young people with "special needs." "Home life," the meeting's summary report asserted confidently, "is the highest and finest product of civilization. It is the great molding force of mind and of character. Children should not be deprived of it except for urgent and compelling reasons."[2] The Children's Bureau based its social welfare policy on the commitment that all children should be provided with a homelife as close as possible to what the agency and its supporters defined as the ideal. This included loving parents and a sanitary home provided by a father who worked as the family's sole breadwinner and a mother who remained at home to devote full attention to her family. The bureau argued that in order to protect "a right to childhood" for children whose circumstances did not meet this criteria, "special" care should be provided by cooperating public and private institutions. The objective: to offer "as nearly as possible" for such children a homelife "like the . . . other children of the community."[3] The practical result was an emphasis on "family" social work and foster care. The Children's Bureau and its supporters maintained that such efforts were not only humanitarian but desirable because they deterred juvenile delinquency and prevented adult dependency. "All society," the Children's Bureau argued, should be "vitally interested" in children whose social welfare involved the state. Children living in circumstances that resulted in legal intervention by local authorities would not grow up to be good citizens unless they received "scientific" direction based on the latest psychological and sociological theories. Insofar as it related to children, the bureau declared that the "law must be oriented to life."[4] The Social Service Division designed programs and lobbied for legislation intended to improve children's health, to end or at least regulate child labor, and to encourage the implementation of compulsory school attendance laws.

During its first two decades much of the Children's Bureau's social welfare efforts encouraged the establishment of state and local juvenile and family courts. These institutions were, as Graham Parker explains, "a hybrid—a legal creation but a social administrative institution, a bridge between law and the social sciences."[5] The family court was an excellent expression of the Children's Bureau's philosophy of relying on scientific investigation and the implementation of its recommended programs by trained professionals at the state and local level. But such services varied under the jurisdiction of the expanding juvenile/family court systems in the United States.

The juvenile court movement had begun long before the establishment of the Children's Bureau. In 1874 Massachusetts created special court procedures for children charged with crimes. In July 1899 Cook County, Illinois, established what is generally recognized as the first "full-fledged" juvenile court system in the world. The county organized a special court designated exclusively to handle cases involving children under a new Illinois law, "An Act to Regulate the Treatment and Control of Dependent, Neglected, and Delinquent Children." The Illinois juvenile court's jurisdiction encompassed any child fifteen years of age or younger who violated any law or ordinance of the state, city, or village. Dependent and neglected children were defined as those who were "destitute or homeless or abandoned; or dependent upon the public for support." Children who lacked good prenatal care or guardianship, were treated cruelly, or lived in a house of prostitution or "with any vicious or disreputable person," including "depraved" parents, could also become wards of the court. As a member of the Illinois Board of Charities, Julia Lathrop had been one of the leaders in this successful effort and played a major role in the establishment of a state reformatory for delinquent girls in 1893.[6] Also in 1899, Judge Benjamin Barr Lindsey organized a similar children's court in Denver, Colorado, under that state's "School Law" that same year.[7] Lindsey, Judge Julian Mack of Illinois and Judge Miriam Van Waters of California became the primary spokespersons for the juvenile court movement. Between 1899 and 1912 a total of twenty states enacted some form of juvenile court law and by 1920 forty-five states had done so. The exceptions were Connecticut, Maine, and Wyoming, but even these states had passed special laws "dealing with some of the problems usually included in the juvenile-court law itself." In fourteen states the courts' jurisdiction extended to children sixteen years of age; in thirteen states to seventeen years of age; and in seventeen states to eighteen years of age. In Maryland its jurisdiction was extended to eighteen for girls and twenty for boys. California used twenty-one for both boys and girls. As with the general definition of childhood, the legal age rose during the first four decades of the twentieth century to as high as twenty-one.[8]

The Children's Bureau and Juvenile Courts

The rationale for juvenile courts held that "children are to be dealt with separately from adults . . . not as criminals but as persons in whose guidance and welfare the State is peculiarly interested." The purpose of such institutions, the Children's Bureau explained, was "not to punish, but to save." The bureau recommended that juvenile courts be conducted informally and, if possible, in separate facilities from adults. In addition, if detention was necessary, children should be held in buildings restricted to juveniles. On the other hand, young people should not be removed from their parents unless absolutely necessary. "Trained" probation officers conducted visits to the family home intended to maintain contact between the child and the court. The bureau warned that leaving the children with their parents did not relieve the state of its responsibility: it was still the state's duty to see that "parental obligations are . . . enforced."[9]

Early juvenile court cases chiefly involved young persons who violated criminal statutes or became dependent on the state for their support. By the turn of the century some reformers began to suggest much broader obligations for courts dealing with children's legal and social welfare. In 1910, Buffalo, New York, organized the nation's first domestic relations court. The court's responsibilities were limited to adults, but its hearings related closely to the juvenile court's jurisdiction. The domestic relations court's caseload included all criminal business relating to domestic or family affairs and "bastardy." New Jersey passed similar legislation two years later. In 1914 Hamilton County, Ohio (Cincinnati), formally combined the jurisdictions of juvenile and domestic relations in the United States' first family court. "The aim of the family court," explained Hamilton County judge Charles W. Hoffman, was "the consideration of all matters relating to the family in one court of exclusive jurisdiction, in which the same methods of procedure shall prevail as in the juvenile court and in which it will be possible to consider social evidence as distinguished from legal evidence." Denying that the idea unduly expanded the role of the judiciary, Hoffman maintained that "providing for a family court is no more than increasing the jurisdiction of the juvenile court and designating it by the more comprehensive term of a family court." The creation of such institutions seemed a logical evolution of the juvenile court movement. However, as Joseph Hawes contends, such developments meant that children actually lost some formal legal guarantees such as due process. But, Hawes concludes, juvenile/family courts were certainly an improvement over former practices which had either neglected such children or treated them as adults.[10]

The Children's Bureau would have agreed. It applauded the trend expanding juvenile courts and thereby encouraged "cooperation between [them and] other social agencies [utilizing] the services of trained social workers." The bureau liked the "tendency to merge the cases of children with those of their families, and to try them before 'family' or 'domestic relations' courts. In this way the child is dealt with as a member of his family and all the family circumstances are taken into account."[11]

The Children's Bureau published forty-nine studies from 1913 through 1930 investigating juvenile delinquency, illegitimacy, children dependent on the state for support, and the mentally handicapped.[12] The bureau advanced family courts (called "tribunals" in some states) as the best way to deal with children in need of "special" care. On May 18, 1923, the Children's Bureau and the National Probation Association (est. 1907) held a conference in Washington which adopted standards for courts dealing with "delinquency or dependency, nonsupport or desertion of minor children, . . . determination of paternity and the support of children born out of wedlock, [and] adoption cases and cases of children in need of protection or custodial care by reason of mental defect or disorder." The conference recognized that the creation of family courts linked the interests of children, their parents, and the state as never before.[13]

In 1925, Katharine Lenroot, then the Children's Bureau's assistant chief, argued that the motivation for juvenile and family courts "is found in the insight, courage and faith of the men and women who saw that the harshness and inflexibility of the criminal law as applied to children and the parental and protective functions of the state were irreconcilable." Quoting from the Chicago Bar Association's committee responsible for drafting the 1899 Illinois act establishing the nation's first juvenile court, she continued: "[The] fundamental idea is that the state must step in and exercise guardianship over a child found under such adverse social or individual conditions as to develop crime. . . . [the juvenile court] proposes a plan whereby he may be treated not as a criminal or one legally charged with a crime, but as a ward of the state to receive practically the care, custody and discipline that are accorded to the neglected and dependent child, and which, as the act states, 'shall approximate as nearly as may be that which should be given by its parents.'"[14]

Katharine Fredrica Lenroot represented a third generation of Children's Bureau staff. She was born in Superior, Wisconsin, on March 8, 1891, the daughter of Clara Pamela Clough and Irvine L. Lenroot. Her father was a prominent Republican senator and also served as a federal judge. Apparently Lenroot's mother maintained the traditional role of wife and mother. Lenroot was closest to her father and decided to choose a more public career. She was a student of John R. Commons at the University of Wisconsin and graduated with a B.A. in economics in 1912. At Wisconsin Lenroot wrote a senior thesis on state laws relating to laundries and prepared a brief on the Australian and English minimum wage laws and court decisions concerning the issue in the United States. She testified before a state joint legislative committee considering the Illinois minimum wage bill and gave an address on the subject at a state Consumers' League convention. In 1913, the Wisconsin Industrial Commission hired Lenroot to conduct cost-of-living surveys in connection with the state's new minimum wage law. The study was conducted under the direction of Children's Bureau Social Service Division head Emma O. Lundberg. At Lundberg's request, in the fall of 1914 Lenroot took the federal civil service examination and joined the Children's Bureau in January 1915 as a special investigator in the Social Service Division. Lenroot was one of twenty-six special agents then employed by the Children's Bureau. Her work included studies concerning "mentally defective children," illegitimacy, juvenile delinquency, and juvenile courts. In 1921, she was named director of the bureau's Editorial Division and in 1922 became assistant chief.[15]

Lenroot and other members of the Children's Bureau recognized that juvenile and family courts dealt "with a complicated group of problems: That of the offending adult, the accused child, the neglectful and degraded parent, the incompetent or unfaithful guardian, [and] the family that is simply poor." Their decisions demanded a careful balancing of the interests of the child, the parents, and the state. The Children's Bureau believed that the rights of children could be "efficiently" protected by uniting social sciences and the law. Since the turn of the century "it has become clear that under the doctrines of equity jurisprudence the rights of the child to a reasonable minimum of care, of decency, of well-being, and of consideration for youth and previous disadvantage might be assured . . . without violating either the constitutional provisions intended to prevent abuse of criminal procedure or the property rights of the father."[16] The Children's Bureau believed that family courts provided the best means to that end.

But merely establishing such institutions was not enough. As in its other programs, the Children's Bureau judged that public attitudes concerning delinquency, illegitimacy, and dependency needed to be changed through education and persuasion in order to protect the best interests of the children involved. Again, the Children's Bureau's policy designers limited the role for the nation's leading advocate for children to investigation, education, and persuasion. In line with this, other efforts of the bureau's Social Service Division focused on juvenile delinquency, illegitimacy, mothers' pensions, and on the needs of all children dependent on the state for support.

Defining and Preventing Juvenile Delinquency

Those involved in the juvenile court movement often cited the prevention of juvenile delinquency as one of their major concerns. They established organizations such as the Chicago Juvenile Protection League (1905) "to keep children out of court by removing many of the demoralizing conditions which surrounded them."[17] Indeed, many reformers believed that a bad environment coupled with youthful immaturity to form the primary cause of juvenile delinquency. Child offenders were "handicapped by immaturity of body and mind [and] by a lack of effective parental control." Many child welfare advocates felt that communities had a responsibility to reform the environment and therefore the children who seemed out of control. California juvenile court judge and active Children's Bureau supporter Miriam Van Waters argued that "a respect for the rights of childhood; the fundamental difference between child and adult, in particular his almost unlimited, unexplored capacity for spiritual growth, for modification, in the right soil, with the right person taking an interest in him—[was] an attitude which . . . places the burden of delinquency and the responsibility for its treatment upon the adult world."[18]

The Children's Bureau's work in this field adhered to this philosophy emphasizing adult responsibility for the reform of children's environment and the care of juvenile delinquents. Shortly after she became Children's Bureau chief, the U.S. attorney general appointed Lathrop to a committee charged with reviewing the District of Columbia's juvenile court. Lathrop's experience with the Illinois Board of Charities and her position as chief of the federal agency responsible for investigating and reporting on juvenile courts made her well suited for this assignment. The committee reviewed judicial appointments and suggested reforms, but Congress ignored the advice and the District of Columbia's juvenile court was not fully "modernized" until 1938.[19]

First, the Children's Bureau collected a history of young people's experiences appearing before Connecticut courts from 1635 to 1917. The study supported the contention of the juvenile court movement that the traditional judicial system failed to protect the best interests of children because it "punished" rather than "saved" them. Lathrop maintained that the "great primary service of the [juvenile] court is that it . . . compels us to see that wastage of human life whose sign is the child in court."[20]

During World War I the Children's Bureau became increasingly concerned with juvenile delinquency and the promotion of juvenile courts. In 1918 the bureau issued a report entitled "Juvenile Delinquency in Certain Countries at War." The study concluded that "the testimony of social workers, judges concerned with children's cases, and students of criminology [revealed] an increasing number of children brought to court and an increasing seriousness in their offenses" in England, France, Germany, and Russia during the war. The causes of this rise in juvenile crime, the Children's Bureau argued, were the departure of fathers to the front, a rise in the number of mothers working outside the home, and the overcrowding of schools caused by a shortage of teachers, some who had taken higher-paying jobs in industry or entered the armed forces. The bureau concluded that "when the normal life of children is broken down, when their needs are neglected by the community, children and community alike must pay the penalty."[21]

The bureau's wartime Children's Year program included efforts designed to prevent a similar rise in juvenile delinquency in the United

States. In the opinion of American judges and other child welfare authorities questioned by the Children's Bureau during 1918, the major causes of juvenile delinquency included "high wages paid child workers . . . and the resulting extravagance, . . . the adoration in which young girls hold soldiers and sailors, . . . the social unrest that is everywhere manifest, . . . the craving for adventure, . . . [and] the entrance of mothers into industry." "Home life and community activities," the bureau argued, "must . . . be upheld in war time. When so many fathers are absent in the service mothers are needed at home even more than in normal times." War must not deprive children of a "normal home life. . . . and surely, the community can maintain its standards of schooling and provide . . . ample opportunity for wholesome play." In addition, "children who have become unruly need the attention which special courts can give." The war should not be "allowed to interfere with the work of [those trained in the] modern methods of care" associated with juvenile and family courts. The Children's Bureau envisioned organizations such as Boston's Judge Baker Guidance Center (established in 1917) as the kind of social work agency for the future.[22]

The Children's Year program also included a recreation drive designed to deter juvenile delinquency. The recreation movement was another Progressive Era child welfare reform effort intended to counter what many believed were undesirable conditions of modernization. These reformers encouraged communities to establish supervised recreational facilities in the form of playgrounds, swimming pools, parks, and other projects in order to provide a wholesome and controlled environment for children's leisure time. The Children's Bureau's recreation drive was a national effort promoting the same kind of environmental changes in behalf of children promoted by the Chicago Juvenile Protection Association, which had been established in 1905 to create "a permanent public sentiment for the establishment of wholesome uplifting agencies, such as parks, playgrounds, gymnasiums, free baths, vacation schools, communal social centers and the like." Grace Abbott had worked for the Chicago Juvenile Protection Association during 1918 and labeled her work there as more "police" effort than anything else.[23] But overlooking this obvious reality the Children's Bureau aggressively supported the national effort to organize children's play with high-minded platitudes and conservationist rhetoric.

In addition, like programs designed to improve the health of mothers and children and the drive to end child labor, the Children's Bureau advocated change in rural as well as urban areas. The agency argued that unorganized play threatened children living the countryside and the nation's cities. Addressing a notion held by many that children growing up in rural areas did not need such services, the Children's Bureau stated that "Country life is no longer a guarantee of good morals." The agency supported its claim that the worst by-products of modernization had also reached the countryside by citing a study of delinquency in rural New York State. The results, contended the Children's Bureau, showed that "the city is not alone in its problem of 'bad' children." Of the 185 children labeled as delinquent by local authorities in the study, "one-fifth were classed as mischievous, incorrigible or wayward, a little less than two-fifths were offenders against decency, and slightly more than two-fifths were offenders against property." Modernization necessitated that Americans in rural and urban areas needed to address juvenile delinquency using "scientific" methods. Every community, urged the bureau, needed more provisions for organized recreation, because "the desire for play is instinctive but not the knowledge how." In a modern world fraught with danger, without supervision "little groups 'with nothing to do' are likely to be transformed into mischief makers; here is often the beginning of the passing from one child to another of forbidden knowledge and practices; and here, too, much of the 'light-fingeredness' and pilfering gets its start." In the Children's Bureau's opinion, "good play leaders, playgrounds and play equipment are as necessary for the rural as for the city child and will go a long way in solving the delinquency problem. Satan does not find mischief for happy hands to do." But children (and their mothers) often resisted attempts to supervise play. Studies conducted by private organizations in New York City (1913) and Milwaukee (1914) revealed that less than 4 percent of school-age children actually used city and school playgrounds outside of school hours.[24]

The Children's Bureau, however, was not deterred. Women volunteers from the General Federation of Women's Clubs, the Congress of Mothers, and other predominately female associations supported the bureau's efforts and organized "Patriotic pageants" as a climax to the Children's Year recreation drive. The pageants served as one way to organize children's play hours in a "constructive manner," but their primary purpose was "to help young people realize more vividly what the aid of the United States means to the peoples of the allied nations, and to show the part to be played by children in furthering the cause of democracy." The Children's Bureau's Mary West wrote the agency's official suggestions for organizing and performing such pageants. West recommended that central figures such as Columbia and Justice could lead the parade and she provided detailed instructions for making appropriate costumes. These characters should be followed by attendants dressed in red, white, and blue and "suffering children draped in gray . . . giving [them] a sorrowful appearance."[25] The General Federation of Women's Clubs and other Children's Year sponsors held the recommended pageants and parades throughout the United States. Instilling patriotic ideals was another way to deter juvenile delinquency and maintain social control. The war provided the perfect opportunity to make this preventive tactic a national effort.

A lack of data made it impossible for the Children's Bureau to determine if juvenile delinquency had actually risen in the United States during the war. However, the agency used what was available to estimate that approximately 175,000 children were brought before U.S. courts during 1918. This was actually only one-seventh of the total number of children then living in the United States, but the agency's wartime study in Great Britain suggested that this may have been a greater percentage than prior to the war. Of those appearing before U.S. courts, approximately 50,000 were in courts not specifically adapted to handling juvenile cases. The Children's Bureau considered this circumstance especially serious because, as noted earlier, many "juvenile" courts were wholly inadequate. Lathrop argued that the circumstances of war and the lack of specialized legal provisions for children made "the duty of studying juvenile courts, which is imposed on the Bureau by statute, one of far-reaching importance."[26]

One of the Children's Bureau's many studies of juvenile courts focused on youthful offenders appearing before federal courts during 1918-19. This was the first study to examine the experience of children (in this case persons under twenty years of age) charged with violating federal laws. The federal government did not follow the Children's Bureau's recommended procedure for juvenile offenders, but instead treated them as adults. The majority of violations (1,108) involved postal offenses including stealing mail and robbing post-offices. The vast majority of cases involved boys. However, fifty-four girls were convicted of postal offenses, which included forgery of mail or of checks contained in the mail (15), larceny of mail (15), and wrongful use of the mail (10, of whom eight sent obscene material and two were involved in schemes to defraud). Slightly more than half (566) of the children were under sixteen years of age. The bureau concluded that the federal government fell far behind many of the states concerning the treatment of juvenile delinquents, since federal district courts provided no separate facilities for children, conducted formal criminal trials, and did not offer segregated penal or reform institutions for juvenile offenders. Julia Lathrop condemned this circumstance and maintained that "the United States [government] should lead not lag far behind the States in the care it gives children who come under its jurisdiction."[27]

Even the accomplishments of the state and local juvenile courts left much to be desired. The Children's Bureau found that during the first six months of 1923, 945 juveniles under eighteen years of age were sent to prisons or reformatories, and 2,445 to jails or workhouses. Most were not segregated from adults. In her 1925 annual report, Children's Bureau chief Grace Abbott lamented that "much yet remains to be done if the ideal of the juvenile court movement—that delinquent children are to be placed under redeeming and not degrading influences—is to be realized." Abbott recommended that the bureau establish a division of delinquency to study the problem. This office, the chief explained, would "conduct research in the field of prevention and proper care of delinquents and on request . . . confer with local agencies on these problems. The present concern over crime and criminal tendencies in the United States makes the creation of this division especially important at this time. Crime begins in delinquency among children." Abbott seemed to feel that many juvenile courts had taken on responsibilities other than juvenile delinquency without the necessary "professional" support network of social workers and other experts. She was disillusioned, but did not call for the abolition of juvenile courts.[28]

As had been the case with infant mortality, there was little national data about children charged with crimes. True to its philosophy, the Children's Bureau believed that data collection and scientific analysis would lead to reform. In late 1926 the bureau began collecting national data on juvenile delinquency from children's courts throughout the United States and started publication of its findings in annual reports beginning in 1927. After five years, the effort showed that juvenile delinquency rates appeared to be rising. During 1931 alone, the ninety-two juvenile courts reporting to the bureau counted 56,110 delinquency cases. The maximum age of children appearing before the courts was twenty-one, but 78 percent fell below sixteen. Boys fourteen and fifteen years of age made up 43 percent of these. Girls of that age group constituted 65 percent of all cases involving females, and were 9 percent of all children under sixteen years of age. Girls' chances of being brought before the court increased as they reached puberty. The number of fourteen-year-old girls in the courts doubled that of thirteen-year-olds. Race was another important factor. Black juvenile delinquency rates were five times that of the total population of all children under sixteen years of age. Black males constituted about one-fifth of the cases involving boys and black girls made up approximately one-fourth of those concerning young females. This is a much higher rate than the proportion of blacks in the general population (less than 10 percent in most areas reporting to the bureau). Furthermore, a higher percentage of black children ten and under appeared before the courts than white children from the same age cohort. This does not suggest that black children were more likely to break the law. Instead, it is possible that local authorities more often charged blacks than whites with juvenile delinquency. The disposition of cases involved racial as well as gender biases. Of all cases involving males, 50 percent were dismissed, adjusted, or held open without further action. The courts dropped 51 percent of the cases involving white boys, but only 46 percent of black males received the same treatment. Interestingly, the courts seemed less likely to take the same action in girls' cases and were more likely to dismiss cases against black rather than white females. Only 39 percent of girls' cases were dropped; 38 percent of those involving white females, but 43 percent of those involving black girls.[29] There are many factors which may have contributed to this circumstance. Perhaps some judges felt that disorderly girls, especially white girls, needed greater attention and control. There may have also been a lack of facilities for black females. The Children's Bureau's 1931 report offers little insight into the causes for these racial and gender biases. However, the agency's studies did show that in general, despite the efforts of juvenile court advocates since the turn of the century, juvenile delinquency remained a problem.

Those attending White House Conference on Child Health and Protection, held between November 19 and November 21, 1930, also expressed concern for "the delinquent child." The Children's Bureau summarized the conference's recommendations in what was identified as "a nontechnical outline of what the citizen needs to know about the prevention and treatment of juvenile delinquency." "The problem of delinquency," the Children's Bureau claimed, "is not a superficial blemish which can be removed with ease. It is an indication of weakness and maladjustment in the whole social organism." Furthermore, "we cannot hope that it will be eliminated in this generation or the next. Conditions of modern living may even tend to increase it." The Children's Bureau concluded that states and local officials formally charged over 250,000 children each year with delinquency and that even more were arrested who never went to court. The bureau restated its contention that although juvenile delinquency was "primarily a city problem . . . it is [also] a serious problem in rural communities." Furthermore, the agency recognized for the first time that class might play a part in the labeling of a child as delinquent. "It is doubtless true," the bureau argued, "that many children of the well-to-do are kept from coming before the courts because their families have greater resources and are often able to obtain special care for their children whereas children of the poor are more likely to be referred to court or committed to institutions." The most usual cases for boys included "stealing, acts of carelessness . . . and traffic violations." For girls, the most common charges were "truancy," "ungovernable[ness]," running away, and "sex offense[s]." It seems clear that sexuality played a major role in the definition of female delinquency charges. But the Children's Bureau did not acknowledge that cultural notions about female sexuality may have influenced its figures. Many people at the time believed that public dance halls exposed girls to immoral behavior. The bureau recommended that while dancing was a desirable recreation for adolescents, dance halls should be supervised and staffed with chaperons to prevent misconduct. Linda Gordon has shown that girls labeled as "sex delinquents" were often the victims of street rape or violence, or unwilling participants in sex acts. Girls who became pregnant by forced or consensual sex might also be charged with sexual offenses.[30]

The bureau's 1930 report also evaluated the causes of juvenile delinquency. "Unhappy home conditions" ranked at the top of the bureau's identified factors leading to delinquent behavior. The Children's Bureau stated that many of the children brought before the courts came from "homes broken by death, desertion, separation, divorce of the parents, and . . . [where] a lack of affection and harmony between parents and other serious emotional problems from adults make it impossible to satisfy the child's fundamental need for security and development." It also argued that some parents contributed to delinquency by failing to understand their children and ignoring the "modern methods of child training and character development." "Gang" membership was also judged to be a factor. The bureau concluded that "an enlightened public opinion [was] one of the most important requirements in any successful program for the prevention of juvenile delinquency." An educated electorate could demand better city planning, more careful zoning, and real-estate developments "that give due consideration to community environment and the provision of such facilities as school sites, playgrounds, parks, and of organized facilities for the constructive use of leisure time." A good preventive program would include "all movements for the improvement of conditions affecting the family and child life." A basic income or a minimum wage for "every family adequate [enough] to insure minimum standards of living" served as one means to protect children from becoming delinquents. In summary, "many children [were] being deprived of their fundamental right to normal home life." In proposing its solution, the Children's Bureau argued that "to promote the stability and happiness in family life is, therefore, to aid in the prevention of juvenile delinquency."[31]

The 1930 White House Conference on Child Health and Protection also published a study in conjunction with the Wickersham National Commission on Law Observance and Enforcement entitled the "Child Offender in the Federal System of Justice." Miriam Van Waters directed the study, which led to passage of a federal law signed by President Hoover in 1931 providing for the transfer of federal juvenile offenders to state courts if the delinquents had also violated a state law. In 1938 Congress further extended legislation to allow federal courts to use juvenile court procedures.[32]

The Children's Bureau's policy concerning juvenile delinquency did lead to more humane treatment of most children under state laws. But the growing bureaucracy also increasingly relied on reform schools as the best (or at least the easiest) solution.[33] As a result, contrary to the Children's Bureau's original suggestion, efforts focused on the individual child rather than the entire family. In addition, rural areas lagged far behind cities and towns in the establishment of special courts for children. Overall, for children whose families could not provide what the Children's Bureau and its supporters judged as an adequate homelife, foster care and institutionalization seemed to be the only choice. In 1933, the Bureau of the Census reported that 28,770 boys and girls under twenty-one years of age in the United States lived in institutions for juvenile delinquents.[34] For these children the state had accepted the role of surrogate parent, but a "normal" homelife was not the end result.

The State as Income Provider: Mothers' Pensions and Dependent Children

Since the mid-nineteenth century the state had also become a source of income if not a "parent" for some of the children living with families unable to provide for their support. A proportion of these children indirectly received relief through veteran's pensions, workmen's compensation programs, or poor relief; but the first two did not relate to the number of recipients' dependents. The 1909 White House conference advocated a new assistance idea for fatherless children. This plan called for the widespread implementation of mothers' pension programs (sometimes called mothers' aid or widows' pensions) at the local level.[35] The White House conference recommended that "children . . . of deserving mothers who are without the support of the normal breadwinner, should, as a rule, be kept with their [mother, with] such aid being given as may be necessary to maintain suitable homes for the rearing of children." As with most of its recommendations, the conference wanted to keep the responsibility for administering this aid at the local level. In addition, aid should be provided "in the form of private charity, rather than of public relief." Many turn-of-the-century child welfare reformers, such as Edward T. Devine, Josephine Shaw Lowell, and Mary Richmond, were suspicious of public relief and questioned the wisdom of mothers' pensions. Others said that the system acted as only a temporary measure that did not do enough to solve the underlying causes of poverty for women and their children. A few worried that mothers' pensions might encourage fathers to desert their families. But child welfare advocates instead focused on the children and discounted such objections by arguing mothers' pensions would help to insure that "except in unusual circumstances, the home should not be broken up for reasons of poverty, but only for considerations of inefficiency or immorality."[36] At least in theory, mothers' pensions protected children's fundamental right to "home life" and in this case the middle-class family ideal was somewhat altered to include children with "worthy mothers" and absent fathers. But it is important to emphasize that the 1909 White House conference did not call for state or federally funded mothers' pensions.

Julia Lathrop had endorsed the mothers' pension idea even before becoming Children's Bureau chief. She argued that "there is not a more pathetic figure, no sadder failure than the mother struggling against insurmountable obstacles for a livelihood. The woman who goes out to work and who attempts to care for her children fails lamentably at both and falls by the wayside."[37] Of course, true to the middle-class family ideal, Lathrop believed that only mothers who were forced to work for wages would do so and that mothers' pensions were one way to help end this circumstance for "deserving" women and their children. It appears that at the time there was actually little need for persuasion. Going beyond the recommendations of the 1909 White House conference, the nation's first state mothers' aid law, entitled "the Illinois Funds to Parents Act," was passed in 1911 and gave administration of the program to the state's juvenile courts. The 1899 Illinois juvenile court law provided for three treatments of dependent children: (1) the return of the child to its own home subject to visitation from a probation officer; (2) the appointment of a "reputable citizen" as guardian for the child; and (3) commitment of the child to an institution. No provision was made for boarding children at state expense in either their own homes or foster homes. The passage of the Illinois mothers' pension act added state support as a possible option for some children with absent fathers.[38] Missouri and other states quickly followed, with most adhering to the system established by Illinois. By 1913 twenty states provided some form of mothers' pension program and by the end of 1921 forty states and the territories of Alaska and Hawaii had done so. During the next ten years six more states enacted such laws, leaving only Georgia and South Carolina without mothers' pension programs by the end of 1931. Isaac Rubinow, the most famous Progressive Era advocate of social insurance, contended that the popularity of mothers' pension programs evidenced the "irresistible development of social insurance principles in the United States."[39] At the same time that states adopted mothers' pension laws, they also enacted workmen's compensation legislation. The Children's Bureau endorsed both, but during its first two decades the agency placed the majority of its emphasis on collecting data and recommending passage of uniform mothers' pension legislation. The Children's Bureau's "whole child" focus shaped this issue. Women's compensation statutes also covered females employed in some industries but most widows and mothers deserted by their husbands did not work in these fields. Labor unions, with their accompanying powerful lobbying systems, and other male-dominated groups served as the primary advocates for workmen's compensation laws. The Children's Bureau's first responsibility was to children. In addition, as Mark Leff argues, the female supporters of mothers' pensions (led by the National Congress of Mothers and the General Federation of Women's Clubs) imposed "upon that system the values of home, family, and moral purity." Lathrop and her Children's Bureau supporters felt that fatherless children living with their widowed or deserted mothers needed an advocate more than the men and their families who generally received veteran's pensions or workmen's compensation. Indeed, the American Federation of Labor endorsed the mothers' pension idea but spent most of its time on efforts to advance workmen's compensation laws.[40] The Children's Bureau also believed that prejudices concerning outdoor relief (poverty relief given directly to families or individuals so they could remain outside institutional care such as "poor houses") could be eliminated in the case of many fatherless children through the careful study and standardization of mothers' pension programs. The Children's Bureau argued in an examination of children in the care of Delaware institutions and agencies during 1920 that "a mothers' pension might have eliminated the necessity for removal [from their homes of] 10 percent of the children" involved.[41] Mothers' pensions might be a means to efficiency and "home life."

Despite what could be seen as a more flexible interpretation of the middle-class family ideal, mothers' pensions reinforced the bureau's narrow definition of the proper roles for women and men within the family. Advocates of mothers' aid held that widows or women deserted by their husbands would be able to remain home with their children if provided an income from the state or through private charity. A bureau expert wrote, "A grant of aid given promptly, with a reasonable assurance of continuance . . . [was] the most help . . . the community could give to mothers [living] under adverse circumstance. A just grant . . . will secure . . . a regular income and relieve them of at least a part of the economic pressure."[42] During World War I the bureau tried to dissuade mothers with young children from entering the work force. Children of wage-earning mothers presented special "problems of social control." It was the "duty of society to find some substitute for the earnings" of an absent father. Most working mothers, the bureau argued, were driven into the work force because of poor earnings available to their husbands or the absence of a male breadwinner. African American mothers were more likely to work outside of the home than whites of the same socioeconomic group. This circumstance, the bureau judged, was partly due to undesirable cultural attitudes among blacks which accepted women as wage earners. But despite the Children's Bureau's stereotype, most black activists also advocated traditional female roles. The bureau's report on wage-earning mothers in Chicago does not clearly define the phrase "social control," but it states that the opposite circumstance for children is "social maladjustment." Providing substitute incomes for families without male breadwinners, training mothers in "modern" methods of child care and home management, and, if absolutely necessary, the organization of sanitary and "intelligent" day nurseries were all ways to keep children under "social control."[43] Further, the agency's efforts to reduce infant mortality urged women to be full-time mothers and housekeepers. Studies of juvenile delinquency suggested that mothers working outside of the home also contributed to that "social" problem. To the Children's Bureau, mothers' aid programs administered through juvenile courts or separate agencies specifically established for that purpose provided the best system for dependent children deprived of a "normal" homelife due to the absence of a father through death, imprisonment, or desertion.

In 1921 the Children's Bureau published a study examining the ten-year administration of the Illinois mothers' aid program. Eligible mothers met specific criteria: standards of moral behavior, physical fitness, and the ability to efficiently and "properly" care for a household and children. Husbands had to be dead, unable to be located, or in prison. "Trained" volunteers or professionals regularly supervised and instructed recipients in child care and other domestic duties such as cooking, cleaning, sewing, and the budgeting of expenses. Budgeting was vital because of the meager payments afforded under the program. Mothers' pensions did not replace the average income of male laborers, which could range from $600 to $800 per year. And perhaps even more importantly, very few children actually received aid and those who did got very little assistance. During January 1917, 778 families got allowances. The number of children was not reported for one family, but the balance consisted of from one to seven children (723 had from two to five). Payments ranged from less than $60 to $720 per year with the largest percentage (36 percent) receiving from $240 to $348 annually. Twenty-seven percent of the incomes of families receiving mothers' pensions fell below what the Children's Bureau suggested was necessary to supply a nutritious diet. The law left administration of the program to county administrators, a policy that resulted in widely disparate application with some counties failing to provide any such relief. The bureau concluded "that all social legislation . . . left to 102 different local authorities to enforce without any supervision [from trained social workers] . . . must fail."[44] The Children's Bureau recommended tight state control of the administration of funds and close supervision of families to solve the problem. However, this trust in the uniform judgment of state authorities was grounded solely in the Children's Bureau's faith that such bureaucrats would follow its recommendations.

Nevertheless, despite its shortcomings, the Children's Bureau maintained that "in the mothers' pension system, if properly organized and safeguarded, may lie the nucleus of a new form of State aid vastly superior to any form of public assistance which our American States have known."[45] But further efforts during the 1920s to secure uniform application of mothers' pension programs failed. In 1922 the Children's Bureau sponsored a mothers' aid conference in cooperation with the National Conference of Social Work. The gathering discussed, among other concerns, the problems of inequity,[46] but made little real progress. Studies conducted in other localities also illustrated wide discrepancies in implementation and funding. In addition, as in Illinois, very few children received any help from such programs.[47] But contrary to these realities, by 1931 the Children's Bureau was encouraged by what seemed an "improved legislation, more liberal local and State funds, and [a] growth in the number of administrative units providing such aid." Most of all, the agency applauded that "back of these developments lie a recognition of the essential values of home life in the rearing of children and acceptance of the principle that no child should be separated from his family because of poverty alone."[48]

Despite this encouragement, in 1931 the Children's Bureau was actually singing the same tune introduced at the 1909 White House conference. Several states had broadened their eligibility requirements to include divorced mothers and their children. Nevertheless, "one qualification for eligibility as expressed in the statutes of all but one of the States (Maryland) . . . [was] that the mother shall be a proper person to have the care of her children." Such requirements left the payment of mothers' aid to the discretion of social workers and authorities. This circumstance opened the door to discrimination based on race and culture and made most never-married mothers ineligible for aid. To its credit, the Children's Bureau recognized that the "provision for Negro families was limited in a number of states." Several counties had lower allowances for African American mothers and their children. Others simply denied any funds to blacks. Average monthly grants for all eligible recipients ranged from $4.33 in Arkansas to $69.31 in Massachusetts. Wisconsin served the greatest percentage of families (24 per 10,000 population) and Maryland the smallest (1 per 10,000). Despite a trend increasing such grants, the Children's Bureau contended that the average allowance of $21.78 per family was below the amount necessary for a "satisfactory standard of living." By the end of 1919 thirty-nine states had passed some form of mothers' aid law. Of these twenty-nine restricted benefits to children born in "wedlock."[49]

According to the Children's Bureau, all mothers needed instruction in the "modern methods" of child care. Children also warranted training. Women and their children who received mothers' aid seemed to be in special need of such attention. But the bureau's limited vision in this field, and its acceptance of rigid "moral" eligibility standards based primarily on recommendations formulated by the 1909 White House conference substantially failed to ease the "economic burden" of many mothers and their children.

Illegitimacy

The Children's Bureau's Social Service Division also addressed illegitimacy as a social welfare issue. During its first two decades of work the agency conducted eleven studies about the condition of children born outside of marriage.[50] "Only within comparatively recent times," wrote Emma Lundberg and Katharine Lenroot in 1920, "has illegitimacy come to be recognized as a definite social problem." However, they suggested, "few topics relating to social welfare have as many ramifications or provoke as many divergent opinions." Controversy concerned the treatment of unwed mothers, whether or not these women should be encouraged to keep their children, the responsibility of fathers, and the compulsory registration of birth parents. The bureau maintained that above all else, illegitimacy's "relation to infant mortality, infant care, child abandonment and neglect, and the care of dependent children . . . demands the attention and concern of all who are engaged in constructive social effort." In this case, true to their constituency, Lundberg and Lenroot recognized that beyond the moral debate the issue had an immediate impact on the lives of the children involved. Again the bureau's staff saw the agency's role as one of encouraging Americans to view the circumstance of these children with "special needs" as a "community problem . . . [a] public responsibility."[51]

A letter from "Mrs." E. to the bureau in May 1915 expressed the likely concern of many young women who found themselves pregnant and alone. "Mrs." E. wrote Lathrop that she was expecting "to become a mother" in two to three weeks and faced circumstances which would "force her to nurse again for a livelihood to provide for my child and myself." She wanted to know if Lathrop could recommend a "private family that will board and room the infant or a private sanatorium or hospital for babies." The woman explained, "I dread infant asylums as I really think the little souls are many times neglected. . . . I want to give my baby the *best* possible even though it is going to call for great sacrifice." She was afraid to tell her "sad tale to a Soul, to not even [her] own mother." Lathrop, she hoped, would be a "*sincere* friend, one whom I can trust or confide in."[52] The chief turned the letter over to Mary West. West assured the young woman that she was "of course, quite right in wishing to do the best you can for the baby, but [that] there is no reason why the father should not bear his share of the burden too. Is it not possible that he could offer you an immediate marriage?"[53] "Mrs." E., a single nursing student, answered that the father of her expected child was "a medical student in Harvard [and] knows naught of my conception or present state." She confided that she was twenty-five years old and had been away from home for eight years. There were "many traps and snares set for me, but my dear mother's home training kept me from harm, but *now* at this late year I find myself led astray." She thanked West for her kindness and for forwarding the bureau's pamphlets on prenatal and infant care. She asked West to please continue looking for a "good place for my expected babe" and requested that West please address all correspondence to "Mrs." E. Apparently West gave "Mrs." E.'s name to the Washington Associated Charities, a Protestant group. This may have resulted in what Lathrop called an "annoyance" for the Catholic young woman who felt that her confidence had been broken. Such intervention was typical of the times and there was actually very little the bureau could do but refer the woman to a local "sanatorium."[54]

The Children's Bureau maintained that "the frequent concomitants of illegitimate birth [were the] absence of a normal home, deprivation of a mother's care, and lack of adequate support." The consequences meant impaired health and vitality, public dependence, and "abnormal character development, producing in many cases waywardness and delinquency."[55] Unmarried mothers were also at high risk. From one-ninth to about one-fifth of unwed mothers and fathers were under eighteen. The bureau also argued that "42 per cent of the mothers of children born out of wedlock in one year [participated in] repeated infractions of the moral code, serious alcoholism, or other antisocial characteristics."[56] Unwed mothers were also much more likely to seek illegal abortions than married women. The bureau's previously discussed study of maternal mortality in fifteen states revealed that 50 percent of 1,588 abortion deaths included in the study resulted from complications from induced abortions given for other than "therapeutic" reasons. For unmarried women, abortions counted for more than one-third of maternal deaths. Infant mortality studies indicated that children of unmarried mothers died at rates two to three times or more that of married parents. A lack of consistent birth registration records made it difficult for the Children's Bureau to report the rate of illegitimacy, but the agency determined that in sixteen states that kept such data during 1915, unmarried women gave birth to 14,217 children. The bureau estimated that between 32,400 and 35,100 illegitimate births took place in the United States each year (over 1 percent of all live births).[57]

Children born to unmarried mothers, argued the Children's Bureau, were in particular need of good health care, provision for a "normal" homelife, and state protection. In the United States, "the child of illegitimate birth often suffers great injustice through being deprived of the care that is his due. Society is forced to bear a burden that properly belongs to the child's parents." As West had suggested to "Mrs." E., the Children's Bureau recommended that fathers be held responsible for their children's support. In addition, the agency maintained that "sentiment [had] ruled largely in the treatment of these cases, often with the result that the emphasis had been placed upon saving the mother from the social consequences, especially if her status or that of her family is likely to be affected." The Children's Bureau included the care of unwed mothers in its general infant and maternal health care strategy, and encouraged states to provide full legal protection to "worthy" unmarried mothers and their children (including the payment of mothers' pensions). In a 1921 report recommending uniform laws concerning illegitimacy among the states, the Children's Bureau advocated juvenile or domestic relations courts as the best place to secure the protection of children born outside of marriage. To its credit, the Children's Bureau recognized illegitimacy, like every other aspect of child welfare investigated by the bureau, as a rural as well as an urban problem. In summary, the Children's Bureau recommended that provisions for unwed mothers and their children should be made in all areas of the country by state, not by federal, action.[58] Newborns should be kept with their mothers, fathers should be held responsible for their support whenever possible, and "worthy" mothers denied support from men due to desertion or imprisonment should be given mothers' aid. The agency also believed that states needed to reform statutory language referring to children born outside of marriage as "bastards."[59] However, the Children's Bureau's adherence to the middle-class ideal in its overall program unintentionally stigmatized children born outside of marriage and the agency made no effort to gain passage of a federal mothers' pension program during its first two decades of work.

The Care of "Defective" Children

The Children's Bureau also investigated the problems of "defective" (mentally handicapped) and other dependent children. Although the Children's Bureau practically ignored the circumstances of physically handicapped children in its early work, Lathrop's professional background did lead to some studies concerning mentally handicapped children. In general, children confined to institutions were sometimes part of the agency's studies, but only mentally impaired children gained any attention from the Children's Bureau.

As early as 1915 the bureau published a report on the circumstances of "mental defectives" in the District of Columbia. The psychological and eugenic theories of the period greatly influenced this study. The bureau judged the "mentally defective woman of child bearing age" a great "danger to society." This was true, the agency contended, because "studies of family records have shown the results of transmission of mental defect from one generation to another." Mentally handicapped girls should be sterilized in order "to cut off at the source a large proportion of degeneracy, pauperism, and crime. It is through prevention that the largest benefits will accrue." It should also be noted that the Children's Bureau concluded that many mentally handicapped children acted as an undue burden on their families, "demanding a large share of the energy of the mother and not only interfer[ing] with the training of the other children but exercis[ing] a demoralizing influence on the family life."[60] By 1932 the Children's Bureau urged that some mentally impaired children could be taught to learn a trade, but the agency still held that institutionalization offered the best choice for such children. This is especially interesting since the Children's Bureau found that as adults many who had been reared in institutions failed "to adjust themselves to either industrial or social conditions in the community."[61] Thus, the Children's Bureau was not willing to insist that "mentally defective" children were entitled to the "normal home life" that was advocated for all other children.

Conclusion

Child welfare advocates recommended mothers' pensions and foster care for most dependent children even before the establishment of the Children's Bureau.[62] Basically reiterating the recommendations of the 1909 White House conference, the Children's Bureau provided very few public policy innovations concerning children whose families seemed to have failed. The aid it did recommend for dependent children was inadequate, varied widely, and was burdened by cultural prejudices and moral judgments. Despite its contention that social welfare policy for children focused on the family, the Children's Bureau devised few strategies for supporting children and their families in a uniform way. The bureau's recommended policies limited the aid mothers and their children received to incomes inadequate for survival. The mothers' pension programs also offered no opportunity to work for economic independence. Instead, the system simply traded women's and children's traditional dependence on men for their dependence on the state. Further emphasizing this circumstance is the fact that poor families headed by single fathers are totally ignored in the Children's Bureau's policies. The bureau ignored or rejected programs which might have helped families toward independence. For example, the agency continued to condemn day care, ignore birth control, focus on child "training," and advocate complete state and community control of the few programs devised to assist dependent children in an era of state-sponsored racial segregation and nativist prejudice. The policies developed did not adequately secure the Children's Bureau's professed fundamental right to a "normal home life" for all children and the programs advocated to ensure this "right" were viewed as charity instead of "social welfare." Even so, the Children's Bureau's limited policies served as a transitional step from private charity programs hindered by nineteenth-century Social Darwinist beliefs to twentieth-century state-sponsored programs for poor children. One widowed mother expressed the feelings of many when she "thank[ed] God for the mothers' pension . . . [and was] thankful that [she could] live in a country where they have it."[63] Despite problems with its efforts, the Children's Bureau had addressed the needs of many while other federal agencies had totally ignored the circumstances of dependent children and their families.

By 1930 the Children's Bureau had faced a number of emotional successes followed by failure. The agency had marshaled a force of supporters behind its maternity and infancy programs, the effort to secure child labor reform, and advocacy of aid to dependent children. But, at the same time, Children's Bureau opponents both inside and outside of the government had also gained strength. Grace Abbott wrote in 1929 that "looking back over fifty years we find evidence . . . that children and child welfare occupy a position of more importance in our national life than a half century ago." But, she lamented, "a survey of present conditions effecting children shows many needs unprovided for and much unnecessary suffering and loss of life."[64]

7

A Policy for Security: The Children's Bureau and the Great Depression, 1929-39

Grace Abbott utilized the health care, child labor reform, and social welfare efforts initiated during the Children's Bureau's first two decades of existence as the blueprint for new programs started during the next ten years. As Abbott acknowledged, the bureau had shown that even its limited efforts had helped some children and their families.[1] But throughout the Great Depression the agency's self-defined role as the nation's chief advocate for "the whole child" was aggressively challenged. The Children's Bureau, like its constituents, was in an increasingly vulnerable position. In 1929 the Children's Bureau lost the administrative power it had held under Sheppard-Towner and the child labor amendment seemed to be stalled. In addition, the Great Depression highlighted the uneven application of recommended reforms as well as the inadequacy of the Children's Bureau's programs constructed on the middle-class family ideal.[2]

The Hoover Years

Republican campaign publicity distributed during the 1928 presidential election urged women to vote for Herbert Hoover because he was "the greatest of humanitarians . . . [had] long helped better homes . . . [and was a] benefactor of children." The Children's Bureau's army of supporters generally agreed. As Grace Abbott's biographer explains, "after eight years of Harding and Coolidge, Hoover seemed to promise renewal of an energetic government and new opportunities for the search for social justice." Indeed, Hoover did have credentials that seemed to suggest he would support the Children's Bureau and child welfare reforms. He publicly endorsed child labor restrictions and had headed the Commission for Relief in Belgium following World War I. Beginning in 1921 he served as president of the American Child Health Association. Grace Abbott's sister Edith wrote Julia Lathrop that she could "hardly believe that anything as good as Herbert Hoover in the White House can come to pass in these days. It is like rubbing the lamp." Lathrop said of Hoover, "He is [by] far the greatest man in the

Republican ranks & one of the ablest men on the planet."[3] In addition, it seemed that Hoover held to an administrative philosophy emphasizing cooperation between government and the private sector that was compatible with the Children's Bureau's strategy devised by Julia Lathrop and Grace Abbott during the agency's first two decades of work.[4] However, there was a subtle point that the Children's Bureau and its supporters missed. Hoover's association with the American Child Health Association placed him tightly under the influence of the AMA. In addition, in 1928 no one foresaw the economic emergency of the next decade. The Children's Bureau responded by calling for greater government involvement in securing "a right to childhood." Hoover chose instead to retain the rhetoric of "voluntarism" and reliance on private charity.

Nevertheless, in 1928 even opponents of the Children's Bureau suspected that Hoover would further the agency's efforts. For example, Elizabeth Lowell Putnam wrote that although a loyal Republican, she was "very much averse to Hoover's election because, though I think he is a very remarkable man . . . he would be a very dangerous one for the country to have as President. . . . I have every reason to know that Mr. Hoover favors the Children's Bureau." She concluded that as much as she dreaded the prospect of a Democratic administration, "it would be less dangerous than to have Hoover."[5]

But after the election it became clear that the new president and his close advisors envisioned a very narrow role for the Children's Bureau. In early 1929 Grace Abbott suggested to Secretary of Labor James J. Davis that it was time to organize another White House conference on children's issues. She reported to Children's Bureau supporter Julius Rosenwald that Davis rejected the idea, replying that the president was too busy to consider organizing a conference at that time.[6] In addition, in his 1929 State of the Union message Hoover called for a reinstatement of "the purpose of the Sheppard-Towner Act [but only] for a limited number of years." This was not an endorsement of the Children's Bureau. Instead, Hoover wanted to eventually replace a federal grant-in-aid infant and maternal health program with one financed solely with voluntary and state funds; a solution palatable to the AMA. During 1929 and 1930 congressional committees, at the request of the Hoover administration, delayed any attempts by Children's Bureau supporters to reinstate even a temporary Sheppard-Towner style program.[7]

In this atmosphere, despite what Davis had told her, Grace Abbott began to hear rumors that the president planned to hold a White House conference on children's issues. Apparently without the Children's Bureau's knowledge, on March 5, 1929, Senator James Couzens (R-Mich.) had asked Hoover if he could speak to him about organizing a White House conference concerning the "problem of the crippled children." The next day Hoover responded that he would like to discuss the issue and added, "we might develop something of rather broad character."[8] Hoover then secured a $500,000 donation from the American Child Health Association to finance the proposed conference and named Secretary of the Interior Ray Lyman Wilbur, M.D., as chair.[9]

Like Hoover, Ray Lyman Wilbur was born in Iowa but spent much of his childhood in California. Wilbur met Herbert Hoover while both attended Stanford University. Wilbur eventually became Stanford's president, but left in 1929 to join Hoover's cabinet. Wilbur had also served as president of the AMA (1923 24). A threat to the Children's Bureau, Wilbur supported the AMA's position maintaining that *all* federal health care work should be the responsibility of the PHS.[10]

Grace Abbott correctly assumed that a White House conference arranged by Secretary Wilbur undermined the Children's Bureau's role as the nation's primary child welfare authority. She suspected that Wilbur intended to expand the PHS and transfer it to the Department of the Interior. Further, in the name of "economic efficiency," Abbott speculated that Wilbur hoped to remove all child health responsibilities from the Children's Bureau and place them with the PHS. Such a change would erase the Children's Bureau's claim to be the single agency equipped to serve the needs of the "whole child." Abbott felt that Wilbur's intentions were obvious because he organized of the White House meeting on children's issues without the Children's Bureau's advice. She protested to the president and he belatedly appointed her to the conference's executive planning committee.[11]

Abbott knew that the bureau was in for a fight. She explained to Julius Rosenwald that she had not at first realized Wilbur's intention to strengthen the PHS at the Children's Bureau's expense, but by late April she felt "quite sure of it."[12] Martha May Eliot, M.D., was the only Children's Bureau representative named to any of the conference's six subcommittees concerned with children's health care.[13] Although a Children's Bureau staff physician (a position usually held by someone outside the heavily male AMA fraternity), Eliot was a highly respected pediatrician who had overcome many of the barriers placed before female physicians. Born in Dorchester, Massachusetts, in 1892, she earned an A.B. from Radcliffe in 1913 and an M.D. from Johns Hopkins Medical School in 1918. From 1921 to 1935 she served on the staff of the Pediatric Department at the Yale University School of Medicine. In 1924 Eliot joined the Children's Bureau as director of the Division of Child and Maternal Health. While in this position, among various other responsibilities, she revised Mary West's "Infant Care" pamphlet, giving it a greater medical perspective and status.[14]

Eliot's appointment to a White House conference health care subcommittee testifies to her high professional status and helped the Children's Bureau retain some influence over the meeting's final recommendations. But the absence of Children's Bureau representatives on other child health care committees revealed the Hoover administration's and specifically Wilbur's attitude toward the Children's Bureau. Abbott received an assignment on the subcommittee on vocational training and child labor. Katharine Lenroot was named to the subcommittee focused on social conditions concerning delinquency and care for handicapped children. While the latter were important issues, it was evident that the Children's Bureau's representatives were confined to narrowly defined social welfare concerns. Abbott again protested to Hoover and the president agreed to appoint her to the subcommittee on public health organization. She also encouraged Hoover to name Julia Lathrop to the conference's general planning committee. The president agreed, but these concessions did not end the controversy.[15]

At about the same time, Lathrop and Clara Mortenson Beyer, a Children's Bureau economist and soon to be named director of the agency's Industrial Division, led an effort to nominate Grace Abbott for secretary of labor.[16]

Lathrop and Beyer took notice of the fact that Abbott's boss, Secretary of Labor James J. Davis, was running for the Senate in Pennsylvania and his victory seemed assured. Beyer collected thousands of signatures and contacted newspapers across the nation to gain support for Abbott's nomination as the next secretary of labor. Women's organizations, a number of university professors, the Urban League, and the Immigrants Protective League in Chicago endorsed Abbott for the job. Abbott also seemed to like the idea, saying, "I will not seek [the position], but I will not shirk it."[17] Some Children's Bureau supporters, however, were wary of the suggestion. They feared that the effort might instead result in Abbott's appointment as assistant secretary, a position that held little authority. Furthermore, some worried that there was no one qualified to replace Abbott and that the Hoover administration's attitude toward the Children's Bureau made it wise for Abbott to remain as the agency's chief. But Clara Beyer felt that it "is hardly good policy to refuse to promote a person because there seems to be no one qualified to carry on her job." Besides, Abbott could refuse to accept the position of assistant secretary if nominated. Beyer maintained that Grace Abbott "in the Cabinet could have a tremendous influence. . . . As Secretary she certainly would be in a better position to tide the [Children's Bureau] over its present difficulties than she is now as Chief." But Abbott's disagreement with the Hoover administration's general policies doomed the effort from the start. The president appointed William Knuckles Doak to the job in December 1930. Julia Lathrop, making the best of the situation, was relieved when Hoover appointed Doak. She wrote, "For my own part I am rather glad Mr. Doak, and not you, has the Secretaryship. It would be a terrible situation for you in many ways and I have no doubt Mr. Doak is quite at ease."[18]

Part of the growing rift between Wilbur and Abbott was a bureaucratic fight over turf, and gender may have influenced the way the battle lines were drawn. But a fundamental philosophical difference between the concept of child protection and advocacy held by the Children's Bureau and that accepted by those supporting Hoover and Wilbur rested at the heart of the matter. As discussed earlier, the Children's Bureau argued that it could not adequately promote "a right to childhood" without considering the "whole child." Paul U. Kellogg, editor of the *Survey,* noted that what "the Children's Bureau has done could have been done years ago by either the PHS or the Bureau of Education. . . . [but] children are bundles of varied possibilities [which] refuse to be cramped into all the neat categories of our adult and scientific scheming."[19] Contrary to this view, the Hoover administration adhered to the already familiar argument that all federal health programs should be consolidated within the PHS and the Children's Bureau restricted to social welfare issues. In an address before the Indiana League of Women Voters, the director of the 1930 White House conference, H. E. Barnard, Ph.D. (former head of the Indiana Department of Public Health), spoke about the idea. Apparently anticipating that he might be facing a hostile audience, he explained that the proposal was merely a way "to perfect the means by which" the federal government could address "the burden for public health administration." Barnard continued, "the president . . . recognizes the several branches of the government and of the states which have a concern in public health and the welfare of women and children but he coordinates these activities as a function of the Government as a whole rather than as the special duty of particular Bureaus." He contended that the administration had "been having splendid cooperation and interest from all the Women's organizations . . . in carrying out the purpose of the White House Conference to create for our children and our children's children a better world in which to live."[20]

Barnard's recommendation for the Children's Bureau simply related the majority opinion of the White House conference's Committee on Public Health Organization, arguing that "the advancement of public health in the United States demands larger appropriations, more adequate and better trained personnel, and a greater opportunity for a career in public health than has existed heretofore." In order to accomplish such goals, "Federal assistance should be given by the United States Public Health Service in cooperation with the official state health agency."[21] A letter to the president accompanying the committee's recommendations "emphasized that the work which has been done by the Children's Bureau had unquestionably accomplished much good. "However, the group believed that the consolidation of federal health functions within the PHS would prove to be "a better administrative procedure and one that is in keeping with much more permanent and larger results in the upbuilding of the general scheme of public health in the United States." Bottom line, the Children's Bureau's "whole child" philosophy was outdated. Barnard tried to persuade the women of the NLWV that the transfer of child health issues from the Children's Bureau to the PHS was not contrary to the best interests of the country's children.[22]

It is unlikely that the women were convinced. Children's Bureau supporters were well aware of Grace Abbott's opposition to the public health committee's final recommendations. In December 1929, Abbott had submitted a minority report protesting the proposal to transfer child health programs to the PHS:

> While I am very much in sympathy with a plan for strengthening the work of the public health service and making possible National, State and local cooperation in promoting public health, I cannot join in all the conclusions reached by the committee. . . . The first White House conference on child welfare which met 20 years ago . . . came to the conclusion that the child and the needs of the child should be considered as a whole by one governmental agency and recommended the creation of a Children's Bureau. . . . The United States Children's Bureau has carefully avoided duplicating work done by any other agency and has endeavored to build up agencies whose proper functioning in the community is important to the welfare of both adults and children. . . . The health of children . . . is the responsibility of parents and particularly mothers who must decide whether the scientific knowledge and skill of the doctor and other specialists will be utilized in the train-

> ing of their children. There is abundant evidence that parents have looked to the Children's Bureau for national leadership in problems relating to the health and general welfare of children.[23]

The White House Conference on Child Health and Protection opened on the evening of November 19, 1930, with little recognition of the controversy between the Hoover administration and the Children's Bureau. Each delegate attending the meeting received a six-hundred-page "confidential" preliminary report stating the recommendations of the various topical committees. This volume did not include Abbott's minority report. President Hoover opened the meeting with an address outlining the purpose of the conference and his goals for its efforts. He stated that "all problems of childhood" were approached with "affection." Children, the president argued,

> are the most wholesome part of the race, the sweetest, for they are fresher from the hands of God. . . . The fundamental purpose of this conference is to set forth an understanding of those safeguards which will assure to them health in mind and body. There are safeguards and services to childhood which can be provided by the community, the State, or the Nation—all of which are beyond the reach of the individual parent. . . . If we could have one generation of properly born, trained, educated, and healthy children, a thousand other problems of government would vanish. . . . The many activities which you are assembled here to represent touch a thousand points in the lives of children.[24]

Hoover maintained that in the United States "progress is the sum of progress of the individuals—that they each individually achieve to the full capacity of their abilities and character . . . [and] the door of opportunity must be opened to each of them." He said that the problems of childhood fell into three categories: "First, the protection and stimulation of the normal child; second, aid to the physically defective and handicapped child; third, the problems of the delinquent child."[25] Such remarks did not reveal much about the Hoover administration's strategy to reach its lofty goal of equal opportunity. But the voluminous preliminary conference report did contain the recommendation to transfer all child health responsibilities to the PHS. Lillian Wald responded in an article in the *Survey* entitled "Shall We Dismember the Child?"[26] To the Children's Bureau and its supporters, this was more than a "turf" battle. The proposal undermined the agency's fundamental "whole child" philosophy.

The bureau's army of advocates again came to its aid. About five hundred conference participants attended the public session where the Committee on Public Health Organization's report was presented (identified as "Section II, Public Health Service and Administration" in the conference program). Martha Eliot noted that "people rose to protest the majority report." For example, Marguerite M. Wells (NLWV) submitted a statement signed by representatives of twelve predominately female organizations protesting the transfer of child health work from the Children's Bureau. Wells argued that "there is no agency of the government and no governmental work that women follow so closely as child health. Probably they know better about the work of the Children's Bureau than about any other part of the government." She explained that women "believe in the work, they think it has been well done, conspicuously well done, and they would be afraid to experiment with it." Martha Eliot remembered that such remarks forced "the chairman [Surgeon General Hugh S. Cumming] . . . to allow Grace Abbott to read her minority report." Then there was a move to replace the majority's report with Abbott's dissent. In the meantime, the chairman ruled that there would be no vote. The "end result was [that both resolutions were] tabled." Abbott and her group of trusted supporters had successfully prevented an endorsement of this "splitting up" of Children's Bureau's responsibilities. Julia Lathrop praised Abbott in a letter written a little over two weeks after the close of the conference. She judged that "already the W.H.C. [White House conference] and your brave victory seems—as it will prove to be—a notable historic episode."[27]

Another outcome of the conference was the adoption of a nineteen-point Children's Charter recognizing "the rights of the child as the first rights of citizenship." Filled with romantic clichés about the rights of childhood, the Children's Charter was reproduced as posters and fliers and distributed throughout the United States. However, such rhetoric did little to solve the crisis facing increasing numbers of children and their families as the economic depression worsened. A December 3, 1930, editorial in the *Nation* regretted that "a gathering of the leading experts on child welfare could not have been allowed to give the public a more inspiring platform than this string of platitudes." The 1930 White House conference, the editorial suggested, resulted in "little tangible achievement." In her 1931 annual report Grace Abbott seemed to agree and called for "a prompt mobilization" and a "consistent social-welfare program" by the federal government to combat the economic crisis gripping the nation.[28]

Consistent with his general social welfare policy of emphasizing individualism and private philanthropy, however, Hoover did not propose any federal aid programs for children. Furthermore, the president and those close to him chose to distrust reports sent by the Children's Bureau to his own Emergency Committee on Employment. Organized in 1930 to work with state and local employment committees designed to encourage the development of private sector jobs, the committee related the suffering of many during the Great Depression.[29] When disastrous floods struck parts of Arkansas, Kentucky, and Tennessee in early 1931, Hoover announced that he had arranged for a "personal report" on the conditions there from the Army Corps of Engineers. These military engineers, whose primary responsibility was flood control, stated that relief services "were adequately meeting the existing need." But studies conducted by the Children's Bureau in many of the same areas a year later (and reported to the president's Emergency Committee on Employment) discovered clear evidence that relief efforts were inadequate to meet the circumstances of flood conditions coupled with the economic depression.[30] In addition, thirty-eight urban areas which regularly provided the bureau with relief cost data had increased their total expenditures nearly 90 percent from 1929 to 1930.[31] The president and his secretary of the interior chose to ignore such evidence. Wilbur stated in 1932 that "unless we descend to a level far beyond anything that we at present have known, our children are apt to profit, rather than suffer, from what is going on." He seemed to believe that economic struggle forced families closer together, kept children from spending their money on entertainment and "unproductive" activities, and led to a more wholesome homelife.[32]

Clearly Abbott and the Children's Bureau rejected such ideas. But the bureau's initial response to the crisis was typical of its earlier efforts concerning child welfare and did little to ease the plight of children. In its usual Progressive-Era-style blueprint, the agency gathered data on the condition of children and their families and promoted local and state programs to deal with these circumstances. Indeed, from 1930 to 1936 the Children's Bureau acted as one of the country's best sources of social welfare statistics.[33] But, as Grace Abbott now recognized, the gathering and reporting of data was obviously not enough to meet the needs of the current emergency. She urged the development of a "flexible" system of unemployment assistance for American families which would provide "not only food and a comfortable home, but . . . above all things security" for children.[34] Abbott's words seem to suggest a more aggressive role for the Children's Bureau and the federal government than one limited to investigation, education, and advocacy. The agency had nibbled at such reform in the past, but only in the case of child labor directly asked for federal intervention through law. Abbott now moved toward advocacy of federal aid to needy children.

Still, Hoover continued to ignore the evidence and Abbott distanced the Children's Bureau from what she believed were the administration's misguided policies. She later said that in general she "avoided public statements about relief except where it was something of that sort on which the bureau could be said to have professional advice to give." She explained that "this was partly because I was not in accord with President Hoover's policy and thought that I should, therefore, not be making public statements, and also because . . . it seemed to me that except where I had definitely cooperated with [the president's Emergency Committee on Employment] in a program, the bureau had better not appear."[35]

Indeed, Hoover continued to deny that a crisis existed. In a December 9, 1931, address to Congress, the president stated that figures from the "Public Health Service show an actual decrease of sickness and infant and general mortality below normal years." He argued that no "greater proof could be adduced that our people have been protected from hunger and cold." Hoover opposed federal aid for ideological and economic reasons. He believed that relief would weaken the character of those receiving help and he felt that such expenditures would worsen the economy. His attitude is reflected in his approval during 1930 of $45 million to feed starving livestock at the same time he opposed $25 million to help starving farmers. The Children's Bureau and its supporters likely abhorred such actions. Lillian Wald and Florence Kelley had often pointed to federal expenditures for livestock and agriculture as evidence that the government valued crops and animals over children.[36] Although such policy seemed appalling to many, Hoover maintained a misguided optimism. The nation's infant mortality rate fell throughout the 1920s from a high of 85.8 per 1,000 live births in 1920 to 61.6 in 1931 and 57.6 in 1932. However, in subsequent years the rate actually increased for the first time since such data had begun to be collected: 58.1 in 1933 and 60.1 in 1934.[37] The Children's Bureau's past experience showed that the consequences of unemployment and malnutrition were not always manifested immediately in infant mortality statistics. An agency study conducted during the economic crisis of 1921-22 had revealed that unemployment seriously affected children and "carries with it immediate deprivation and hardship [while] leav[ing] a burden of debt and discouragement for the years to come. . . . Children suffering . . . through depression and uncertainty of what the future may mean, . . . are more to be dreaded than the discomforts of the immediate present." The bureau concluded that "unemployment, then, because it means lowered family standards and anxiety and dread, the loss of savings, and the mortgaging of the future, has a direct and disastrous effect upon the welfare of children."[38] Abbott contended that Hoover "like some other public men . . . distrusted the trained sympathies of the social workers and their estimates of existing needs."[39] The Children's Bureau staff felt betrayed by the administration and turned to its friends in Congress in an effort to provide some form of federal aid for unemployed Americans and their children.

On February 2, 1932, Senator Robert M. La Follette (R-Wis.) provided Congress with a Children's Bureau report examining the effects of the worsening economy on children. It argued that despite Hoover's contentions, malnutrition was a serious problem among the nation's children and that this condition "had increased over the past year." The bureau maintained that diminished milk sales and testimony by teachers and school officials supported this conclusion. There was a growing inability on the part of existing social service and health agencies to provide for children's basic needs. For example, the bureau cited a National Organization for Public Health Nursing study that noted that "although demands on public-health nurses had increased enormously during the past two years, 41 percent of the agencies have suffered reduction, 33 percent are operating on the same budgets, [and only] 25 percent have had increases." La Follette warned Congress that failure to institute a federal relief program for unemployed parents would mean that "we would be paying the toll in malnutrition and its effect upon adults and children for 50 years to come." Child welfare organizations outside the Children's Bureau agreed. For example, the Welfare and Relief Mobilization of 1932, a private social welfare group organized by authorities from children's institutions, hospital officials, summer camp directors, nutritionists, and public health nurses to address the economic emergency, argued that the apparent reduction in infant mortality was a consequence of "well-organized health work over a number of years." However, the group contended that such data did "not show the havoc being wrought by a lack of food, clothing, fuel, medical care and recreation." The group predicted that "we shall reap a harvest of tuberculosis and other diseases in the next ten years from what the children to-day are suffering."[40]

Buoyed by the obvious, La Follette used the Children's Bureau's report to urge passage of the La Follette-Costigan bill (S. 3045) proposing $375 million for relief and the creation of a Federal Board of Unemployment Relief headed by the chief of the Children's Bureau. The board would also consist of the director of public extension work in the Department of Agriculture, and the chief of the Vocational Rehabilitation Service of the Federal Board for Vocational Education. La Follette explained that the Children's Bureau was chosen as the chief administrator of the program because of its "large experience" gained through the Sheppard-Towner Act. Bureau and federal aid opponents responded that the bill would send "some little girl who had just taken a course in some social service school" to local communities to make decisions concerning state relief services. Ultimately the La Follette bill failed to pass (35H48).[41] The bill's connection with the Children's Bureau was not the only reason for the proposal's failure, but this fact added strength to traditional opposition contesting any federal aid program. Prejudice against an agency controlled almost entirely by women also added to Congress's rejection of the bill. Interestingly, the proposal contained no special provisions for children, but La Follette's plan to place administrative responsibility in Abbott's bureau signaled that any national relief program should benefit children as well as adults. In addition, even in the face of adversity, it is likely that Abbott and her staff felt bolstered by their successful defeat of the White House conference committee's recommendations and the national attention drawn to the Children's Bureau by La Follette's proposal.

In this atmosphere, Abbott and her staff believed that the "people of the country want[ed] the Children's Bureau to proceed with its [current] line of work."[42] Perhaps the effort to give the bureau responsibility for the administration of what would have been the first federal unemployment relief program made the agency's traditional role of investigation, education, and advocacy seem less controversial. Rising public pressure as well as lobbying by politicians probably influenced the Hoover administration to soften its stance against Abbott and her agency. Hoover's 1932 campaign strategists dismissed as "absolutely untrue" accusations made by the Women's Division of the Democratic National Campaign Committee that the president had not supported the Children's Bureau. The Republican campaign also stated that the recommendation to transfer the health activities of the Children's Bureau to the PHS had been withdrawn at Hoover's request. The Children's Bureau and its supporters remained skeptical. Katharine Lenroot wrote Grace Abbott that she believed Hoover's "statements about human suffering *unbearable*. I am *so* afraid of the outcome of the election! Another five years are too much to contemplate!" The support for Hoover among Children's Bureau supporters, so evident in 1928, had evaporated by 1932.[43]

Hoover had not given the Children's Bureau the "free hand" that Lathrop believed would have made "all the row . . . worthwhile." Meanwhile, the circumstances of children, as well as many adults, was worsening. Drawing on its past experience, at the depth of the depression (during the winter of 1932-33) the Children's Bureau asked for a $100,000 appropriation "to help the states conduct demonstrations of county child welfare work." Hoover's budget bureau denied the request.[44] Even in a time of crisis it appeared that many policy makers rejected the idea that children, unlike some other recipients of federal money, were a public responsibility. Grace Abbott recognized the neglect of child welfare policy in a speech she delivered in 1931:

> Sometimes when I get home at night in Washington I feel as though I had been in a great traffic jam. The jam is moving toward the Capitol where Congress sits in judgment on all administrative agencies of the Government. In that traffic jam there are all kinds of vehicles, for example, that the Army can put into the streets—tanks, gun carriages, trucks, the dancing horses of officers, and others which I have not even the vocabulary to describe. They all finally reach the Hill and they make a plea that is a very old plea—one which I find in spite of the reputation for courage that they bear, men respond to rather promptly. The Army says to them, "Give, lest you perish"; and fear as a motive is still producing results on a scale which leave the rest of us feeling very anxious of the kind of eloquence the Army and Navy can command. But there are other kinds of vehicles in this traffic jam—great numbers of them which, coming from Nebraska as I do, do not seem to me to get they attention they should as they move down the street. There are the hayricks and the binders and ploughs and all the other things that the Department of Agriculture manages to put in the streets. But when the drivers get to the hill they have an argument which Congressmen understand. They say to them when they ask for appropriations for research in animal husbandry, in the chemistry of soils, or in agricultural economies, "Dollars invested on this side of the ledger will bring dollars in geometrical or arithmetical progression— . . . on the other side." And, if there is one thing that a Congressman, and for that matter people in general understand, it is a balance on the profit side of the ledger. . . .
>
> Then there are other vehicles. The handsome limousines in which the Department of Commerce rides . . . the barouches in which the Department of State rides with such dignity . . . the noisy patrols in which the Department of Justice officials sometimes appear. . . . I stand on the sidewalk watching it become more congested and more difficult, and then because the responsibility is mine and I must, I take a very firm hold on the handles of the baby carriage and I wheel it into the traffic. There are some people who think it does not belong there at all, there are some who wonder how I got there with it and what I think I am going to be able to do, and there are some who think the baby carriage is a symbol of bolshevism instead of a symbol of the home and the future of America.[45]

Abbott knew that new Children's Bureau programs, even those consistent with its past limited role of investigation and advocacy, would have to wait for another administration.

Efforts for Children in the Early New Deal

Initially it looked as though the election of Franklin D. Roosevelt would do little to help gain "security" for children. The Children's Bureau, like other agencies, expected a 25 percent budget cut ($100,000) under the Roosevelt administration's 1933 Economy Act.[46] However, during the first "100 Days" the Roosevelt administration ignored the proposed cut and the Children's Bureau's Social Statistics Project expanded. In fact, the Social Statistics Project provided data utilized to support many New Deal programs. In addition, the Roosevelt administration seemed interested in an overall strengthening of the Children's Bureau. When Lenroot told Second Assistant Labor Secretary Arthur J. Altmeyer about the bureau's earlier unsuccessful attempt to secure $100,000 from the Hoover administration, he called her concern "silly" and told her to dismiss any worries she held for the future of such programs. Altmeyer assured her, "we'll get . . . much more money than that." In May 1933, Congress established the Federal Emergency Relief Administration (FERA), the first federal unemployment aid program. The Children's Bureau collected data for the FERA, thereby helping to administer its $500 million annual appropriation.[47] Altmeyer's assurances seemed well founded. Calls by the Children's Bureau and others for federal assistance to the unemployed were beginning to have an effect.

Following Roosevelt's election, Abbott began to push aggressively for federal programs designed specifically to assist needy children. Two *New York Times* articles illustrate the chief's new strategy of moving the Children's Bureau's role beyond investigation, education, and advocacy. Addressing the question of the depression's effect on children, Abbott maintained that there had been 6,000,000 undernourished children in the United States at the time of Hoover's 1930 White House conference. She estimated that the "number undoubtedly was very much larger" in 1932 and argued that "one-fifth of . . . preschool and school children were showing the effects of poor nutrition, of inadequate housing, and of the lack of medical care." To lessen this problem Abbott called for a federally funded program to aid children in both health and welfare matters. Children were "showing the effects of the anxiety and the sense of insecurity that prevails when the father is unemployed for long periods." She worried that "the strain of living in a state of uncertainty week after week, month after month, and year after year deepens and intensifies the serious effects on the children in the family group." Using evidence gathered for the Children's Bureau's 1932 report presented in the Senate by Robert La Follette, Abbott cited deep economic cuts in existing state and local programs for children. The effect of greater need and diminished funds, according to the Children's Bureau chief, "has discouraged some communities and individuals from doing what they could in the emergency."[48] The Children's Bureau could no longer rely on parents or the states and local communities to serve as the primary providers for children's needs.

As might be expected, the Children's Bureau's first New Deal efforts emphasized nutrition and health care. With Grace Abbott's urging, the newly appointed secretary of labor, Frances Perkins, called for a Child Health Recovery Conference to be held in Washington on October 6, 1933. Since the new secretary was already known to those in the child welfare reform network, Abbott felt confident that Perkins would look out for the Children's Bureau and its recommended programs. From 1910 to 1912 Perkins had worked closely with Florence Kelley as secretary of the New York Consumers' League. She was a Democratic party political insider and close friend of Eleanor Roosevelt. With Perkins's appointment as secretary of labor in 1933, Abbott and the Children's Bureau had a friend in the cabinet.[49]

Perkins's "informal" 1933 Child Health Recovery Conference was attended by representatives from a wide variety of federal agencies along with one hundred and forty individuals from state departments of health, private health organizations, medical societies, and relief agencies. Eleanor Roosevelt also participated at Perkins's request.[50] The conference's purpose was "to stimulate a movement for the recovery of ground lost, during the Depression, in conditions affecting the health and vitality of children." Proposals focused attention on the effects of malnutrition and inadequate health care. As a result of the meeting's discussions, conference participants advocated that the FERA, headed by Harry L. Hopkins, should be responsible for "encouraging" emergency plans within the states to feed hungry children. Further, conference members resolved that Grace Abbott and the Children's Bureau should "promote" complementary state health care projects, especially in the country's depressed rural areas. School lunch programs, reimbursement plans for private physicians, and nurses' salaries paid through the proposed Civil Works Administration were also to be part of this combined effort to "take care" of the more than 6,000,000 children of families on federal and state relief.

During the conference, Secretary Perkins presented informal "greetings" from President Roosevelt stating his support for a federal child welfare program and for the Children's Bureau. She said that Roosevelt recognized the conference as "an opportune time for us all to remember once more how valuable has been the Children's Bureau in development of consciousness in the United States of the health of our children."[51]

Following this meeting, the FERA and the Children's Bureau instituted the Child Health Recovery Program (CHRP), which concentrated on providing emergency food and medical care to the country's neediest children. Funds came from existing FERA, Civil Works Administration (after its establishment in November 1933), and Children's Bureau appropriations. As with the bureau's experience under Sheppard-Towner, limited funding necessitated the extensive cooperation of public and private health care and relief organizations. With its funds the Children's Bureau made available five physicians for consultation, and the Civil Works Administration employed as many as two hundred full- and part-time public health nurses per state. In addition, private physicians, nutritionists, and home economics teachers, in cooperation with manufacturers and retailers, contributed expertise, supplies, and food. Schools played an important role in identifying and distributing help to the children in greatest need.[52] CHRP was the New Deal's first and only federal "relief" program for young children until implementation of the 1935 Social Security Act.

Ultimately, despite some success, CHRP did not live up to expectations. Its major handicap was a lack of funds for full-time medical and nursing personnel. Despite the decided need, states under great economic stress had little money to pay for an additional health care and nutrition program. As noted by Abbott, the effort's most successful result was to "show the urgent need of a more extensive and permanent program for maternal and child health," as well as other aspects of child welfare.[53]

In December 1933, Perkins authorized the Children's Bureau to call state relief officials to Washington to discuss other important relief issues. This conference, "Present Emergencies in the Care of Dependent and Neglected Children," found that considerable ground had been lost in the area of mothers' pensions. Thirty-three counties in Michigan, ten in Illinois, six in Wisconsin, four in Pennsylvania, and two in New York had discontinued mothers' aid payments due to a shortage of revenue. These families were either left helpless, dependent on private charity, or placed on local or federal-state relief rolls. Such practices ran contrary to the Children's Bureau's philosophy that mothers' pensions were not "charity" relief but a preventive entitlement. In a March 1934 *Survey* article, Abbott noted that there were "some 300,000 children, most of them fatherless and all of them dependent, . . . supported by mothers' pensions." She argued that the needs of these children should not be answered with emergency relief, but with "the same kind of security . . . as is now being sought for the aged in old age pensions." Abbott warned that "in the long future, our democracy will have to pay in perhaps arithmetical or even geometrical progression for our failure to bring security and stability to the care of these especially disadvantaged children."[54] The chief and her supporters asserted that the nation's dependent children needed more than emergency relief.

The Committee on Economic Security and Children

President Roosevelt responded to growing pleas for an "economic security" plan by establishing the Committee on Economic Security (CES) on June 29, 1934 (Executive Order #6757). The president instructed executive committee members (Frances Perkins, chair; Harry L. Hopkins, FERA head; Henry Morgenthau, Jr., secretary of the treasury; Homer S. Cummings, attorney general; and Henry A. Wallace, secretary of agriculture) to "formulate . . . sound legislation [with] these three great objectives—the security of the home, the security of livelihood, and the security of social insurance." Subordinate committees included an advisory council composed of representatives from industry, labor, and "social welfare"; a technical board; an actuarial consultants committee; a medical advisory committee; a public health advisory committee; a hospital advisory board; and a dental advisory committee. Roosevelt named economist Edwin E. Witte, Ph.D., executive director and executive committee secretary. Although clearly a qualified nominee, Witte had no direct connections with the child welfare reform network.[55]

After consulting with Witte and others, Roosevelt selected members of the CES executive committee and the cabinet committee chose subordinate committee participants. The July 1934 announcement concerning the CES's creation cites the major issues to be addressed by the group: unemployment compensation, old age insurance, workmen's compensation, mothers' pensions, maternity benefits, health care, and public relief. "The reason for creating the organization," the announcement explained, "is a conviction that neither time nor automatic economic readjustments will solve the problems [of insecurity], but that active measures undertaken cooperatively by the Federal, State, and local governments can control and direct economic changes."[56]

By 1934, it appeared that the welfare of children should be a recognized part of New Deal concerns. Some child welfare issues had been established two years before Roosevelt's election during the Hoover administration's 1930 White House conference, and later during the two Children's Bureau-sponsored meetings held in 1933. An article in *Parents Magazine* outlined the "hopes" Roosevelt administration officials had for children under the New Deal. "Security" for families was at the center of their efforts. However, children's welfare was not initially addressed by the CES. Homer Folks, longtime Children's Bureau ally and chair of the CES Public Health Advisory Committee, noted this circumstance at the National Conference on Economic Security held in Washington, D.C., on November 14, 1934. He complained that the specific subject of children's welfare did not enter into general discussions about economic security "until the announcement of a subcommittee" on children five months after the president's executive order establishing the CES. In fact, no formal announcement confirming the formation of the Advisory Committee on Child Welfare was made until November 19, 1934.

It is not clear why this delay occurred, especially since Lenroot recalled that Altmeyer had assured her in the fall of 1933 that there would be a lot of money available for child welfare "through the economic security program."[57] It is fair to speculate that most policy makers in the Roosevelt administration failed to understand the Children's Bureau's "whole child" philosophy, and instead planned to integrate child welfare efforts into its general security program. Further underscoring this possibility, in 1933 the Children's Bureau had to fight another federal reorganization attempt that threatened its principle of serving the "whole child." Responding to rumors of such a move, Mary F. "Molly" Dewson, director of the Democratic National Committee's Women's Division, wired Roosevelt that "nothing would upset women more all over the country than to take health work away from the Children's Bureau. This is a cause celebre. Hoover attempted to do this and was defeated. . . . such an idea is fundamentally unwise and impractical. I have my finger on this pulse." Roosevelt took Dewson's advice and quickly dropped the issue.[58] Whatever the reason for the delay, a child welfare committee was finally organized in November and Secretary Perkins enthusiastically praised its existence. "There can be no economic security for a nation . . . while its children are economically or socially insecure. There are about seven million children under the age of 16 years in families on relief. Many of these children are mal-nourished, crippled, blind; children suffering from tuberculosis and heart disturbances; children living under conditions of physical and moral neglect. For these children there should be more adequate protection."[59]

As Perkins's words suggest, it looked by December 1934 as if the Children's Bureau could fully recover from its loss of "power" during the Hoover years. This was a great relief to bureau supporters since Grace Abbott, ill with tuberculosis, had sent a letter of resignation to President Roosevelt on June 13, 1934, effective July 1. At the time some bureau supporters feared that Abbott's leaving would hinder the agency's efforts to regain its status as the nation's chief lobbyist for children. But Abbott was not worried. She explained, "I have always planned not to stay in the Bureau indefinitely." However, "for a considerable period of time I did not feel free to resign because I did not feel sure that the program of the Bureau would be safeguarded if I did." By June 1934 her attitude had changed, "With Miss Perkins as Secretary this is no longer true and I am sure that the Bureau's programs will be safeguarded and developed."[60] Eleanor Roosevelt expressed the disappointment felt by many at Abbott's decision to leave the Children's Bureau. "I only heard yesterday of your decision that you must resign. I can quite see your point of view and I know how desperately tired you must be. . . . For so long I have thought of you as a tower of strength in the Children's Bureau that I can hardly bear to think of anybody else trying to take your place, but what must be must be!"[61] The chief noted that she "felt a special responsibility to" the first lady and thanked Eleanor Roosevelt for her kind words. Abbott concluded, "I admire the leadership you have given us in the whole field of social welfare these eighteen months and I look forward to following the Roosevelt banner whether I am in Washington or Chicago."[62]

In her letter of resignation, Abbott, who although ill was only fifty-six years old, explained that she was leaving the Children's Bureau to accept a position as professor of public welfare at the School of Social Service, University of Chicago. She felt that "year by year evidence has accumulated of the [Children's Bureau's] importance in our national life." She argued "that a final test of our recovery program may well be what it does to remove the injustices from which children have suffered in the past." "But," she warned, "as children are not merely pocket editions of adults, special health and protective services for children are essential for their optimum growth and development as well as measures which will bring security to the wage earner and the farmer." Abbott said that she left "in the belief that the Bureau will be developed and expanded during this administration."[63]

Upon accepting Abbott's resignation, President Roosevelt praised her service and noted that while he regretted losing her, "it is with satisfaction that I learn you and your long-time friend, the Secretary of Labor, have worked out a plan whereby you will maintain an advisory relationship to the Children's Bureau." This circumstance, the president felt, "gives us assurance of carrying on the Bureau with the same practical and effective policies."[64] Indeed, it again appeared that the Children's Bureau's overall program started under Julia Lathrop would continue without missing a beat. In addition, Roosevelt's response shows that he believed Abbott would continue to serve as an important influence in the Children's Bureau. But there was considerable delay surrounding appointment of a new chief. Katharine Lenroot and Martha Eliot were the top candidates for the job. Lenroot's father's position as a powerful Republican somewhat hindered her nomination. For example, a prominent Democrat wrote Abbott in July 1934 that Harry Hopkins had said "Lenroot could not have the job [of chief] because of political considerations—that Miss Perkins would not appoint her." But Molly Dewson denied that party politics caused the delay. More likely the problem stemmed from Grace Abbott's belief that Martha Eliot might be able to ease some of the tension between the Children's Bureau and physicians. Abbott also seemed to lack confidence in Lenroot's abilities. Other candidates were also considered, but the choice narrowed to Lenroot or Eliot. Social workers favored Lenroot, and members of the American Pediatric Society endorsed Eliot. There was "a lot of gossip" about the whole affair. Despite the uncomfortable situation, Eliot and Lenroot remained friends. Lenroot was finally named chief in November 1934, perhaps because of support from traditional Children's Bureau allies combined with the experience she gained serving as acting chief during Abbott's absences in 1931-32 and 1934. Abbott was able to appease some members of the medical community by naming Eliot assistant chief. As Julia Lathrop had done, Grace Abbott chose her successor; but, unlike Lathrop, Abbott intended to continue to directly influence Children's Bureau policy.[65]

As demonstrated by her coauthorship of "Special Measures for Economic Security of Children," Grace Abbott was able to contribute to the development of the most comprehensive program for children the federal government had ever implemented, despite the fact that she had resigned as chief of the Children's Bureau. Thomas H. Eliot, no relation to Martha Eliot but the man responsible for the legal drafting of the Social Security bill, says that he asked his "colleague" Katharine Lenroot to write the child welfare sections. Lenroot quickly formed a committee composed of herself, Martha Eliot, and Grace Abbott. These women quickly designed the New Deal programs intended to assure "security" for "whole child."[66]

As a first step they established a subcommittee composed of both public health and social workers. Homer Folks, already head of the CES Public Health Advisory Committee, was named as chair. This subcommittee also included New York City's Bureau of Catholic Charities' Father Bryan McEntegart, someone Lenroot identified as "a great friend of the Children's Bureau." CES committees intentionally included Catholic officials in order to avoid the kind of criticism from the Catholic hierarchy that had plagued past efforts for health care and social welfare reforms. Lenroot, Eliot, Abbott, and their subcommittee used the data collected and the experience obtained during the bureau's twenty-two years of work to devise their recommendations for a New Deal program for children. They assumed that the programs they designed would be administered by the Children's Bureau when the economic security bill became law.[67]

According to Lenroot, the president and his advisors used the following criteria to decide which issues would be included in the CES program: "It was felt that it would be most logical and most reasonable to select . . . those parts of the child welfare or child health problems which were closely related to the problem of unemployment; in the second place, measures which would attempt to meet the basic needs of children throughout the country, such as the need for economic security when the father is absent from the home, and the need for a measure of health protection."[68] With these criteria in mind, the three women devised a three-part plan providing "security" for children.

First, they designed a federally aided mothers' pension plan called aid to dependent children. After federal and state relief became available in 1933 through the FERA, many families eligible for mothers' aid were instead on FERA emergency relief rolls. This was largely due to the fact that mothers' aid funds in most states had already been reduced or depleted. By 1934, although mothers' pensions were "authorized by the laws of 45 States . . . [such funds were] actually granted by less than half the local units empowered to provide this form of care."[69] This circumstance was contrary to the Children's Bureau principle that mothers' aid and public relief were not interchangeable. The Children's Bureau argued that these families were entitled to "long time care." Mothers' aid, Grace Abbott maintained "should not be administered in connection with or as part of general relief and must have a different standard of adequacy than emergency relief."[70] The Children's Bureau held that "experience shows that this security and the assistance given to the mother in meeting the problems of family life and child-rearing are important influences in preventing juvenile delinquency and other social difficulties."[71] As has been shown, the Children's Bureau contended that mothers' aid was a form of preventive social welfare, not poor relief. Security for these children and their mothers included federal and state aid to dependent children.

In 1934 the bureau estimated that there were three times more families eligible for mothers' aid than the number actually receiving it. State relief officers found it economically expedient to place families on emergency relief, subsidized by FERA funds, rather than on mothers' aid payrolls funded exclusively by the states. Lenroot and her staff calculated that 358,000 households headed by widowed, separated, or divorced women with one or more dependent children received emergency relief. There were 719,500 children under sixteen years of age (approximately 4 percent of the age cohort) living in those households. Such families made up 8.8 percent of all rural relief cases and 10.0 percent of all urban ones. A study funded by the Children's Bureau in Cincinnati specifically supported this estimate. It found that 478 families received mothers' aid and another 2,153 families were probably eligible for mothers' aid but instead remained on FERA rolls.[72] Such findings meant that the federal government provided $45 million and state and local governments added another $15 million in emergency relief payments to families that should have been eligible for mothers' aid. State and local governments also spent $37.5 million on mothers' aid funds. The Children's Bureau argued that this appropriation should be much higher and that the federal government should help fund this social insurance effort. The situation was especially critical because by 1934 state and local governments had largely run out of revenue for mothers' aid programs.

After examining the data collected by the Children's Bureau, Lenroot, Eliot, and Abbott submitted their recommendations concerning aid to dependent children to the CES. They proposed that local and state governments increase their contribution to mothers' aid programs (which should then be renamed aid to dependent children) to $40 million. To ease the burden, the federal government should provide $40 million in matching grants. In a further attempt to distinguish aid to dependent children from unemployment relief, Lenroot, Eliot, and Abbott recommended that the "shift from emergency relief to aid to dependent children must be somewhat gradual." This was because trained staffs needed to be hired to distribute the funds. Mothers' aid involved social welfare casework as well as long-term financial assistance. It was not simply temporary "charity" relief. Like old age pensions, aid to dependent children was an entitlement. The CES proposal urged a federal appropriation of $25 million for the first two years with an increase of not more than $50 million per year thereafter.[73] According to this plan, all families eligible for aid to dependent children would then be "properly" included in a program separate from emergency relief. Furthermore, it would be a program "equalized" by the federal government's contributions, but one which maintained state and local control of funds: "The Federal, State and local governments should share in the program, through a system of Federal and State cooperative and equalization funds. Since it would be a long-time, not an emergency undertaking, Federal administration should be vested in the Children's Bureau, U.S. Department of Labor, State administration in departments of public welfare, and local administration, wherever possible, in local public welfare or child welfare boards or departments."[74]

The discussions within the CES cabinet committee concerning the proposed plan did not focus on the program's cost or suitability. Instead, conflict arose between the Children's Bureau and the FERA over the bureaucratic administration of the program. As Linda Gordon explains, Abbott viewed FERA head Harry Hopkins as something of an "imperialist, attempting to control more and more." But again, arguments over administration were more than simply "turf" disputes or fears that women would lose control of child welfare. The two agencies had contrasting notions about the purpose of the aid to dependent children program. Hopkins argued that all relief efforts, whether temporary or long term, should be administered through the FERA. He and many of his supporters thought that in the future a permanent federal department of public welfare might be established to administer all federal relief programs. In addition, the FERA believed that the aid to dependent children program had a much broader scope than did the Children's Bureau. For the FERA, the term "dependent children" meant "children under sixteen in their own homes, in which there is not an adult person, other than one needed to care for the child or children, who is able to work and provide the family with a reasonable subsistence compatible with decent health."[75] This definition was not as specific as the Children's Bureau's, which required that male breadwinners in families eligible for aid to dependent children be absent through death, separation, or desertion. The

FERA's broader interpretation ran contrary to the Children's Bureau's concept of a program designed specifically for "worthy fatherless" families that needed long-term care. According to the bureau, such children, through their mothers, were entitled to a "pension" or benefit. Furthermore, the Children's Bureau's viewpoint maintained that the rearing of children by worthy widowed, divorced, or abandoned mothers was a service just as vital to the national security as military service. Economic security for mothers and children was as much an entitlement as old age or veterans' pensions and should not be confused with relief. They argued that the very phrases "mothers' aid" and "mothers' pensions" misconstrued the intention of such laws. These were "not primarily aids to mothers but defense measures for children." According to Lenroot, Eliot, and Abbott, aid to dependent children was "designed to release from the wage-earning role the person whose natural function is to give her children the physical and affectionate guardianship necessary not alone to keep them from falling into social misfortune, but more affirmatively to rear them into citizens capable of contributing to society."[76]

Witte, Perkins, Hopkins, Wallace, Altmeyer, and Treasury Department Assistant Secretary Josephine Roche held an "informal" meeting at Secretary of Labor Perkins's home on December 22 or 23, 1934, to work out a final draft of the CES proposal. There are apparently no minutes of the meeting, but it is clear that during this session the group decided to include the Children's Bureau's interpretation of the aid to dependent children proposal in the CES's final report. However, the committee also recommended that the FERA administer the new program. The group felt that giving the Children's Bureau responsibility for administering aid to dependent children would not effectively induce states to contribute their own funds to the program since they already got a higher proportion of relief funds from the FERA. States received half of their expenditures from the federal government under FERA programs but only one-third in the proposed aid to dependent children plan. The group at Perkins's house agreed that consolidation of all relief efforts within the FERA would better achieve the desired end of increased aid to dependent children rolls. As Marshall Dimock, then assistant secretary of labor, remembers, Lenroot, Eliot, and Abbott were very upset that the CES report did not recommend that the Children's Bureau administer the program. But, according to Dimock, supporting Roosevelt and the New Deal took first priority for the three. Dissension within the Roosevelt ranks might have threatened the entire economic security proposal.[77]

The second program devised by Lenroot, Eliot, and Abbott for the CES also had its roots in the Children's Bureau's first two decades of work. This proposal centered on children with "special needs" not necessarily related to unemployment or an absent parent. The 1934 definition of this group included a much broader range of dependent children than the agency's earlier meaning: "situations of neglect in homes, feeblemindedness in parents or children, cruel and abusive parents, illegitimate children without competent guardians, children who are delinquent, truant, or wayward, or who suffer from mental disturbances or handicaps."[78] The Children's Bureau estimated that there were approximately 300,000 dependent and neglected children in the United States, approximately 1 percent of all Americans nineteen and under. Of these three-fifths lived in institutions, and the rest in foster homes. In addition, 200,000 more children fell under juvenile court supervision and another 75,000 children were born to unmarried parents each year. Local services, although modest, were generally available for children living in cities of 100,000 or more. But in smaller localities "services of this kind [were] extremely limited, or non-existent." Only one-fourth of the states had statewide county welfare boards.[79]

At first, Abbott proposed requesting $1 million for a program designed to address children with special needs. However, Lenroot and Eliot increased the recommended appropriation by 50 percent. Abbott was somewhat taken aback by the suggestion fearing that this asked for too much. But the new chief and her assistant dismissed Abbott's objections and asked for $1.5 million; $1 million to be distributed in automatic grants-in-aid to the states ($10,000 to each state with the rest proportional according to population) and $500,000 to states with the greatest need, especially those with large rural populations. It is important to note that this program, unlike the Sheppard-Towner Act, required no matching funds from the states. It also included a plan to equalize care as much as possible. Not surprisingly, the women recommended that the Children's Bureau be made responsible for this new program. There apparently was no disagreement, and the CES submitted the proposal in its final draft exactly as presented by Lenroot, Eliot, and Abbott.[80]

The third program recommended by Lenroot's committee also related to the Children's Bureau's previous experience, this time focusing on maternal and child health care. The loss of Sheppard-Towner combined with the economic depression to cause an extreme drop in the expenditure of public health funds. This was particularly true of programs intended to reduce infant and maternal mortality rates. During 1928 the states used approximately $2,158,000 in combined state and federal funds (of which $1,018,000 was federal money) for use in maternity and infancy work under Sheppard-Towner. By 1934, funds for the promotion of good infant and maternal care had been reduced to $1,157,000 and nine states reported no special appropriations for such work. Twenty-two states funded less than 50 percent of the total amount spent in 1928.[81] Lenroot, Eliot, and Abbott developed a plan to reverse this trend. Modeled on Sheppard-Towner, the program would utilize diagnostic clinics and educational work, but go further by permitting the distribution of actual medical care for needy children and their mothers. In addition, the plan also covered older children. In an interview conducted years later, Eliot explained that it was her idea to expand the proposal to include "children" up to twenty-one years of age. She felt that the CES needed to "think in broader terms—what do children need all through their school years until they are adults." This concept was "a little overwhelming to Grace Abbott; but I being very young and naive, thought 'Why not?' and [Abbott] agreed that we would then title our proposal 'Maternal and Child Health'" instead of maternal and *infant* health care.[82] The Children's Bureau's studies conducted during the previous two decades showed that children needed good health care throughout their lives and those living in rural areas had even less access to good medical care than did urban children. But at the same time that this proposal broadened Sheppard-Towner, the addition of means testing made it a program accessible to a much smaller constituency. As might be expected, some felt that the PHS should be given responsibility for the proposal. However, the CES's final recommendation designated that the Children's Bureau act as the program's administrator.

Lenroot, Eliot, and Abbott recognized "crippled" children as another group needing uniform health care. During the first years of its existence the Children's Bureau had examined the circumstances of mentally handicapped children living in institutions or seen in public diagnostic clinics.[83] Nevertheless, since its establishment the bureau had actually spent little effort on the concerns of other physically handicapped youngsters. Unable to give an exact number, the bureau estimated that approximately one in every one hundred children was physically handicapped.[84] According to Martha Eliot, Grace Abbott came up with the idea to incorporate a "crippled" children's program into the CES proposal. Eliot said that Abbott believed a plan for handicapped children would not be as controversial as maternal and child health care and that the president might have a particular interest in the issue. In a letter written to Perkins in 1955, Lenroot explained that "the President wished the Committee to include in its considerations the subjects of the health and welfare of children." Stricken by polio, Roosevelt received many letters like the one from Jane Deuel praising him for "overcoming" his "physical disability." But as Witte and Lenroot later acknowledged, the White House did not instruct the CES to include handicapped children as a separate item in the proposal. Perhaps, as Hugh Gallagher suggests, Roosevelt rarely initiated discussions about the handicapped because he did not want to draw attention to his own situation.[85] A program for handicapped children was not a revolutionary idea. Thirty-five states already had some provision for such children in 1934, "although in several of these states the appropriations were so small that only a few . . . could be cared for." States and counties spent approximately $5,500,000 annually on the care of handicapped children. However, this only touched a small percentage of the estimated 300,000 to 500,000 physically handicapped youngsters living in the United States. Many were difficult to locate and it was hard to offer follow-up health care for those living in rural areas, especially those residing two hundred miles or more from the closest hospital.[86] Initially Abbott planned to include services for handicapped children within the maternal and child health proposal. But pressure from advocacy groups such as the National Society for Crippled Children influenced the women to make this program a separate section of their plan. They asked for $3 million in federal grant-in-aid funds which would be matched dollar for dollar by the states. The CES's proposal slightly reduced this request to $2,850,000 and recommended that the Children's Bureau be responsible for administering the program.[87]

Ironically, a controversy that materialized even before the child health and "crippled" children proposals were submitted to the CES cabinet committee helped the bureau to retain control of such programs. A preliminary report by the CES Medical Advisory Committee, a body with no Children's Bureau representative, issued on September 26, 1934, echoed some of the same arguments used by the AMA, the Hoover administration, and earlier opponents of the Children's Bureau's maternal and child health promotional efforts. This CES committee, chaired by a member and later president of the AMA, Walter L. Bierring, M.D., initially appeared to support AMA policy. The committee's preliminary report recommended that children's health care should be "properly and adequately" incorporated into the PHS as a part of a general program of medical care and public health. But by November 1934 the addition of three new members to the CES committee weakened the AMA's influence and the group's recommendations changed dramatically.[88]

By late 1934 the Medical Advisory Committee and its technical staff formulated ten general principles concerning health care. For a time a few members of the Roosevelt administration attempted to include a national health care program as part of the New Deal. The committee's statement suggested making "good health services and medical care [available] to all of the population" including those who "cannot otherwise secure them." Providing such benefits, the committee's members argued, is an "obligation of society." The committee also recommended that "responsibility for the quality of medical services should be borne by the professions [and that] all medical services should be under the control of the medical professions," provided that such care be "properly remunerated." Patient freedom to choose a "properly qualified doctor" must be maintained and "health and medical care should be furnished at the lowest cost consistent with the maintenance of adequate quality of service." These were radical suggestions coming from federal policy makers and they show the diminished influence of the AMA among committee members. The group concluded that in order to successfully uphold these principles a compulsory health insurance plan should be part of the CES's final proposal.[89] The plan also included cash maternity benefits to encourage women "to abstain from employment for some time before or after birth . . . [and] to receive competent prenatal and postnatal, as well as delivery care." According to the committee, these suggestions maintained the control of health care by doctors by giving "recognition to the physician as the central and preeminent person responsible for the furnishing of service."[90]

But keeping the power over medical care in the hands of physicians did not quiet objections from the AMA. Two AMA members of the committee objected to the majority report and countered with ten principles of their own, proclaiming that "medical service must have no connection with any cash benefits." Furthermore, "no third party must be permitted to come between the patient and the physician. . . . all responsibility for the character of medical service must be borne by the profession" (meaning the AMA). By February 1935, Medical Advisory Committee chair and AMA president Walter Bierring seemingly rejected his committee's recommendation and wrote Witte that he was as "firmly convinced as ever that the delivery of medical service under Federal or State control is not advisable or adaptable for this country."[91]

Ultimately, Perkins, Witte, Hopkins, and Altmeyer removed compulsory health insurance from the CES's final draft because they believed it too controversial and feared that retaining it in the proposal might jeopardize the entire program.[92] The attention focused on compulsory health insurance benefited the Children's Bureau and its constituents by drawing attention away from the child health proposals. The AMA and its supporters worried much more about the implementation of national health insurance than the skimpy maternal and child health proposals given to the Children's Bureau. In addition, the CES's final child health plan emphasized the "close cooperation" of the Children's Bureau with "medical and public welfare agencies." At the same time, the PHS's role expanded through a proposed $8 million annual appropriation designed to assist the states in development of "adequate public health services" and an additional $2 million yearly for "public health investigations."[93] It appears that this strengthening of the PHS may have allayed any concerns its supporters had expressed in the past concerning competition from the Children's Bureau. Both the PHS and the Children's Bureau argued that their programs were complimentary and that they planned to work together to provide health "security" for mothers and their children.

A strong desire among the plan's designers to gain passage of the entire CES proposal also made such cooperation possible. Witte testified that "no member of the technical board ever publicly (or, as far as I know, privately) expressed any dissent from any recommendations made by the committee." In fact, in House hearings held in January 1935, even Bierring testified in support of the final CES package.[94]

But, on December 24, 1934, before the proposal reached Congress, Perkins and Hopkins briefed Roosevelt on the CES's recommendations. After a conference lasting several hours, Roosevelt accepted the CES program as submitted. The final signed report, along with a draft of the Economic Security bill, was filed with the president on January 15, 1935. Two days later, Roosevelt sent a special message to Congress recommending that the program be enacted "with a minimum of delay." The Wagner-Lewis bill (S. 1130, H.R. 4120) was introduced on January 18, 1935, and sent to the House Ways and Means Committee and the Senate Finance Committee for hearings three days later. During congressional hearings the bill was renamed the Social Security bill and its organization and content changed.[95]

Public and political attention focused generally on the old age pension and public relief sections of the bill. But during House committee hearings, the aid to dependent children proposal also drew some objections. The first concern focused on the FERA's role as administrator. Some members had previously objected to the FERA, a temporary agency, administering the old age assistance section of the bill. These critics argued that permanent "security" programs should not be given to an emergency agency. Giving the Children's Bureau, a permanent agency, the administrative responsibility for the aid to dependent children program would have muted such criticisms against the children's section, but no one offered such an amendment. Instead, the House committee amended the bill by calling for the establishment of the Social Security Board, a permanent agency that would be responsible for both the old age and aid to dependent children programs. Interestingly, this time objections to a child welfare program focused on the bureaucratic technicalities of the plan and not on the need for or constitutional aspects of federal assistance for mothers and their children. But this change in strategy signaled a rejection of the Children's Bureau's notion that aid to dependent children was a form of social insurance similar to old age pensions, or payments for service (an earned benefit) like veterans' pensions. In addition, the change showed a rejection of the agency's "whole child" philosophy. According to Thomas Eliot, members of the House Ways and Means Committee did not believe that grants-in-aid programs designed to help the needy were insurance or an earned benefit. Instead they viewed programs such as aid to dependent children as noncontributory and therefore a form of "charity" relief. This has become the foundation of the two-tiered U.S. social insurance system. In other words, popular belief holds that the Social Security old age benefit program is a form of savings account in which individuals get back what they paid in. But all FICA (Federal Insurance Corporation of America) taxes are part of a general revenue fund and payments are only partially related to how much an individual has contributed (most people get much more than they paid in). Furthermore, veterans' pensions, funded solely through the federal government, are generally viewed as a benefit for service, while aid to dependent children payments granted to single mothers are stigmatized as relief.[96] Consequently, despite the Children's Bureau's apparent victory over the FERA's interpretation in CES debates, even in 1935 aid to dependent children was viewed as "welfare."

A second concern expressed by House committee members posed a more practical problem for mothers and children who would benefit from the program. In the final CES proposal there had been no limitation on the maximum grant per child appropriated by the federal government if matched by the required amount of state funds. However, the House committee established the maximum grants at $18 per month for the first child and $12 per month for each additional child. They used this standard because it was the same amount allowable under the veterans' pension acts paying benefits to children of servicemen killed during World War I. But committee members ignored the fact that under the veterans' pension acts widows were granted a $30 per month allowance in addition to children's benefits. The aid to dependent children program did not include an allowance to mothers or other caretakers, but it was still written with the intention of keeping women at home to care for "dependent" children. The term "dependent child" was legally defined under Title IV, Section 406 of the 1935 Social Security Act as "a child under the age of sixteen who has been deprived of parental support or care by reason of the death, continued absence from the home, or physical or mental incapacity of a parent, and who is living with his father, mother, grandmother, brother, sister, stepfather, stepmother, stepbrother, stepsister, uncle, or aunt, in a place of residence maintained by one or more of such relatives as his or their own home." Noting the lack of financial support for mothers, Witte reported that the members of the House committee "acknowledged [the discrepancy] to be a justifiable criticism . . . [but said that] there was so little interest on the part of any of the members in aid to dependent children that no one thereafter made a motion to strike out the section." Grace Abbott noted that "dependent children did not have a large voting lobby."[97] This objection, coupled with the apparent lack of controversy surrounding the children's proposals in the Social Security bill, provides evidence that these sections were largely ignored by most legislators. Even the bill's major designer, Thomas Eliot, admits that the child welfare sections of the bill received little of his attention and were "edited far too hastily." In addition, Edwin Witte maintained that "there was little interest in Congress in . . . aid to dependent children." It was his belief that "nothing would have been done on this subject if it had not been included in the report of the Committee on Economic Security."[98]

On August 14, 1935, President Roosevelt signed the Social Security Act into law (49 *Stat.* 620). The program is often cited as a watershed in American social welfare history, but, like Congress, the press, the public, and the program's designers, most scholars have focused on the old age and unemployment insurance aspects of the law and generally ignored the programs for children included in the act under titles IV, V, and VII.[99] But the children's programs developed under the Social Security Act would touch the lives of more young people in the United States than all the Children's Bureau's investigative and educational efforts during its previous twenty-two years. In addition, under the law, the Children's Bureau changed from an agency responsible for the distribution of $337,371 in 1930 to one dispensing $8,644,500 in 1938 and $10,892,797 by the end of the decade. Its staff grew from 143 to 438.[100] Perhaps most significantly, although believed to be a minor concern at the time, the aid to dependent children program has become one of the most controversial legacies of the New Deal.

Several factors contributed to the successful effort to include programs for children in the 1935 Social Security Act. First, the Great Depression changed the minds of many Americans concerning the role of the federal government in social welfare. Proposals that seemed radical to many Americans only a few years earlier, now appeared necessary. Second, those involved in drafting the proposals skillfully negotiated compromises in order to achieve success. Third, as already indicated, the effort to avoid public debate on a compulsory health insurance proposal drew attention away from the Children's Bureau's programs. But, at the same time, this lack of attention may have weakened the Children's Bureau's role in the final product. Perhaps preferring to be "good soldiers," Lenroot and the Children's Bureau staff did not turn to their usual army of supporters, namely women's organizations and child welfare reform groups, for fear that controversy within the government might put successful passage of the entire program at risk. It is also possible that the "maternalist" politics of the past proved inadequate to deal with the growing federal bureaucracy influenced by growing numbers of powerful professional lobbyist groups.

In addition, it is interesting that Martha Eliot and Katharine Lenroot both suggested that Grace Abbott was somewhat surprised by some of their proposals. For two decades the Children's Bureau had limited its role to investigation, education, and advocacy. The New Deal brought the federal government and the Children's Bureau more aggressively into the effort to protect "a right to childhood." Ironically, activists at the time paid little attention to this dramatic change for children. Unlike the heated 1920s debates over Sheppard-Towner, during the 1930s maternal and infant health care for poor women and their children became a joint federal-state responsibility with relative ease. Services for handicapped children entered the federal scheme. The Social Security Act's aid to dependent children program, a decided improvement over mothers' pensions, for the first time instituted a permanent federal program advancing money to fill the needs of poor children. Between 1934 and 1939, the average mothers' pension-style benefits (now ADC) increased from $22.31 per month to $32.12 and the number of recipients rose from 300,000 to 700,000 (approximately 3 percent of American children). In the original version ADC benefits extended only to children up to sixteen. Amendments in 1939 expanded the program to those eighteen and under. But the program continued to address only the needs of children living in "deserving" families. Mothers who had never married and their children need not apply. Divorced mothers or those hindered by racial or ethnic prejudice could also be excluded. In addition, changes in administrative responsibility for the bill influenced the law's effectiveness for children. Although the designer of the New Deal's child welfare program, the Children's Bureau was not its sole administrator. Instead, the Social Security Board, a federal agency more interested in old age insurance than children's aid, implemented and directed the future of the important aid to dependent children program. The Children's Bureau's had won the battle but lost the war. The loss of administrative responsibility for the aid to dependent children program showed that the agency had not successfully convinced policy makers of its "whole child" strategy. In the post-World War II era, the aid to dependent children program (later renamed Aid to Families with Dependent Children [AFDC]) became the cornerstone of child welfare efforts and the most controversial aspect of the New Deal's Social Security Act.[101]

The New Deal and Child Labor Reform

Child labor reform was another issue that had historically been a part of the Children's Bureau's effort to secure "a right to childhood." At the onset of the Great Depression the Children's Bureau continued its program of urging parents to keep their children in school rather than allowing them to work for wages. By 1929 the child labor amendment still lacked the necessary thirty-six states for ratification and the 1930 census showed that two million children were gainfully employed despite the Children's Bureau's efforts during the previous two decades. Among individuals ten to thirteen years of age, the Bureau of the Census reported that 235,328 children, or one out of every forty-one, was employed. Of children fourteen and fifteen years old, 431,790 or one out of every eleven worked for pay. Making things worse, this was actually only a portion of those children working during 1930.[102] In December 1932, the Children's Bureau called "an emergency" conference in Washington to review the "whole question of child labor." Several in attendance presented evidence of increasing numbers of children worked in "new sweated industries which had sprung up during the depression."[103] But attendees decided that the time was not right for ratification of the federal child labor amendment. They instead agreed to work for the adoption of state laws requiring a sixteen-year age minimum for employment. As Walter Trattner argues, the conclusion of those present at the meeting "was a misjudgment of public opinion."[104]

In reality, the depression drew increasing public attention to the abuses of child labor. Sweatshops looking to cut costs hired children for little or no pay. Labor unions blamed such practices for lowering wages and reducing the number of jobs open to adults. The 1933 National Recovery Act (NRA) (48 *Stat.* 195) helped to reverse this trend. The NRA child labor codes, developed in cooperation with the Children's Bureau, set the general minimum age for employment at sixteen, and eighteen in forty-nine occupations judged as dangerous. The codes prohibited all full-time industrial employment of children under sixteen and young people aged fourteen through sixteen could work only when school was not in session. In addition, in cooperation with the Federal Farm Security Administration, the Children's Bureau set codes prohibiting the employment of children under fourteen in the sugar beet industry. This was the first successful, although temporary, effort to reform agricultural child labor practices.[105] It was not clear from the start that child labor regulations would be included in the NRA codes. The first one adopted concerned the cotton textile industry and initially contained no minimum employment age or other reference to child labor. After a protest by the NCLC and the Children's Bureau the "Code of Fair Competition," effective July 17, 1933, prohibited employment of persons less than sixteen years of age. This code, written for an industry with traditionally high child labor rates, set the standard for others. Even the newspaper business, another strong opponent of child labor regulation in the past, agreed to set a fourteen-year age minimum for its street vendors. Over the next year, the Children's Bureau and the NCLC worked with representatives from various industries to write the forty-five codes involving child workers. The bureau claimed success and agreed with the NRA's judgment that the codes "resulted in the practical elimination of child workers from industry."[106] Likely, a plentiful supply of adults willing to take such jobs for low wages turned the tide in favor of child labor restrictions.

However, on May 27, 1935, the Supreme Court declared the NRA unconstitutional. Thereafter the Children's Bureau encouraged manufacturers to continue to abide by the codes, but with no means of federal enforcement the Children's Bureau and the NRA estimated that child labor rates rose during the second half of 1935.[107] In response, the bureau again stepped up its efforts to gain ratification of the child labor amendment.

Contrary to the expectations of those attending the December 1932 Children's Bureau conference in Washington, fourteen states ratified the child labor amendment during 1933. Molly Dewson, director of the Democratic National Committee's Women's Division, wrote President Roosevelt in December 1933 that "the ratifications are coming so fast I believe that with a little interest on your part, the amendment can be ratified in 1934." Indeed, Roosevelt sometimes urged passage of the child labor amendment in his public addresses but did not take a consistently aggressive stand until 1937.[108] That January, at the request of Frances Perkins, the president sent letters to the governors of the nineteen states that had not yet ratified the amendment. He urged them to pressure their state legislatures for ratification.

> I am sure you will agree with me that one of the most encouraging developments of the past few years is the general agreement that has been reached that child labor should be abolished. Outstanding gains were made under the N.R.A. codes which have been maintained in many establishments through voluntary cooperation of employers. . . . However, it is clearly indicated that child labor, especially in low paid unstandardized types of work is increasing. I am convinced that Nation-wide minimum standards are necessary. . . . Do you not agree with me that ratification of the child labor amendment by the remaining twelve States whose action is necessary to place it in the Constitution is the obvious way to early achievement of our objective?[109]

Four more states (Kansas, Kentucky, Nevada, and New Mexico) ratified the amendment during 1937, but this was not enough.[110] Opposition from organizations such as the National Committee for the Protection of Child, Family, School, and Church (established in St. Louis in 1934 and well financed by business interests) avidly worked to defeat ratification in the remaining states. Continuing criticism from seventy newspapers including the powerful *New York Sun, New York Herald Tribune,* and the *St. Louis Post-Dispatch* also contributed to the amendment's defeat. A new editor at the *Chicago Tribune* changed that paper's stand from support to opposition of the amendment. In addition, the American Bar Association had gone on record opposing the amendment in 1933 contending that it was "a communistic effort to nationalize children."[111]

The passage of the 1938 Fair Labor Standards Act, which virtually replicated the earlier NRA codes, finally achieved federal regulation of much child labor. The Children's Bureau received responsibility for the enforcement of the law (52 *Stat.* 1060).[112] However, as Katharine Lenroot acknowledged, the Fair Labor Standards Act applied only to establishments producing goods shipped across state lines. The Children's Bureau estimated that only 6 percent of child laborers held jobs regulated by the law, which did not affect children working in strictly intrastate enterprises such as restaurants, beauty parlors, garages and repair shops, or working as newsboys or as actors. Federal law also exempted most agricultural employment. The Federal Sugar Act of 1937 required that sugar beet workers be at least fourteen and that those from fourteen to sixteen work no more than eight hours a day. But no federal law helped pickers of other agricultural products. As Lenroot concluded, "Although the Fair Labor Standards Act of 1938 marks a long step forward in the establishment of a national child labor standard, it leaves many children unprotected."[113] This should not be surprising since it was consistent with other New Deal efforts. For example, the Social Security Act excluded agricultural workers (and domestic laborers).

A New Deal for Children?

In a 1940 article examining child welfare during the 1930s, Katharine Lenroot used a cliché borrowed from Charles Dickens to describe the Children's Bureau's experience during the Great Depression. "It was the best of times, it was the worst of times, it was the age of wisdom, it was the age of foolishness, it was the epoch of belief, it was the epoch of incredulity, it was the season of Light, . . . it was the winter of despair." Indeed, the Great Depression resulted in "the deepening sense of public responsibility for children and the accompanying realization that this responsibility must be developed on a nationwide basis."[114] The Children's Bureau moved from its limited role of investigation, education, and advocacy to federally administered, regulated, and funded programs for some of the nation's infants, children with special needs, and those working in the nation's cities, farms, and factories.[115] The Children's Bureau also expanded its topical recommendations with publications such as "Are You Training Your Child to Be Happy? Lesson Material in Child Management" (1929, no. 202), "Posture and Physical Fitness" (1931, no. 205), and "Development of a Leisure-Time Program in Small Cities and Towns" (1937, no. 241). Renewed attention focused on the economic reasons for the loss of "a right to childhood," in the agency's study of homeless children, "Temporary Shelter for Homeless or Transient Persons and Travelers Aid" (1932, addendum to no. 209).

Funds for the Social Security Act's maternal, child health, and handicapped children's provisions became available in February 1936 ($3,800,000 for maternal and child health, $2,850,000 for handicapped child services). By April 1, 1937, forty-two states, Alaska, Hawaii, and the District of Columbia cooperated in the maternal and child health sections of the Social Security Act. By June 1940 every state participated in the program offering services and medical care to handicapped children. The maternal and child health provisions received an even more enthusiastic response. By October 1936 all forty-eight states, Alaska, Hawaii, and the District of Columbia cooperated in the program. In 1939 the Children's Bureau oversaw the distribution of $3,724,362.29 to state health departments to pay for the services of physicians, dentists, public health nurses, medical social workers, and nutritionists working in public clinics and conducting home visits to mothers and children living primarily in rural areas. Amendments passed by Congress in 1939 extended benefits to Puerto Rico and Hawaii effective January 1, 1940. Part of the program regulated midwives, but the program's major emphasis rested on physician-directed care. Clearly, the efforts of the Children's Bureau contributed to the switch of childbirth from home to hospital and promoted physician-administered care for mothers and babies. Better education about obstetric and infant care has saved many lives, but the cost of having a baby has risen faster than inflation and the infant mortality rate in the United States remains one of the highest in the industrialized world.[116]

The Children's Bureau sponsored what it called a "Conference on Better Care for Mothers and Babies" in Washington, D.C., on January 17-18, 1938. The meeting was attended by 481 individuals representing eighty-six child health care organizations and state agencies. Conference participants "consider[ed] the existing resources for the care of mothers and newborn infants in the United States, the extent to which maternal and infant mortality may be reduced, the measures successfully undertaken in certain localities and among certain groups, and the ways by which such services may be made available everywhere."[117] The committee evaluating the evidence disclosed during the meeting found an "inadequacy of maternal and infant care." During 1936, 248,000 babies (about 10 percent of total births) were born without a physician present; neighbors and relatives assisted in the delivery of 15,000 and midwives aided the birth of 223,000. The Children's Bureau judged most midwives "untrained and ignorant." Seventy-one percent of all urban births occurred in hospitals, but only 14 percent of those babies born in rural areas were born in hospitals. The nation averaged one public health nurse for every 5,000 persons in cities with more than 10,000 population, but only one for every 14,000 persons in rural areas. Even more significantly, many rural public health nurses traveled long distances under difficult circumstances to reach the women and children within their jurisdictions. A great need for state and federally assisted health care for all classes existed because "the purchase of health services is still mainly a matter of private and individual action." While "rich and poor alike have benefited [from] the progress of public health and the medical sciences . . . the poor have more sickness and more disability and need more health services than the rich." The Children's Bureau and those attending the conference believed that the deaths of mothers and/or infants in 150,000 families every year were largely preventable, and therefore recommended an expansion of medical care to "needy" mothers through Social Security funds. In response, Congress increased the 1939 appropriations under Title V.[118]

However, the Social Security program, like the Fair Labor Standards Act, had fundamental limitations. State and local authorities had wide discretion concerning the expenditure of funds, thereby opening the door to racial discrimination and moralistic judgments, as well as other inequities. In addition, limiting child health services to "needy" children left many families of the working poor ineligible for aid, and the quality of services varied widely. As the bureau found in its 1933-35 study of infant and maternal mortality among blacks, race and class played significant roles in the actual care afforded to children in America. The Social Security Act did not directly address this historic pattern. For example, about 22,000 (8.8 percent) of all black children died before their first birthday and almost half of these in the first month of life. Maternal mortality was also much higher for African American mothers than for whites (96.7 versus 56.4 per 10,000 live births). Even absent blatant discrimination, of the more than 250,000 black babies born each year, almost two-thirds were born in rural areas of the South severely lacking medical services.[119] Although overall infant and maternal mortality rates continued to decline, race and class played a large part in the deaths of mothers and babies.

Local discretion in implementation of the aid to dependent children program and other child welfare services also shows that the bureau did not accomplish its goal to "equalize" opportunity for children under its New Deal proposals. In reality, the agency had little authority to enforce its recommendations and lost control of the program's social security insurance for children. Furthermore, the plan establishing economic security for "a right to childhood" was not designed and therefore not viewed in the same way as the plan for instituting a secure old age. Designed as an entitlement for all American citizens, the Social Security Act's old age pension plan contained no means test or "worthiness" qualifications.[120] Despite the Children's Bureau's arguments to the contrary, from its inception AFDC was seen as "welfare"—charity, a handout, not intended for all American children. The program's basic design functions on the notion that only a limited number of children were in need of government assistance and even among those, families must be judged "worthy." Furthermore, contributions to the fund played little role in this perception since historically most elderly recipients collect far more than they ever contribute (especially the earliest beneficiaries).

The Children's Bureau accepted the popular cultural values concerning the importance of mothers in children's lives. Lenroot, Eliot, and Abbott intended that in exchange for ADC payments for children, widowed, (worthy) divorced, and abandoned mothers would renounce outside employment and instead provide a service to the nation by staying at home to nurture their children fulltime. However, the very idea of ADC ran contrary to the economic value society had traditionally placed on "women's work," a fact that must have been part of the reason why mothers received no benefit for themselves. In addition, the money provided through the Social Security Act's ADC program did not offer adequate support nor the opportunity to better a family's circumstance. The program ignored educational and employment training for mothers and day care for those who wanted to work, and condemned wage labor for either children or mothers as a threat to "a right to childhood." Hence, the only escape from poverty for many single mothers was remarriage, driven by economic necessity, not for the emotional fulfillment of themselves or their children. In 1939, federal aid to dependent children contributions increased from one-third to one-half of the total, the same as old age assistance, unemployment relief, and aid to the blind. In addition, children living with relatives other than their mother could also receive benefits, but "suitability" was still determined by the states. These broadened the program but the stigma of "welfare" became increasingly entrenched. The program never received the "insurance" status of old age pensions or the "service" status of veteran's pensions. Furthermore, children living with never-married mothers were ignored as generally ineligible for aid. Overall, during the 1930s the Children's Bureau's experience, as well as the welfare of many American children, was, as Lenroot noted, uneven.[121]

Involvement in a persistent fight with those who wanted to reorganize the federal government on a "functional" rather than "constituent" basis also hampered the Children's Bureau's effectiveness. The refusal to give administrative responsibility for the Social Security Act's AFDC program to the Children's Bureau denied the agency's principle that child welfare for the "whole child" must emanate from a single government agency. It appears that even some of the agency's traditional network of supporters, social workers and family policy advocates, abandoned the Children's Bureau's "whole child" strategy in light of the creation of the semi-welfare state. This circumstance also ignored the fact that children are a particularly vulnerable constituency that must rely on powerful surrogates to lobby on their behalf. Although it is now a lost concept, perhaps a single agency such as the Children's Bureau could more effectively promote the best interests of children than a diverse collection of government bureaucracies answering to an ever growing variety of powerful interest groups. Despite its apparent influence in 1939, the Children's Bureau's power diminished at a time when the federal government's role in protecting the social welfare of its citizens expanded. Apparently oblivious to the consequences of the changing political climate for the Children's Bureau, Katharine Lenroot continued to rely on the agency's past network of supporters. In addition, efforts to entice the backing of new groups, such as physicians, failed. Ironically, although the Children's Bureau acted as the chief architect of New Deal programs for children, the implementation of such plans undermined permanently its blueprint for protecting "a right to childhood."

8

"Children in a Democracy": The Children's Bureau and World War II, 1940-46

Hindsight provides a clear view of the Children's Bureau's weakened role and fading blueprint in its effort to protect "a right to childhood" by 1940. Nevertheless, the successful inclusion of programs for children in the second New Deal and the expanding role of the federal government at the onset of World War II served as a smoke screen which temporarily camouflaged the diminishing influence of the Children's Bureau and its "whole child" philosophy. From 1936 through 1940, federal grants authorized under the Social Security Act's maternal and child health, aid to handicapped children, and general child welfare programs rose 73 percent. Even more than during World War I, the new wartime crises highlighted the vulnerability of children and brought new attention to the federal agency mandated to investigate, report, and advocate on their behalf.

White House Conference on Children in a Democracy

Encouraged by new appropriations under the 1939 amendments to the Social Security Act and the implementation of the 1938 Fair Labor Standards Act, Children's Bureau chief Katharine Lenroot optimistically called the fourth White House conference on children. Unlike the 1930 conference, the meeting was organized and directed by the Children's Bureau. It was held January 18-20, 1940, in Washington, D.C., and was attended by 676 health professionals, child and family welfare bureaucrats, and interested academics. Frances Perkins acted as chair, Katharine Lenroot served as executive secretary, and Homer Folks headed the report committee. The meeting's theme, "Children in a Democracy," reflected attitudes held in the "phoney war" period, but specific topics were reminiscent of earlier White House conferences on children: attendees lauded the establishment of the economic and emotional security of children as the primary insurance for America's future; they embraced the middle-class family ideal as the "threshold of democracy," continued to call for ratification of the child labor amendment, and lamented rising juvenile delinquency rates, comparatively high maternal and infant mortality rates, and inadequate child health care.[1] Participants urged increased "social services for children with special needs" and claimed that the continuing lack of economic opportunities for many families remained an obstacle to the effort to provide "a right to childhood." While the conference was topically consistent with the past, the report also reflected new trends in child welfare reform strategies developed or expanded during the 1930s.

First, the report praised the federal role in New Deal child welfare programs. The report committee argued that "the complexities of modern life . . . require far-reaching modifications . . . in the relative responsibilities of local community, State, and Nation" and called for "more awareness of the Nation as a unit and of goals national in scope." Specifically this meant the expansion of federal-state aid grant programs designed to assure security for children and their families.[2]

Second, the Great Depression had revitalized Progressive Era arguments pointing to poverty as a threat to family stability and therefore child welfare. The conference report underscored the need for well-paying jobs for fathers so that mothers could remain at home with their young children, thereby helping to insure a "normal" homelife. During the 1920s, with the exception of a single study, the Children's Bureau had almost ignored the issue of poverty as a problem in child welfare. The onset of the Great Depression brought renewed attention to the conditions of poor children and their families and expanded the Children's Bureau's role beyond investigation, education, and advocacy. The 1940 White House conference furthered this trend and reestablished economic concerns as an important aspect of child welfare reform. Folks and his committee contended that "in the pursuit of happiness all men should have as nearly equal economic opportunity as their unequal natural endowment and the slow process of economic change permit." They found that despite an improving economy, "far too many American children belong to families that have no practical access to economic opportunity." They argued that federal contributions to relief programs should continue because "legal safeguards alone are not sufficient to insure liberty, unless the individual also has a reasonable degree of economic opportunity." Equal opportunity "is less easily provided in an industrial society than under pioneer conditions with unlimited free land."

The Great Depression had also altered attitudes about the federal government's responsibilities in the effort to secure the economic stability for families. Placing less stress on the importance of hard work and rugged individualism, the conference report held that poor children and their families "living in actual distress or in constant insecurity, are trapped in circumstances from which their knowledge and initiative cannot extricate them." Accordingly, only "outside help" could solve the problem of unequal economic opportunity. Families residing in rural areas, where half of the nation's children aged fifteen and under lived in 1940, appeared particularly vulnerable. Citing a 1934 U.S. Department of Agriculture study, the Folks committee reported that of 620,000 farm dwellings surveyed, 18 percent were more than fifty years old and very few had modern conveniences: only 18 percent had electricity, 17 percent had running water, 12 percent had bathtubs, and a mere 8 percent had central heating. To deal with such problems, the conferees advocated the continuation and expansion of federal housing and home loan programs, a rising minimum wage, laws safeguarding the right of collective bargaining, unemployment compensation, old age and survivors benefits, increased aid to dependent children, and higher public works spending in order to afford "flexible work programs for the unemployed." Therefore, "unless some other way, not yet suggested can be found, the Conference believes that the Federal Government will need to [take] steps to strengthen general-relief systems in the States, including standards of administration, through financial participation in these programs."[3] For these activists the federal government played a central part in the effort to provide "a right to childhood." But, as this discussion also reveals, the Children's Bureau no longer acted as the sole federal agency designated to deal with problems facing children and their families.

Third, the meeting placed a much greater emphasis on childhood education than earlier White House-sponsored child welfare conferences. Since its founding, the Children's Bureau had left the topics of schools and pedagogy to the Office of Education. Although concerned with the "whole child," by its silence on educational issues the Children's Bureau apparently signaled approval of the Office of Education's handling of such concerns. As Julia Lathrop testified before Congress many times during her tenure as chief, the Children's Bureau did not intend to "duplicate" work already being done by another federal agency. On the other hand, the Children's Bureau's jurisdiction over infant and maternal mortality was justified because the PHS, the federal agency normally associated with public health concerns, had ignored the problem. Whatever the reasoning, from the onset the exclusion of education from Children's Bureau responsibilities undermined the agency's "whole child" philosophy.

The inclusion of education in the 1940 conference reflected the modernization of traditional social welfare views, showed the "phoney war" atmosphere of the time, and further underscored the belief by many that the Children's Bureau was no longer the sole federal agency concerned with the nation's children. Many Americans suggested that schools should be used to counter threats to democracy brought about by the Great Depression and the apparent success of totalitarian governments in Europe and Asia. Conference participants looked to the Office of Education to encourage greater attention to schools and associated activities.[4] Exhibiting such notions, the report stated, "We wish to rear [American children] so that they may successfully participate in our democratic way of life. We seek to develop in them an appreciation of the expanding forms of civic responsibility and an understanding of the nature of social life and the satisfaction of cooperative enterprise." By the time of the conference, over 90 percent of American children had access to elementary schools and enrollment in secondary schools had doubled in every decade since 1890. But conference participants also worried about the time children spent outside of the classroom. Organized recreational and leisure time activities "should reflect the values that are implicit in the democratic way of life." Federal aid to schools, playgrounds, and recreational programs would encourage states to "equalize tax burdens" and reduce "educational inequities" especially for "minorities." Advocates believed that with the help of federal funding, states would be able to provide free schooling, libraries, and recreational facilities for children as young as three and youth up to twenty years of age.[5] The conference committee now deemed education, a field outside of the Children's Bureau's authority, a proper area of federal participation in the interest of the "whole child."

Fourth, the conference report reflected the new trend in child welfare policy of placing greater importance on children's emotional health. During the Progressive Era, World War I, and the 1920s discourse touting emotional security and the value of children for the future of democracy had resulted in protectionist legislation such as the Sheppard-Towner Maternity and Infancy Act, child labor legislation, and mothers' pension laws. This time, discussions about children's emotional security were also linked with political rhetoric common in the "phoney war" period and later to the cold war era. "It is essential to democracy," explained the report, "that self-respect and self-reliance, as well as respect for others and a cooperative attitude be fostered." However, responsibility for maintaining the ideal rested "not alone upon the care provided within the family, but also upon the safeguards and services provided by community, State, and *Nation* [emphasis added]." In order to help nuclear families provide the essentials necessary for the emotional security of their children, participants called for the continuation of federal housing programs for rural areas, government-subsidized loans for public housing projects in urban areas, "safeguarding of credit for housing purposes" in order to protect the availability of low interest mortgages for moderate income families, and "adequate regulatory laws . . . enforced by competent inspection departments in every city." Such programs were necessary, argued the report, because ideally "the single-family house with its own yard is unquestionably the best type." The house should include "indoor and outdoor play space, at least for children not old enough to reach recreational places unaccompanied by an older person, and accessibility to school, doctor, church, library facilities, recreational opportunities, and neighbors are important."[6] However, as noted by the Department of Agriculture study, few children lived in such a world and the housing needs created by the Great Depression intensified under wartime shortages in the years to come. New Deal programs alone could not possibly meet the needs of every family that diverged from this narrow model, which became the mainstay of postwar American suburban design.[7]

Another section of the report also foreshadowed postwar culture. For the first time a White House conference included discussions about organized religion's "proper" role in the lives of children. Here too the family and the community must take an active role. The report's authors complained that approximately half of the children and youth in the United States received no religious instruction outside of the home. Parents, teachers, and others responsible for guiding children "provide the occasions for vital and creative religion to function. Adult leaders of children should be persons of the utmost personal integrity and of the highest ideals who have themselves a vivid appreciation of spiritual values." In movies, the press, and on radio "religion should be treated frankly, openly, and objectively." This rhetoric included no effort to endorse a single organized church or doctrine, but instead urged that "churches and synagogues need to emphasize the common ends which they share . . . [and thereby] constitute a bulwark against factionalism and antagonism in local communities." Finally, the conference committee recommended that "a critical study be made . . . to discover how [to] provide a total program of education, without in any way violating the principle of the separation of church and state."[8] Religion could be used to secure the emotional health of children and to encourage conformity to "desired" values. "Good" American parents included church attendance as a part of the effort to provide the best environment for their children. The government, the community, and the media should fill this role if parents failed to do so. Reliance on organized religion as a source of morality and social stability was certainly nothing new. However, perhaps the economic crisis of the 1930s, which highlighted the divisive possibilities of a capitalist system, and the growing threats to democracy in Europe and Asia led those attending the 1940 White House conference to endorse organized religion, even at the risk of violating such a fundamental constitutional principle.

Ultimately, the 1940 White House conference offered little innovation in its recommended strategies for securing "a right to childhood." But the conference report clearly signaled a permanently altered role in child welfare policy for the federal government and the Children's Bureau. As the conference's summary concludes, the federal government now set standards *and* provided aid to "State and local groups interested in children for both war and post-war periods."[9] Although the Children's Bureau's staff organized the conference and the agency's chief served as the meeting's executive secretary, Lenroot did not use the meeting as a means to reinstate the agency's original "whole child" philosophy. In fact, this time conference attendees, unlike the Children's Bureau supporters who waged the bitter battle during the 1930 meeting, endorsed the idea that several federal agencies should share in the effort to secure "a right to childhood." Katharine Lenroot, Grace Abbott, and Martha Eliot had quietly complained when the bureau lost responsibility for the Social Security Act's ADC program in 1935. By 1940, Lenroot and her staff appeared resigned to the fact that the Children's Bureau now operated under a revised blueprint which dispersed responsibility for the administration of post-New Deal programs for children through several federal agencies. Instead of feeling threatened, it appears that the Children's Bureau and its supporters felt optimistic about the agency's future within the Roosevelt administration.

In a radio address broadcast on January 19, President Roosevelt heartily endorsed the conference report, but cautioned that "the Federal treasury has a bottom to it, and that mere grants in aid constitute no permanent solution to the problem of our health, our education, or our children." He urged, "we should address ourselves to two definite policies: first, to increase the average incomes in the poorer communities, in the poorer groups and in the poorer areas of the nation; and, second, to insist that every community should pay taxes in accordance with ability to pay." Roosevelt noted that he had recently read John Steinbeck's *Grapes of Wrath* and used the novel to promote his plan to resettle migrants to the Columbia Basin as the type of long-term solution he envisioned to help poor children and their families in America. He also endorsed the idea that religion and the nuclear family were the "threshold[s] of democracy." For mothers and babies the president hoped that "within the next ten years every part of the country . . . will have complete and adequate service for women during maternity and for all new-born infants. That we can do." Roosevelt asked "all our fellow citizens who are within the sound of my voice to consider themselves identified with the work of this Conference." He urged everyone "to study and discuss with friends and neighbors the program that it has outlined . . . [so that] the security and the happiness of every boy and girl in our land be our concern, our personal concern, from now on."[10]

The *New York Times* reported daily on the conference's activities and proclaimed "almost unprecedented zeal for the program of action which it proposes to implement." The newspaper judged that Frances Perkins "epitomized the sentiment reflected in pledges of cooperation from many of the largest and most influential organized groups of the nation" when she concluded, "This conference has been a demonstration of democracy in its finest sense. . . . The program which it contemplates is one which I predict will be worked upon not only for the ten years that will intervene before another conference is held, but for thirty years to come, when a new generation, pray God, is better born, better educated and better trained than any group of people that has ever walked the earth."[11]

The *American Journal of Public Health* explained that "because of the special emphasis put upon child health at the [White House] Conference in 1930, it was surprising to some delegates to find the emphasis so largely on subjects other than child health." But, this seemed reasonable because the first two White House conferences held in 1909 and 1919 had "treated health rather incidentally . . . as but one part of the interests of children in a democracy." Overall, the conference received positive reports and the *American Journal of Public Health* quoted Sadie Orr Dunbar, president of the General Federation of Women's Clubs, praising the meeting's efforts and follow-up program as "not a matter of creating new agencies . . . but of providing continuing sources of information and direction for existing agencies."[12] For all involved, effective child welfare policy meant cooperation among a variety of federal and state agencies.

The onset of war further disrupted the lives of American children and their families over the next five years. In response, the Children's Bureau developed and implemented programs based on its new blueprint "in an effort to cushion for children the effects of an emergency."[13]

The wartime emergency expanded the role of the federal government and therefore offered the Children's Bureau the opportunity to experiment within its altered status.

The U.S. Children's Bureau and Europe's Refugee Children during the War

During July and August 1939, the Children's Bureau's Elsa Castendyck, director of the agency's Delinquency Division and bureau representative to the League of Nations' Advisory Committee on Social Questions, visited Switzerland, France, Holland, and Great Britain in an effort to secure information about refugee children. She went to several refugee camps and collected data on a small number of children being cared for in Belgium. Castendyck found that private charities coordinated with haphazard government responses to provide services for families fleeing war zones. Some lived in camps and hostels, others were taken into private homes. Holland and Switzerland had received children from the anti-Semitic violence in Germany. Children from Spain primarily escaped to France. English authorities reported the most specific data. By early July 1939, the World Movement for the Care of Children from Germany (established in 1938) reported that 7,752 children (3,920 boys and 3,832 girls) had emigrated from "greater" Germany to England without their parents. Castendyck concluded that "without exception workers in all of the countries visited stressed the need of the United States offering some form of help, either financial or actual hospitality to these children."[14]

During the next year, several private charities located in the United States and Canada worked to stimulate public interest in the plight of European children living in war zones. The United States Committee for the Care of European Children (CCEC) was organized June 19, 1940, in New York City. Eleanor Roosevelt chaired the meeting and was named honorary president. The group elected department store mogul Marshall Field as acting president, and he also served as the organization's main fund-raiser. Members hoped to raise $5,000,000 to care for an anticipated 20,000 children they believed would come to the United States. But unlike the refugees fleeing from anti-Semitic violence identified in Castendyck's report, the CCEC expected most of those evacuated to the United States to be British. The group dismissed criticism of its "apparent unconcern for any but British children" by contending that its very name implied that it had been "set up to aid European children of whatever nationality." However, the CCEC said that "immigration regulations . . . tied its hands as far as any but British children are concerned [because] the new visas may be used only for those children whose country will guarantee to accept their return" after the war. This "practically eliminated the chances for bringing over children from any of the occupied countries or foreign children in England." The French and Belgian quotas were still open, so those children who could be granted visas to come to the United States under normal immigration policy, but each must have an individual sponsor guaranteeing support before arrival.[15]

After consulting with the Canadian government, which had already organized an evacuation plan for British children, the CCEC made the Children's Bureau responsible for maintaining "identifying records" for evacuated British children and for the "placement and supervision of [such] children to child-caring agencies" and foster families within the United States. Early on the group anticipated that perhaps as many as 15,000 children would be evacuated from Great Britain. In order to ease immigration procedures for such a potentially large group, the Children's Bureau coordinated its efforts with those of the Commission of Immigration and Naturalization, the Department of State, and the Department of Justice. By July 5, 1940, the CCEC ran 177 branches in communities throughout the United States and reported that according to Gallup polls and its own contacts "millions of persons in the United States were willing to provide hospitality for British children who might be evacuated to this country."[16]

On July 8, 1940, President Roosevelt wrote that he was "entirely sympathetic with the situation of the unfortunate refugees in the distressed areas of Europe" and that Eleanor had familiarized him with the CCEC's intentions. But he worried that visas were being issued faster than transportation for evacuated British children became available. A *Washington Daily News* editorial expressed similar sentiments by urging "let's save the children."[17] On July 14, 1940, the Department of Justice and the Department of State announced the adoption of simplified procedures for the admission of children from war zones. The new regulations applied only to children under sixteen years of age who sought to enter the United States "to escape the dangers of war" and did not specify British or southwestern European children, but apparently few Jewish and no Asian or African children ever entered under the program. "Refugee" children could come to the United States on either visitors' or quota visas with the accompaniment of a "corporate affidavit" from an organization such as the CCEC stating that the child would not become a public charge. Groups such as the CCEC were required to form a fifty dollar trust fund for each child, pay an eight dollar "head tax," and pay a $2.50 visa charge. Sponsors were asked to pay these fees and an additional $2.50 to cover the cost of a personal credit investigation. Any charitable corporation acting under the new regulations must be approved by the attorney general and assure that children under its care would be maintained "in conformity with the standards of the Children's Bureau of the Department of Labor."[18]

In January 1941, the CCEC reported that 1001 refugee children had arrived in the United States and claimed 900 under its auspices. Most of the rest entered with "consular affidavits" or private sponsorship. The CCEC discouraged the immigration of children outside of CCEC authority because, it claimed, some independent sponsors later wished to be relieved of their responsibilities. For example, a man telephoned the CCEC asking for aid in placing a two-year-old child who had come to live with his grandparents. The grandfather died and the grandmother could no longer afford to keep the child. Another case involved two Jewish girls, fifteen and nine, sponsored by their uncle. According to the CCEC, almost immediately the uncle wrote his sister, the girls' mother, expressing dissatisfaction with the situation. The mother appealed to the American Committee in London. The problem seemed to arise from the fact that the girls were Jewish. Their uncle, although a Jew, had married a gentile and kept his ancestry unknown to the community. He repeatedly wired his sister demanding that the girls be removed from his home.[19] Neither the Children's Bureau or the CCEC reported such problems with the children directly placed under CCEC auspices. But, as noted earlier, the group generally limited its assistance to British evacuees. Anti-Semitism, official immigration policy, the fall of France to the Nazis, and ethnic prejudices probably made it initially easier and politically popular for the CCEC to focus its efforts on British children. U.S. immigration policy contained no special provisions for admittance of "refugees" until passage of the 1948 Displaced Persons Act. As Roger Daniels has shown, when Felix Frankfurter or Raymond Moley asked Franklin Roosevelt to send representatives to a 1936 League of Nations conference on Jewish and non-Jewish refugees, the president instead followed the advice of Secretary of State Cordell Hull, who said "there is no latitude left to the Executive to discuss questions concerning the legal status of aliens. It does not appear advisable, therefore, for the Government to place itself in the position of even appearing to have any authority or discretion in connection with the status of other than American citizens." In two other incidents in 1935 and 1936 Roosevelt expressed "sympathetic interest" for the plight of those fleeing Nazi aggression but in reality ignored evidence that German Jews were having difficulty getting visas from American consulates in Germany. In fact, Roosevelt's Department of State made it difficult for most refugees to enter the United States, and during the war the Children's Bureau, like the rest of the Roosevelt administration, generally ignored the crisis facing many European children, especially Jews.[20]

Even the evacuation of British children became increasingly difficult. By January 1941 the CCEC concluded that "the outlook for a mass evacuation of children from either Great Britain or Southwestern Europe is virtually unsurmountable,"[21] as growing submarine activity threatened the safety of all ships traveling from England to the United States. Although many fewer than American authorities had expected, more than eight thousand unaccompanied European children came to the States during the war. Of those, five thousand were British evacuees. By April 1945 about thirty-five hundred such children had returned to England. Most of the others had immigrated from Germany and Austria, and the majority of these children returned to Europe by the summer of 1945. A minority from both groups became U.S. citizens. The Children's Bureau claimed that "placing these children [during the war] required the highest skill of child-welfare workers," but concluded that "in most of the placements, the difficulties were met and overcome and the boy or girl was soon taking his place with other children in the family, the school, the church or synagogue, and the community."[22]

In October 1945, the United Nations' Relief and Rehabilitation Administration reported that about 100,000 children under fourteen years of age resided in refugee camps in Germany. Many of these children were Polish, Hungarian, and Romanian Jews. Some were with relatives but about 3,800 unaccompanied children lived in camps in the American and British zones. The CCEC made plans to bring up to 2,000 of these children to the United States. President Harry Truman issued a directive on December 22, 1945, concerning displaced persons and refugees, thereby assisting the CCEC as well as other groups. Overall, the United States admitted about 450,000 immigrants from 1948 to 1953 as "displaced persons." Many of the children sponsored by the CCEC after 1945 were concentration camp survivors, of whom 80 percent were adolescents and therefore difficult to place. By March 31, 1948, the CCEC and the Children's Bureau reported that 1,275 refugee children had arrived in the United States and lived in homes in thirty separate states.[23] Little is known about the circumstances of these arrivals once they reached their new homes and neither the CCEC nor the Children's Bureau conducted any follow-up work.

The Children's Bureau's cooperation with the CCEC was consistent with its past efforts on the international level. Although mandated "to investigate and report" primarily on children in the United States, the Children's Bureau had been somewhat concerned with the development of international policies for children and youth since World War I. Julia Lathrop, Grace Abbott, Katharine Lenroot, and members of the Children's Bureau staff served as advisors to the League of Nations on child welfare issues and as representatives at the various Pan American conferences held since 1916. But the agency's World War II experience through its efforts with the CCEC and participation during the same period in maternal and child health programs with other nations in the Americas established the Children's Bureau as an official participant in the international child welfare field. During the postwar years, the United Nations, the World Health Organization, and the U.S. Department of State called upon the Children's Bureau to assist in furthering international efforts in refugee relocation and maternal and child health programs.[24]

The Children's Bureau and World War II on the Home Front

On the domestic scene, the Roosevelt administration's general wartime mobilization effort also underscored the federal role in child welfare. Approximately a year after the war began in Europe and about two months after the initiation of a draft in the United States, the Children's Bureau began to plan for the possible effects of World War II on American children. On December 20, 1940, Katharine Lenroot wrote Eleanor Roosevelt thanking the first lady for her interest in the Children's Bureau and stating that she felt encouraged by the administration's general concern for social welfare issues. As noted previously, Eleanor Roosevelt served as a sympathetic and influential lobbyist for the Children's Bureau within the White House. But changes brought on by the war abroad stretched the resources of Lenroot's agency and that of state child welfare departments to the limit. Lenroot also feared that gains achieved through the New Deal might be rescinded if the United States was drawn into the war. The chief asked Eleanor Roosevelt to urge the president to request "greater resources" for the Children's Bureau in order to "enable it more fully to serve children in the present critical period, and to strengthen the permanent services for children for which a foundation has been so strongly laid through the Social Security program." She reported "first-hand evidence of needs of mothers and children arising out of defense measures, and urgent requests for assistance in developing State and local resources to meet them."[25]

Lenroot cited several field reports and requests from state officials to show some of the problems exacerbated by the nation's "defense measures." For example, the state health officer in Georgia confronted problems in communities near the four large military encampments in his state. Worst of all, the construction of Camp Stewart, located about forty miles north of Savannah, had attracted 22,000 workmen and their families to Hinesville, a town of 450 people. The construction workers and their families lived in tents, trailers, and large conduits normally used in drainage and sewer construction. Others had no protection from the elements and simply did "as best they can" out-of-doors. No sanitary facilities for the transients existed, and Hinesville had only one public toilet. Making the situation worse, Camp Stewart was located in "the worst malarial district in Georgia." He also reported another familiar concern, "prostitution, is an ever present problem at each of the camps." The official warned the Children's Bureau's chief that he urgently needed more nursing and medical care personnel. State directors in Mississippi, Virginia, and California told similar stories about urban and rural military districts in their states. Another problem concerned areas where military camps were already built. There, increased population made maternal and child welfare funds supplied through the Social Security Act wholly inadequate or unavailable to many who needed aid. For example, California law required three years' residence in the state and one year's residence in the county for eligibility for county-provided medical care. A San Diego official explained that "in the past [the] Army and Navy have supplied medical services including maternity care to families of officers but usually not to families of privates. Now even officers' wives must seek private care." Lenroot estimated that the Children's Bureau required an additional appropriation of $28,000,000 to meet the various states' maternal and child health needs.[26] Health care was only one problem exacerbated by the war. The Children's Bureau's experience during World War I revealed that many other social welfare concerns affected children on the home front.

Acknowledging the Children's Bureau's past experience and federal jurisdiction, in February 1941 President Roosevelt named Martha Eliot to the United States Defense Mission to Great Britain. While in England, Eliot helped to devise strategies to deal with the war's effects on children. The Children's Bureau hoped that the program devised by child welfare officials in that country might serve as a model for American civil defense policy concerning children if the United States entered the war. Eliot's report, completed in April 1941, focused on the effects of warfare ("bombardment") and the British evacuation program on children and adolescents.[27] She produced an interesting study of governmental responses to perceived emotional and physical effects of war on children mainly by conducting interviews with British government officials, local authorities, and representatives from volunteer organizations. She also observed children in day nurseries and clinics, and those participating in evacuation plans. Eliot concluded that because the British government had instituted an extensive social welfare program during the previous twenty years, British children had an advantage over young people in the United States if a similar crisis occurred. She warned that "the relative inadequacy in the United States of facilities and services for child health and welfare and maternity care, especially in small cities, towns, and rural areas, and the greater distances between cities and potential reception areas make our problem of planning for the protection of children a far greater one than that encountered in England."

Eliot also felt that greater numbers of mothers entering the work force and rising juvenile delinquency rates were other "problems" escalated by wartime circumstances. Here again she cautioned that much needed to be done in the United States, urging that "advance planning, advance preparation, and advance training of personnel should be undertaken at once." Eliot believed that early preparation, coordination, and a general commitment to children's welfare on the part of government officials had helped to reduce deaths and lessen the war's terrible social effects on British children. She credited the British Women's Voluntary Services, organized in June 1938, with playing a major role in civil defense and children's protection. Eliot concluded that the protection of children in wartime was a complicated matter which demanded inventive strategies.[28] Armed with the results of Eliot's study, Lenroot and the Children's Bureau staff felt well qualified to develop plans for American children threatened by wartime conditions.

Other government officials agreed. On May 29, 1941, Charles P. Taft, a conservative Republican from Cincinnati and then head of the Office of the Coordinator of Health, Welfare, and Related Defense Activities, recognized the Children's Bureau as the "appropriate agency to develop . . . comprehensive plans for assuring proper safeguards to children whose health and well being are of primary importance in the program of national defense." Taft asked Lenroot to assign a member of the Children's Bureau's staff to his office as a "liaison officer in matters relating to children." Lenroot quickly consented, naming her assistant, Charles I. Schottland, as liaison to Taft's office. As a next step, Lenroot hoped that the Children's Bureau could quickly sponsor a Washington conference designated to deal with a variety of issues relating to child welfare and defense. Nevertheless, as the chief explained, "time was pressing and [the] subject of children of working mothers seemed to be one on which there was need for very prompt consideration." Consequently, the Children's Bureau hastily organized the Conference on Day Care of Children of Working Mothers, held in Washington, D.C., July 31-August 1, 1941.[29]

As shown previously, the shortage of affordable quality day care for children was not a new problem. But since its founding, the Children's Bureau had argued that only mothers who were "forced" to work for wages should do so. During the 1930s, economic need had driven many married women into the paid labor force. But like most people in the United States, the Children's Bureau continued to reject the idea that it was proper for mothers with young children to work outside of the home. In 1930, 8 percent of mothers with children under ten years of age worked for wages. During the Great Depression, Congress had funded the Works Progress Administration's (WPA) Lanham Act, which provided federal funds to establish day nurseries. But the Lanham Act was primarily a welfare measure designed to furnish jobs for unemployed teachers and other child welfare workers. The program's benefits for working mothers and their children were secondary or even nonexistent in the minds of many. The placement of the first federal day care program with the WPA, and not the Children's Bureau, is one indication of the general attitude concerning such programs.

In addition, as a lobbyist for children, the Children's Bureau did not view such programs favorably. The bureau's attitude simply reflected its times. Although a minority touted the positive effects of day care and mothers working outside of the home, public sentiment against day care, the employment of married women in general, and specifically of mothers with young children strengthened during the 1930s. A 1936 public opinion poll reported that 82 percent of those questioned (including 75 percent of the women) believed that wives should not work for wages if their husbands had jobs. Support for laws prohibiting the employment of women dropped to 56 percent if the husband's earnings were less than $1,000 per year, but this statistic still reflects strong resistance to the employment of married women, even those from poor families.[30] Census data, unavailable to those attending the Children's Bureau's summer 1941 conference, shows that in 1940, only 7.8 percent of all mothers with children under ten worked outside of the home, and the rate for mothers of children under six rose only from 9 percent to 12 percent during the war.[31] But to their credit, Lenroot and those attending the bureau's 1941 conference anticipated an increase in the employment of mothers. Clearly, manufacturers in the United States were already beginning to relax their prohibitions against the employment of wives and preliminary census data showed that more than two million American women had joined the paid labor force since 1930. In addition, the Children's Bureau knew that employment rates among women between the ages of twenty-five and forty-four rose from 25.4 percent in 1930 to 30.2 percent in 1940. This data, coupled with Eliot's discovery of rising employment rates among women in Great Britain, led the Children's Bureau to warn that a rise in the employment of mothers in the United States was inevitable.

Mary Anderson, director of the U.S. Women's Bureau, agreed. She maintained that "since the defense emergency . . . married women are now by some employers taken in preference to any others because they feel that when the emergency is over these married women can be discharged much more easily." Anderson recognized that employed mothers were a growing reality and it seems logical that she would advocate the establishment of government-funded day care facilities. Instead, Anderson endorsed the Children's Bureau's condemnation of this growing practice and maintained in her report to the Children's Bureau's conference on day care, "I do not think that the employment of women with small children is necessary at the present time." Anderson stated that no community should encourage employers to establish nurseries within factories or "urge . . . that women with small children go to work unless it was absolutely necessary." She later modified her stand, but in 1941 the Women's Bureau and the Children's Bureau both rejected the notion of mothers with young children working outside of the home. However, mandated to investigate and lobby on behalf of the "whole child," the Children's Bureau could not ignore its past studies showing that some mothers were "forced" by economic necessity to take jobs outside of the home. "We don't want to get employment managers to thinking in terms of discriminating against mothers with children," Lenroot cautioned, "because even with reference to such mothers the individual situation determines what should be done." Therefore, the bureau recommended that communities where mothers *must* be employed develop day care services for children over two years of age. Underlying the assumption that only mothers forced to work outside the home would do so, Lenroot argued that day care "activities should be integrated with the whole community program for public and private family assistance."[32]

Linking day care to poverty, the Children's Bureau's policy stigmatized working mothers who put their children in day care facilities and failed to recognize the reality for many children and their families. In August 1942, the War Manpower Commission issued its "Policy on Employment in Industry of Women with Young Children." Influenced by the Children's Bureau and its supporters, the commission maintained that "the first responsibility of women with young children, in war as in peace, is to give suitable care in their own homes to their children." The Office of Defense, Health, and Welfare Services did receive $400,000 from the President's Emergency Fund in order to provide grants to states for local "advisory services," but the agency did not use the money to operate day care centers. During the war, 1.5 million mothers, 12.1 percent of women with children under ten years of age, entered the paid labor force.[33] Despite this circumstance, the Children's Bureau continued to advocate policies making it difficult for mothers with young children to work outside the home and negatively stigmatizing those who choose to do so. Child welfare experts feared that employed mothers would neglect their children, a situation which they believed resulted in antisocial behavior and eventually emotionally unstable adults.[34] In 1942 the Children's Bureau established standards for day nurseries, but maintained that "mothers of preschool children and especially of those under 2 years of age *should not be encouraged* to seek employment; children of these ages should in general be cared for by their mothers and in their homes."[35]

Even as the wartime labor shortage intensified, the Children's Bureau continued to ignore reality. In July 1944, the Children's Bureau sponsored another conference on day care attended by psychiatrists, nursery school educators, and child welfare and child development professionals who evaluated how the needs of children under two years of age could be met as more of their mothers took jobs in the wartime economy. Again, these authorities contended that "every effort must be made to preserve for the baby his right to have care from his mother." But faced with the fact that increasing numbers of such mothers entered the labor force every day, conference attendees insisted that foster family day care was preferable to group care for children under three years of age and that the minimum age for admission to group care should be fixed at "2½ to 3 years."[36] While this policy moved closer to the real situation faced by many families, such statements still contributed to popularly held negative stereotypes of working mothers. Martha Eliot had reported during the bureau's 1942 conference that the British government had a policy "stimulating" the establishment of day nurseries in industrial areas and approved of such efforts. But, throughout the war, the Children's Bureau did not feel the need or desire for similar facilities in the United States. As Susan Hartmann has shown, "it was married women with children who faced the most social disapprobation" during the war years if they worked outside the home. Despite Lenroot's contention to the contrary, women who sought employment were often questioned about their provisions for the care of their children, "a practice recommended by government officials."

Children also lost. Employed mothers, fearing negative judgment from others, most often avoided the issue by securing the services of a family member or neighbor, or by leaving a child unattended at home or even in the family car parked in the factory lot. Children left home alone were called "latch-key kids" or "eight hour orphans" by the press. The few existing public day care centers were frequently overcrowded, substandard, and charged high fees. Daily costs ranged from fifty to seventy-five cents, nearly one-tenth of a typical day's wage. The Census Bureau estimated in 1944 that 2.75 million mothers working outside of their homes had 4.5 million children under age fourteen. The problem was at its peak in 1945, when 1,600,000 children were enrolled in federally subsidized nursery schools and day care centers. Organizers poorly coordinated hours of operation with factory shifts, costs remained high, and facilities were often located far from the workplace, making it undesirable or impossible for workers to use the centers. Many mothers had real or imagined fears about the shortcomings of group care. Consequently, despite the need, federally funded and private group-care facilities remained underutilized. Children's Bureau's policies contributed to this circumstance.[37]

The Children's Bureau's traditional attitude about day care was consistent with past policies and somewhat understandable for its times. However, child welfare activists outside the Children's Bureau offered more realistic and innovative solutions. For example, Henry L. Zucker, a child welfare advocate and member of the national advisory committee on day care of the Child Welfare League of America, estimated that on April 18, 1944, there were 16,850,000, women employed outside the home, including approximately 2,000,000 mothers with small children. Zucker sympathized with women who sought employment and believed that they did so for emotional as well as economic reasons. He agreed with the Children's Bureau that ample evidence existed to suggest that "large numbers of children are being neglected while parents are working." However, he argued that "though some small children, particularly those under two years, should not be separated from their parents for a considerable part of the day, others can be separated without serious effect." Furthermore, Zucker insisted that "most mothers do, in fact, exercise sound judgment about the care of their children. . . . [and he urged that] the logical person to judge the propriety of a mother's working is the mother herself." Consequently, Zucker maintained that a day care program should first be thought of "less as a means of releasing womanpower for war work and more as a service to children whose mothers, for good, bad, or indifferent reasons, are at work." Furthermore, an extensive public education program relative to what constituted good day care might publicize existing but underutilized centers. Above all, "a substantial number of children are suffering deprivations because of the employment of both parents, and for many of these children the emergency child care program would offer some compensation."[38]

Despite the Children's Bureau's policies, wartime labor shortages led to an expansion of day care services.[39] Finally in early 1945 the Children's Bureau varied slightly from its stance by recommending "supervised homemaker service . . . [as the] best solution" to the day care problem for women with young children. The basic idea was nothing new. During the 1920s a few state and local welfare departments established homemaker services (temporary domestic and child care help). At that time advocates contended that a supervised homemaker service acted as an alternative to foster care and as "one way to preserve family life for children in homes where the death of the mother or her absence because of illness had disrupted the normal family life and created serious problems in the care of the children." It is interesting that monetary assistance through aid to families with dependent children or mothers' pensions was judged adequate to replace absent fathers, but the absence of mothers required a female stand-in. A variety of factors, including high costs, a limited pool of "trained" workers, and general resistance to the idea of assigning public employees to work in private homes, hindered the success of such programs. Such an idea intended to fill the nation's children's growing need for adequate day care during World War II was even less pragmatic. High wages in industry and other types of production-based employment created a shortage of domestic and other service workers. As Sherna Gluck explains, especially "for many black women, the war was a turning point. The expansion of jobs in the defense industries, coupled with Roosevelt's executive order prohibiting discrimination in hiring, helped black women get out of the white women's kitchens." Furthermore, the cost of such a program remained much higher than group care, an alternative already excessive for most parents. Basically, despite the problem, the Children's Bureau continued to cling to its 1941 day care recommendations.[40] In the case of child care, the Children's Bureau did not use the model established in Britain and instead provided inadequate solutions to pressing wartime conditions, thereby neglecting the needs of many American children throughout the war.

Within one month following the close of the Children's Bureau's 1941 conference on day care, the United States entered World War II. In the months that followed, trends identified in Martha Eliot's study of the war's impact on children in Britain became increasingly apparent in the United States. As Lenroot had hoped, on March 16-18, 1942, the Children's Bureau held the first of three annual meetings of the National Commission on Children in Wartime. Sixty child welfare professionals and "lay" individuals, all chosen by the Children's Bureau, were instructed to identify and recommend programs to "safeguard" children. At its first meeting the commission adopted a "Children's Charter in Wartime" which guided bureau policies throughout the war. In "patriotic" language typical of the period, this document states that "both as a wartime responsibility and as stepping stones to our future . . . we call upon citizens, young and old, to join together to . . . guard children from injury in danger zones, protect children from neglect, exploitation and undue strain in defense areas, strengthen . . . home life . . . , [and] conserve, equip, and free children of every race and creed to take their part in democracy." The president of the Child Welfare League of America, Leonard Mayo, served as the commission's chair. Mayo appointed an executive committee which included the heads of nine of the thirteen Children's Bureau advisory committees.[41]

Consistent with the Children's Bureau's New Deal responsibilities, Mayo's executive committee recommended programs that could be undertaken through the Social Security Act's Title V provisions. These included the "appropriate immunization of all children against communicable disease, . . . helping children to meet the anticipation and realities of wartime," and the endorsement of plans for the "evacuation of children from danger zones" designated under the civil defense program. Above all, urged the committee, "children [should be] first in all plans for protection."[42] As time progressed it also became apparent that the bureau could expand its maternal and child health responsibilities through the Title V program.

Initially the Children's Bureau planned to investigate and report on the circumstances of American children in wartime so that parents and communities could devise programs to protect "a right to childhood." However, soon after the United States entered the war, all federal agencies dropped research programs which could not be justified as contributing directly to the war effort. This resulted in a weakening of the Children's Bureau's original mandate to "investigate and report." Children's Bureau researcher Dorothy Bradbury noted in 1962 that "never since the war years has the Bureau recovered its research program."[43] After 1942, the Children's Bureau relied more than ever on information supplied by other federal agencies, state and local child welfare departments, and private organizations. In addition, as Lenroot had feared in 1941, the federal government reduced its social welfare contributions during the war.

Hence, much of the Children's Bureau's wartime work, and that undertaken in the postwar period, centered on advice literature and media presentations. As it had done during World War I, the Children's Bureau stepped up its efforts to promote good maternal and child health care, urged children to stay in school, designed programs to reduce juvenile delinquency, and developed minimum standards for the employment of youth under eighteen who joined the labor force. During 1942-43, the Children's Bureau produced a series of radio broadcasts entitled "Children in Wartime" and also worked with magazines and newspapers to bring public attention to the physical and emotional needs of children on the home front.[44]

Unlike its advice during World War I, the Children's Bureau, obviously influenced by the 1940 White House conference and general trends in child welfare, this time also emphasized the psychological impact of wartime conditions on children and their families. A 1942 publication, "To Parents in Wartime," justified this attention to children's emotional needs because "as armies march, planes fly, ships sail, and factories hum with the tremendous effort of total war, the security, the protection, and the morale of families at home are fundamental to our success." Accordingly, parents could take solace in the fact that "nowhere in the world have children held the place of prime importance in the scheme of living and in the thoughts and consideration of adults as in the United States." It also offered reassurance that "children are as much a concern of our Government in this emergency as are the soldiers and munitions workers who carry on the war directly." The Children's Bureau provided two principal suggestions for parents: (1) prepare yourselves to face whatever may come, and (2) help your children to continue living their everyday lives with as little change as possible. In order to accomplish the second goal, the bureau advocated honesty as the best policy and warned, "above all, don't suppress or banish from family conversation all reference to war." Besides, argued the Children's Bureau, "We have more deaths from automobile accidents than England had from air raids in the same length of time." But recognizing that the war disrupted "normal" family life, the Children's Bureau maintained that fathers absent from the home "can still remain in the thoughts and conversations as an important part of the children's lives and an essential part of the family itself." Parents were urged to allow their children to express their fears frankly. Advice varied somewhat according to a child's age. The Children's Bureau prescribed care, patience, and personal comfort for small children. Grade-school children needed such assurances too, but the older ones might also view the war with "considerable excitement and fun." For example, the bureau suggested that the "time-honored game of prisoner's based *[sic]* cops and robbers" would likely be changed to the real life excitement of "air raids and ambulance and stretcher drills and real war games." But when away from their "gang," cautioned the bureau, grade-school children might be subject to "daydreams and nightmares of very real terror." Their fears could be lessened by giving them productive "duties and responsibilities." Adolescents offered a special challenge. They, "more than any other group in the community," are likely to have their lives "profoundly changed and their difficulties increased by war. . . . Little as we are likely to think so," insisted the Children's Bureau, "the adolescent group is going to require our understanding and support as much as the other two." During wartime adolescents are forced to "grow up almost overnight." Some might quit school to join the military or choose early marriage. Others, due to the rising availability of jobs, become economically independent at a much earlier age. "Parents," warned the Children's Bureau, "cannot expect the same rules and behavior to be maintained now as in other days." This sensitivity to the emotional needs of children and adolescents was virtually absent from the agency's World War I Children's Year program, and the change reflects the growing influence of child psychology.[45]

Another concern on the home front, juvenile delinquency, seemed a more difficult problem. As earlier bureau efforts had indicated, there was no comprehensive data available to accurately determine national juvenile crime rates. But, as previous chapters have shown, there was a rising public interest in juvenile delinquency by the 1930s and the war years brought even more attention to the issue. By one count, in just the first half of 1943 an estimated twelve hundred articles on the subject appeared in national magazines. Apparently, many people felt that the wartime disruption of the family and local community further encouraged antisocial behavior among the nation's young people. Despite the fact that only 1 to 2 percent of all adolescents appeared before the nation's juvenile courts on delinquency charges, the press sensationalized stories of youthful violence.[46] For example, in 1942, hundreds of national newspapers reported the murder of a New York City schoolteacher by "zoot-suited" adolescents. In another article the *New York Times* contended that more than five hundred youth gangs armed with brass knuckles, blackjacks, broken bottles, ice picks, and guns made from four-inch pipe roamed that city's streets. As Steven Mintz and Susan Kellogg maintain, "most observers believed that the war had weakened traditional controls on the young and heightened the problem of rearing responsible and well-adjusted young people."[47]

Mirroring this popular notion, Lenroot and her staff urged that under wartime stresses American youth faced greater risk of perpetrating antisocial behavior. The Children's Bureau based its conclusions on research conducted during World War I, an ongoing study concerning juvenile delinquency begun in 1937 in St. Paul, Minnesota, and Eliot's 1941 fieldwork completed in Great Britain.[48] In 1943 the agency used 1940-43 data reported by four hundred juvenile courts to estimate juvenile delinquency trends in the United States. In the eighty-two reporting courts serving communities with populations of at least 100,000 the agency found a 52.1 percent increase in the number of juvenile delinquency cases. The greatest rise, 59.3 percent, occurred in thirty-eight war production centers. Population growth alone did not seem to explain this increase. There was a 40.5 percent rise in the forty-four towns and counties in the sample with stable or declining populations.[49]

In December 1943, Katharine Lenroot argued before the Senate Committee on Education and Labor that wartime conditions escalated social problems contributing to antisocial behavior among young people. The bureau's St. Paul project showed that both minor and more serious delinquent behavior in children could be prevented and corrected with the effective use of adequately funded community-based social services for children and their families. But wartime conditions threatened such services. Lenroot also maintained that children awaiting court action experienced delays for "considerable periods of time" and their situations were more "tragic than usual." In November 1943 and May 1944, the Children's Bureau sponsored conferences in Washington, D.C., on training police to work with young people. Lenroot called on parents, community agencies, and the federal government to unite in rescuing "the hundreds of children in jail, the thousands on the threshold of jail, and the many more thousands who are in danger of tangling with the law because grown-ups have neglected their needs." Highlighting the possible consequences of neglect, Federal Bureau of Investigation director J. Edgar Hoover contended that conditions on the home front set the stage for a postwar crime wave led by youngsters deprived of a stable homelife.[50]

In this atmosphere, the Children's Bureau implemented a wartime program designed to define, discover the causes of, and control juvenile delinquency. During its first three decades of work the Children's Bureau had held that strong child labor laws, compulsory school attendance legislation, and standardized juvenile court systems went hand in hand with family assistance programs to secure a reduction in juvenile delinquency rates. The Children's Bureau maintained that there was no single cause for delinquent behavior but that instead a combination of factors led to rising instances of juvenile crime.[51]

Therefore, to Lenroot and like-minded individuals, the wartime emergency was exactly the wrong time to cut back child welfare programs, educational services, or loosen child labor restrictions. Rationing of other activities might be necessary, but as Secretary Perkins argued, reductions in child welfare efforts would result in the country's "winning the war but losing the peace." According to the Children's Bureau, "in wartime, as in peacetime, juvenile delinquency results from our failure to satisfy the basic needs of children and youth—the need for security and the opportunity for growth and achievement."[52] Nevertheless, wartime conditions seemed to create social circumstances which contributed to the problem. An increasing number of fathers were absent from home because of military service or distant war work. Mothers working in wartime employment, and therefore away from home for most of the day, gave children the opportunity for activities that might lead to "unacceptable behavior." Rising youth employment rates, "in many instances under unwholesome conditions that impede their growth, limit their educational progress, or expose them to moral hazards," encouraged a "premature sense of independence" on the part of some youth. Widespread migration of families to crowded centers of war industry uprooted children from familiar surroundings and subjected them to life in communities overtaxed by population increases. The bureau also believed that wartime prosperity had led to the establishment of more "dance halls, beer parlors, and other 'attractions' that flourish in industrial centers near military establishments . . . [and] frequently exert a harmful influence on youth." And finally, "the general spirit of excitement and adventure aroused by war and the tension, anxiety, an apprehension felt by many parents or other adults are reflected in restlessness, defiance, emotional disturbances, and other negative forms of behavior on the part of children and young people." Lenroot and her staff believed that the primary responsibility for children and youth rested with parents, but wartime conditions had placed a special strain on families. "Hence," concluded the Children's Bureau, "the community, now more than ever, has responsibility to assist parents in fulfilling their obligations toward their own children." As part of an overall program to protect "a right to childhood," Lenroot and her staff encouraged, communities with the help of federal and state government must develop services to combat juvenile delinquency.[53]

During the war, although limited by research restrictions, the Children's Bureau gathered information concerning juvenile delinquency from local officials in ten cities with war industries or military facilities. The agency published its findings in the March 1944 issue of the *Survey*. None of the communities were prepared for the population influx experienced during the war and in each, authorities were concerned with what appeared to be increasing instances of antisocial behavior among young people. Reports included "boisterous boys and girls" congregating on corners, girls thirteen and fourteen years old strolling along late at night in twos and threes and sometimes even alone, and rising instances of runaway children and truancy.[54] For girls, the primary concern centered on sexual misconduct. Indeed, as several historians have shown, premarital pregnancy, illegitimacy, and venereal disease rates did rise during the war. Due to the era's popular perceptions of the unwritten codes defining proper sexual behavior, adolescent girls seemed particularly vulnerable to the relaxed sexual standards of the period. Girls and young women who frequented areas around military bases and liberty centers were popularly called "khacky-whacky girls, victory or V girls, or good time Charlottes."[55] The Children's Bureau found a 47.3 percent increase in the number of boys charged with delinquency, but a 76 percent rise in the number of girls' cases disposed of by local juvenile courts. Although five times less likely to be arrested than boys, adolescent girls, argued the Children's Bureau, posed a particular problem in war industry and military centers. Not surprisingly, the vast majority of females brought before the local juvenile courts were charged with sex delinquency or disorderly conduct.[56] Memphis juvenile court judge Camille Kelley reported similar data in a study conducted in 1941. Kelley stated that twenty-one of the twenty-six white children appearing before the Memphis juvenile court on sex delinquency charges were girls. It is also interesting to note that of the twenty-four black children appearing before the court on the same charge, only thirteen were girls.[57]

As previously noted, gender had historically played a significant role in juvenile delinquency charges and court decisions. It is probable that adolescent boys also experienced greater sexual freedom during the war. Popular culture notes that young men in the military had few restraints over their sexual behavior. But many young men outside of the military also experienced a lessening of parental authority and greater sexual freedom that generally went unpunished by local authorities. For example, one seventeen-year-old male described his experience in a war industries town as "a real sex paradise." He explained, "the plant and the town were full of working girls who were on the make. Where I was, a male war worker became the center of loose morality." A male high school student reported that he had sex with a married thirty-year-old woman whose husband was overseas. "We weren't in love," he contended, "the times were just conducive for this sort of thing." Such behavior for girls was condemned as promiscuous or defined as statutory rape. It is also likely that male prostitution rates rose during the war. However, that topic, like homosexuality, was rarely discussed by community leaders or the popular press. Enveloped by the sexual double standard of the time, the Children's Bureau and other authorities ignored or dismissed "improper" sexual activity committed by young males.[58] In fact, there is no discussion of adolescent male sexual behavior in the Children's Bureau studies on wartime juvenile delinquency.

However, although lacking sensitivity to gender influences, the Children's Bureau did recognize that race and class affected juvenile delinquency rates.[59] Throughout the United States, about one-fifth of male delinquency cases and approximately one-fourth of the female delinquency cases involved blacks. This is a rate almost twice the proportion of blacks in the total population. Furthermore, as the bureau acknowledged, "many delinquents come from families whose financial status is insecure."[60] But perhaps not wanting to irritate local officials or question community standards, the Children's Bureau failed to suggest that authorities were more likely to arrest adolescents and children new to a community than those native to the area, or that blacks were more likely to be arrested than whites. Indeed, the tremendous influx of "outsiders" and the resentment felt toward these newcomers and their children may have further contributed to the perception of increased antisocial behavior among young people. The Children's Bureau did identify transient and runaway youth as a particular problem, but did not conclude that the war intensified the situation. Instead, the agency maintained that the reasons why "runaways" left home were likely much the same as in the past. But, as the Children's Bureau argued, opportunities for work, a greater mobility, "the restlessness of youth," desires for the "excitement of living in the vicinity of service camps and other crowded war centers" combined with the "lessening of parental supervision due to the absence of parents in the armed forces and increased employment of mothers" to make the problem of juvenile delinquency "sizeable" during the war years. Few states provided funds for the return of runaways to their homes; juvenile courts assisted by local Travelers' Aid societies attempted to deal with the circumstance. The Children's Bureau reported increasing problems with runaway youths ("children" from age eight to twenty-one) in Arkansas, Alabama, California, Florida, Kentucky, Michigan, Massachusetts, Ohio, Oklahoma, Pennsylvania, Tennessee, and Wisconsin.[61] While transient youth might be most vulnerable, the Children's Bureau believed that wartime conditions created circumstances which might increase unacceptable behavior among all young people.

Beginning in November 1942, the Children's Bureau in cooperation with the Social Security Board's Bureau of Public Assistance sponsored a project in Newport News, Virginia, aimed at preventing and reducing juvenile delinquency. Assisted by the Social Security Act's Title V funds, the two federal agencies placed Paul R. Cherney in the city manager's office in March 1943 through July 1, 1944 (when he entered the military), to direct the program. After Cherney's departure local officials continued to report to the Children's Bureau until March 1, 1945. For a program designed to help lower wartime stress on families, and therefore reduce juvenile delinquency rates, Newport News seemed to be a good area since it had experienced some of the most extreme wartime demographic changes of any region in the United States. The city's prewar population of 37,000 had nearly doubled by 1942 and the Children's Bureau expected the employment of women, including mothers, to "increase drastically in the shipyards and civilian services due to the withdrawal of men for military service." In addition, the city did not have an existing child welfare program. The bureau argued that "the conclusions drawn" from this study were "in a large measure applicable to planning for any community service for children."[62]

The final report from this effort shows the Children's Bureau's continued adherence to its "whole child" strategy. But the agency's cooperation with the Bureau of Public Assistance further underscores the fact that the Children's Bureau was no longer the sole authority on the needs of children and their families. The project's initial purpose brought "together the appropriate Federal, State, and local agencies to work on the problem of the prevention and control of juvenile delinquency." But the Children's Bureau soon altered the original plan, explained the agency, to better fit the American social welfare system in which local governments served as the strategic place to plan and implement juvenile delinquency prevention efforts. Consequently, "the federal agencies acted only as observers and consultants and, except for financial support, the project became to all intents and purposes a local effort such as any community might make with expert local leadership."[63] This approach offered real possibilities for strengthening children and their families. Placing the child at the center of social welfare services left the door open for the creation and execution of innovative programs which could fortify families and therefore help children. But leaving the design and implementation for such efforts entirely in the hands of local communities could result in a patchwork of services open to discriminatory practices and neglect.

Ironically, despite the beliefs held by Children's Bureau officials at the time, the agency revised its wartime report on juvenile delinquency in 1949, and concluded that contrary to popular perceptions, the available statistics showed "no alarming tendency to increased 'juvenile crime,' as newspapers perennially claim[ed]" during the war and after.[64] Even during the war, the Children's Bureau recognized that the vast majority of young people responded in "acceptable" ways to the war emergency. As William Tuttle has chronicled in his recent study of children on the American home front, young people participated in scrap drives and patriotic programs, and volunteered their time to the local Red Cross chapter and other service organizations.[65] But, as the Children's Bureau feared, the war also served to set the stage for a reversal of some of the progress made on social welfare issues during the New Deal.

Child labor was one of the areas in which some of the ground gained during the 1930s was lost. As noted earlier, the 1938 Fair Labor Standards Act prohibited the employment of children in industries producing materials for interstate commerce. But the onset of World War II and its accompanying labor shortage enticed young people back into the paid work force. In March 1940, the census counted 872,314 adolescents aged fourteen to eighteen working for wages. In April 1944, the number had risen to 2.9 million and an estimated 2,000,000 additional workers from the age cohort entered the work force during the summer of 1944. Although they are not entirely reflective of actual employment, from 1940 through 1943 applications for Social Security numbers by those under eighteen rose 203 percent, 166.3 percent for boys and 266.6 percent for girls.[66] Katharine Lenroot wrote Eleanor Roosevelt, who was preparing a speech to the New Hampshire legislature, that employment certificates issued for boys and girls fourteen through seventeen in that state had increased from 1,330 in 1940 to 7,762 in 1944 (an increase of just under 500 percent). Lenroot also noted that while fewer girls worked for wages than boys, their rate of increase grew much more dramatically than that of boys during the war. This fact seems to have been a particular worry for the Children's Bureau since it felt that girls were more vulnerable than boys to "outside influences" introduced through paid employment.[67] A wartime labor market short of workers tempted young people with relatively high wages and patriotic rhetoric asking those on the home front to support the military forces abroad by working in the nation's factories and on its farms. The federal government's termination of the Civilian Conservation Corps in 1942 and the National Youth Administration in 1943 also encouraged many under eighteen to get a job in the private sector.[68]

Contrary to its historic hardline stand, the Children's Bureau recognized that it must adjust child labor policies to wartime conditions. In an October 12, 1942, radio address, President Roosevelt stated that "grown" boys and girls were one of the nation's "sources of manpower" but he cautioned that they should be used where "reasonable."[69] On the same theme a Children's Bureau report quotes Roosevelt as suggesting that plans be worked out to enable high school students "to take some time from their school year and to use their summer vacations to help farmers raise and harvest their crops, or to work in the war industries." But the bureau did not want the complete removal of the child labor protections achieved during the previous decade. It cautioned that due to the wartime hysteria "in many cases schools have been closed for weeks at a time and education disrupted; many younger children have been employed when older youth could have been made available." The agency surmised that this situation existed not because of necessity but partly because it was easiest for employers to recruit workers from schools "—a group found all together in one place, a group naturally eager for new experiences and for what seems an exciting part in the war effort, a group inexperienced in employment relationships and often willing to accept any wages offered." The employment of adolescents, claimed the bureau, had often been unreasonable "from the point of view of the best interests of youth or of the Nation or from the long-range point of view of winning both the war and the peace." The Children's Bureau urged that young people must be "regarded primarily as the reservoir for the trained minds of tomorrow" and developed guidelines for the employment of youth during the wartime emergency.[70]

Indeed, during the war years industries and the public exerted pressure on the federal and state governments to repeal child labor laws. This atmosphere resulted in a modification of child labor restrictions during the war. For example, on November 11, 1942, the secretary of labor, in consultation with the Children's Bureau, granted an exemption from the provisions of the Public Contracts Act to permit the employment of girls sixteen through eighteen, making it equal to the basic minimum age protection for boys. This legislation applied to employment in industries producing goods for the federal government under contracts in excess of $10,000 and required a maximum eight-hour day and a thirty-minute lunch period, and prohibited night work between 10:00 P.M. and 6:00 A.M. The Children's Bureau also issued exemptions relaxing the Fair Labor Standards Act "for the duration." These permitted the employment of fourteen- and fifteen-year-olds outside of school hours until 8:00 P.M. in heading and peeling shrimp, and until 10:00 P.M. packing fresh fruits and vegetables. The bureau also temporarily amended the 1938 act's hazardous occupation sections by allowing the employment of sixteen- and seventeen-year-olds in small arms and munitions plants and permitting seventeen-year-olds to work on road maintenance and railroad crews. The Children's Bureau explained that such changes were made "at the request of the Federal departments most concerned with the war, [in order] to prevent retardation of essential production." Furthermore, some states weakened child labor restrictions by lengthening permissible work hours or relaxing prohibitions on night work. During 1943 alone, state legislatures passed sixty-two acts lowering restrictions on the employment of minors. Fifteen states lowered maximum hour standards, permitted night work, and shortened the length of the meal period for sixteen- and seventeen-year-olds. Several also lowered minimum age requirements and extended the hours for night employment of children in bowling alleys and other service businesses. For example, in Delaware, a change in the law which was justified as part of the war effort but was clearly outside of wartime production allowed bowling alley pin boys as young as twelve to work until midnight and fourteen-year-olds to work until midnight and as early as 5:00 A.M. delivering milk. Florida lowered the minimum age for nonfactory employment during school hours from sixteen to fourteen and set a minimum age of twelve for work conducted outside of school hours. States also made provisions for students under sixteen who wished to leave school for agricultural work during planting and harvesting periods. Some set a minimum age of fourteen for such exemptions, but several states established no age standards. Although most state statutes applied "only for the duration of the war," some, like an Ohio law allowing canneries to employ girls over sixteen for unlimited hours, were not restricted to the war period.[71]

Even with the relaxation of standards, the illegal employment of children rose during the war. The Children's Bureau reported that 4,334 establishments involving 12,000 young workers had violated the Fair Labor Standards Act's child labor regulations during the law's first five years. Illegal child laborers worked in virtually every industry in which inspections were made. The highest number of violations occurred in the food canning and packing industry, where some workers were as young as eight.[72] During the summer of 1943 the New York Department of Labor conducted a study of child labor included in industries under state minimum wage orders—hotel, restaurant, beauty service, and confectionery. The sample included 1,764 establishments employing 7,117 minors, and investigators found that more than 50 percent of those under eighteen were working illegally. Forty-three percent of those had no employment certificates and approximately 33 percent worked illegal hours. Twenty-four children were under fourteen. Others worked in jobs where the law forbade their handling hazardous machinery. The New York State Department of Labor estimated that these findings reflected a 400 percent increase in the illegal employment of minors during the war.[73]

The Children's Bureau feared that growing numbers of young people worked in "dangerous occupations" or at least under unsafe conditions. The agency reported several examples of youths under eighteen years of age injured or killed on the job. The story of a thirteen-year-old boy who caught his arm in a bakery dough-mixing machine and died as a result of his injuries seemed all too typical. A sixteen-year-old farm worker was seriously injured when he fell asleep at 4:00 A.M. while driving a truck to market. In another case, a fifteen-year-old boy had his arm torn off above the elbow while working on the night shift in a laundry. He had tried to remove a tangled sheet from a machine while it was operating. The Children's Bureau also suggested that many children worked long hours in clear violation of its recommended standards. A fourteen-year-old boy in the ninth grade attended school Monday through Friday from 8:15 or 8:30 A.M. until 2:00 P.M., then sold candy in a theater from 2:00 P.M. to 10:00 P.M. six days a week. The Children's Bureau surmised that he "worked" either at school or his job 73.5 hours per week. Another thirteen-year-old set pins in a bowling alley until 11:00 P.M. on school days and until midnight on Saturday and Sunday. In one city, employed students constituted from 31 to 41 percent of the students enrolled in the three local high schools. The majority were sixteen and seventeen but many were younger. This situation, argued the Children's Bureau, resulted in many cases where the "pupil's health is impaired, and he either fails in his school work, or discouraged with the lack of school progress and lured by the pay envelope, he drops out of school." The agency suggested that the consequences of such practices might also include weariness, poor work in school, truancy, and delinquency.[74]

The Children's Bureau continued to emphasize the links between child labor laws, compulsory school attendance, education, and healthy and productive adults. According to the 1940 census, one of every eight adults twenty-five or older had less than five years of schooling. A survey conducted in March 1940 found that 10 percent of all fourteen- and fifteen-year-olds did not attend school and among rural youth in the same age group the rate was 18 percent. School dropout rates were highest in the rural South, where 80.3 percent of fourteen-year-old males and 84.3 percent of females attended school. These figures fell to 70.6 percent and 76.3 percent for fifteen-year-olds. By age seventeen only 40.3 percent of boys and 47.4 percent of girls enrolled in school. Among fourteen-year-olds 11.1 percent of boys and .07 percent of girls worked for wages in 1940. At fifteen the percentage increased to 19.1 percent and 5.4 percent respectively. By age seventeen, 47.6 percent of males and 16.9 percent of females were employed. Overall, rural nonwhites were more likely to work for wages and less likely to attend school than whites. The highest school attendance and lowest employment rates existed in northeastern states. There 96.6 percent of fourteen-year-old boys and 96.5 percent of girls attended school. At fifteen the proportion dropped slightly to 94.9 percent and 94.1 percent. Even at seventeen, 66.1 percent of boys and 64.8 percent of girls remained in school. Only 1.0 percent of white fourteen-year-old males and 0.5 percent of females worked for wages. At fifteen only 2.5 percent of boys and 1.2 percent of girls were employed. Nonwhites were as likely to remain in school as whites in urban areas.[75] From April 1942 through March 1943, the military rejected approximately two of every one hundred white and ten of every one hundred black recruits due to "educational deficiency." The Children's Bureau maintained that "our past failure to assure, even for the generations now young, adequate educational opportunity and the foundations for good health, is evident in the record of rejections under the Selective Training and Service Act of 1940." Of the first two million men examined, nearly half failed to meet the physical and mental requirements for general military service. Overall, during the war the military rejected more than one-third of its recruits.[76]

In March 1943, as part of its effort to protect the interests of young workers as well as fill the country's defense needs, the Children's Bureau devised a statement of principles and standards for young workers in war industries. This policy concluded that although "many young persons are needed in the labor force . . . careless and unsupervised use of youth power is a waste of the most precious resource of the Nation." The most important premise, according to the Children's Bureau and the War Manpower Commission, rested on the notion that the "first responsibility and obligation of young people even in wartime is to take full advantage of their educational opportunities in order to prepare themselves for war and post-war services and for the duties of citizenship." The policy reemphasized the federal mandate establishing fourteen as the minimum age for entrance to the hired labor force (in most fields), sixteen as the minimum for factory work, and eighteen as the minimum for hazardous work. Boys and girls should be employed during school hours only if the area or regional manpower director determined that needs cannot be met with other labor sources. Such work should also be "suitable to their strength and age." The policy also recommended paying young workers the same wages as adults so as to prevent employers from hiring minors as a cheap labor source. For industrial work requiring children to live away from home, the policy urged no recruitment of children under sixteen and provision for suitable living conditions.[77] In September 1943, the Children's Bureau, the War Manpower Commission, and the United States Office of Education issued a joint statement concerning the part-time employment of minors. It recommended that all student workers fourteen through seventeen receive one day off in seven, "adequate" meal and rest periods, "adequate" sanitary facilities, and "good" supervision and safety measures. Part-time workers sixteen and seventeen years of age should be limited to a twenty-eight-hour workweek when school was in session and a forty-eight-hour week during vacation periods. In no case should these youngsters work a combined school and employment schedule of more than nine hours a day or work after 10:00 P.M. The workweek should be limited to eighteen hours for fourteen- and fifteen-year-olds during school sessions and no more than forty hours otherwise. In addition, the combined school and work schedules for the younger group should not exceed eight hours per day and they should not work after 7:00 P.M. or before 7:00

A.M. In February 1944, at the urging of the Children's Bureau, the War Department set standards for minors employed in war department installations controlled by the army. This pronouncement prohibited the employment of workers under sixteen, established protections against hazardous occupations for those under eighteen, prohibited night work between 10:00 P.M. and 6:00 A.M., and provided for one day's rest in seven in war department facilities.

Indeed, as the aforementioned data shows, many young people labored in the nation's factories and on farms during the war. Children engaged in industries falling under the jurisdiction of the Fair Labor Standards Act were protected by federal law. But, most children worked in industries outside federal authority. Realizing that minors would also be used to "get in the 1943 crop," the Children's Bureau, in cooperation with the Department of Agriculture, the United States Office of Education, the War Manpower Commission, and the Office of Civilian Defense, published "Guides to Successful Employment of Non-Farm Youth in Wartime Agriculture." But here the agency was limited to rhetoric. Child labor laws protecting agricultural workers varied by state and the federal government had no regulatory authority. The Department of Agriculture's War Food Administration estimated that 700,000 youths under eighteen worked farm jobs during the 1943 summer season alone and that the number would rise to 1,200,000 in 1944.[78] The Children's Bureau argued that while such employment was necessary during the wartime emergency, recruitment should be limited "to boys and girls old enough and sufficiently well-developed physically to work efficiently and without undue strain . . . [this] will help to give satisfactory results to both farmers and young people." The agency recommended a minimum age of fourteen for agricultural workers who could live at home or work as part of a "camp program" conducted by a recognized youth-serving agency, and sixteen for those living away from their families. Consistent with its earlier child labor efforts, the Children's Bureau also recommended physical examinations, adequate rest periods, availability of sanitary facilities, clean drinking water, eight-hour workdays (not more than six for workers fourteen and fifteen years old), and six days or less per workweek. Morning and evening "chores" were permissible on the seventh day. The bureau's guidelines included methods to prevent accidents and instructed employers to carry "adequate liability insurance."[79] Such standards supposedly sheltered adolescent workers from exploitive situations all too common in agricultural labor, but the Children's Bureau's Industrial Division acknowledged that public agencies in some states still recruited children as young as nine or ten for agricultural work.[80]

Without the power of enforcement, the Children's Bureau's recommendations were simply ignored by many who employed migrant farm labor. Lenroot's staff knew well the poor circumstances of many agricultural workers and their families. The agency's 1941 investigation of migrant agricultural workers residing in Hidalgo County, Texas, showed that children and their families worked long hours at low pay and had poor health care as well as substandard educational opportunities. Of youths fourteen to seventeen years of age nearly 95 percent worked for wages. Of those between ten and fourteen, four-fifths had worked for hire sometime during 1941. The same was true for more than one-fourth of the children between six and ten years of age.[81] Wartime employment of adolescents may have eased family poverty for some, but it is also likely that employers abused many minors, particularly those working in agriculture, during the war years. The wartime emergency seemed to justify the exploitation of young workers, particularly children of color and those living in rural areas. The Children's Bureau's guidelines, although well intentioned, seem almost comical when compared to its own findings. In the end, despite the Children's Bureau's advocacy of continued and strengthened child labor restrictions, many young people left school for full-time employment, and it appears that the illegal use of young workers rose during the war years.[82] Public pressure and calls for change from defense industries, farmers, the War Manpower Commission, and the Department of Agriculture apparently outweighed the Children's Bureau's earlier efforts at investigation and advocacy. Most Americans, and most historians, have turned a blind eye to the contributions and sacrifices of young workers on the home front during the war.[83]

Maternal and child health was another area where the Children's Bureau feared that previous social gains might be reversed by wartime conditions. But here Title V, Part I, of the Social Security Act opened the door to a much more active effort to save the lives of mothers and babies.

Emergency Maternal and Infant Care Program

The Children's Bureau had its greatest impact during the war in the area of infant and maternal health care. Since its inception, the Children's Bureau had focused much of its efforts on the promotion of good health care for mothers and babies. The bureau's early investigation of maternal and infant mortality rates in the United States revealed that many mothers and babies did not receive adequate medical care. Title V, Part I, of the 1935 Social Security Act annually provided $5,820,000 for maternal and child health services conducted by the states under plans approved by the Children's Bureau. Title V, Part I, provided $3,840,000 from Fund A ($20,000 to each state with the balance distributed on the basis of percentage of live births). These federal dollars had to be matched with state funds. Fund B did not require matching funds and was allotted by the Children's Bureau according to financial need after taking into account the number of live births in each state. State health departments used Title V money to provide prenatal and child health clinics and medical examinations for school-age children, to pay the salaries of public health nurses designated to care for mothers and children, and to provide dental and nutritional services. Some counties also used Title V, Part I, funds to pay for medical and/or hospital care for maternity cases and sick children.[84] In addition, the Children's Bureau continued to publish its popular manuals on infant and maternal health care. The wartime emergency offered Lenroot and her staff the opportunity to expand the program and become powerful administers of health care for some American mothers and children, albeit only temporarily.

By late 1940, the commanding officer at Fort Lewis found himself faced with a new dilemma. Many of his men had brought their young wives to the base area, and some of these women became pregnant and were in need of maternity care. During peacetime the post hospital had taken care of such cases. But as the nation's defense efforts grew after the passage of the October 1940 Selective Service and Training Act, the hospital was soon unable to care for the families of enlisted men without jeopardizing its ability to care for soldiers. Because they did not meet local residency requirements, military wives were generally ineligible for county department of health programs. Married to men in the military services' four lowest pay grades (grades 4-7), most wives could not afford to purchase private care nor did they have adequate resources to return to their hometowns. Under the Selective Service Act married enlisted men in the armed services were paid $28 per month, $40 if they had a wife and one child, and $10 for each additional child. According to the Children's Bureau these amounts were insufficient to cover the costs of maternity care and the care of sick children. Suitable medical and nursing services during pregnancy and after the baby was born were judged to average $70-$80.[85] Private charities were generally inadequate or absent for military personnel. The commander felt that this circumstance harmed the soldiers' morale, and he appealed to the state health officer for help. This official then had to ask the Children's Bureau for an exception to use Title V, Part I, funds to care for these women, because, as already noted, wives of servicemen generally did not fit the normal eligibility requirements established under most state assistance programs. In August 1941, the Children's Bureau agreed to the plan. From then through July 1942, 677 women in the Fort Lewis area, most between the ages of seventeen and nineteen and expecting their first child, registered for obstetrical care under the extended program. Of those, 193 delivered their babies and 432 received prenatal care.[86] The Children's Bureau released a memorandum to all state health departments on May 1, 1942, describing its plan to expand the Fort Lewis program to all states if given adequate funding by Congress.[87]

Interestingly, although public demand grew once the program was instituted, not a single health department reported that a serviceman or his wife had contacted it for help prior to the establishment of the program at Fort Lewis. The Children's Bureau contended that despite the absence of requests, there was a great need for such service. Approximately four hundred babies a day were being born to the wives of men in the military. The American Red Cross reported that in just one month (July 15-August 15, 1942), 3,262 servicemen had asked its representatives stationed at 240 U.S. Army posts for help in securing obstetric care for their wives. Another 2,601 wives of servicemen asked for help in obtaining maternity care or medical care for sick children. The Children's Bureau estimated that 25,000 soldiers' and sailors' wives sought assistance in securing obstetric and pediatric care each month. Apparently, most people did not think of state health departments as dispensaries of maternal and child health care. This is not inconsistent with the Children's Bureau's or the PHS's previous efforts to reduce the nation's maternal and infant mortality rates. These federal agencies in cooperation with state health departments had been primarily involved in investigation, education, immunization, and standardization, not in providing medical care. As an analyst of the Title V program maintained in 1948, it was not until after the extended efforts under Title V were launched that "the department of health became much more real to servicemen and their wives [because] then they had a government agency to which they could make their needs known and from which they could expect help."[88]

Although the need seemed great, Lenroot contended that after December 1942 the Children's Bureau had no more money to allocate to an extended Title V program. She estimated that the agency needed an additional $1,1817,200 to adequately fund an expanded program through June 30, 1943, when a new fiscal budget could be secured.

Lenroot felt optimistic about the future of the extended Title V program as well as other Children's Bureau child welfare efforts. On August 22, 1942, President Roosevelt had sent letters to the chairmen of the House Ways and Means Committee and the Senate Finance Committee proposing an amendment to Title V permitting additional appropriations of $7,500,000 for grants to states for the duration of the war and six months thereafter. The president's proposal was introduced in Congress as bills S. 2738 and H.R. 7503 and was initially intended to "safeguard" the children of "our fighting men and of our war workers."[89]

In December 1942, the Bureau of the Budget agreed to include a request for $1,200,000 for supplementary funding for the Children's Bureau's expanded Title V, Part I, efforts in the Roosevelt administration's first deficiency appropriation bill of 1943 (H.R. 1975). On February 11, 1943, Lenroot and Eliot testified before the House subcommittee on appropriations in support of what was to be called the Emergency Maternity and Infant Care program (EMIC).[90] Perhaps seeking the easiest path, Lenroot and Eliot argued that this was not a new program, simply an expansion of existing services available under the Social Security Act. Indeed, the effort did not require additional state matching funds because federal money could be allocated from Title V Fund B and could be enacted immediately. Furthermore they argued that the war had led to the need for the expanded program, a circumstance similar to many other adjustments made by government agencies on the home front. Emphasizing the war's role, Lenroot and Eliot suggested that the program be available only to the wives and infants of servicemen in the military's four lowest pay grades. Instead of primarily a child welfare effort, this would be a way to promote good morale within the military. Lenroot and Eliot explained that many state health agencies were unable to accept all requests for care due to existing fund limits. The Children's Bureau already had a maternity and infancy program in the states, but up to that point the funds from Title V, Part I, had been used primarily for prenatal and postnatal care, not for hospital costs and medical care during the mother's ten-day to two-week confinement. While Lenroot's and Eliot's testimony seemed to be effective, the committee was not convinced that this was simply the expansion of an existing program and questioned the fact that the federal government funded the program entirely, without matching state allocations. And finally, the committee asked about the lack of a financial need test for recipients. As a result, the February 24, 1943, House Committee of Appropriations Report denied the Children's Bureau's request.[91]

When the bill reached the Senate, Lenroot and Eliot again tried to justify the need for the expanded Title V program. The same concerns mentioned in the House report surfaced during Senate hearings on the bill. Lenroot again asserted that the program was "not a new activity" and she estimated that the bureau would need $6,000,000 to carry the effort for a full year. It appeared that although such a program for the general public was unlikely, senators were not willing to deny care for the wives and babies of servicemen. On March 12, 1943, the Children's Bureau's request was put back into the bill. Although it had been only three weeks since the House committee had denied the Children's Bureau's request, on March 18, 1943, the House agreed that the program had merit and both houses of Congress unanimously approved the 1943 Deficiency Appropriation Bill. The president quickly signed the bill into law (Public Law 11).[92] The Children's Bureau relied on the American Legion, the Veterans of Foreign Wars, the Red Cross, and its usual network of supporters to exert pressure on Congress for passage of the appropriation bill. Although it is not entirely clear why representatives made such an abrupt about-face on the issue, it is likely that lobbyists for the American Legion and the Veterans of Foreign Wars convinced members of the House that the EMIC program's benefits for uplifting morale in the military far outweighed its potential negative aspects or high cost. In addition, it was depicted as a wartime emergency program for the nation's most patriotic Americans—soldiers. Unlike earlier maternal and child welfare programs endorsed by the Children's Bureau, EMIC was not marketed as a service for women and children. This proved an advantage that would have made such a program impossible to pass during peacetime. Lenroot expressed her pleasure at the expanded EMIC program's prospects in a letter to Eleanor Roosevelt on the day the deficiency bill became law. Her thoughts show that although the bill probably passed because it benefited soldiers, Lenroot knew that the money would most directly help American women and children. Other women thought so too. As Lenroot wrote Eleanor Roosevelt, "I know you will rejoice with us in the passage through Congress of the item for maternity care of wives of service men and medical care for their infants. This item was included in the First Deficiency Appropriation Bill which I understand is now before the President for his signature. The Women's Christian Temperance Union, the General Federation of Women's Clubs, and the Women's Joint Congressional Committee helped greatly in enlisting the interest of Congress in the bill."[93]

After the bill's passage, the Children's Bureau in cooperation with the military services promoted the program through the popular press and by the insertion of flyers describing EMIC benefits in servicemen's pay envelopes. The first of five such "stuffers" was enclosed in the August 1943, payroll, letting servicemen know that EMIC provided medical services which included at least five prenatal examinations, a minimum of ten days' hospital care at the time of delivery and immediately postpartum, and an unspecified number of postpartum medical examinations to the wives of servicemen in the four lowest pay grades. The babies born to these women were also eligible for medical, nursing, and hospital care up to one year of age. Applicants submitted one form in order to receive authorization for care of the mother and newborn. Physicians' services averaged $35 (with a low of $34.50 in Illinois and a high of $55.29 in New York). The program set hospital charges at the actual per diem cost of operating the hospital (ward rates, no "luxury services," ranging from $40.92 in Georgia to $73.41 in New York). The Children's Bureau approved all charges paid from state-allocated Title V, Part I, funds, and patients contributed nothing.[94] The program clearly encouraged hospital births and the use of medical doctors over midwives, osteopaths, and other alternatives. For example, 92 percent of all EMIC mothers delivered in hospitals, while the overall rate for all births in the United States by 1945 was 79 percent. Licensed doctors of medicine attended 97 percent of EMIC births while osteopaths assisted only 2.5 percent and a mere 0.5 percent involved "others."[95] EMIC also provided many American couples with their first introduction to insured health care. From its inception until its conclusion on June 30, 1949, EMIC paid the medical expenses of 1,200,000 maternity patients and over 230,000 infants. The Children's Bureau estimated that 85 percent of those eligible applied and that from 1943 through 1946 one in every seven babies was born under the EMIC program. The last appropriation bill for EMIC passed on July 26, 1946. Overall, Congress had provided $130,500,000 for EMIC from 1943 to 1949. Clearly the Children's Bureau gained new administrative authority and influence during the program's existence. At the beginning of the war the Children's Bureau had been spending only about $11,000,000 in all of its child welfare efforts. Furthermore, hospitals and doctors had to meet Children's Bureau minimum standards in order to receive EMIC funds.

It is more difficult to determine what direct effect EMIC had on the lives of mothers and babies. The national maternal mortality rate fell from 37.6 deaths per 10,000 live births in 1940 to 20.7 in 1945. Similarly, infant mortality declined from 47.0 per 1,000 live births in 1940 to 38.3 in 1945. Rates for blacks remained roughly twice those of whites.[96] Furthermore, the program did not cover most American women. Nevertheless, although Lenroot and Eliot made public statements to the contrary, it appears that the Children's Bureau hoped that an EMIC style program would become permanent and be expanded to include all mothers and babies. As early as July 15, 1942, an internal Children's Bureau memo suggested that there should be a "post-war expansion of tax-supported hospital maternity and pediatric services."[97] This slide toward national health care was exactly what the critics of the Children's Bureau had accused the agency of intending since its first efforts to reduce the deaths of mothers and their children. Beginning with the 1921 Sheppard-Towner Maternity and Infancy Act, the Children's Bureau's health care efforts had been soundly criticized by the AMA and its supporters as inappropriate and "socialized" medicine. Among professional medical societies, only the Women's Medical Association and the American Academy of Pediatrics were consistent supporters of the Children's Bureau. As previously discussed, in 1934 Grace Abbott had tried to heal the rift between the Children's Bureau and many within the physician-led medical community through her appointment of Martha Eliot as associate chief. But despite Abbott's effort to sway the agency's critics, the AMA and its supporters criticized the popular EMIC program.

The AMA grumbled through its journal and congressional lobbying, but its members participated in EMIC during the war,apparently because they viewed the war years as an emergency period which allowed for such dramatic measures. In addition, the program paid for obstetric care for many women who might otherwise have been unable to afford the services of a medical doctor. Besides, even from a conservative perspective EMIC was a wartime necessity whose primary purpose was to maintain military morale and only as a side benefit provided for women and babies. It is important to note that the federal government did not institute EMIC style programs for the wives and children of civilians. This was true despite the fact that a Senate committee investigation examining the civilian population's physical and educational condition as it related to national defense capabilities found that many American women and infants lacked adequate medical care.[98] However, although the program was developed amid evidence of need, cloaked in patriotic rhetoric, and implemented with requirements favoring licensed medical doctors, the AMA and its affiliated societies in several states warned that EMIC was only acceptable as an emergency measure. The AMA contended that steps should be taken to insure that the program would not open the door to socialized medicine after the war. Some also argued that although the program was a potential good during the war, federal funds for EMIC should go directly to the servicemen's wives as cash allotments that could then be used to purchase medical care from hospitals and physicians. The Children's Bureau feared that under such a plan some women might be swayed to use hospitals and doctors that did not meet minimum standards. In addition, wives of enlisted men might be tempted to pay debts rather than purchase maternity care. The agency also worried that physicians and hospitals might raise prices above those amounts approved by the Children's Bureau, thereby forcing pregnant mothers to contribute to their care.[99]

Even the Children's Bureau's longtime ally, the American Academy of Pediatrics, criticized the agency for wanting to extend the EMIC program after the war. As Franklin P. Gengenbach, M.D., 1944 president of the American Academy of Pediatrics, explained, "We definitely agreed to go along with [the Children's Bureau] in carrying out the EMIC program for the duration but we did object to . . . efforts to continue that program after the war. . . . the Bureau became bureaucratic in this program." In August 1945, Joseph S. Wall, M.D., then president of the American Academy of Pediatrics, wrote, "In my opinion . . . proposed legislation [to extend the EMIC program after the war] is purely and utterly a piece of socialistic endeavor." With this, the American Academy of Pediatrics withdrew its support and recommended the transfer of all child health related activities to the PHS.[100] Martha Eliot's mentor, Yale University pediatrician Grover F. Powers, M.D., wrote several letters in support of the Children's Bureau. Another prominent pediatrician, Edwards A. Park, contended that "the E.M.I.C. under the Children's Bureau has been a most unqualified and brilliant success . . . [and therefore] it would be difficult to think of a more bungling and stupid action than for the Academy to base their sabotage of the Children's Bureau on one of the most successful achievements . . . with the lay public." But Ashley A. Weech, M.D., of Cincinnati's Children's Hospital Research Foundation, while sympathetic to the bureau, acknowledged that he believed that Martha Eliot "regards the moves which have been taken in extending the EMIC program as merely an opening wedge from which the program can be extended to children of all ages, whether or not they are connected with the military forces."[101] Indeed, it appears that Eliot did hope that the EMIC program opened the door to compulsory federal health care for all American mothers and children. While it is true that the Children's Bureau requested an $8,000,000 reduction in the EMIC program on October 2, 1945, it is also possible that Lenroot and Eliot believed that a permanent national maternal and infant health care could be established in place of the wartime program. When confronted with complaints that the Children's Bureau had overstepped its authority with EMIC, Eliot claimed that the Children's Bureau did not "participate in medical practice" but that in carrying out its responsibilities under the Social Security Act the Children's Bureau did set standards and pay for medical care conducted by private physicians. These were purely administrative responsibilities authorized within the limits of Title V. In congressional testimony Eliot noted that "the Children's Bureau has accepted the fact that [the EMIC] is a wartime service." But she explained further, "We also appreciate very fully that in peacetime as well as in wartime there are many mothers in this country who are in need of the kind of service that has been provided in this program." Eliot said that it was up to Congress to decide whether the federal government will "in the future will make it possible for the mothers and children of this country to have the kind of care that they should have during the maternity period and during the period of childhood when proper growth, development, and health means so much to the health of future citizens of this country."[102]

It was not to be. EMIC was the most extensive federally funded health care program for mothers and children to date. Although popular and operated with few administrative problems, it was not accepted as a peacetime measure. During the 1940s and 1950s, as had been the case previously, all attempts to pass any form of national health insurance failed. Medical procedures and hospital care were enhanced by the war, but the distribution of medical care in the United States was limited to those who could afford it or to holders of private health insurance. Again, the medical lobby had succeeded in stopping the Children's Bureau's primary dream of providing good quality and affordable medical care for all American mothers and babies. After 1946, government public health efforts on all levels focused on research rather than prevention or the provision of health care.[103]

Although EMIC was the most extensive maternal and infant care program to date, it had several fundamental limitations. Even women contributing directly to the war effort as wives of defense workers or those employed as "Rosies" outside the home, women enlisted in the military, and unmarried mothers whose babies were fathered by men in the military were not eligible for EMIC funds. Furthermore, the program remained tied to traditional definitions of family which placed women and children as dependents of men and made men responsible for their care and protection. Perhaps this is not surprising for the times in light of the fact that even the Women's Bureau did not call for an extension of the program to pregnant working women, unmarried females, or women in the military.[104] These exceptions, although perhaps unintentionally, fueled the arguments of critics of national health insurance who maintained that all Americans should be responsible for purchasing their own health care. Even maternal and infant care was not a fundamental right nor a national interest. Advocates of private insurance argued that responsible, "worthy," and productive families could afford good medical care in America. While Eliot and Lenroot may have seen EMIC as an opening wedge to national maternity and infant insurance, in the end the program was viewed as only one of many federal interventions necessary during the war. EMIC was not "a right to childhood." Instead, it was a military measure instituted solely to improve the morale of men in the military.[105] Although the program represented a heroic try, the bureau's efforts were limited by the same arguments that had hindered its work since the agency's inception.

Protecting Children in a Democracy?

The Children's Bureau's wartime experience was a mixed bag for its own future and for the children it sought to help. On October 26, 1940, Katharine Lenroot wrote Eleanor Roosevelt expressing concern that the administration was developing a plan whereby all responsibility for the social welfare of families of men in the military would be vested in the American Red Cross. The Children's Bureau's chief acknowledged that voluntary organizations were important, but said she felt that "through the Social Security Program and other programs of the Federal Government, carried on in cooperation with the States and local communities, a foundation of public service has now been laid which was not in existence in 1917." She urged that public child welfare services established and monitored by the Children's Bureau should be strengthened to help serve the needs of the families of men in the armed forces. The first lady replied that she had inquired and found that the Red Cross was "only going to be used in the way it had always been used. All the other bureaus [including the Children's Bureau] will be expected to function" as authorized under the Social Security Act. She was sure this meant that "there would be less for the Red Cross to undertake than ever before."[106] Certain aspects of the Children's Bureau's efforts to protect "a right to childhood" had been strengthened by the 1935 Social Security Act, and certainly the wartime emergency did offer the opportunity to expand some of those responsibilities, particularly in the area of maternal and child health care. As William Tuttle has shown, the postwar baby boom actually began in 1940.

Between 1939 and 1946 the U.S. birth rate rose from 79.6 to 85.9 births per 100 women of child-bearing age. This fact alone put the Children's Bureau's major constituency in the limelight. Furthermore, the agency's interest in preventing juvenile delinquency and other social problems received greater public attention during the war. Although its basic program did not change, appropriations for the Social Security Act's Title V, Part II, program for handicapped children rose from $732,493 in 1936 to over $4,300,000 by the war's end.[107] From 1939 to 1946 the Children's Bureau also became involved in a more direct way in international child welfare policy development.

However, the additional appropriations and expanded programs did not necessarily act in the interests of "the whole child." As might be expected, the agency continued to adhere to the middle-class family ideal which generally ignored the children of mothers employed outside of the home. Wartime pressures also led to the relaxation of child labor laws. In addition, the Children's Bureau, the nation's chief advocate for children, did not protest or do much to improve the conditions for Japanese American children forcibly removed from their homes by the War Relocation Authority. Those interned included babies, handicapped children, and orphans—groups for whom "loyalty" was not much of an issue. The Children's Bureau's records offer little insight into the agency's policy concerning Japanese American children during the war. On August 4, 1942, Katharine Lenroot sent a memorandum to Secretary Perkins citing several "problems" with the evacuation of Japanese Americans from the West Coast. She said that housing conditions were congested and should be improved. In addition, the Children's Bureau hoped that the promotion of good maternal and infant health care would be facilitated under Title V. She also urged better nutritional and educational opportunities. However, there is no further evidence in the Children's Bureau's records of special attention given to this group of children whose "right to childhood" was directly affected by the war. Like most people in the United States, even in the face of such outrageous violation of civil liberties the Children's Bureau remained silent.[108] Perhaps most importantly, the Children's Bureau's wartime experience did not restore the agency's fundamental philosophy designed to protect the needs of the "whole child." Programs within the United States remained uneven and out of reach for many children.

Conclusion: The Children's Bureau and "A Right to Childhood"

The vulnerability of the Children's Bureau resurfaced by the end of World War II. In 1939 rumors spread that President Roosevelt was again considering a reorganization of the Children's Bureau's functions and transfer from the Labor Department to the Federal Security Agency (FSA). Plans for federal reorganization were a consistent part of the Roosevelt New Deal. Some contended that the growing federal government should be organized according to function; others, such as the Children's Bureau and the Veteran's Administration, argued that constituency was the more effective structure.[1] When the issue came up again in 1939 Lenroot lobbied Eleanor Roosevelt to help keep the Children's Bureau intact. She argued that "our position as a bureau serving the interests of all children, and especially the children of working people of the Country, is stronger in the Department of Labor than it would be in any other department." To support her claim, Lenroot sent Eleanor Roosevelt and a number of other bureau supporters copies of a confidential report investigating the Children's Bureau's relationship with other agencies on the federal, state, local, public, and private levels. Mrs. Roosevelt forwarded the report to her husband noting that "perhaps you'd like to glance through before making up your mind."[2] For undetermined reasons the president did nothing further about the proposal.

The Children's Bureau again faced a reorganization threat in 1944. Representative A. L. Miller (R-Nebr.) introduced a bill in the House of Representatives (H.R. 4663) in April proposing the transfer all the Children's Bureau's health services to the PHS, then located within the FSA.[3] Miller was a physician and former president of the AMA's affiliated society in his state. In response, Lenroot again wrote Eleanor Roosevelt. The chief believed that the Miller bill was part of the AMA's effort to thwart the Children's Bureau's administration of the EMIC program. She maintained that "of course the essence of the Children's Bureau is its ability to approach all the problems of children. . . . The Bureau would be destroyed if its health functions were transferred."[4] The Miller bill never left the House committee on expenditures, but as Lenroot suspected, the old problem of reorganization would not go away. Democrats within the Administration, influenced by the advice of bureaucratic efficiency experts, constituted the real danger. Lenroot believed that the Children's Bureau "was not in danger of losing everything," but she urged that "a careful study of the whole situation in the Federal Government with reference to children and youth should be made."[5]

Just as Lenroot had feared, the enactment of the president's Reorganization Act in December 1945 set the stage for a dramatic change in the administrative responsibilities and bureaucratic location of the Children's Bureau. This legislation authorized President Harry Truman to put into effect any reorganization plan as long as both houses of Congress did not defeat the proposal within sixty days of its introduction. Feeling uncomfortable with the new Truman administration, Edith Abbott (Grace Abbott's sister) established an Emergency Committee to Save the Children's Bureau. Abbott's committee called on the historic network of Children's Bureau supporters to come to the agency's aid. Completely dismissing the arguments in favor of the move to the FSA, Lenroot and Abbott's emergency committee hoped that any reorganization plan would give the aid to dependent children program to the Children's Bureau. At the same time the emergency committee worked to reinstate the agency's "whole child" philosophy, the Bureau of the Budget, the PHS, and the FSA circulated memoranda openly calling for the Children's Bureau's transfer. In addition, the American Public Welfare Association, a professional organization of state welfare and health department officials, also lobbied for the recommended change. Already dealing with the bureaucratic legacy of the New Deal, this group maintained that having a single federal agency for all social welfare and health grant-in-aid programs was the most efficient system for state officials. As the calls for transfer intensified, Lenroot fought back by dismissing claims that the current system was inefficient, citing examples of improved cooperative efforts among the Children's Bureau and other federal agencies during the war.[6] The 1945 reorganization plan was not enacted but such ideas continued to surface.

Reorganization Plan No. 2, sent to Congress on May 16, 1946, also called for the Children's Bureau to be transferred to the FSA. While this move alone did not call for a reduction of bureau responsibilities, the plan, consistent with authority placed in the hands of most federal agency heads, gave the FSA administrator, Watson Miller, complete authority to determine the future of the Children's Bureau. Lenroot had a special meeting with the president where she gained his written assurance that the FSA would "discuss with [her] any plans for any major reorganization affecting the basic operations of the Children's Bureau." Further, Truman wrote that he was "fully confident that the [Children's] Bureau will have its interests well protected and . . . it will, indeed, be strengthened." Despite the uncertainty, things appeared to be looking up. Lenroot felt that the president's letter was sufficient protection and believed that it meant all current administrative duties and functions held by the Children's Bureau would be transferred with her agency in any future reorganization plan.[7]

However, her confidence was premature. Watson Miller periodically met with Lenroot, but he offered no specific details of his intentions for the Children's Bureau. Lenroot remained confident that these meetings, combined with the president's letter and her longtime friendship with Arthur Altmeyer, then chair of the Social Security Board and soon to be commissioner of the Social Security Administration, would protect the Children's Bureau's interests. But Congress had to reject Reorganization Plan No. 2 by July 16 in order for Lenroot's agency to remain untouched. Knowing that Lenroot was unhappy with the proposal and fearing that the Children's Bureau might be able to defeat the plan if given sufficient notice, Miller waited until Friday, July 12, to give Lenroot the details. The Children's Bureau would be placed under the direct authority of Arthur Altmeyer's Social Security Administration along with the bureaus of Old Age and Survivors' Insurance, Unemployment Compensation, and Public Assistance. Four principal agencies composed the FSA: Altmeyer's Social Security Administration, the PHS, the Office of Education, and a catchall unit called the Office of Special Services. In this structure the Children's Bureau's status was lowered one step within the federal bureaucracy because the agency's chief and her staff had no direct contact with a cabinet officer. In addition, the Children's Bureau would have to compete from this new position with much larger federal programs located within the Social Security Administration as well as the FSA. Perhaps most distressing to Lenroot, the Children's Bureau lost all authority over existing grant-in-aid programs and the agency's Industrial Division, responsible for child labor regulation and enforcement, remained in the Department of Labor. Thus, the Children's Bureau's responsibility was limited to its original mandate to investigate and report on child life. Katharine Lenroot and Martha Eliot tried to come up with a last-minute strategy to save the Children's Bureau's "whole child" philosophy, but it was too late and the reorganization plan went into effect on July 16, 1946. Miller contended that "the grouping of the various bureaus into four operating branches is necessary in order to simplify the administrative structure of the Agency and enable the Administrator to function effectively." He urged that "everything possible will be done to facilitate the work of the Children's Bureau and its relations with other Bureaus."[8]

Lenroot, Eliot, and their supporters were unconvinced. To add insult to injury, "U.S." was removed from the Children's Bureau's name. While this may seem trivial and consistent with steps taken earlier concerning the PHS and the Office of Education, the Children's Bureau's staff and supporters saw the move as "a psychological weapon in the battle against their institutional identity."[9] Eliot also believed that the (mostly male) federal bureaucrats in charge of the Social Security Administration did not understand how to deal with an agency as diverse (and mostly female) as the Children's Bureau. She believed that the bureaucrats in the FSA treated the Children's Bureau's staff like a "huge corps of clerical workers" instead of the nursing, social work, medical, and other professionals who made up about 40 percent of the agency's employees. She explained in an interview conducted twenty years later that this was "a very hard period of adjustment, as you can tell from my tone of voice."[10] Marshall Dimock, assistant secretary of labor in the Roosevelt administration, reported that Lenroot and Eliot were very upset by the change. He surmised that the general government reorganization plan, designed according to "function rather than constituency," negated the Children's Bureau's fundamental principles. He also guessed that growing "anti-labor sentiment" contributed to the transfer because the move also weakened the Department of Labor. While the transfer may have made bureaucratic sense and followed political trends of the postwar period, it completely destroyed the Children's Bureau's "whole child" philosophy as the best way to protect "a right to childhood." The agency was again transferred on April 1, 1953, to the newly created Department of Health, Education, and Welfare, where it has remained with diminishing influence.[11]

The 1946 bureaucratic reshuffle ended the life of the Children's Bureau as a largely self-governing federal enclave for children's interests. From 1912 to 1946 the Children's Bureau transformed itself from an agency limited to research and promotion to an administrator in the American "semiwelfare" state. In a 1921 address entitled "Our Nation's Obligation to Her Children," Julia Lathrop maintained that "under the Constitution it is the right of the state to make laws regarding . . . children and the family. [However,] the [federal] government has a restricted function—it can [only] investigate and report." During the 1920s Grace Abbott generally continued this policy, but the economic depression of the 1930s led the agency's second chief to call for more aggressive action by the federal government on behalf of America's young people. She argued that while states still had the primary responsibility for collecting money for child welfare programs, "if they cannot raise the necessary funds, I am in favor of the Federal Government raising it all." Abbott's successor, Katharine Lenroot, shaped the development of programs implementing this new federal role. Lenroot maintained that "the experience of the depression years will have been sterile indeed, in relation to the future, [if] it does not develop in the minds and hearts of the public . . . that never again must economic crisis find us so unprepared." Building upon the models constructed by her predecessors, Lenroot speculated in 1935 that in the future "means shall be taken through the cooperation of the federal government and the states to assure American wage-earners and their families some measure of security in jobs and earnings, and more adequate community services for child welfare and public health."[12]

A history of the Children's Bureau offers an excellent example of the link between the Progressive and New Deal eras. The Children's Bureau provided a national focus for child welfare reform and designed the model upon which public child welfare policy developed throughout the twentieth century. Although many reformers disagreed about the specific strategy, the establishment of the Children's Bureau in 1912 recognized federal responsibility for the social welfare of children in the United States. Furthermore, the work of the Children's Bureau helped to define childhood as a special period with specific needs. A report completed using data collected by the 1950 census defined childhood and youth in five distinct stages: 0-4 years (preschool age), 5-9 (early school ages), 10-14 (middle school ages), 15-19 (latter school ages), and 20-24 (constituting those years at the threshold of their working lives and/or marriage).[13] In 1900 childhood was generally defined as the period of life up to fourteen years of age. By 1950 this definition was more distinct and expanded to include young adults. The Children's Bureau's work also highlighted the widely varying circumstances of children living in the United States and the need for more federal assistance.

But despite these successes, the Children's Bureau's leadership never converted policy makers to its "whole child" philosophy. The agency's "dismemberment" in 1946 is indicative of post-New Deal bureaucratic trends emphasizing "function rather than constituency." As a result, since 1946 no federal agency has lobbied exclusively for the interests of children. As the *American Journal of Public Health* noted in October 1946, "from a 'functionalist' point of view, the

Children's Bureau is and always has been illogical in its organization as an independent unit of government." The journal supported the Children's Bureau's philosophy, stating that the needs of the "'child as a whole' must be the center of our attention." But apparently not fully understanding the idea, the journal also praised the transfer of the Children's Bureau to the FSA and called the consolidation of all federal child health programs to the PHS as an "advance" in federal health organization.[14] The journal's editorials show that functional organization strategies had triumphed even among those sympathetic to the Children's Bureau and its work. The traditional network of women's organizations and child welfare advocates which had lobbied on the bureau's behalf in the past were weakened and dispersed by 1946.[15] Consequently, the agency's earlier successful strategy identifying child welfare as primarily a women's issue became a liability in the postwar period.

Throughout its first thirty-four years, predictable and powerful opposition to Children's Bureau efforts came from conservative male politicians, the male-controlled AMA, male industrialists opposed to child labor regulation, and most members of the Catholic Church's hierarchy. But by emphasizing the role gender played in the agency's history scholars have generally overlooked the conservative women who also opposed the Children's Bureau. For example, although active herself in the effort to reduce the nation's infant mortality rate and an early supporter of the Children's Bureau's efforts, during the 1920s Elizabeth Lowell Putnam became one of the agency's most visible critics. She condemned the bureau for focusing on social and not medical problems. Arguing instead that the deaths "in the first month of life . . . are caused almost entirely by prenatal conditions and conditions of the birth [which] can be prevented only by medical care," Putnam believed that extension of the Sheppard-Towner Act "was a cruel measure, because it would lull the public with a false sense of security and so prevent measures of real value from being undertaken." Opposing child labor reform as a usurpation of individual and states' rights, Putnam denounced the Children's Bureau's staff as a group most interested in ensuring their own future employment. In 1927 she urged President Calvin Coolidge to appoint her Children's Bureau chief so that she "might secure its abolishment."[16] Similarly, the Woman Patriots chose to direct much of their ire at the Children's Bureau after ratification of the Nineteenth Amendment granting women's suffrage. Perhaps they were "sore losers," but it should also be acknowledged that female antisuffragists such as Putnam and the members of the Woman Patriots believed that the Children's Bureau's staff and supporters held ideals contrary to "democratic" family values. Historians studying women's experiences need to recognize that female critics of the Children's Bureau included many voices that are often neglected. Such recognition also helps to explain why women did not vote as a bloc, as anticipated by suffrage advocates, after gaining the vote. Still, in the end, it was the bureau's "friends" within the Democratic administration who led to its demise.

At the same time a history of the Children's Bureau's first thirty-four years shows that women played primary roles as architects of child welfare policy, formed the basic network of reform-minded supporters, and acted as the agency's largest group of adult constituents from the presuffrage era through the end of World War II. Women associated with the Children's Bureau worked successfully with like-minded men who agreed that child welfare was a proper topic for female attention. The agency provided an avenue for professional women, but its leaders also worked to lock out those who did not adhere to its reform strategies. For example, in 1931 members of the Children's Bureau aggressively opposed the reappointment of Judge Kathryn Sellers to the District of Columbia's juvenile court. Although the *Washington Post* called Sellers's work in the juvenile court "outstanding in child reform," Grace Abbott and Clara Beyer felt that the judge did not understand the importance of social case work in the prevention of juvenile delinquency. Beyer wrote that the "Juvenile Court should be a coordinating agency for the social work of the District. . . . There is no cooperation or sympathy between the various social agencies and the Court. . . . Judge Sellers has again and again in open court referred to the child labor and school attendance laws as 'rotten statutes.'" Beyer and Abbott also questioned whether Sellers was physically up to the job, since the judge had "apparently [suffered] some kind of stroke a few years ago from which she apparently has not completely recovered." Abbott maintained that "it ought to be possible to find someone in the District of Columbia who could do more for the reduction of our delinquency problem . . . than Judge Sellers." Beyer judged that two other women seeking the job were also not qualified.[17] Although interested in advancing roles for women within the male-dominated policy making structure, the women of the Children's Bureau were most interested in reforms consistent with their "whole child" philosophy.

Perhaps most importantly, a history of the Children's Bureau from 1912 to 1946 reveals some of its successes and failures in the effort to secure "a right to childhood." Even during its most influential years, the policies developed and implemented by the sole federal agency mandated to advocate for the best interests of children did not consistently offer children and their families effective solutions. As might be expected for the time, the Children's Bureau largely adhered to traditional gender roles and the ideals of the agency's well-educated middle-class leaders. This left little room for the development of innovative strategies which might have better addressed the needs of children whose circumstances did not conform to the middle-class family ideal. By promoting the notion that women's and children's welfare was dependent upon men, the Children's Bureau limited its options as a child welfare advocate. The bureau not only "standardized" what it identified as "good" family life but also set other physical and behavioral expectations for children. In addition, states had the primary responsibility for implementing and financing child welfare programs. As a result, the effort to promote "a right to childhood" varied widely. For example, in 1949 Mississippi reported the nation's lowest median annual income at $1,200. The median in Arkansas, Alabama, Georgia, South Carolina, and Tennessee also dipped below $2,000. At the same time New Jersey, Connecticut, Illinois, Michigan, California, Nevada, and Washington reported annual median incomes above $3,500. Regional differences, influenced by historical prejudices and discriminatory economic patterns, continued to impact the lives of children in the United States. Ultimately, child welfare policy often placed the "best" interests of children behind those of adults, or at least perpetuated existing social structure.[18]

The Children's Bureau's advocacy of programs for "dependent" children highlights the dual circumstance of its policies designed to promote "a right to childhood." For example, the Children's Bureau promoted foster care as the best means to secure a "normal home life" for children whose families had "failed." Before the Children's Bureau's establishment few Washington policy makers had paid any attention to the undesirable nineteenth-century-style institutions where many poor, orphaned, or abandoned children lived. But foster care did not necessarily supply the access to "normal home life" that the bureau suggested was the right of every child. Although altered in the Progressive Era to advance the interests of minors, many state statutes still protect the rights of biological parents over security for children. On the issue of adoption, as E. Wayne Carp argues, the Children's Bureau served as "the center for authoritative information" when little attention was given to the topic by reformers or government policy makers. However, adoption and foster care received little attention compared to other child welfare reform efforts.[19] This is a serious legacy for today's children languishing in ineffective foster care programs or lost in custody fights between biological and adoptive parents due to the lack of a federal adoption statute. Another issue is that mothers' pensions and eventually aid to dependent children funds were inadequate from their inception. Even though the agency recognized wide regional and professional disparity in existing public and private programs designed to meet the needs of "dependent" children, it only advocated federal intervention after the emergency conditions experienced during the Great Depression. Even then, federal aid was limited to those identified by local authorities as eligible. Consequently, this failure to develop adequate programs for youngsters with "special needs" ultimately meant that the Children's Bureau's work promoted "a right to childhood" for middle-class children more successfully than for those in greatest distress. For example, the bureau's best-selling instructional pamphlets, "Infant Care" and "Prenatal Care," emphasized "traditional" values and lifestyles that were often inappropriate or impossible for poor families to obtain.

Nonetheless, at the time of its establishment and for the next thirty-four years the Children's Bureau served as the only federal agency interested solely in the needs of children. Under Julia Lathrop and her successors, the agency's investigative and reporting work served as its most important contribution. "Scientific studies" raised public awareness about the needs of children and their families in both urban and rural areas. This is most evident in the Children's Bureau's efforts to reduce the nation's maternal and infant mortality rates. The country's maternal mortality rate dropped from 60.8 deaths per 10,000 live births in 1915 to 15.7 in 1946. The infant mortality rate fell from an estimated rate of 132 deaths per 1,000 live births in 1912 to 99.9 in 1915 and to 33.8 in 1946 (see table 5).[20] Though difficult to measure, Children's Bureau efforts on behalf of mothers and babies probably contributed to these trends, thereby saving many lives. When the Children's Bureau was established in 1912, the PHS gave no attention to why mothers and babies died. The Children's Bureau pioneered infant and maternal mortality studies and designed and implemented the 1921 Sheppard-Towner Maternity and Infancy Act, the epochal 1935 Social Security Act, and the capstone of its efforts for mothers and their children, the EMIC program operated during World War II. Poor mothers and children have since benefited from the maternity and child health sections of the 1935 Social Security Act and the standards established by EMIC. During the war, the pregnant wives and newborn children of servicemen benefited directly from the good medical care provided by EMIC, but everyone profited through improved medical standards encouraged by the Children's Bureau's reg-

Table 5. Infant and Maternal Mortality Rates for Death Registration Area, 1915-46

Years	Infant Rate[a]	Maternal Rate[b]	Years	Infant Rate[a]	Maternal Rate[b]
1915	99.90	60.80	1931	61.60	66.10
1916	101.00	62.80	1932	57.60	63.30
1917	93.80	66.20	1933	58.10	61.90
1918	100.90	91.60	1934	60.10	59.30
1919	86.60	73.70	1935	55.70	58.20
1920	85.50	79.90	1936	51.70	56.80
1921	75.60	68.20	1937	54.40	48.90
1922	76.20	66.40	1938	51.00	43.50
1923	77.10	66.50	1939	48.00	40.40
1924	70.80	65.60	1940	47.00	37.60
1925	71.70	64.70	1941	45.30	31.70
1926	73.30	65.60	1942	40.40	25.90
1927	64.60	64.70	1943	40.40	24.50
1928	68.70	69.20	1944	39.80	22.80
1929	67.60	69.50	1945	38.30	20.70
1930	64.60	67.30	1946	33.80	15.70

Source: U.S. Bureau of the Census. *Historical Statistics of the United States, Colonial Times to 1970, Bicentennial Edition, Part 1* (Washington, D.C.: Government Printing Office, 1976), p. 57.

a. Deaths under one year of age per 1,000 live births.
b. Deaths per 10,000 births.

ulation of hospital services. Further, the Children's Bureau hoped to expand obstetric and pediatric care to all mothers and babies in the United States after the war. But, in a more conservative postwar political atmosphere, the evolution of Children's Bureau infant and maternal policy unintentionally encouraged the growth of private health insurance companies, placed the AMA in an even stronger position to oppose any form of national health insurance, stigmatized government-assisted health care for mothers and babies as "charity," and strengthened traditional gender roles by making women's and children's welfare dependent on their attachment to men.

As already noted, the promotion of mothers' pensions was another major policy effort adopted by the Children's Bureau during its first thirty-four years that relied primarily on traditional gender roles. Here again, the agency had mixed success. Building on the bureau's early experience, Katharine Lenroot, Martha Eliot, and Grace Abbott developed the aid to dependent children sections of the 1935 Social Security Act. Although it received little attention at the time, ADC has become one of the most controversial and unwieldy aspects of the American "semiwelfare" state.[21] The Children's Bureau's efforts gained attention for a program that was received with little enthusiasm by other federal reformers. Since its inception this program has helped many poor children, even though it was never adopted as the social insurance Lenroot, Eliot, and Abbott envisioned. Mothers' pensions and the subsequent ADC program were an attempt to recognize children's "right" to care and security. But ADC families have had limited opportunity to become independent or improve their economic circumstances. Perhaps over time the Children's Bureau would have been in a better position to advocate for the interests of poor children and their families if the agency had retained control of this program. Instead, implementation of ADC under the Social Security Board destroyed the Children's Bureau's fundamental "whole child" philosophy and placed children's interests in competition with those of much more powerful groups. Children might have also benefited from the advocacy and coordination a single agency could provide during the development of Lyndon Johnson's Great Society programs.

Despite its self-induced weaknesses and those failures over which it had no control, the Children's Bureau did try to examine the needs of "all" children in the United States. While most social activists focused on cities, the Children's Bureau also conducted studies and promoted child welfare reform in rural areas. Furthermore, in a time when such viewpoints were absent from most social reform agendas, many of the Children's Bureau's studies recognized race, ethnicity, class, and region as factors in the experiences of children.

In addition, the bureau responded more positively than most federal bureaucracies to the requests of its constituents. Children, parents, and reformers wrote the agency as many as 125,000 letters a year requesting help and offering suggestions. The bureau sent its instructional pamphlets and wrote individual responses to such inquiries. The Sheppard-Towner program and Title V, Part I, of the Social Security Act were direct responses to requests for help from women living in rural America. The inclusion of services for handicapped children under Title V, Part II, was also a response to suggestions from child welfare advocates and parents.

In a more general sense, as Walter Trattner maintains, the establishment of the Children's Bureau "marked a significant departure in public policy. It was the first time the federal government recognized not merely the rights of children, but also the need to create a permanent agency to at least study, if not yet protect them." An examination of the Children's Bureau's history also supports Viviana Zelizer's argument that during this period the value of children was transformed from "useful worker to sacred child."[22] Childhood was sentimentalized and children gained new significance. The bureau and its supporters were able to convince many adults that children had worth beyond what they could contribute to the family's immediate economic circumstances. Child labor regulations, better educational opportunities, recreational facilities, the development of juvenile courts, and the equalized legal status of children born outside of marriage resulted from bureau efforts to promote a new way of valuing children and their "right to childhood."

But ultimately, Lathrop and her successors were unable to convince the public and policy makers that the best interests of the "whole child" should be undertaken by a single federal agency. Perhaps they were unwilling to hear, but there was also a lack of commitment on the part of many in authority and a rejection of the idea by some citizens that public responsibility included the welfare of all children. Throughout its existence, the Children's Bureau and its constituency faced an atmosphere of neglect. Even during the development and passage of the Social Security Act, the inclusion of children in the effort to provide "security" for everyone in the United States drew little attention. The most innovative federal program implemented during the period, EMIC, served only as a temporary wartime effort designed primarily to benefit adult males (or the military) rather than children.

Today one child in five in the United States lives in poverty and as the 1991 final report of the National Commission on Children, *Beyond Rhetoric,* shows, creative initiatives to deal with the difficulties faced by many children are rare. A recent analysis conducted by the Luxembourg Income Study indicates that poor children in the United States are poorer than the children in fifteen other Western industrialized nations. Only poor children in Israel and Ireland fair worse. Public debate about "welfare reform" has intensified but there are no clear solutions. An examination of the U.S. Children's Bureau's first thirty-four years of work highlights some of the successes and failures of the past which continue to plague current child welfare policy. Perhaps most fundamentally maternal and infant mortality rates for the United States remain skewed by race and class, and continue to rank poorly among comparable nations.[23] From the Progressive Era through World War II the Children's Bureau's staff and supporters acted as the movers and shakers responsible for much of twentieth-century U.S.

child welfare policy development. But after 1946 children did not have a powerful advocate within the federal government solely concerned with their interests. After its transfer to the FSA in 1946, the Children's Bureau continued to investigate and report on behalf of children. But since it no longer had administrative status in a growing postwar bureaucracy, the Children's Bureau's efforts were largely negated. As Stephen R. Graubard, editor of the Academy of Arts and Sciences' *Daedalus,* contends in his introduction to the journal's 1992 special issue concerning America's childhood, "if major changes are to take place there must be a more candid acknowledgment of any number of circumstances, many with deep historical roots, that make the lives of American children so precarious."[24] A powerful federal agency mandated solely to care for the needs of the "whole child" might best protect the diverse interests of America's children.

Notes

Abbreviations

ACHAP	American Child Health Association Papers, Herbert Hoover Presidential Library, West Branch, Iowa
CBP	Records of the U.S. Children's Bureau, National Archives, Washington, D.C.
CESP	Records of the Committee on Economic Security, National Archives, Washington, D.C.
CMBP	Clara M. Beyer Papers, Schlesinger Library, Radcliffe College, Cambridge, Mass.
COHP	Columbia Oral History Project, Social Security Project, Columbia University Library, New York City
DLP	Records of the U.S. Department of Labor, National Archives, Washington, D.C.
EGAP	Edith and Grace Abbott Papers, Regenstein Library, University of Chicago, Chicago, Ill.
ELPP	Elizabeth Lowell Putnam Papers, Schlesinger Library, Radcliffe College, Cambridge, Mass.
ERP	Eleanor Roosevelt Papers, Franklin D. Roosevelt Presidential Library, Hyde Park, N.Y.
FDRP	Franklin D. Roosevelt Papers, Franklin D. Roosevelt Presidential Library, Hyde Park, N.Y.
HHP	Herbert Hoover Papers, Herbert Hoover Presidential Library, West Branch, Iowa
JLP	Julia Lathrop Papers, Rockford College Library, Rockford, Ill.
MMEP	Martha May Eliot Papers, Schlesinger Library, Radcliffe College, Cambridge, Mass.
NCLCP	National Child Labor Committee Papers, Library of Congress, Washington, D.C.
WHTP	William Howard Taft Papers, microfilm, University of Cincinnati Langsum Library, Cincinnati, Ohio

Introduction

1. This study primarily relies on the following works for its interpretation of the general development of the U.S. "semiwelfare" state: Robert H. Bremner, *From the Depths: The Discovery of Poverty in the United States;* Walter I. Trattner, *From Poor Law to Welfare State: A History of Social Welfare in America;* James T. Patterson, *America's Struggle against Poverty, 1900-1985;* Michael B.

Katz, *In the Shadow of the Poorhouse: A Social History of Welfare in America;* and Edward D. Berkowitz, *America's Welfare State: From Roosevelt to Reagan.*

2. In 1937 Newton Edwards warned, "The aging character of the population will tend to reduce the influence of youth in the areas of politics, economy, ethics—in short, in the whole area of human relations" ("Youth as a Population Element," p. 8). Edwards did not foresee the upcoming baby boom, but he did correctly predict the competition between social welfare programs for children and those of older adults in a postwar America; on the effects of an aging population on social welfare policy see W. Andrew Achenbaum, *Shades of Gray: Old Age, American Values, and Federal Policies since 1920.*

3. A good examination of the changing status of children during the late nineteenth and early twentieth centuries is Vivana A. Zelizer, *Pricing the Priceless Child: The Changing Social Value of Children.*

4. Trattner, *From Poor Law to Welfare State,* p. 196.

5. For example see Bremner, *From the Depths,* pp. 221-22; Clarke A. Chambers, *Seedtime of Reform: American Social Service and Social Action, 1918-1933,* pp. 27-58; Trattner, *From Poor Law to Welfare State,* pp. 195-200; Katz, *In the Shadow of the Poorhouse,* p. 122; and Theda Skocpol, *Protecting Soldiers and Mothers: The Political Origins of Social Policy in the United States,* pp. 10, 46, 47, 304, 486-94.

6. Stephen B. Wood, *Constitutional Politics in the Progressive Era;* and Walter I. Trattner, *Crusade for the Children: A History of the National Child Labor Committee and Child Labor Reform in America.*

7. Richard A. Meckel, *Save the Babies: American Public Health Reform and the Prevention of Infant Mortality, 1850-1929.*

8. Molly Ladd-Taylor, *Mother-Work: Women, Child Welfare, and the State, 1890-1930.*

9. Joseph B. Chepaitis, "The First Federal Social Welfare Measure: The Sheppard-Towner Maternity and Infancy Act, 1918-1932"; Skocpol, *Protecting Soldiers and Mothers,* pp. 480-524; for details on the implementation of Sheppard-Towner in one state see Kriste Lindenmeyer Dick, "Saving Mothers and Babies: The Sheppard-Towner Maternity and Infancy Act 1921-1929, with Emphasis on Its Effects in Ohio."

10. Studies that discuss the programs leading to the Social Security Act but pay little attention to the children's welfare aspects include: Roy Lubove, *The Struggle for Social Security, 1900-1935;* Daniel Nelson, *Unemployment Insurance: The American Experience, 1915-1935;* Bremner, *From the Depths,* pp. 263-64; William Graebner, *A History of Retirement: The Meaning and Function of an American Institution, 1885-1978;* and Edward Berkowitz and Kim McQuaid, *Creating the Welfare State: The Political Economy of Twentieth-Century Reform,* pp. 96-113; on the development and implementation of the early program see Charles McKinley and Robert W. Frase, *Launching Social Security: A Capture-and-Record Account, 1935-1937;* W. Andrew Achenbaum, *Social Security: Visions and Revisions;* and Trattner, *From Poor Law to Welfare State.* James Patterson discusses the development of aid to dependent children briefly in *America's Struggle against Poverty,* pp. 65-77.

11. Edwin E. Witte, *The Development of the Social Security Act;* Winifred Bell, *Aid to Dependent Children;* Leroy Ashby, "Partial Promises and Semi-Visible Youths: The Depression and World War II"; Thomas H. Eliot, *Recollections of the New Deal: When the People Mattered;* and Linda Gordon, *Pitied but Not Entitled: Single Mothers and the History of Welfare, 1890-1935.*

12. One exception is the recently published detailed study of children's experiences in the United States during World War II, William M. Tuttle, Jr., *"Daddy's Gone to War": The Second World War in the Lives of America's Children.*

13. Nancy Pottishman Weiss, "Save the Children: A History of the Children's Bureau, 1903-1918"; and Louis J. Covotsos, "Child Welfare and Social Progress: The United States Children's Bureau, 1912-1935."

14. Sheila M. Rothman, *Woman's Proper Place: A History of Changing Ideals and Practices, 1870 to the Present,* pp. 126-52; J. Stanley Lemons, *The Woman Citizen: Social Feminism in the 1920s,* pp. 153-80; Robyn Muncy, *Creating a Female Dominion in American Reform, 1900-1935;* and Skocpol, *Protecting Soldiers and Mothers,* esp. pp. 311-524.

15. Molly Ladd-Taylor, *Raising a Baby the Government Way: Mothers' Letters to the Children's Bureau, 1915-1932,* p. 5; see also Molly Ladd-Taylor, "Women's Health and Public Policy."

16. Gordon, *Pitied but Not Entitled,* p. 6.

17. "Children or Parsimony: Which Shall Prevail," pp. 313-15.

18. "Misplaced Priorities," p. 28.

Chapter 1: The Origins of a Federal Bureau for Children, 1900-1912

1. Robert H. Wiebe, *The Search for Order, 1877-1920.*

2. Owen Lovejoy, "Letter to the Editor"; Lillian Wald, "The Idea of the Federal Children's Bureau," pp. 33-37; Covotsos, "Child Welfare and Social Progress," pp. 1-12; James A. Tobey, *The Children's Bureau: Its History, Activities, and Organization,* p. 1; Robert L. Duffus, *Lillian Wald, Neighbor and Crusader,* p. 35; Weiss, "Save the Children," pp. 4, 48; Josephine Goldmark, *Impatient Crusader: Florence Kelley's Life Story,* pp. 94-96; James Johnson, "The Role of Women in the Founding of the United States Children's Bureau," pp. 183-84; Alice Elizabeth Padgett, "The History of the Establishment of the United States Children's Bureau," pp. 1-22; Alexander McKelway, chief lobbyist for the NCLC, found mention of a proposal for a children's bureau in the *New York World* a early as July 27, 1866. This editorial opted for a children's bureau instead of a Freedman's Bureau ("Communications," cited in Weiss, "Save the Children," p. 72).

3. Florence Kelley, *Some Ethical Gains through Legislation,* pp. 99-101.

4. Dorothy E. Bradbury, "Four Decades of Action for Children: A Short History of the Children's Bureau," p. 1.

5. Steven Mintz and Susan Kellogg, *Domestic Revolutions: A Social History of American Family Life,* p. xv.

6. Homer Folks, *The Care of Destitute, Neglected, and Dependent Children;* Emma O. Lundberg, *Unto the Least of These: Social Services for Children;* and John Spargo, *The Bitter Cry of the Children;* Jacob Riis, *How the Other Half Lives: Studies among the Tenements of New York,* p. 134.

7. Bremner, *From the Depths;* U.S. Bureau of the Census, *Historical Statistics of the United States, Colonial Times to 1970, Bicentennial Edition, Part I,* p. 57.

8. National Child Labor Committee, *Twenty-fifth Anniversary of the National Child Labor Committee, 1904-1929,* p. 5; Ronald D. Cohen, "Child Saving and Progressivism, 1885-1915," p. 274; and Joseph M. Hawes, *The Children's Rights Movement: A History of Advocacy and Protection,* pp. 26-53.

9. "Chronology," in *American Childhood: A Research Guide and Historical Handbook,* ed. Joseph M. Hawes and N. Ray Hiner, pp. 619-26; adolescent medicine was not recognized as a specialty until the 1950s.

10. G. Stanley Hall, *Adolescence: Its Psychology and Its Relations to Physiology, Anthropology, Sociology, Sex, Crime, Religion, and Education;* Samuel McCune Lindsay, "Exploring the New World for Children," pp. 459-63; Weiss, "Save the Children," pp. 8-47.

11. U.S. Bureau of the Census, *Historical Statistics of the United States,* p. 15; Covotsos, "Child Welfare and Social Progress," p. 17. While eighteen is generally recognized as adulthood, the Bureau of the Census compiles statistics for those nineteen years of age and under. Zelizer, *Pricing the Priceless Child,* defines children as those fourteen years and under. This is an acceptable definition for the early child welfare movement, but the most extreme wing of the child labor movement defined persons eighteen and under as children (Robert H. Bremner et al., eds., *Children and Youth in America: A Documentary History,* 2:vii; Trattner, *From Poor Law to Welfare State,* pp. 103-28).

12. The best overview of the infant health movement is Meckel, *Save the Babies;* on the New York City efforts see S. Josephine Baker, *Fighting for Life;* Wiebe, *Search for Order,* p. 169; on the link between glorified motherhood and child welfare see Ladd-Taylor, *Mother-Work,* esp. pp. 43-73. For evidence of the "scientific" trend in child welfare work see Frank J. Bruno, *Trends in Social Work, 1874-1956: A History Based on the Proceedings of the National Conference of Social Work;* Trattner, *From Poor Law to Welfare State,* pp. 103-28, 211-29; Hamilton Cravens, "Child Saving in the Age of Professionalism, 1915-1930," pp. 415-88; and Susan Tiffin, *In Whose Best Interest? Child Welfare Reform in the Progressive Era,* pp. 253-80.

13. Sara M. Evans, *Born for Liberty: A History of Women in America,* p. 146; Daniel J. Walkowitz, "The Making of a Feminine Professional Identity: Social Workers and the 1920's," p. 1055; Muncy, *Creating a Female Dominion,* pp. 66-92; and Seth Koven and Sonya Michel, "Womanly Duties: Maternalistic Politics and the Origins of Welfare States in France, Germany, Great Britain, and the United States."

14. Julia Lathrop noted the connection between Florence Kelley, Lillian Wald, and Jane Addams in a letter to Graham Taylor, Dec. 13, 1927, Graham Taylor Papers, Newberry Library, Chicago, Ill., Ta, file Julia Lathrop to Graham Taylor, July 26, 1918-June 1932.

15. Sybil Lipschultz, "Social Feminism and Legal Discourse: 1908-1923"; Bremner et al., *Children and Youth in America,* 2:1524; *American Childhood,* ed. Hawes and Hiner, pp. 621-22; Kathryn Kish Sklar, ed., *Notes of Sixty Years: The Autobiography of Florence Kelley,* pp. 85-86; and Hawes, *Children's Rights Movement,* pp. 39-53.

16. Ellis W. Hawley, "Social Policy and the Liberal State in Twentieth-Century America," pp. 117-40.

17. Kelley, *Some Ethical Gains through Legislation,* p. 101.

18. John D. Lindsay to Representative James Kennedy, Jan. 8, 1909 (copy), EGAP, box 38, folder 1; *Senate Documents,* 60th Cong., 2d sess., report no. 2144, "Establishment of a Children's Bureau," p. 3; Covotsos, "Child Welfare and Social Progress," pp. 35-36; and Weiss, "Save the Children," pp. 61-63.

19. Edward T. Devine to Lillian Wald, Sept. 15, 1903, EGAP, box 38, folder 1; see also Weiss, "Save the Children," p. 48; Wald, "Idea of a Federal Children's Bureau," p. 34; Bradbury, "Four Decades of Action for Children," p. 2; the date for the meeting may be found in Theodore Roosevelt Papers (microfilm, University of Cincinnati Langsam Library), daily desk diary, Fri., Mar. 31, 1905, 12:30 P.M., microfilm series 9, reel 430.

20. Roosevelt to Jane Addams, Jan. 24, 1906, Theodore Roosevelt Papers (microfilm, University of Cincinnati Langsam Library), series 2, vol. 61, p. 16. Concerning the deer head episode, Roosevelt's secretary cautioned Wald upon her receipt of the unusual gift, "not to make [the gift] public in any way or it will bring a flood of requests for like donations" (William Loeb to Lillian D. Wald, Nov. 4, 1903, and William Loeb to Lillian Wald, Feb. 15, 1904, Lillian D. Wald Papers, Columbia University, New York; cited in Mina Carson, *Settlement Folk: Social Thought and the American Settlement Movement, 1885-1930,* pp. 147, 245-46); for a revealing article on the attitudes of some reformers concerning Roosevelt's support for social workers' interests see Jane Addams et al., "TR—Social Worker."

21. Senate, "President's Annual Message," Dec. 6, 1904, *Congressional Record,* 58th Cong., 3d sess., p. 13.

22. Edward T. Devine, "The Message," pp. 449-50; Roger Daniels, *The Politics of Prejudice: The Anti-Japanese Movement in California and the Struggle for Japanese Exclusion,* pp. 31-45.

23. The original forty-three members of the NCLC included Felix Adler (chair), Jane Addams, Grover Cleveland, Homer Folks, James Cardinal Gibbons, Florence Kelley, Ben B. Lindsey, Edgar Gardner Murphy, Gifford Pinchot, Graham Taylor, and Lillian D. Wald. Trattner, *Crusade for the Children;* NCLC, "Minute Book, First to Twentieth Meeting," Apr. 15, 1905, NCLCP; Samuel McCune Lindsay, "Child Labor—A National Disgrace," p. 302.

24. I have discovered no evidence for this meeting in either the NCLCP or Roosevelt's desk diary, but Bradbury contends this was the sequence of events ("Four Decades of Action for Children," p. 2). For a discussion of the NCLC's role in the effort to establish a federal children's bureau see Carmen R. Delle

Donnie, "Two-Handed Engine at the Door: Social Workers and the Agitation for a National Children's Bureau"; and Trattner, *Crusade for the Children,* pp. 95-98; Covotsos, "Child Welfare and Social Progress," pp. 20-39; quotation from Edward T. Devine, "Congress and the Children," p. 588.

25. Senate, *Congressional Record,* 59th Cong., 1st sess., p. 892, and House, p. 6001; Trattner, *Crusade for the Children,* pp. 95-98; Covotsos, "Child Welfare and Social Progress," p. 23; James Johnson, "Role of Women," p. 184.

26. Typed summary of editorial, "Children's Bureau and State Control," *Providence Journal,* Mar. 18, 1906, included in EGAP, box 38, folder 1; however, it should be noted that in 1906 the children's bureau proposal received little attention in the popular press.

27. Duffus, *Lillian Wald,* p. 95.

28. Owen R. Lovejoy to Jane Addams, Apr. 29, 1908; *Minutes of the Board of Trustees Meeting, National Child Labor Committee, 48th Meeting to the 65th Meeting, November 9, 1916 to June 29, 1921,* NCLCP, p. 1.

29. Lindsay, "Child Labor—A National Disgrace," p. 303; House, *Congressional Record,* 60th Cong., 2d sess., H.R. 24148, p. 296, and Senate, S. 8323, p. 747; Alisa C. Klaus, "Babies All the Rage: The Movement to Prevent Infant Mortality in the United States and France, 1890-1920," pp. 181-84; Meckel, *Save the Babies,* pp. 140, 151.

30. Child welfare advocates believed that all children were dependent on their parents and communities to "protect" them during childhood, but the term "dependent" usually referred to children without parents, or those in families unable to provide for them. Physically and mentally handicapped children were also often included.

31. Roy Lubove, "James E. West," pp. 871-73.

32. Addams, "TR—Social Worker," pp. 525-26; James E. West et al. to Theodore Roosevelt, Dec. 22, 1908, reprinted in *Proceedings of the Conference on the Care of Dependent Children, Held at Washington, D.C., January 25, 26, 1909* (hereafter cited as *Proceedings 1909 White House Conference*), Senate Document 721, 60th Cong., 2d sess., 1909, pp. 17-18; the following eight men signed the letter: Homer Folks, secretary, New York State Charities Aid Association; Hastings H. Hart, superintendent, Illinois Children's Home and Aid Society, and chair, Study of Child Placing, Russell Sage Foundation; Thomas M. Mulry, president, St. Vincent de Paul Society of the United States; Edward T. Devine, editor, *Charities and the Commons,* general secretary, Charity Organizing Society, and professor of Social Economy, Columbia University; Julian W. Mack, judge, Circuit Court of Chicago, and former president, National Conference of Jewish Charities; Charles W. Birtwell, general secretary, Boston Children's Aid Society; Theodore Dreiser, editor, *Delineator;* and James E. West, secretary, National Child-Rescue League; Dorothy Bradbury, "The Children's Advocate: The Story of the U.S. Children's Bureau, 1903-1946," unpublished manuscript in MMEP, MC 229, box 13, file 184, p. 17; Weiss, "Save the Children," p. 77; Harold A. Jambor, "Theodore Dreiser, the *Delineator* Magazine, and Dependent Children: A Background Note on the Calling of the 1909 White House Conference," pp. 33-40.

33. *Proceedings 1909 White House Conference,* a list of individuals invited to the conference and their affiliations appears on pages 20-31; note: "All of the above, with a few exceptions, accepted the invitation and were present at the sessions of the conference" p. 31. The list includes Catholics, Jews, and Protestants; thirty of the invitees were clearly women; race is much more difficult to determine, but Booker T. Washington attended and presented an address entitled "Destitute Colored Children of the South," pp. 113-17; for a brief summary of the conference's ideology see Weiss, "Save the Children," pp. 59-60.

34. *Proceedings 1909 White House Conference,* p. 174; Walter I. Trattner, *Homer Folks: Pioneer for Social Justice,* pp. 292-93; Weiss, "Save the Children," pp. 65-71; further analysis of this debate is addressed in chap. 6.

35. *Proceedings 1909 White House Conference,* pp. 6, 114-15.

36. Ibid., p. 171.

37. Ibid., pp. 171, 174-75.

38. Ibid., p. 9; the conference recommendation for a private committee was not realized until the 1916 establishment of the Child Welfare League of America.

39. Ibid.; Trattner, *From Poor Law to Welfare State,* pp. 194-95.

40. These individuals included Jane Addams, Edward T. Devine, Homer Folks, Florence Kelley, Samuel McCune Lindsay, Judge Ben B. Lindsey, Judge Julian Mack, Alexander McKelway, and Lillian D. Wald, among others; see "Arguments before the Committee on Expenditures in the Interior Department, House of Representatives, Jan. 27, 1909, H.R. Bill 24148," EGAP, box 38, folder 1. For a complete list of those who testified see House Committee on Expenditures in the Interior Department, *Establishment of Children's Bureau: Report to Accompany H.R. 24148,* 60th Cong., 2d sess., 1909, House Report 2144, hereafter cited as House Report 2144; Senate, Senate Committee on Education and Labor, *Establishment of a Children's Bureau in the Interior Department: Hearings on S. 8323,* 60th Cong. 2d sess., Senate Report 974, hereafter cited as Senate Report 974.

41. House Report 2144, p. 3.

42. Ibid., p. 4; Covotsos, "Child Welfare and Social Progress," pp. 26-27.

43. Covotsos, "Child Welfare and Social Progress," pp. 21-29; see also Senate Report 974; House Report 2144, pp. 3-13.

44. *Congressional Record,* vol. 43, Feb. 22, 1909, 60th Cong., 2d sess., pp. 2897-98.

45. House Report 2144, pp. 2-3.

46. *Congressional Record,* 60th Cong., 2d sess., Feb. 15, 1909; McKelway wrote Roosevelt's message; L. Moody Simms, Jr., "Alexander McKelway," pp. 530-32.

47. House Report 2144, p. 3.

48. Committee on Expenditures in the Department of Commerce and Labor, *Establishment of Children's Bureau, June 21, 1910,* 61st Cong., 2d sess., House Report no. 1675; Covotsos, "Child Welfare and Social Progress," pp. 32-34.

49. Covotsos, "Child Welfare and Social Progress," pp. 28-30; Edward Devine to Lillian Wald, Sept. 15, 1903, EGAP, box 38, folder 1.

50. Senate, *Congressional Record,* 62d Cong., 1st sess., p. 105; House, p. 173.

51. P. P. Claxton to Secretary of the Interior, Jan. 3, 1912, WHTP, microfilm, reel 370, case file 161; Claxton to Secretary of the Interior, Jan. 2, 1912, EGAP, box 38, folder 2; Alexander J. McKelway to P. P. Claxton, Dec. 19, 1912, EGAP, box 38, folder 2; Lillian Wald to William Allen, Feb. 10, 1912, EGAP, box 38, folder 2.

52. Lillian Wald to Owen Lovejoy, Feb. 1, 1912, EGAP, box 59, folder 2; Padgett, "History of the Establishment of the United States Children's Bureau," p. 69; Senate, *Congressional Record,* 62d Cong., 2d sess., pp. 1573-79.

53. Owen Lovejoy to Lillian Wald, Jan. 31, 1912, EGAP, box 38, folder 2; A. J. McKelway to Charles D. Hilles, Apr. 5, 1912, WHTP, microfilm, reel 370, case file 161; National Child Labor Committee, "Minute Book, New York, May 1st, 1912," NCLCP, box 7, p. 67.

54. Florence Kelley to Julia Lathrop, Nov. 19, 1930, EGAP, box 39, folder 2.

55. National Child Labor Committee, "NCLC Minute Book, Twentieth to Forty-Seventh Meeting, May 1st, 1912," p. 2. It is likely that a number of individuals were mentioned for the position. Pauline Goldmark and Alexander McKelway were just two of those considered by the NCLC; also see Weiss, "Save the Children," pp. 106-7.

56. Grace Abbott, "Notes on the Establishment of the Children's Bureau," EGAP, box 25, folder 10, p. 7.

57. Telegram from Jane Addams and Julius Rosenwald to Lillian Wald, Apr. 12, 1912, EGAP, box 38, folder 2; similar telegram sent to Judge Julian W. Mack, Apr. 12, 1912, WHTP, microfilm, reel 370, case file 161; Jane Addams to Lillian Wald, Apr. 12 1912, EGAP, box 38, folder 2.

58. Louise C. Wade, "Julia Clifford Lathrop," in *Notable American Women,* 2:370-72.

59. National Child Labor Committee, "NCLC Minute Book, May 1, 1912," p. 2; William Howard Taft to Jane Addams, Apr. 15, 1912, WHTP, microfilm, reel 370, case file 161; telegram from Julia Lathrop to Lillian Wald, Apr. 19, 1912, EGAP, box 59, folder 1; Julia Lathrop to William Howard Taft, May 7, 1912, WHTP, microfilm, reel 370, case file 161a. In an article in the *New York Evening Post* Lathrop is quoted as expressing some fear at her appointment: "The responsibilities are great and I do not know that I am equal to them" (Jan. 18, 1913, clipping in EGAP, box 25, folder 10).

60. Grace Abbott, "Notes on the Establishment of the Children' Bureau," p. 7.

61. *Survey,* 28 (Apr. 13, 1912): 176-77; quotation from telegram sent by Jane Addams and Julius Rosenwald to Lillian Wald, Apr. 12, 1912.

62. Because many were unfamiliar with Lathrop, Graham Taylor, editor of the *Survey,* wrote enthusiastically concerning her qualifications for the job; see also Grace Abbott, "Notes on Julia Lathrop's Appointment, May 4, 1912," EGAP, box 25, folder 10; Linda Gordon, "The New Feminist Scholarship on the Welfare State," p. 9.

Chapter 2: The Bureau Goes to Work, 1912-13

1. Belgium, Czechoslovakia, Germany, the Soviet Union, Poland, and Yugoslavia created similar government agencies during the next decade (Grace Abbott, "Ten Years' Work for Children," p. 190).

2. Julian W. Mack, "The President's Address," *Proceedings of the National Conference of Charities and Correction, 39th Annual Session, June 12-19, 1912,* pp. 1, 5 (hereafter cited as *NCCC Proceedings, 1912*); Julia Lathrop, in same, p. 33; Julia Lathrop to John Glenn, Apr. 24, 1912, EGAP, box 57, folder 2.

3. Trattner, *From Poor Law to Welfare State,* pp. 62-63, 78-79, 194; Tiffin, *In Whose Best Interest?* pp. 237-38; and Barbara Finkelstein, "Uncle Sam and the Children: A History of Government Involvement in Child Rearing."

4. "Children's Bureau Bill" (Apr. 13, 1912): 83; see also "Notes on Julia Lathrop's Appointment," EGAP, box 25, folder 10; "Governor Wilson and the Social Worker"; Addams, "TR—Social Worker"; "Children's Bureau Bill" (May 7, 1912): 83-84; Mary Drier to Lillian Wald, n.d. [ca. 1912], Lillian Wald Papers, New York Public Library, New York, New York, cited in Weiss, "Save the Children," p. 109, n. 2.

5. Aileen S. Kraditor, *The Ideas of the Woman Suffrage Movement, 1890-1920,* pp. 70-71; Julia Lathrop, "Suffrage and the Home," undated essay sent to N. K. Murdock from Julia Lathrop in response to Murdock's request for "a line . . . as to why you think Women need the vote?" June 3, 1917, EGAP, box 59, folder 3.

6. The National Anti-Woman's Suffrage Organization's publication, *The Woman's Protest:* unsigned, "Is Woman's Own Work So Well Done?"; Mrs. William Forse Scott, "Woman and Government"; O. J. Campbell, "Woman Suffrage and Social Welfare"; Margaret C. Robinson, "Discriminating against Mother"; and William J. Magie, "Civilization Based upon the Family."

7. Lillian Wald, "The Right Woman in the Right Place"; Graham R. Taylor, "Personals"; Clara Dennis, corresponding secretary of the National Daughters of the American Revolution, to William Howard Taft, n.d. (received May 9, 1912), Anna Garlin Spencer to William Howard Taft, May 1, 1912, and Lulu L. Echman to Julia Lathrop, May 7, 1912, all three in WHTP, microfilm, reel 370, case file 161; in her survey of 1912 and 1913 newspapers and magazines Padgett found supportive editorials in *Life and Labor,* the *Journal of the Association of Collegiate Alumnae, Woman's Progressive Weekly,* the *Woman's Journal,* the *Standard,* the *Los Angeles Times,* the *Philadelphia North American,* the *New York Evening Post,* the *Baltimore Sun,* the *Chicago Tribune,* the *Herald,* the *Home Town Magazine,* of Naperville, Illinois, *Coal Age,* and the *Washington Star* ("History of the Establishment of the United States Children's Bureau," pp. 20-55). A review of publications which later became ardent Children's Bureau opponents, such as the *Journal of the American Medical Association* and the *Woman's Protest* (published by the National Association Opposed to Woman Suffrage, renamed the Woman Patriots after passage of the Nineteenth Amendment) revealed no mention of the bureau's founding; James Burrow maintains that despite the AMA's later opposition, in 1912 the orga-

nization, as well as most public health advocates, were "largely indifferent" to the bureau's establishment (James G. Burrow, *Organized Medicine in the Progressive Era,* p. 101).

8. From the bureau's founding in 1912 through 1969 five women served as its chief: Julia C. Lathrop (1912-21), Grace Abbott (1921-34), Katharine F. Lenroot (1934-51), Martha May Eliot (1951-56), and Katherine B. Oettinger (1957-69). In 1969 the Children's Bureau was transferred to the Office of Child Development in the Department of Health, Education, and Welfare. Frederick C. Green, associate chief, headed the bureau in the interim between Oettinger's retirement and Zigler's appointment. Green was the first African American to serve as associate chief.

9. Jacqueline K. Parker and Edward M. Carpenter, "Julia Lathrop and the Children's Bureau: The Emergence of an Institution," p. 62; Julia Lathrop, "The Children's Bureau," *NCCC Proceedings, 1912,* pp. 30-33.

10. Lathrop, "Children's Bureau," pp. 30-33.

11. Children's Bureau's actual expenses for 1912 were the salary appropriation of $25,640, and an allotment for "contingent expenses of $4,500 and a printing fund of $3,500" for Aug. 23, 1912, to June 30, 1913 (Lewis Meriam, "The Aims and Objectives of the Federal Children's Bureau," p. 324).

12. Lathrop, "Children's Bureau," p. 31; Bradbury, "Four Decades of Action for Children," p. 9; Parker and Carpenter, "Julia Lathrop and the Children's Bureau," p. 62; Weiss, "Save the Children," p. 178.

13. Edward Bunnell Phelps, "A Statistical Study of Infant Mortality," p. 272.

14. Lathrop, "Children's Bureau," p. 31.

15. Patricia Mooney Melvin, "Milk to the Motherhood: The New York Milk Committee and the Beginning of Well Child Programs"; Judith Walzer Leavitt, *The Healthiest City: Milwaukee and the Politics of Reform;* Kriste Lindenmeyer Dick, "The Silent Charity: The Cincinnati Maternity Society"; Kriste Lindenmeyer, "'To Begin with Babies': The Early Years of the Babies' Milk Fund Association of Cincinnati, 1880-1929"; George Rosen, *A History of Public Health,* p. 358; George B. Mangold, *Problems of Child Welfare,* p. 133; Benjamin K. Rachford, "A Reliable Milk Supply for Babies"; Burrow, *Organized Medicine in the Progressive Era,* pp. 95-97, which relies most heavily on the excellent overview of the U.S. infant welfare movement found in Meckel, *Save the Babies.*

16. Klaus, "Babies All the Rage," pp. 179-84; Judith Walzer Leavitt and Ronald Numbers, "Sickness and Health in America: An Overview"; Covotsos, "Child Welfare and Social Progress," pp. 70-86; John J. Hanlon, *Principles of Public Health Administration;* and Louis I. Dublin, *After Eighty Years: The Impact of Life Insurance on the Public Health,* pp. 38-40.

17. Ralph Chester Williams, M.D., *The United States Public Health Service, 1798-1950;* Fitzhugh Mullan, *Plagues and Politics: The Story of the Unites States Public Health Service,* pp. 32-57.

18. Memorandum, Homer Folks to Julia Lathrop, May 15, 1912, CBP, RG 102, CBP, file 9-1-0-2, cited in Parker and Carpenter, "Julia Lathrop and the Children's Bureau," pp. 63-65.

19. Julia Lathrop to Clifford Beers, June 12, 1915, RG 102, CBP, file 9-1-0-2; cited in Parker and Carpenter, "Julia Lathrop and the Children's Bureau," pp. 63-65; U.S. Children's Bureau, *First Annual Report of the Chief* (1914), p. 7.

20. Senate, Committee on Appropriations, *Hearings on the Legislative, Executive, Judicial Appropriations Bill,* 62d Cong., 2d sess., Dec. 14, 1912, p. 65.

21. Jane Addams, "Miss Lathrop's Letter," typed essay, July 18, 1901, EGAP, box 58, folder 11; Julia Lathrop to Lillian Wald, Jan. 20, 1913, EGAP, box 59, folder 1.

22. Charles Nagel to Lillian Wald, Sept. 12, 1912, EGAP, box 59, folder 1; U.S. Children's Bureau, *First Annual Report of the Chief* (1914); quotation on political pressure from Lewis Meriam, "A Great Bureau Chief," cited in Weiss, "Save the Children," p. 176. It appears that there is nothing concerning Children's Bureau appointments other than Lathrop's nomination in the Taft papers.

23. Ethelbert Stewart moved to the newly created Bureau of Labor Statistics in March 1913 and actually had little influence on the bureau. Lewis Meriam remained with the Children's Bureau from its establishment until 1916. While at the Bureau of the Census Meriam had written three publications including child welfare data: Bureau of Labor Statistics, "Marriage and Divorce," "Paupers in Almshouses, 1910," and "Insane and Feebleminded in Institutions, 1910"; Lathrop, "Children's Bureau," p. 32.

24. As Muncy argues, Lathrop did, in general, use her position to ensure that the field of child welfare would be dominated by women (*Creating a Female Dominion,* pp. 50-53); nevertheless, Lathrop's own comments indicate that the decision to employ Lewis Meriam met with her approval. She endorsed the Meriam and Stewart appointments in her speech before the NCCC in June 1912; see Lathrop, "Children's Bureau," p. 32; and "Minutes and Discussions," *Proceedings of the National Conference of Charities and Correction, 1894,* cited in Covotsos, "Child Welfare and Social Progress," p. 50.

25. Lathrop, "Children's Bureau," p. 32; Parker and Carpenter contend that Meriam's experience "introduced Lathrop to the bureaucratic maze of checkpoints and bargaining counters and steadied the fragile enterprise with a sober hand" ("Julia Lathrop and the Children's Bureau," p. 62). Lewis Meriam and Helen Sumner, "Memorandum, Civil Service Examination for the Children's Bureau," 1914, RG 102, CBP, 3-0; "Immediate Work of the Children's Bureau"; Grace Abbott, "Ten Years' Work for Children," p. 191.

26. Julia Lathrop to Lillian Wald, Jan. 15, 1913, EGAP, box 59, folder 1; Lillian Wald to Julia Lathrop, Jan. 18, 1913, EGAP, box 59, folder 1.

27. N. Lucile Covington to Woodrow Wilson, Mar. 18, 1913, General Records of the Department of Labor, Chief Clerk's File, 1907-42, DLP-CCF, RG 174, box 5, file 1.

28. Harriett Dunn to Woodrow Wilson, Mar. 19, 1913, DLP-CCF, RG 174, box 5, file 4-1; files containing correspondence concerning Wyckliffe and Davis are included in DLP-CCF, RG 174, box 5, file 4-2, 4-5; W. David Lewis, "Katharine Bement Davis, (1860-1935)."

29. Laura Holmes Reilly to Secretary of Labor William B. Wilson, Mar. 20, 1913, DLP-CCF, RG 174, box 5, file 4-1.

30. Public No. 426, 37 *Stat. L.,* 736.

31. Julia Lathrop to Lillian Wald, Mar. 10, 1913, EGAP, box 59, folder 1; Lillian Wald to Julia Lathrop, Mar. 11, 1913, EGAP, box 59, folder 1; "Governor Wilson and the Social Worker," p. 640.

32. Correspondence from Fannie Fisk to Julia Lathrop, Oct. 19 and 30, 1913, EGAP, box 59, folder 1.

33. Meriam, "Aims and Objectives of the Federal Children's Bureau," pp. 317-24; for a review of the Children's Bureau's first year of work see U.S. Children's Bureau, *First Annual Report of the Chief* (1914); and U.S. Department of Labor, *First Annual Report of the Secretary of Labor, Mar. 4, 1913 to June 30, 1913,* pp. 44-46. While the five volume "handbook" Meriam first envisioned never materialized, the Children's Bureau did later become the major source of data outlined in the assistant chief's NCCC address. Under Meriam's direction the Children's Bureau published a "Handbook of Federal Statistics of Children."

34. Meriam, "Aims and Objectives of the Federal Children's Bureau," p. 322.

35. U.S. Children's Bureau, "Birth Registration: An Aid in Protecting the Lives and Rights of Children," p. 5.

36. Edward Bunnell Phelps, "Statistical Study of Infant Mortality," p. 246; Mangold, *Problems of Child Welfare,* p. 57.

37. U.S. Children's Bureau, "Birth Registration," pp. 7, 10.

38. From 1913 through 1923 the Children's Bureau published ten infant mortality community studies, in Johnstown, Pa.; Montclair, N.J.; Manchester, N.H.; Waterbury, Conn.; Brockton, Mass.; Saginaw, Mich.; New Bedford, Mass.; Akron, Ohio; Pittsburgh, Pa.; and Gary, Ind. (Emma Duke, "Infant Mortality: Results of a Field Study in Johnstown, Pa., Based on Births in One Calendar Year"; U.S. Children's Bureau, "Infant Mortality, Montclair, N.J.: A Study of Infant Mortality in a Suburban Community"; Beatrice Sheets Duncan and Emma Duke, "Infant Mortality: Results of a Field Study in Manchester, N.H. Based on Births in One Year"; Estelle B. Hunter, "Infant Mortality: Results of a Field Study in Waterbury, Conn., Based on Births in One Year"; Mary V. Dempsey, "Infant Mortality: Results of a Field Study in Brockton, Mass., Based on Births in One Year"; Nila F. Allen, "Infant Mortality: Results of a Field Study in Saginaw, Mich., Based on Births in One Year"; Jessamine S. Whitney, "Infant Mortality: Results of a Field Study in New Bedford, Mass., Based on Births in One Year"; Theresa S. Haley, "Infant Mortality: Results of a Field Study in Akron, Ohio, Based on Births in One Year"; Glenn Steele, "Infant Mortality in Pittsburgh: An Analysis of Records for 1920 with Six Charts"; Elizabeth Hughes, "Infant Mortality: Results of a Field Study in Gary, Ind., Based on Births in One Year"; Anna Rochester,

"Infant Mortality: Results of a Field Study in Baltimore, Maryland, Based on Birth in One Year"). Each project generally followed the pattern established by the first investigation done in Johnstown, but after the creation of a child hygiene division (in 1916), headed by a female physician, medical causes for infant deaths also became a part of bureau research; each study resulted in a bureau report; another infant mortality study published by the bureau was implemented by local officials assisted by Children's Bureau staff; Covotsos, "Child Welfare and Social Progress," pp. 87-89.

39. Julia Lathrop, "Letter of Transmittal," in Duke, "Infant Mortality," pp. 5-9, 11-13.

40. Of the 1,551 mothers interviewed, 854 were listed as native-born white, 6 African American, 394 Slovak or Polish, 76 Serbo-Croatian, 75 Italian, 53 German, 38 Magyar, 33 British, 12 Syrian and Greek, and 10 Hebrew; Serbo-Croatian babies had the highest infant mortality rate of 263.9 and those of native-born mothers (whites and blacks) the lowest, of 104.3 (ibid., pp. 27-31, 7).

41. Meriam, "Aims and Objectives of the Federal Children's Bureau," pp. 321; when funds were unavailable to pay interpreters, Lathrop paid them herself (Weiss, "Save the Children," p. 178).

42. Duke, "Infant Mortality: Results of a Field Study in Johnstown, Pa.," pp. 12-14.

43. Ibid, pp. 11-85; for a statistical summary see tables throughout the text and general tables on pp. 57-77; statements of mothers appear on pp. 81-85.

44. Lathrop, "Letter of Transmittal," pp. 8-9, 45-49.

45. Mrs. Max (Mary) West, "Prenatal Care" and "Infant Care." According to a Children's Bureau press release, "Mrs. West is herself the mother of five attractive children whom she has been supporting since the death of her husband several years ago, and her bulletins combine practical experience and detailed study." She was born in Minnesota and was graduated from the University of Minnesota (untitled press release, RG 102, CBP, file 8-2-1-0-3).

46. Elizabeth Lowell Putnam to Mary West, Mar. 17, 1913, ELPP, MC 360, box 30, file 511; Putnam later became one of the bureau's strongest opponents, an issue addressed in chap. 4.

47. Meriam, "Aims and Objectives of the Federal Children's Bureau," p. 321; Duke, "Infant Mortality: Results of a Field Study in Johnstown, Pa.," pp. 14-26, 89-93.

48. Klaus, "Babies All the Rage," pp. 179-89; Ladd-Taylor, *Mother-Work,* pp. 46-55, 86-89.

49. U.S. Children's Bureau, "Baby-Saving Campaigns: A Preliminary Report on What American Cities Are Doing to Prevent Infant Mortality," pp. 5, 9.

50. Meriam, "Aims and Objectives of the Federal Children's Bureau," p. 318.

51. Alisa Klaus, "Perfecting American Babyhood: Race Betterment and the Baby Health Contest," p. 3; press release, U.S. Children's Bureau, "Baby

Saving Campaigns," June 16, 1913, ELPP, MC 360, box 30, folder 511; Parker and Carpenter, "Julia Lathrop and the Children's Bureau," pp. 70-73.

52. U.S. Children's Bureau, *First Annual Report of the Chief* (1914).

53. Meriam, "Aims and Objectives of the Federal Children's Bureau," p. 318.

Chapter 3: Expanding the Bureau through a Blueprint for Maternal and Child Health, 1914-20

1. Julia Lathrop to Graham Taylor, Apr. 14, 1914, EGAP, box 59, folder 2; U.S. Department of Labor, "Children's Bureau," *Annual Report of the Secretary of Labor, 1915,* p. 75; Zelizer, *Pricing the Priceless Child,* pp. 138-68; and Meckel, *Save the Babies,* pp. 124-58.

2. House, *Committee on Appropriation Report,* Apr. 2, 1914.

3. Lillian Wald to Jane Addams, Apr. 3, 1914, EGAP, box 38, folder 2; Muncy, *Creating a Female Dominion,* pp. 62-64.

4. Telegram from Lillian Wald and Florence Kelley to Owen Lovejoy, Apr. 3, 1914, EGAP, box 38, folder 2; National Child Labor Committee, *Minute Book, Meetings 20 to 47, October 29, 1908 to March 29, 1916,* "Annual Report of the National Child Labor Committee, 10th Fiscal Year Ending September 30, 1914," p. 8; see also Owen Lovejoy to Julia Lathrop, Apr. 9, 1914, CBP, file 2-1-2-3.

5. "Children or Parsimony."

6. Owen Lovejoy to Julia Lathrop, Apr. 10, 1914, EGAP, box 59, folder 2.

7. On another occasion Lathrop reluctantly agreed to remain on the NCLC's advisory committee. She contended, "I don't belong on anybody's advisory committees, and I am trying to get off of them all" (Julia Lathrop to Owen Lovejoy, Nov. 24, 1916, EGAP, box 59, folder 3). On the increasing role of government in child welfare during the Progressive Era see Katz, *In the Shadow of the Poor House,* pp. 121-24.

8. Lillian Wald to Julia Lathrop, Apr. 3, 1914, EGAP, box 59, folder 2.

9. House, *Congressional Record,* 63d Cong., 3d sess., Apr. 14, 1914, pp. 6709-13.

10. Ibid, pp. 6798-6812.

11. Julia Lathrop to Lillian Wald, Apr. 15, 1914, EGAP, box 59, folder 2.

12. House, *Congressional Record,* 63d Cong., 3d sess., p. 6830.

13. Julia Lathrop to Florence Kelley, probably Apr. 1914, box 59, folder 2.

14. Senate, *Congressional Record,* 64th Cong., 2d sess., 1917, pp. 1667-68, 1672-75.

15. U.S. Department of Labor, "Children's Bureau," *Annual Report of the Secretary of Labor, 1915,* pp. 74-82.

16. Lathrop to Secretary of Labor Wilson, Aug. 1913, DLP, RG 174, box 5, 4-23; "Frank S. Drown," Nov. 3, 1916, CBP, RG 102, 8-2-1-0-3; Lathrop to Dr. Walter S. Cornell, Oct. 10, 1914, CBP, RG 102, 4-15-1-3-0, cited in Parker and Carpenter, "Julia Lathrop and the Children's Bureau," pp. 65-66; Lundberg, *Unto to the Least of These;* Peter Romanosfsky, "Emma

Octavia Lundberg"; see also Lundberg's obituary in the *New York Times,* Nov. 18, 1954.

17. U.S. Department of Labor, "Children's Bureau," *Annual Report of the Secretary of Labor, 1915,* pp. 74-82.

18. Marshall Dimock (who served as assistant secretary of labor during Franklin Roosevelt's administration) explained that men and women benefited from connections with the "Chicago network" (interview conducted by the author with Marshall Dimock at the University of Cincinnati, Jan. 19, 1990, notes in author's possession); Caroline Fleming to Jesse H. Evans, Central Bureau of Planning and Statistics, "Children's Bureau Employees Who Have Left," May 20, 1919, CBP, RG 102, 3-3-1-1.

19. Meriam and Sumner, "Memorandum, Civil Service Examinations for the Children's Bureau"; Grace Abbott, "Ten Years' Work for Children," p. 191.

20. Meriam and Sumner, "Memorandum, Civil Service Examinations for the Children's Bureau."

21. Ibid.; two letters from Julia Lathrop to Secretary of Labor Wilson, both dated July 22, 1914; John A. McIlhenny to Secretary of Labor Wilson, July 31, 1914, all in CBP, RG 102, file 3-0.

22. Memorandum, "Employees in the Children's Bureau, Nov. 20, 1918," CBP, RG 102, box 14, 3-0; memorandum, "Positions in the Children's Bureau U.S. Department of Labor," 1917, CBP, RG 102, box 20, 3-3-1-1; untitled questionnaire, Feb./Mar. 1918, CBP, 3-3-2.

23. "Employment and Staff," Feb./Mar. 1918, CBP, RG 102, box 21, 3-3-2; for an example of female networking see Caroline Fleming (assistant chief) to Grace Abbott, June 11, 1920, CBP, RG 102, 3-0-2.

24. Eleanor Taylor, "The Story of the Children's Bureau," p. 4; although instituted under Lathrop's tenure, the last of the Children's Bureau's infant mortality studies was actually published in 1923.

25. Etta R. Goodwin to Mrs. Maud Hemingway, Aug. 5, 1915, CBP, RG 102, file 4-0-1, cited in Muncy, *Creating a Female Dominion,* p. 60, n. 102.

26. U.S. Children's Bureau, *Tenth Annual Report of the Chief* (1923), p. 30; in 1915 the national birth registration area included Connecticut, Maine, Massachusetts, Michigan, Minnesota, New Hampshire, New York, Pennsylvania, Rhode Island, Vermont, and the District of Columbia; all existing states had joined by 1933.

27. Press release, Children's Bureau, July 14, 1920, CBP, RG 102, 8-2-1-0-4; Rochester, "Infant Mortality: Results of a Field Study in Baltimore, Maryland," pp. 100-105.

28. Julia Lathrop, "Income and Infant Mortality"; U.S. Department of Labor, *Sixth Annual Report of the Secretary of Labor, 1918,* p. 183.

29. Julia Lathrop, "Public Protection of Maternity"; Meckel, *Save the Babies,* pp. 178-99.

30. Lathrop, "Income and Infant Mortality," p. 274.

31. Bremner, *From the Depths,* p. 138; Patterson, *America's Struggle against Poverty,* pp. 20-36; Meckel, *Save the Babies,* p. 193; press release, Children's Bureau, July 14, 1920, CBP, RG 102, 8-2-1-0-4.

32. Gordon, *Pitied but Not Entitled,* pp. 46-47, 84-88; Helen A. Tucker, "The Negroes of Pittsburgh," p. 607; Jacqueline Jones, *Labor of Love, Labor of Sorrow: Black Women, Work, and the Family from Slavery to the Present,* pp. 184-85; and Dorothy Salem, *To Better Our World: Black Women in Organized Reform, 1890-1920,* pp. 106-10.

33. Covotsos, "Child Welfare and Social Progress," p. 97; U.S. Department of Labor, *Sixth Annual Report of the Secretary of Labor, 1918,* p. 185.

34. "Conference of the Home Economics Department," *Official Report, Thirteenth Biennial Convention, General Federation of Women's Clubs* (1916), pp. 599-600, cited in Covotsos, "Child Welfare and Social Progress," p. 100; Grace L. Meigs, "Maternal Mortality from All Conditions Connected with Childbirth in the United States and Certain Other Countries"; U.S. Bureau of the Census, *Historical Statistics of the United States,* p. 59.

35. U.S. Bureau of the Census, *Historical Statistics of the United States,* pp. 10-12, 24-26; Lathrop, "Public Protection of Maternity," p. 31.

36. See the following Children's Bureau publications: Elizabeth Moore, "Maternal Mortality and Infant Care in a Rural County in Kansas"; Frances Sage Bradley, M.D., and Margaretta A. Williamson. "Rural Children in Selected Counties of North Carolina"; Viola I. Paradise, "Maternity Care and the Welfare of Young Children in a Homesteading County in Montana"; Florence Brown Sherbon, M.D., and Elizabeth Moore, "Maternity and Infant Care in Two Rural Counties in Wisconsin"; Helen M. Dart, "Maternity and Child Care in Selected Rural Areas of Mississippi"; and Glenn Steele, "Maternity and Infant Care in a Mountain County in Georgia."

37. The Kansas study, the only exception to the general trend, reported a relatively low maternal mortality rate of 2.9 per 10,000 and an infant mortality rate of 40 per 1,000 live births; here socioeconomic class may have contributed to lower mortality rates (Moore, "Maternal Mortality and Infant Care in a Rural County in Kansas"); for similar conclusions about lower infant and maternal mortality in the Midwest, see Samuel H. Preston and Michael R. Haines, *Fatal Years: Child Mortality in Late Nineteenth-Century America,* pp. 111, 114, 133-34, 151-54, 168.

38. Mrs. A. P. to Julia Lathrop, Oct. 19, 1916, CBP, RG 102, 4-3-0-3; transcription included in MMEP, MC 229, box 11, file 151; for a copy of this letter and examples of letters from other women expressing anxiety concerning their lack of medical care and pregnancy see Ladd-Taylor, *Raising a Baby the Government Way,* pp. 47-61.

39. Mrs. A. P. to Julia Lathrop, June 5, 1917 (copy), MMEP, box 11, file 151.

40. Most letters to the bureau concerning maternal and early infant care during this period are housed throughout the Children's Bureau's records in category 4. An excellent sampling of such correspondence is included in Ladd-Taylor, *Raising a Baby the Government Way,* esp. pp. 47-70; quotations used here are from this book.

41. Mrs. G. S. to Julia Lathrop, Mar. 30, 1916, EGAP, box 59, folder 3.

42. Julia Lathrop to Mrs. G. S., Apr. 4, 1916 (copy), EGAP, box 59, folder 1.

43. Ladd-Taylor, *Raising a Baby the Government Way,* pp. 9, 14, 26, 52, 68, 174, 179, 180-84; Mrs. D., Sweetgrass, Mont., to Julia Lathrop, Apr. 17, 1917, and Lathrop's response, Apr. 24, 1917, EGAP, box 59, folder 4.

44. Nancy Pottishman Weiss, "Mother, the Invention of Necessity: Dr. Benjamin Spock's *Baby and Child Care.*"

45. Julia Lathrop to General Federation of Women's Clubs, Aug. 10, 1916, CBP, RG 102, cited in Covotsos, "Child Welfare and Social Progress," p. 109; see also Julia Lathrop's *Fourth Annual Report of the Chief, Children's Bureau* (1916) and U.S. Children's Bureau, *Fifth Annual Report of the Chief* (1917); "Press Release, Patriotism and Babies," CBP, RG 102, 8-2-1-0-4.

46. Muncy, *Creating a Female Dominion,* p. 97; William J. Breen, *Uncle Sam at Home: Civilian Mobilization, Wartime Federalism, and the Council of National Defense, 1917-1919,* pp. 4-9, 94, 115-17.

47. Wilson's letter quoted in Anna E. Rude, "The Children's Year Campaign," p. 346.

48. On threats to the milk supply see clipping "High Milk Prices Cause U.S. Warning," Dec. 16, 1917; "Babies Get Less Milk," *Baltimore Sun,* Apr. 18, 1918; see also Janet M. Geiser to Grace Meigs, May 7, 1918; and letter to Herbert C. Hoover from Council of National Defense, June 18, 1917; on the problem of public health nurses see correspondence from Julia Lathrop to Major General William C. Gorgas, Mar. 22, 1918; Dora E. Thompson, Mar. 27, 1918; and Dora E. Thompson to Julia Lathrop, Mar. 27, 1918; all in CBP, RG 102, box 47, file 4-16-4-0 and 4-16-5-0.

49. The three other members of the committee were J. H. Mason Knox, Jr., M.D. (chair), W. C. Woodward, M.D, and Gertrude B. Knipp (secretary); J. H. Mason Knox, Jr., and Gertrude B. Knipp to F. S. Simpson, Chief of Medical Section, Council of National Defense (copy), and attached proof "Report to Council of National Defense," May 25, 1917; Grace L. Meigs, "Memorandum on Report of the Committee to the Council of National Defense"; Gertrude Knipp to Grace Meigs, May 29, 1917; all in CBP, RG 102, box 47, 4-16-0-1.

50. Dorothy Reed Mendenhall, "Milk, the Indispensable Food for Children."

51. U.S. Children's Bureau, *Sixth Annual Report of the Chief* (1918), pp. 21-24; ibid., "Save 100,000 Babies: Get a Square Deal for Children"; ibid., "Children's Year Working Program"; ibid., "Children's Year: A Brief Summary of Work Done and Suggestions for Follow-up Work"; Covotsos, "Child Welfare and Social Progress," pp. 121-22.

52. Fred S. Hall, ed., *Social Work Yearbook, 1935,* p. 252; Muncy, *Creating a Female Dominion,* p. 100.

53. Rude, "Children's Year Campaign," pp. 347-51.

54. For an overview of the second White House conference and the regional conferences held as a result see Elvena Bage Tillman, "The Rights of Childhood: The National Child Welfare Movement, 1890-1919," pp. 214-52.

55. U.S. Children's Bureau, *Fifth Annual Report of the Chief* (1917), pp. 47-49.

Chapter 4: Saving Mothers and Babies

1. The legislative history of the Sheppard-Towner Maternity and Infancy Act has been examined by a number of scholars. This overview is a compilation of those efforts and further historical investigation. The most detailed legislative history of the bill is Chepaitis, "First Federal Social Welfare Measure"; various aspects of the legislative effort and implementation of the bill also appear in Nathan Sinai and Odin W. Anderson, *EMIC: A Study of Administrative Experience,* pp. 10-17; Edward R. Schlesinger, "The Sheppard-Towner Era: A Prototype Case Study in Federal State Relationships"; Joseph B. Chepaitis, "Federal Social Welfare Progressivism in the 1920's"; James G. Burrow, *AMA: Voice of American Medicine,* pp. 157-65; Lemons, *Woman Citizen;* and Covotsos, "Child Welfare and Social Progress." Other historians have focused on the role women played in the passage and implementation of Sheppard-Towner, see esp. J. Stanley Lemons, "The Sheppard-Towner Act: Progressivism in the 1920's"; Muncy, *Creating a Female Dominion,* pp. 93-123; and Ladd-Taylor, "Women's Health and Public Policy," pp. 393-405. The following works place greater emphasis on the long-term consequences of Sheppard-Towner: Joan E. Mulligan, "Three Federal Interventions on Behalf of Childbearing Women: Sheppard-Towner, EMIC and the 1963 Maternal Health Amendments"; Sheila M. Rothman, *Woman's Proper Place,* pp. 136-53; Kristine Siefert, "An Exemplar of Primary Prevention in Social Work: The Sheppard-Towner Act of 1921"; Ladd-Taylor, *Raising a Baby the Government Way;* Ladd-Taylor, *Mother-Work,* pp. 167-96; Meckel, *Save the Babies,* pp. 200-219; and Skocpol, *Protecting Soldiers and Mothers,* p. 480; for an examination of Sheppard-Towner on the state level see Elissa Miller, "A History of Nursing Education in Arkansas"; and Dick, "Saving Mothers and Babies."

2. Julia Lathrop to Jeannette Rankin, Nov. 17, 1916, EGAP, box 59, folder 3.

3. Baker, *Fighting for Life;* Leona Baumgartner, "Sara Josephine Baker," pp. 85-86.

4. House Committee on Labor, *A Bill to Encourage Instruction in the Hygiene of Maternity and Infancy and to Extend Proper Care for Maternity and Infancy, Hearings before the Committee on Labor on H.R. 12634,* 65th Cong., 3d sess., 1919 (hereafter cited as *Hearings on H.R. 12634*), p. 32.

5. Kriste Lindenmeyer, "Dorothy Reed Mendenhall"; Lois Decker O'Neill, ed., *The Women's Book of World Records and Achievements,* p. 212; Elizabeth D. Robinton, "Dorothy Reed Mendenhall."

6. U.S. Children's Bureau, *Fifth Annual Report of the Chief* (1917), pp. 47-49; Lemons, *Woman Citizen,* p. 154.

7. House, *Congressional Record,* 65th Cong., 2d sess., July 1, 1918, pp. 8599-8600; and Senate, pp. 8544. Joseph T. Robinson, although from a southern state, was a vocal supporter of the 1916 Keating-Owen child labor act and had voted in favor of past Children's Bureau appropriation requests (House Committee on Labor, *Hearings: Hygiene of Maternity and Infancy,*

H.R.12634, 65th Cong., 3d sess., Jan. 15 and 28, 1919 [hereafter cited as *Hearings, H.R. 12634*]).

8. *Hearings, H.R. 12634;* for a detailed description of the bill's provisions see Chepaitis, "First Federal Social Welfare Measure," pp. 19-24.

9. Section 15 of the bill stated that "the act is not a charity." Covotsos suggests that this was an important point since an earlier draft had limited the act's benefits to those unable to pay ("Child Welfare and Social Progress," p. 123).

10. Individuals testifying before the House committee included Jeannette Rankin, Bradford Knapp (States Relations Service, Department of Agriculture); R. S. Sexton (legislative representative of the American Federation of Labor); Florence Kelley (National Consumers' League), S. Josephine Baker, M.D. (then president of the American Child Health Association); Lee M. Frankel (president, American Public Health Association); and Children's Bureau employees Caroline Fleming (assistant chief); Mary West (author of the bureau's instructional pamphlets); Anne E. Rude, M.D. (director of the Division of Hygiene); and Dorothy Reed Mendenhall, M.D (staff physician) (*Hearings on H.R. 12634*); Chepaitis, "First Federal Social Welfare Measure," p. 24.

11. Joseph Chepaitis concludes that the PHS proposal failed because of greater popular support for the Children's Bureau bill ("First Federal Social Welfare Measure," p. 34).

12. Senate, *Congressional Record,* 66th Cong., 1st sess., 1919, p. 6314; and p. 7157; Chepaitis, "First Federal Social Welfare Measure," pp. 34-35; and Lemons, *Woman Citizen,* p. 155; Covotsos, "Child Welfare and Social Progress," p. 128; "Morris Sheppard," p. 1592.

13. Senate Committee on Public Health and National Quarantine, *Protection of Maternity and Infancy,* Senate Report no. 650, 66th Cong., 2d sess., 1920; for details of this report see Chepaitis, "First Federal Social Welfare Measure," pp. 39-40.

14. "Horace Mann Towner," p. 1723; House, *Congressional Record,* 66th Cong., 2d sess., Dec. 5, 1919, p. 214; David Burner, *The Politics of Provincialism: The Democratic Party in Transition, 1918-1932,* pp. 161-66; Muncy, *Creating a Female Dominion,* p. 103; Chepaitis, "First Federal Social Welfare Measure," pp. 30-31; Lemons, *Woman Citizen,* pp. 154-55.

15. Muncy, *Creating a Female Dominion,* pp. 102-3; Chepaitis, "Federal Social Welfare Progressivism in the 1920's," p. 216; Lemons, *Woman Citizen,* pp. 157-58.

16. Herbert Hoover, "Speaking for the Swiss Woman," address at the 1st Annual Meeting of the American Child Health Association, Oct. 1920, CBP, RG 102, 11-0-3.

17. Kirk H. Porter, ed., *National Party Platforms,* pp. 425; Lemons, *Woman Citizen,* p. 155.

18. Helen T. Woolley to Carrie Chapman Catt, May 10, 1919, EGAP, box 62; Grace Abbott contended that women made the issue of significant "national importance" ("A Record of Achievement for Children," memo, May 24, 1921, CBP, RG 102, 0-5-4-8-0 to 1-3-4, file 1-2).

19. Nancy F. Cott, *The Grounding of Modern Feminism,* pp. 97-99.

20. Charles A. Selden, "The Most Powerful Lobby in Washington," p. 95. Associations which endorsed the Sheppard-Towner Maternity and Infancy bill included (* designates membership in the WJCC): American Association of University Women*, American Child Health Association, American Home Economics Association*, Association of Collegiate Alumnae, Daughters of the American Revolution*, Federation of Colored Women's Clubs, General Federation of Women's Clubs*, League of American Pen Women, Life Insurance Institute of New York, National Child Welfare Association, Women's Christian Temperance Union*, National Consumers' League*, National Council of Jewish Women*, National Congress of Mothers and Parent-Teachers Associations*, National Education Association*, National Federation of Business and Professional Women*, National League of Women Voters*, National Organization of Public Health Nursing, National Women's Trade Union League*, National Women's Association of Commerce, Women's Foundation for Health, Service Star Legion, Women's League for Peace and Freedom*, Women's National Democratic Committee, Women's National Republican Committee, Women's Press Club, Young Women's Christian Association*. The Daughters of the American Revolution withdrew its support in late 1921. This list has been compiled from the following: papers of the Women's Joint Congressional Committee, Manuscript Division, Library of Congress; Chepaitis, "Federal Social Welfare Progressivism in the 1920's," p. 218; House, *Congressional Record,* 66th Cong., 3d sess., 1920, p. 418; U.S. Children's Bureau, "Promotion of the Welfare and Hygiene of Maternity and Infancy, the Administration of the Act of Congress of November 23, 1921, Fiscal Year Ended June 30, 1929."

21. For a detailed examination of these debates see Chepaitis, "First Federal Social Welfare Measure," pp. 41-49; Senate, *Congressional Record,* 66th Cong., 3d sess., Dec. 1920, esp. pp. 379-581; House Committee on Interstate and Foreign Commerce, *Public Protection of Maternity and Infancy, Hearings on H.R. 10925,* 66th Cong., 3d sess., Dec. 20-23, 28-29, 1920 (hereafter cited as *Hearings on H.R. 10925*).

22. *Hearings on H.R. 10925,* p. 29; summary from Chepaitis, "First Federal Social Welfare Measure," p. 47; House Committee on Interstate and Foreign Commerce, *Protection of Maternity and Infancy,* 66th Cong., 3d sess., H. Report 1255 to accompany S. 3259, 1921; "President's Message," Joint Session of Congress, *Congressional Record,* 67th Cong., 1st sess., 1921, p. 172; House, *Congressional Record,* 67th Cong., special sess., Apr. 11, 1921, p. 98, and Senate, p. 172.

23. Women's Joint Congressional Committee, "Yearly Report of the Secretary of the Woman's Joint Congressional Committee, November 1920, to December 1921," box 6, Library of Congress; Harriett Taylor Upton to Warren G. Harding, June 18 and July 30, 1921, both in Warren G. Harding Papers, Ohio Historical Society, Columbus, box 157, file 117-1; for further evidence of pressure from women on Harding see Lemons, *Woman Citizen,* p. 157.

24. Mary G. Kilbreth to Warren G. Harding, Nov. 25, 1921, Warren G. Harding Papers, Ohio Historical Society, Columbus, box 157, file 117-1, Ohio Historical Society, Columbus; Covotsos, "Child Welfare and Social

Progress," p. 139; the antisuffrage publication *Woman's Protest* was renamed the *Woman Patriot* in 1918. It was published regularly until 1932; Lemons, *Woman Citizen,* pp. 156-57, 209-27.

25. For an example of Putnam's early positive attitude toward the bureau see her letter in support of the bureau's request for a larger appropriation for fiscal 1915 (Elizabeth Lowell Putnam to Owen R. Lovejoy, Apr. 10, 1914, ELPP, MC 360, box 30, file 511; see also "Elizabeth Lowell Putnam" obituary clipping, *Herald Tribune,* n.d. (probably June 5, 1935), ELPP, MC 360, box 1, file 2; Putnam to Mr. Taylor, Jan. 9, 1931, on women and suffrage, ELPP, MC 360, box 30, file 483; Putnam to Richard A. Bolt, M.D., n.d. (sometime in 1922), ELPP, MC 360, box 16, file 281; Elizabeth Lowell Putnam to James P. Mahr, Feb. 3, 1919, ELPP, MC 360, box 16, file 288; Elizabeth Lowell Putnam, "Why the Appropriation for the Extension of the Sheppard-Towner Act Should Not Be Granted," privately published pamphlet, n.d. (probably 1926), ELPP, MC 360, box 4, file 53.

26. Elizabeth Lowell Putnam to Alice Mary Robertson, Aug. 24, 1921, ELPP, MC 360, box 30, file 484; Ladd-Taylor, *Mother-Work,* pp. 173-74.

27. Meckel, *Save the Babies,* p. 208; Chepaitis mistakenly interprets Winslow's attitude toward the bill ("First Federal Social Welfare Measure," p. 60, n. 113).

28. Senate, *Congressional Record,* 67th Cong., 1st sess., 1921, pp. 8759-67, 4207; Chepaitis shows that even the *New York Times,* which then opposed the Sheppard-Towner bill, called Reed's accusations "doubly fallacious" (editorial, "His Argument Doubly Fallacious," *New York Times,* July 25, 1921, p. 12; cited in Chepaitis, "First Federal Social Welfare Measure," p. 56).

29. Joseph Chepaitis contends that such accusations came from "the 'lunatic fringe' of conservatism"; see Chepaitis, "Federal Social Welfare Progressivism in the 1920's," pp. 220-21; and "First Federal Social Welfare Measure," p. 140.

30. Burrow, *AMA,* pp. 157-58; Lemons, *Woman Citizen,* p. 780; Covotsos, "Child Welfare and Social Progress," pp. 135-37; "Federal Care of Maternity and Infancy: The Sheppard-Towner Bill," p. 383.

31. *Hearings on H.R. 10925,* pp. 15-19.

32. Siefert, "Exemplar of Primary Prevention in Social Work," p. 92.

33. Letter to the editor, Ella Oppenheimer, *JAMA,* 76 (May 21, 1921): 1418-19, cited in Covotsos, "Child Welfare and Social Progress," p. 137.

34. Sheila M. Rothman, "Women's Clinics or Doctors' Offices: The Sheppard-Towner Act and the Promotion of Preventive Health Care," pp. 181, 193-94; Rosemary Stevens, *In Sickness and in Wealth: American Hospitals in the Twentieth Century,* pp. 80-104; Sydney A. Halpern, *American Pediatrics: The Social Dynamics of Professionalism, 1880-1980.*

35. The Medical Women's National Association published a journal, the *Woman's Medical Journal* (1917-19), renamed the *Woman's Medical Journal* (1920-32); Regina Morantz-Sanchez, "Physicians."

36. *Hearings on H.R. 10925,* pp. 15-19; Dick, "Saving Mothers and Babies," pp. 110-11.

37. J. S. Eichelberger, letter to the editor, *Survey,* 46 (Aug. 1, 1921): 567.

38. Senate, *Congressional Record,* 67th Cong., 1st sess., July 22, 1921, pp. 4215-17.

39. A comparison of the Rankin and Sheppard-Towner bills is included in Siefert, "Exemplar of Primary Prevention in Social Work," pp. 125-28; Ladd-Taylor, *Mother-Work,* pp. 174-76; by 1920 twenty-eight states had established distinct state divisions of child hygiene or welfare (Grace Abbott, "The Federal Government in Relation to Maternity and Infancy," pp. 92-94).

40. Senate, *Congressional Record,* 67th Cong., 1st sess., July 22, 1921, pp. 4215-17.

41. For examples of AMA arguments see "Again, the Sheppard-Towner Bill," p. 696; "Editorial," p. 383; and Burrow, *AMA,* pp. 146-58; O'Neill, *Women's Book of World Records and Achievements,* pp. 202-3, 209.

42. Julia Lathrop, "Memorandum on an Interview with Dr. Blue," May 24, 1919, EGAP, box 62, folder 1; see also Covotsos, "Child Welfare and Social Progress," p. 127; and Robert D. Leigh, *Federal Health Administration in the United States,* pp. 490-91; Surgeon General Cumming testified before the House committee conducting hearings on H.R. 10925 (*Hearings on H.R. 10925,* pp. 15-19).

43. Chepaitis, "Federal Social Welfare Progressivism in the 1920's," p. 217.

44. *Congressional Record,* 67th Cong., 1st sess., pp. 7990, 8036-37, 8052-53, 8115, 8154, 8178.

45. *New York Times,* Nov. 20, 1921, cited in Chepaitis, "First Federal Social Welfare Measure," p. 75.

46. "The Sheppard-Towner Program," *America,* 26 (Dec. 10, 1921): 182, cited in Chepaitis, "First Federal Social Welfare Measure," pp. 85-87; House Committee on Interstate and Foreign Commerce, *Hearings on H.R. 2366, a Bill for the Public Protection of Maternity and Infancy,* 67th Cong., 1st sess., 1921 (hereafter cited as *Hearings on H.R. 2366*).

47. Lemons, *Woman Citizen,* p. 153; *Hearings on H.R. 2366,* pp. 246-51.

48. Florence Kelley, "Congress and the Babies," *Survey,* 46 (1921): 200.

49. Julia Lathrop to Grace Abbott, June 4, 1921, EGAP, box 57, folder 7.

50. Abbott never married but acted for sixteen years as guardian and "surrogate" mother for her niece Charlotte (Jill Kerr Conway, "Grace Abbott," 1:2-4; Zona Gale, "Great Ladies of Chicago"; Edith Abbott, "A Sister's Memories"; "Grace Abbott Hull House, 1908-21"; Helen Wright, "Three against Time: Edith and Grace Abbott and Sophonisba P. Breckinridge"; Lela B. Costin, *Two Sisters for Social Justice: A Biography of Grace and Edith Abbott;* and "Champion of Women and Children: The Story of Grace Abbott" [this article has no byline but is likely written by Edith Abbott]).

51. Costin, *Two Sisters for Social Justice.*

52. Frank O. Lowden to Julius Rosenwald, copy forwarded by William C. Graves (secretary to Julius Rosenwald) to James J. Davis, May 4, 1921, Herbert Hoover Secretary of Commerce Files, Herbert Hoover Library box 362, file "Labor Department, Children's Bureau 1921-1926"; see also correspondence between Robert La Follette and Julia Lathrop, July 20 and 23,

1920, JLP, microfilm, reel "correspondence 1911 July-Dec. to Correspondence 1924 Oct.-Dec."

53. Clipping from the *New York Nation,* Aug. 31, 1921, EGAP, box 5, folder 7.

54. Julia Lathrop to Graham Taylor, Sept. 13 [1921], Graham Taylor Papers, Newberry Library, Ta, file "Julia Lathrop to G.T., July 26, 1918-June 1932."

55. Grace Abbott, "Steps to Be Taken by Women's Organizations to Secure the Benefits of the Sheppard-Towner Act for a State," Jan. 18, 1922, cited in Covotsos, "Child Welfare and Social Progress," p. 141.

56. U.S. Children's Bureau, "Promotion of the Welfare and Hygiene of Maternity and Infancy: The Administration of the Act of Congress of November 23, 1921 for the Period March 20, 1922 to June 30, 1923," pp. 4-5.

57. Lemons, "Sheppard-Towner Act," pp. 782-83.

58. Julia Lathrop to Florence Kelley, microfilm of correspondence in the Jane Addams Papers, 1872-1935, Swarthmore College Peace Collection, Swarthmore, Pa.; cited in Covotsos, "Child Welfare and Social Progress," pp. 142-43.

59. *Massachusetts v. Mellon* and *Frothingham v. Mellon,* 262 U.S. 447; Melvin I. Urofsky, "*Massachusetts v. Mellon,*" p. 531.

60. Florence Kelley, "The Children's Amendment," p. 170; state responses gathered from U.S. Children's Bureau, "The Promotion of the Welfare and Hygiene of Maternity and Infancy," Children's Bureau pub. nos. 137, 146, 156, 178, 186, 194, 203 (1924-31). Grace Abbott to Marjory Cheney, Jan. 21, 1924, CBP, RG 102, box 241, 11-0; Lemons, "Sheppard-Towner Act," pp. 782-83.

61. U.S. Children's Bureau, "Promotion of the Welfare and Hygiene of Maternity and Infancy" (1931).

62. U.S. Children's Bureau, "Promotion of the Welfare and Hygiene of Maternity and Infancy" (1924); only the 1926 conference resulted in a published report—U.S. Children's Bureau, "Proceedings of the Third Annual Conference of State Directors in Charge of the Local Administration of the Maternity and Infancy Act, Act of Congress of November 23, 1921, Held in Washington, D.C., Jan. 13, 1926"; no such conference was held in 1922 or 1929, the first and last years federal funds were available under Sheppard-Towner.

63. U.S. Children's Bureau, "The Promotion of the Welfare and Hygiene of Maternity and Infancy" (1925), pp. 12, 42-44.

64. Muncy, *Creating a Female Dominion,* p. 108; U.S. Children's Bureau, "Promotion of the Welfare and Hygiene of Maternity and Infancy" (1927), p. 7; and (1924), pp. 8-9.

65. I am aware of only two studies evaluating the implementation of Sheppard-Towner at the state level, so it is difficult to generalize about such details. However, it appears from the Children's Bureau's summaries that Ohio was the rule rather than the exception; an overview of the primary activities undertaken by each state is included in U.S. Children's Bureau,

"Promotion of the Welfare and Hygiene of Maternity and Infancy" (1931); data on Ohio from Dick, "Saving Mothers and Babies," pp. 113-14; the first woman director of a municipal board of health was Esther Pohl Lovejoy, M.D., who served as head of the Portland, Oregon, Board of Health from 1907 to 1909 (O'Neill, *Women's Book of World Records and Achievements,* p. 226). State board of health directors were generally members of the AMA and, as far as I can tell, until at least the post-World War II period, always male.

66. S. Josephine Baker estimates that in 1922, where child welfare programs existed, women headed all but three, but in 1939 men headed three-fourths of such state efforts. Her 1922 estimate is likely an exaggeration, but as salaries for such positions rose there was a shifting of men into many of these jobs (*Fighting for Life,* p. 201).

67. Frances E. Kobrin, "The American Midwifery Controversy: A Crisis in Professionalization"; Judy Barrett Litoff, "Midwives and History."

68. Grace Abbott, "The Midwife in Chicago"; Neal Devitt, "The Statistical Case for the Elimination of the Midwife: Fact versus Prejudice, 1890-1935"; Joyce Antler and Daniel M. Fox, "The Movement toward a Safe Maternity: Physician Accountability of New York City, 1915-1940"; and Muncy, *Creating a Female Dominion,* p. 116.

69. Molly Ladd-Taylor, "'Grannies' and 'Spinsters': Midwife Education under the Sheppard-Towner Act"; Ladd-Taylor, *Mother-Work,* pp. 179-83; Muncy, *Creating a Female Dominion,* pp. 116-18; U.S. Children's Bureau, "Promotion of the Welfare and Hygiene of Maternity and Infancy" (1931), p. 121.

70. U.S. Children's Bureau, "Promotion of the Welfare and Hygiene of Maternity and Infancy" (1931), p. 26.

71. For an overview of state Sheppard-Towner programs see ibid., pp. 26-29; Anna Rude, M.D., to R.G. Leland, M.D., Aug. 14, 1923, RG 102, CBP, 11-37-1.

72. U.S. Children's Bureau, "The Best Fed Baby," ca. 1920s, and "Our Children," filmed in Gadsen, Ala., ca. 1917; "Sun Babies," filmed in New Haven, Conn., ca. 1920s; all housed in Film Archives, National Archives, Washington, D.C.; H. E. Kleinschmidt, "Leaves from the Diary of a Healthmobile," p. 141; U.S. Children's Bureau, "Promotion of the Welfare and Hygiene of Maternity and Infancy" (1931), pp. 26-29.

73. U.S. Children's Bureau, "Promotion of the Welfare and Hygiene of Maternity and Infancy" (1931), pp. 75-77.

74. Ibid.; U.S. Children's Bureau pamphlets reviewed here include "What Builds Babies? The Mother's Diet in the Pregnant and Nursing Periods" (1925), CBP, folder no. 4; "Minimum Standards of Prenatal Care" (1923), CBP, folder no. 1; "Why Children Sleep? Sleep Helps Children Grow" (1929), CBP, folder 11; and "Breast Feeding" (1926), CBP, folder no. 8, all issued by the Children's Bureau. The bureau's "Prenatal Care," first published in 1914 and written by Mary West, was revised by a bureau physician after 1919.

75. U.S. Children's Bureau, "Promotion of the Welfare and Hygiene of Maternity and Infancy" (1931), pp. 26-29.

76. "Maternity Act Extension Seekers Claim President's Support."

77. "President's Message," *Congressional Record,* 68th Cong., 2d sess., 1924, p. 36; Lemons, *Woman Citizen,* pp. 172-73.

78. U.S. Children's Bureau, "Promotion of the Welfare and Hygiene of Maternity and Infancy" (1925), pp. 32-33; House Committee on Interstate and Foreign Commerce, *Extension of Public Protection of Maternity and Infancy: Hearings on H.R. 7555,* 69th Cong., 1st sess., Jan. 14, 1926; and Senate, *Maternity and Infancy Act: Letters and Extracts from Letters Commending the Maternity and Infancy Act,* 69th Cong., 1st sess., 1926, Sen. Doc. 120.

79. The WJCC consisted of representatives from the National Board of the Young Women's Christian Association, National Council of Jewish Women, National Consumers' League, National Council of Women, General Federation of Women's Clubs, National League of Women Voters, American Association of University Women, National Women's Trade Union League, National Congress of Parent-Teachers, and Women's Christian Temperance Union; compiled from National League of Women Voters Papers, Library of Congress.

80. Julia Lathrop, "Mothers and Babies First!" pp. 41-42; on the mood of fiscal conservatism during the 1920s see Walter Thompson, *Federal Centralization;* and Austin F. McDonald, *Federal Aid: A Study of the American Subsidy System.*

81. "Controversy Develops over Alleged Coolidge Support," p. 19.

82. "AMA House of Delegates Proceedings," 73d annual session (May 1922), p. 44; cited in Burrow, *AMA,* p. 157.

83. For example see L. R. Williams, "Correlation of Federal Health Agencies," pp. 1479-80; "The Perpetuation of the Sheppard-Towner Idea," pp. 1833-34; "The President and the Sheppard-Towner Act," p. 2097.

84. Elizabeth Lowell Putnam to Alice Robertson, Jan. 22, 1927, ELPP, MC 360, box 30, file 484; "A Petition to the United States Senate," p. 117; Mrs. Frederick Schoff, "Children's Bureau Absolutely Unnecessary," pp. 20-21; S. 5250, Feb. 5, 1927, introduced by Senator William H. King (D-Utah); H.R. 17377, Mar. 1, 1927, by Representative Piatt Andrew (R-Mass.); H.R. 17399, Mar. 3, 1927, by Representative Gordon Browning (D-Tenn.).

85. "Address to Sentinels," p. 36; *Hearings on H.R. 7555,* pp. 22-23.

86. House, *Congressional Record,* 69th Cong., 1st sess., Jan. 25, 1926, p. 6920; May 3, 1926, pp. 8573-74; and June 15, 1926, p. 11271.

87. Senate, *Congressional Record,* 69th Cong., 2d sess., Jan. 13, 1927, pp. 1584-85; the opposition included six who had voted against the 1921 act, three who had not voted earlier, and three who had first supported Sheppard-Towner: Peter G. Gerry (D-R.I.), Carter Glass (D-Va.), and Thomas D. Walsh (D-Mont.).

88. Grace Abbott to Florence McKay, Jan. 18, 1927, EGAP, box 62, folder 7; see also Costin, *Two Sisters for Social Justice,* p. 148.

89. Martha May Eliot reported that this was the driving force behind this study, "Martha May Eliot, M.D.," Rockefeller Colloquia, May 9, 1975, transcript, Schlesinger Library; U.S. Children's Bureau, "Maternal Deaths, a Brief Report of a Study Made in Fifteen States" and "Maternal Mortality in Fifteen States."

90. For a detailed history of the Jones-Cooper bill see Chepaitis, "First Federal Social Welfare Measure," pp. 278-366; the bill passed the Senate (56-10) on Jan. 10, 1931, but failed to gain approval in the House and died.

91. *Hearings on H.R. 10925,* p. 23; Ray Lyman Wilbur and Arthur Mastic Hyde, *The Hoover Policies,* pp. 68-74; Costin, *Two Sisters for Social Justice,* p. 166.

92. *Hearings on H.R. 10925,* p. 23; U.S. Bureau of the Census, *Historical Statistics of the United States,* p. 49.

93. U.S. Bureau of the Census, *Historical Statistics of the United States,* p. 57.

94. Alabama, California, Kentucky, Maryland, Michigan, Minnesota, Nebraska, New Hampshire, North Dakota, Oklahoma, Oregon, Rhode Island, Virginia, Washington, and Wisconsin participated in the study. The bureau published two reports from this effort: U.S. Children's Bureau, "Maternal Deaths, a Brief Report of a Study Made in Fifteen States" and "Maternal Mortality in Fifteen States."

95. U.S. Children's Bureau, "Maternal Mortality in Fifteen States"; ibid., "Standards of Prenatal Care, an Outline for the Use of Physicians."

96. This report defined abortion as "the termination of a previable uterine pregnancy" and included "all terminations of uterine pregnancies before the seventh month . . . whether . . . spontaneous or self induced" (U.S. Children's Bureau, "Maternal Mortality in Fifteen States," pp. 103, 105, 114-15).

97. Caroline Hadley Robinson, *Seventy Birth Control Clinics,* pp. 31-32; John D'Emilio and Estelle B. Freedman, *Intimate Matters: A History of Sexuality in America;* Kriste Lindenmeyer, "Taking Birth Control to the Hinterland: Cincinnati's First Birth Control Clinic as a Test Case, 1929-1931."

98. Dick, "Saving Mothers and Babies," pp. 133-34; for a similar argument concerning the national program see Sheila M. Rothman, "Women's Clinics or Doctors' Offices," p. 195.

99. The Committee on the Cost of Medical Care, "The One Great Outstanding Problem," ca. 1927, pamphlet included in JLP, microfilm, reel "Correspondence 1927-1928; the committee included physicians, nurses, economists, business executives, and other professionals; the officers were Ray Lyman Wilbur, M.D., chairman; C. E. A. Winslow, M.D., vice chairman; Chellis A. Austin, treasurer; and Harry H. Moore, Ph.D., director of study; John Duffy, *The Sanitarians: A History of American Public Health,* pp. 257, 275.

100. U.S. Children's Bureau, "Promotion of the Welfare and Hygiene of Maternity and Infancy" (1931), pp. 37-38; Duffy, *Sanitarians,* pp. 239-55.

101. Meckel, *Save the Babies,* pp. 218-19.

Chapter 5: The Children's Bureau and Child Labor Reform, 1912-30

1. David K. Wiggins, "The Play of Slave Children in the Plantation Communities of the Old South, 1820-60," p. 175; Ross W. Beales, Jr., "In Search of the Historical Child: Miniature Adulthood and Youth in Colonial New England," p. 9; Edith Abbott, "Child Labor in America before 1870," 1:270-76; Christine Stansell, *City of Women: Sex and Class in New York, 1789-1860,* esp. pp. 115-22. To the disgust of the Children's Bureau, Wisconsin and eleven other states continued to use apprenticeship for children under sixteen as late as 1923 (U.S. Children's Bureau, "Children Indentured by the Wisconsin State Public School"; Neva R. Deardorff, "Bound Out," p. 459; Weiss, "Save the Children," p. 226.

2. On the transformation of children's work during the nineteenth century see Mintz and Kellogg, *Domestic Revolutions,* pp. 87-91; for a more positive view concerning children's labor in turn-of-the-century urban areas see David Nasaw, *Children of the City at Work and at Play;* National Child Labor Committee, "Changes and Trends in Child Labor and Its Control," pp. 6-7.

3. Chambers, *Seedtime of Reform,* p. 3; Irwin Yellowitz, *Labor and the Progressive Movement in New York State,* p. 76; Samuel McCune Lindsay, "Seventh Annual Child Labor Conference."

4. Florence Kelley, "Obstacles to the Enforcement of Child Labor Legislation," 1:438-42; Dorothy E. Bradbury, "Five Decades of Action for Children," p. 19; Kelley, *Some Ethical Gains through Legislation,* pp. 103-4.

5. Spargo, *Bitter Cry of the Children,* pp. 125-56, 174-95; Mangold, *Problems of Child Welfare,* pp. 290-93; Trattner, *Crusade for the Children,* pp. 21-49; Kelley, *Some Ethical Gains through Legislation,* pp. 82-85, 89; Richard K. Caputo, "Welfare and Freedom American Style: A Study of the Influence of Segmented Authority on the Development of Social and Child Welfare Reform through an Examination of the Role and Activities of the Federal Government, 1900-1940," pp. 63-74; Tiffin, *In Whose Best Interest?* pp. 144-46.

6. The NCLC's papers located in the Library of Congress contain a fascinating collection of editorial cartoons and other media depictions of children as exploited victims at the turn of the century, NCLCP, box 18; for an overview of reformers' attitudes concerning the causes of child labor see Mangold, *Problems of Child Welfare,* pp. 271-83.

7. Robert Willard McAhren, "Making the Nation Safe for Childhood: A History of the Movement for Federal Regulation of Child Labor, 1900-1938," pp. 5-6; U.S. Children's Bureau, "Child Labor Facts and Figures," p. 2.

8. National Child Labor Committee, "Changes and Trends in Child Labor and Its Control," pp. 7, 13; U.S. Children's Bureau, "Child Labor Facts and Figures," p. 2; and Grace Abbott, *Child and the State,* vol. 1, esp. parts 3 and 4.

9. McAhren, "Making the Nation Safe for Childhood," pp. 4-5; Trattner, *Crusade for the Children,* p. 30; Mintz and Kellogg, *Domestic Revolutions,* pp. 56, 88-89; and Tamara K. Hareven, "Family Time and Historical Time," pp. 64-66; Claudia Goldin, "Family Strategies and Family Economy in the Late

Nineteenth Century: The Role of Secondary Workers," p. 298; Priscilla Ferguson Clement, "The City and the Child, 1860-1885," pp. 247-50.

10. The Working Men's party and the Knights of Labor argued as early as 1876 that child labor effectively forced down wages for adult males (Trattner, *Crusade for the Children,* pp. 32, 47-49, 71-75); Owen R. Lovejoy, "In the Shadow of the Coal Breaker"; for a brief overview of the coal strike see George E. Mowry, *The Era of Theodore Roosevelt and the Birth of Modern America, 1900-1912,* pp. 134-40; Mangold, *Problems of Child Welfare,* pp. 297-318; National Child Labor Committee, "Why Conserve Our Natural Resources and Not the Generations that Are to Use Them?"

11. U.S. Bureau of Labor Statistics, "An Investigation of Woman and Child Wage-Earners in the United States"; Gertrude Folks Zimand, "Child Labor Facts," p. 5.

12. U.S. Bureau of Labor Statistics, "Investigation of Woman and Child Wage-Earners in the United States: Cotton Textile Industry," vol. 1; 61st Cong., 2d sess., Senate Doc. 645.

13. John R. Kemp, ed., *Lewis Hine: Photographs of Child Labor in the New South;* Trattner, *Crusade for the Children,* p. 106; on Hine's work as propaganda and an educational tool see Eugene F. Provenzo, Jr., "The Photographer as Educator: The Child Labor Photo-Stories of Lewis Hine"; and Alan Trachtenberg, *Reading American Photographs: Images as History, Mathew Brady to Walker Evans,* pp. 190-209; a collection of Hine's photographs is included in the NCLC's papers at the Library of Congress and in the Records of the U.S. Children's Bureau, RG 102, Still Pictures Branch, National Archives.

14. Edwin Markham, Benjamin B. Lindsey, and George Creel, *Children in Bondage: A Complete and Careful Preservation of the Anxious Problem of Child Labor—Its Causes, Its Crimes, and Its Cure,* p. 15; Weiss, "Save the Children," pp. 226-28; Parker and Carpenter, "Julia Lathrop and the Children's Bureau," pp. 62-65; Trattner, *Crusade for the Children,* pp. 96-98.

15. Trattner, *Crusade for the Children,* pp. 50-51.

16. John Braeman, "Albert J. Beveridge and the First National Child Labor Bill"; Grace Abbott, *Child and the State,* 1:461, 472-76; Senate, *Congressional Record* 59th Cong., 2d sess., part 2.

17. Trattner, *Crusade for the Children,* pp. 87-93; Bremner, *From the Depths,* p. 224; National Child Labor Committee, "Annual Report of the National Child Labor Committee, 10th Fiscal Year Ending September 30, 1914," Minute Book, NCLCP, box 7, pp. 9-10.

18. Grace Abbott, "Ten Years' Work for Children," p. 191; for a discussion on the selection of infant mortality as the bureau's first area of work see chap. 2.

19. U.S. Children's Bureau, *First Annual Report of the Chief* (1914), pp. 9-10.

20. Meriam, "Aims and Objectives of the Federal Children's Bureau," p. 322; press release, U.S. Children's Bureau, "Can You Prove Your Right to Vote?" Aug. 9, 1920, CBP, RG 102, box 74, 8-2-1-0-4; Cressy L. Wilbur, M.D., Chief Statistician, U.S. Bureau of the Census, "Needs and Present Status of Birth Registration," *Proceedings of the National Conference of Charities*

and Corrections, 41st Annual Session, May 8-15, 1914, pp. 257-62; Tiffin, *In Whose Best Interest?* p. 145; and Hawes, *Children's Rights Movement,* p. 51.

21. Helen L. Sumner and Ella A. Merritt, "Child Labor Legislation in the United States"; Helen L. Sumner and Ethel E. Hanks, "Administration of Child-Labor Laws: Part I, Employment-Certificate System, Connecticut." From 1915 to 1924 the Children's Bureau conducted fifteen similar child labor studies resulting in four publications: Helen L. Sumner and Ethel E. Hanks, "Administration of Child-Labor Laws: Part 2, Employment Certificate System, New York"; Francis Henry Bird and Ella Arvilla Merritt, "Administration of Child-Labor Laws: Part 3, Employment Certificate System, Maryland"; Ethel E. Hanks, "Administration of Child-Labor Laws: Part 4, Employment Certification System, Wisconsin"; and Helen Sumner Woodbury, "Administration of Child-Labor Laws: Part 5, Standards Applicable to the Administration of Employment Certificate Systems."

22. Trattner, *Crusade for the Children,* pp. 87-93; Bremner, *From the Depths,* p. 224; McAhren, "Making the Nation Safe for Childhood," pp. 70-72; Thomas George Karis, "Congressional Behavior at Constitutional Frontiers: From 1906, the Beveridge Child-Labor Bill, to 1938, the Fair Labor Standards Act," pp. 1-39.

23. National Child Labor Committee, "Annual Report of the National Child Labor Committee, 10th Fiscal Year ending September 30, 1914," Minute Book, NCLCP, box 7, pp. 9-10; *Congressional Record,* 63d Cong., 3d sess., Feb. 15, 1915, pp. 3827-28; Stanley Coben, *A. Mitchell Palmer: Politician,* pp. 84-89.

24. House Committee on Labor, *To Prevent Interstate Commerce in the Products of Child Labor: Hearings on H.R. 12292,* 63d Cong., 2d sess., Mar. 9, 1914; Covotsos, "Child Welfare and Social Progress," pp. 170-71; Karis, "Congressional Behavior at Constitutional Frontiers," pp. 44-58; McAhren, "Making the Nation Safe for Childhood," pp. 73-76; Coben, *A. Mitchell Palmer,* p. 88; Arthur S. Link, *Woodrow Wilson and the Progressive Era, 1910-1917,* p. 59; Bremner et al., *Children and Youth in America,* 2:695-701.

25. House, *Congressional Record,* 64th Cong., 1st sess., Jan. 1916, pp. 699 and 2035; and Senate, pp. 12194-220; Alexander J. McKelway to Woodrow Wilson, July 17, 1916, Alexander J. McKelway Papers, Library of Congress, box 1; 39 *Stat. L.,* 675.

26. House Committee on Labor, *To Prevent Interstate Commerce in the Products of Child Labor: Hearings on H.R. 8234;* Wood, *Constitutional Politics in the Progressive Era,* pp. 41-48; McAhren, "Making the Nation Safe for Childhood," pp. 76-87.

27. Grace Abbott describes Lathrop's strategy in an untitled speech located in EGAP, box 25, folder 11; see also Costin, *Two Sisters for Social Justice,* pp. 103-5.

28. U.S. Department of Labor, *Annual Report of the Secretary of Labor, 1918,* p. 178; Grace Abbott to Edith Abbott, May 9, 1917, EGAP, addenda.

29. U.S. Children's Bureau, "Administration of the First Federal Child-Labor Law," p. 8; Muncy, *Creating a Female Dominion,* p. 90.

30. U.S. Children's Bureau, "Administration of the First Federal Child-Labor Law," pp. 7-9; "Administrative Practice and Costs under the Federal Child Labor Act of 1916," undated memorandum, EGAP, box 35, also cited in Covotsos, "Child Welfare and Social Progress," p. 174; "Enforcement of the Child Labor Law," memorandum, Feb. 9, 1924, EMF-CBP, RG 102, box 9, file 11.

31. McAhren, "Making the Nation Safe for Childhood," pp. 88-91; Alexander J. McKelway to Julia Lathrop, June 22, 1917, AMP, box 1, and Alexander McKelway to Owen Lovejoy, Sept. 1, 1917, box 1; Costin, *Two Sisters for Social Justice,* pp. 105-6.

32. U.S. Department of Labor, *Annual Report of the Secretary of Labor, 1918,* p. 179. The state officials attending the conference were from Alabama, Arkansas, California, Connecticut, Delaware, Georgia, Illinois, Indiana, Iowa, Kansas, Kentucky, Louisiana, Maine, Maryland, Massachusetts, Missouri, New York, North Carolina, Ohio, Oregon, Pennsylvania, Rhode Island, South Carolina, Tennessee, Vermont, Virginia, West Virginia, and Wisconsin; U.S. Children's Bureau, "Administration of the First Federal Child-Labor Law," p. 53; Owen Lovejoy, "What Remains of Child Labor," p. 39; also in Bremner et al., *Children and Youth in America,* 2:705.

33. U.S. Children's Bureau, "Administration of the First Federal Child-Labor Law," pp. 8, 21, 28, 53; Tobey, *Children's Bureau,* p. 6.

34. U.S. Children's Bureau, "Administration of the First Federal Child-Labor Law," pp. 29-37; see also Covotsos, "Child Welfare and Social Progress," pp. 165-67; U.S. Children's Bureau, "Physical Standards for Working Children"; press release, U.S. Children's Bureau, untitled, Aug. 2, 1920, CBP, RG 102, 8-2-1-0-4.

35. U.S. Children's Bureau, "Administration of the First Federal Child-Labor Law," pp. 29-35.

36. Ibid., pp. 37-38.

37. Ibid., p. 8.

38. David Clark, ed., *Southern Textile Bulletin,* 110 (Apr. 1933): 226-27, cited in Katharine DuPre Lumpkin and Dorothy Wolff Douglas, *Child Workers in America,* pp. 204-5.

39. McAhren, "Making the Nation Safe for Childhood," pp. 93-96; Trattner, *Crusade for the Children,* pp. 136-41; *New York Times,* Sept. 1, 1917, p. 16.

40. For evidence of the controversy see correspondence from Alexander McKelway to Thomas Parkinson, Aug. 11, 1917; Julia Lathrop to Alexander McKelway, Aug. 25, 1917; Felix Adler to Alexander McKelway, Aug. 27, 28, and 29, 1917; Alexander McKelway to Julia Lathrop, Aug. (no day), 1917, all in AMP, box 1; McAhren, "Making the Nation Safe for Childhood," pp. 94-95.

41. "Majority Opinion," *Hammer v. Dagenhart,* 247 U.S. 251 (1918); Stephen B. Wood, "*Hammer v. Dagenhart,*" pp. 359-60.

42. "Minority Opinion," *Hammer v. Dagenhart,* 247 U.S. 251 (1918), pp. 268-81; also "U.S. Supreme Court Declares the Act Unconstitutional, 1918," in Bremner et al., *Children and Youth in America,* 2:712-16.

43. *Child Labor Bulletin,* 7 (Nov. 1918): 150-51, 213; postcard from Grace Abbott to Libby Abbott, June 4, 1918, EGAP, addenda, cited in Costin, *Two Sisters for Social Justice,* p. 111; U.S. Children's Bureau, *Sixth Annual Report of the Chief* (1918), p. 7; and U.S. Department of Labor, *Annual Report of the Secretary of Labor, 1918,* p. 181; "Minutes of Department Cabinet Meetings," Aug. 6, 1918, CBP, RG 102, box 1, 1-2-5-1; U.S. Department of Labor, *Annual Report of the Secretary of Labor, 1918,* p. 180.

44. U.S. Children's Bureau, "Administration of the First Child-Labor Law," p. 8; U.S. Department of Labor, *Annual Report of the Secretary of Labor, 1918,* p. 180; McAhren, "Making the Nation Safe for Childhood," pp. 101-3; U.S. Department of Labor, *Annual Report of the Secretary of Labor, 1918,* p. 180.

45. Owen Lovejoy to Julia Lathrop, Apr. 11, 1917, CBP, RG 102, no box number, 12-1-2-6; for another example of the opinion that the war might encourage an increase in child labor see "Hope for War Profits Increases Child Labor," *New York Times,* Nov. 24, 1918, in Bremner et al., *Children and Youth in America,* 2:719-20.

46. Press release, U.S. Department of Labor, Children's Bureau, Feb. 24, 1919; press release, U.S. Children's Bureau, "Children Now in School Urged to Stay There," Feb. 10, 1919, both in CBP, RG 102, 8-2-1-0-4; press release, U.S. Children's Bureau, "One Million Children from 14 to 16 Leave School Yearly," Feb. 7, 1919; press release, U.S. Children's Bureau, "Why Children Leave School," Dec. 23, 1918, both in CBP, RG 102, 8-2-1-0-4; this file contains other similarly worded press releases for the Back to School Drive.

47. Press release, U.S. Children's Bureau, "Uncle Sam Says 'Back to School!'" Dec. 2, 1918; "Back to School," Nov. 2, 1918; "Children's Year: Looking Backward and Forward," Mar. 8, 1920, all in CBP, RG 102, 8-2-1-0-4.

48. U.S. Bureau of the Census, *Historical Statistics of the United States,* p. 368; U.S. Bureau of the Census (Frank Alexander Ross), "School Attendance in 1920," pp. 189-90.

49. George Alger to Julia Lathrop, June 7, 1918; Florence Kelley to Julia Lathrop, Aug. 19, 1918; Ernst Freund to Grace Abbott, June 18, 1918; Alger, "Memorandum on Federal Child Labor Bill," all in CBP, RG 102, 26-1-1; McAhren, "Making the Nation Safe for Childhood," pp. 104-12; and Karis, "Congressional Behavior at Constitutional Frontiers," pp. 155-79.

50. Owen Lovejoy to Julia Lathrop, Dec. 5, 1918, and Owen Lovejoy to Grace Abbott, Dec. 9, 1918; both in CBP, RG 102, 26-1-1; Karis, "Congressional Behavior at Constitutional Frontiers," pp. 176-92; Ernst Freund to Grace Abbott, June 29, 1918, and Roscoe Pound to Grace Abbott, July 1, 1918, both in CBP, RG 102, 26-1-1; Costin, *Two Sisters for Social Justice,* pp. 116-18.

51. *Bailey vs. Drexel Furniture Co.,* 259 U.S., 20 (1922), only Justice Clarke dissented; Stephen B. Wood, "*Bailey v. Drexel Furniture Co.,*" p. 56; Owen Lovejoy to Edward Clopper, Jan. 3, 1921, Minute Books, 1916-21, NCLCP,

box 7, cited in McAhren, "Making the Nation Safe for Childhood," p. 116; Trattner, *Crusade for the Children,* p. 163.

52. On Grace Abbott's appointment and Lathrop's resignation see chap. 4.

53. Groups represented at the AFL meeting included the National Consumers' League, National Women's Trade Union League, General Federation of Women's Clubs, Women's Joint Congressional Committee, Federal Council of Churches of Christ in America, and the National Catholic Welfare Council; see Costin, *Two Sisters for Social Justice,* pp. 150-51; and Trattner, *Crusade for the Children,* pp. 163-64; Florence Kelley to Grace Abbott, July 29, 1922, EGAP, box 5, folder 5.

54. Julia Lathrop to Grace Abbott, EGAP, box 57, folder 8; for a discussion of the NCLC's stand see Trattner, *Crusade for the Children,* pp. 165-66; Florence Kelley to Grace Abbott, July 29, 1922, EGAP, box 5, folder 5; Florence Kelley to Grace Abbott, Dec. 28, 1926, EGAP, same box and file; Chambers, *Seedtime of Reform,* pp. 33-34.

55. House, *Congressional Record,* 68th Cong., 1st sess., 1924, p. 7295; and Senate, p. 10142.

56. 43 *Stat. L.,* 670.

57. Kirk H. Porter and Donald B. Johnson, eds., *National Party Platforms, 1840-1960,* pp. 252, 262; Trattner, *Crusade for the Children,* p. 169; McAhren, "Making the Nation Safe for Childhood," pp. 135-45.

58. "Editorial," *New Republic,* 42 (May 20, 1925): 330.

59. "The Proposed Amendment to Give the Federal Government Complete Control over the Nation through Child Legislation," *Manufacturers' Record* (Baltimore), July 10, 1924: 67, copy located in EGAP, box 5, folder 11.

60. "Health and Happiness Number," p. 1; "Exposure of Despicable Methods Being Used," *Utica Press,* Feb. 9, 1925, clipping included in EMF-CBP, RG 102, box 22, file 1.

61. Philip S. Tuley to David Clark, Oct. 16, 1924, and David Clark to Secretary of Labor James J. Davis, Sept. 26, 1923, both in EMF-CBP, RG 102, box 11, file 38.

62. George S. Graham in *Manufacturers' Record,* 84 (Dec. 1924): 10; and *Republican Record* quoted by *Manufacturers' News,* 26 (Aug. 30, 1924): 45, both cited in Anne Kruesi Brown, "Opposition to the Child Labor Amendment Found in Trade Journals, Industrial Bulletins, and Other Publications for and by Business Men," pp. 45-46.

63. Trattner, *Crusade for the Children,* pp. 171-72; Vincent A. McQuade, *The American Catholic Attitude on Child Labor since 1891,* esp. pp. 1-30; Monsignor Peter M. H. Wynhoven, "Why Do Catholics Oppose the Ratification of the Federal Child Labor Amendment," pamphlet included in CBP, RG 102, 7-0-9.

64. Ned Weissberg, "The Federal Child Labor Amendment—A Study in Pressure Politics," pp. 170-84; and Trattner, *Crusade for the Children,* pp. 109-14.

65. Goldmark, *Impatient Crusader,* pp. 117-19; Trattner, *Crusade for the Children,* p. 172; Mrs. William Lowell Putnam [Elizabeth Lowell Putnam], "No," Oct. 5, 1924, pamphlet included in ELPP, MC 360, box 16, file 294.

66. U.S. Children's Bureau, "Child Labor Facts and Figures," p. 1.

67. U.S. Children's Bureau, "Administration of the First Federal Child-Labor Law," pp. 48-51.

68. Nettie P. McGill, "Children in Street Work"; Nasaw, *Children of the City,* pp. 103-5; two brief references to girls in street work are included in McGill, ibid., pp. 46, 48.

69. Summarized from McGill, "Children in Street Work"; on the growing consumer culture directed at urban children see Nasaw, *Children of the City,* pp. 115-37.

70. Nettie P. McGill, "Children in Agriculture."

71. Ibid., pp. 1-5; the fourteen states in the Children's Bureau studies were Michigan, Colorado, Texas, New Jersey, Maryland, Virginia, Illinois, Washington, Oregon, North Dakota, Kentucky, South Carolina, Massachusetts, and Connecticut; California, an important agricultural state, did not become part of Bureau studies until the 1930s.

72. Ibid., pp. 1-15.

73. Tilda Kemplen, *From Roots to Roses: The Autobiography of Tilda Kemplen,* p. 9.

74. McGill, "Children in Agriculture."

75. U.S. Children's Bureau, "Child Labor Facts and Figures," p. 19; Arkansas, Arizona, California, Michigan, Montana, Colorado, Oregon, Washington, North Dakota, Michigan, Ohio, New Hampshire, New Jersey, Oklahoma, and Illinois had ratified the amendment by 1930.

76. Grace Abbott, "Child Labor Amendment," p. 225.

77. Lowell Mellet, "The Sequel of the Dagenhart Case" (also in Bremner et al., *Children and Youth in America,* 2:716-17); and Lowell Mellett, "How Sharper than a Serpent's Tooth It Is to Have a Thankless Child," *Labor,* Nov. 17, 1923, reprinted in Grace Abbott, *Child and the State,* 1:515-17; see also Lowell Mellett, "The Dagenhart Boys," clipping, EMF-CBP, RG 102, box 9, file 16; on child labor reform as a civil rights issue see Hawes, *Children's Rights Movement,* pp. 39-53.

78. For examples of the bureau's suggested solutions see U.S. Children's Bureau, "Employment-Certificate System: A Safeguard for the Working Child"; ibid., "Advising Children in Their Choice of Occupation and Supervising the Working Child"; and ibid., "Scholarships for Children."

Chapter 6: When Families Fail

1. Tobey, *Children's Bureau,* pp. 28, 33; Covotsos, "Child Welfare and Social Progress," pp. 198-232; Sophonisba P. Breckinridge and Helen R. Jeter, "A Summary of Juvenile-Court Legislation in the United States," p. 19.

2. Bruno, *Trends in Social Work,* pp. 169-76; "An Act to Regulate the Treatment and Control of Dependent, Neglected and Delinquent Children," Illinois, 1899; and Julia Lathrop, "The Background of the Juvenile Court in Illinois," in *The Child, the Clinic and the Court,* ed. Julia Lathrop et al., pp. 290-95, reprinted in Bremner et al., *Children and Youth in America,* 2:504-11; Covotsos, "Child Welfare and Social Progress," pp. 203-4; Anthony Platt, *The Child Savers: The Invention of Delinquency,* pp. 124-25, 131-36; Robert M. Mennel, *Thorns and Thistles: Juvenile Delinquents in the United States, 1825-1940,* p. 129.

7. Trattner, *From Poor Law to Welfare State,* p. 117; Platt, *Child Savers,* pp. 9-10; Joseph M. Hawes, *Children in Urban Society: Juvenile Delinquency in Nineteenth-Century America;* Bremner et al., *Children and Youth in America,* 2:439-41; Alexander W. Pisciotta, "Benjamin Barr Lindsey," pp. 503-6; and Charles Larsen, *The Good Fight: The Life and Times of Ben B. Lindsey;* D'Ann Campbell, "Judge Ben Lindsey and the Juvenile Court Movement, 1901-4."

8. Breckinridge and Jeter, "Summary of Juvenile-Court Legislation in the United States," pp. 15-16; Mennel, *Thorns and Thistles,* p. 132.

9. Flexner, Oppenheimer, and Lenroot, "Child, the Family, and the Court," p. 12.

10. "An act providing for the hearing and determination of disputes or matters affecting the domestic relation, and conferring jurisdiction upon the county courts," 1912, *Acts in the State of New Jersey,* p. 543, in Bremner et al., *Children and Youth in America,* 2:543-44; Flexner, Oppenheimer, and Lenroot, "Child, the Family, and the Court," pp. 14-15; Charles W. Hoffman, "Courts of Domestic Relations," *Proceedings of the National Conference of Social Work,* 1918, pp. 125-26, in Bremner et al., *Children and Youth in America,* 2:543-45; Hawes, *Children's Rights Movement,* pp. 37-38.

11. U.S. Children's Bureau, press release, "Juvenile Courts in the United States," Dec., 15, 1920, CBP, RG 102, 8-2-1-0-4.

12. See U.S. Children's Bureau, "Handbook of Federal Statistics of Children"; ibid., "Mental Defectives in the District of Columbia: A Brief Description of Local Conditions and the Need for Custodial Care and Training"; ibid., "Baby-Week Campaigns: Suggestions for Communities of Various Sizes"; Leifur Magnusson, "Norwegian Laws concerning Illegitimate Children"; Kate Holladay Claghorn, "Juvenile Delinquency in Rural New York"; U.S. Children's Bureau, "Juvenile Delinquency in Certain Countries at War: A Brief Review of Available Foreign Sources"; Ernst Freund, "Illegitimacy Laws of the United States and Certain Foreign Countries: Analysis and Index"; Evelina Belden, "Courts in the United States Hearing Children's Cases: Results of a Questionnaire Study Covering the Year 1918"; Emma O. Lundberg and Katharine F. Lenroot, "Illegitimacy as a Child-Welfare Problem, Part I: A Brief Treatment of the Prevalence and Significance of Birth out of Wedlock, the Child's Status, and the State's Responsibility for Care and Protection"; Breckinridge and Jeter, "A Summary of Juvenile-Court Legislation in the United States"; Lundberg and Lenroot, "Illegitimacy as a Child-Welfare Problem, Part II: A Study of Original Records in the City of Boston

and in the State of Massachusetts"; U.S. Children's Bureau, "Standards of Legal Protection for Children Born out of Wedlock: A Report of Regional Conferences Held under the Auspices of the U.S. Children's Bureau and the Inter-City Conference on Illegitimacy, Chicago, Ill., February 9-10, 1920"; Charles L. Chute, "Probation in Children's Courts"; Edith Abbott and Sophonisba P. Breckinridge, "The Administration of the Aid-to-Mothers Law in Illinois"; William Healy, M.D., "The Practical Value of Scientific Study of Juvenile Delinquents"; U.S. Children's Bureau, "Proceedings of the Conference on Juvenile-Court Standards Held under the Auspices of the U.S. Children's Bureau and the National Probation Association, Milwaukee, Wisconsin, June 21-22, 1921"; Bernard Flexner and Reuben Oppenheimer, "The Legal Aspect of the Juvenile Court"; Ruth Bloodgood, "The Federal Courts and the Delinquent Child: A Study of the Methods of Dealing with Children Who Have Violated Federal Laws"; Helen Rankin Jeter, "The Chicago Juvenile Court"; "County Organization for Child Care and Protection"; U.S. Children's Bureau, "Proceedings of the Conference on Mothers' Pensions Held under the Auspices of the Mothers' Pension Committee Family Division of the National Conference of Social Work and the Children's Bureau, U.S. Department of Labor, Providence, R.I., June 28, 1922"; Florence Nesbitt, "Standards of Public Aid to Children in Their Own Homes"; U.S. Children's Bureau, "Juvenile-Court Standards: Report of the Committee Appointed by the Children's Bureau, August, 1921, to Formulate Juvenile-Court Standards. Adopted by a Conference Held under the Auspices of the Children's Bureau and the National Probation Association, Washington, D.C., May 18, 1923"; ibid., "List of References on Juvenile Courts and Probation in the United States and a Selected List of Foreign References"; ibid., "Illegitimacy as a Child-Welfare Problem, Part III: Methods of Care in Selected Urban and Rural Communities"; Emma O. Lundberg, "State Commissions for the Study and Revision of Child-Welfare Laws"; Katharine F. Lenroot and Emma O. Lundberg, "Juvenile Courts at Work: A Study of the Organization and Methods of Ten Courts"; U.S. Children's Bureau, "The Welfare of Infants of Illegitimate Birth in Baltimore as Affected by a Maryland Law of 1916 Governing the Separation from Their Mothers of Children under Six Months Old"; Reuben Oppenheimer and Lulu L. Eckman, "Laws Relating to Sex Offenses against Children"; U.S. Children's Bureau, "Juvenile-Court Statistics: A Tentative Plan for Uniform Reporting of Statistics of Delinquency, Dependency, and Neglect"; ibid., "Dependent and Delinquent Children in North Dakota and South Dakota: A Study of the Prevalence, Treatment, and Prevention of Child Dependency and Delinquency in Two Rural States"; ibid., "Dependent and Delinquent Children in Georgia: A Study of the Prevalence and Treatment of Child Dependency and Delinquency in Thirty Counties with Special Reference to Legal Protection Needed"; Emma O. Lundberg, "Public Aid to Mothers with Dependent Children: Extent and Fundamental Principles"; Dorothy Reed Mendenhall, "Milk, the Indispensable Food for Children" (1926 ed.); Emma O. Lundberg, "Children of Illegitimate Birth and Measures for Their Protection"; H. Ida Curry, "Public

Child-Caring Work in Certain Counties of Minnesota, North Carolina, and New York"; William J. Blackburn, "Child Welfare in New Jersey, Part 1—State Supervision and Personnel Administration"; Ruth Berolzheimer and Florence Nesbitt, "Child Welfare in New Jersey, Part 2—State Provision for Dependent Children, the Work of the Board of Children's Guardians of the New Jersey State Department of Institutions and Agencies"; Neva R. Deardorff, "Child-Welfare Conditions and Resources in Seven Pennsylvania Counties"; U.S. Children's Bureau, "Child Welfare in New Jersey, Part 4—Local Provisions for Dependent and Delinquent Children in Relation to the State's Program"; Mary F. Bogue, "Administration of Mothers' Aid in Ten Localities: With Special Reference to Health, Housing, Education, and Recreation"; A. Madorah Donahue, "Children of Illegitimate Birth Whose Mothers Have Kept Their Custody"; U.S. Children's Bureau, "List of Psychiatric Clinics for Children in the United States"; ibid., "Juvenile-Court Statistics, 1927, Based on Information Supplied by 42 Courts"; Dorothy Williams Burke, "Youth and Crime: A Study of the Prevalence and Treatment of Delinquency among Boys over Juvenile-Court Age in Chicago"; U.S. Children's Bureau, "Juvenile-Court Statistics, 1928, Based on Information Supplied by 65 Courts"; ibid., "Juvenile Delinquency in Maine"; ibid., "Juvenile-Court Statistics, 1929, Based on Information Supplied by 96 Courts"; and ibid., "Juvenile-Court Statistics, 1930, Based on Information Supplied by 92 Courts."

13. U.S. Children's Bureau, "Juvenile-Court Standards"; ibid., *Eleventh Annual Report of the Chief* (1923), p. 23; Flexner, Oppenheimer, and Lenroot, "Child, the Family, and the Court," p. 13; Dorothy E. Bradbury, "The Children's Bureau and Juvenile Delinquency: A Chronology of What the Bureau Is Doing and Has Done in This Field," pp. 5-6; the recommendations formulated by the 1923 conference were adopted as Children's Bureau policy in this field until revised in 1954 (Bradbury, ibid., p. 6).

14. Katharine F. Lenroot, "The Place of the Juvenile Court in a Community Program for Child Welfare," p. 60.

15. Lenroot and Lundberg remained close and lived as housemates from 1935 to 1954; biographical material gathered from "Katharine Lenroot," pp. 428-29; George Kennedy, "Katharine Lenroot and Her Times," *Washington Star,* July 10, 1951; Thomas L. Stokes, "A Notable Career of Service," *Washington Star,* July 11, 1951; Lowell Mellett, "Tough Bureaucrat Takes a Rest," *Washington Star,* July 12, 1951; Nicha Searle, "She Came for One Year and Stayed 36," *Washington Post,* July 15, 1951; "Children's 'Foster Mother' Approves Present Generation," *Madison, Wisconsin, Capital Times,* ca. July 10, 1951; and Children's Bureau, "Background Information on Katharine F. Lenroot," typed memo, n.d. (ca. 1951); all in MMEP, MC 229, box 12, file 162; "Katharine F. Lenroot, Chief of the Children's Bureau," *United States News,* Dec. 24, 1934: 8, and Elizabeth F. Fisher, "Katharine F. Lenroot," typed biography prepared for the Committee on Research of Rho Chapter of Delta Kappa Gamma, 1968, both included in Irwin L. Lenroot Papers, box 30, file "Material about Katharine F. Lenroot," Library of Congress; "Statement in Re

Miss Lenroot's Academic and Professional Background," EGAP, box 37, folder 1; and "Katharine Lenroot," *Columbia Oral History Project,* part 3.

16. Breckinridge and Jeter, "Summary of Juvenile-Court Legislation in the United States," pp. 7-8.

17. Quotation from Louise deKoven Bowen, cited in Costin, *Two Sisters for Social Justice,* p. 39.

18. Miriam Van Waters, "The Juvenile Court from a Child's Point of View," in *Child, the Clinic, and the Court,* ed. Lathrop et al., reprinted in Bremner et al., *Children and Youth in America,* 2:542; and Miriam Van Waters, "Juvenile Delinquency and Juvenile Courts," p. 529.

19. Bradbury, "Children's Bureau and Juvenile Delinquency," p. 2; memorandum from Julia Lathrop to William Howard Taft in care of Charles Hilles, Jan. 16, 1913, WHTP, microfilm, reel 433, case file 2624; Mennel, *Thorns and Thistles,* p. 180.

20. William B. Bailey, "Children before the Courts in Connecticut"; Lathrop quotation from "Introduction," in Sophonisba P. Breckinridge and Edith Abbott, *The Delinquent Child and the Home.*

21. U.S. Children's Bureau, "Juvenile Delinquency in Certain Countries at War," pp. 7, 24.

22. Bradbury, "Children's Bureau and Juvenile Delinquency," p. 3; U.S. Children's Bureau, *Sixth Annual Report of the Chief* (1918), pp. 17-21; Julia C. Lathrop, "Children's Bureau in Wartime"; on the Baker Center see Linda Gordon, *Heroes of Their Own Lives: The Politics and History of Family Violence,* esp. pp. 12-13.

23. Nasaw, *Children of the City,* pp. 35-36; Dominick Cavallo, *Muscles and Morals: Organized Playgrounds and Urban Reform, 1880-1920,* pp. 1-2; *Annual Report of the Board of Commissioners of Cook County* (1907), cited in Platt, *Child Savers,* p. 148; Costin, *Two Sisters for Social Justice,* p. 39.

24. U.S. Children's Bureau, press release, "No Play," Nov. 25, 1918, CBP, RG 102, 8-2-1-0-4; Kate Holloday Claghorn, "Juvenile Delinquency in Rural New York"; on children's disdain for such efforts to control their play see Nasaw, *Children of the City,* pp. 36-38.

25. Mrs. Max [Mary] West, press release, "Teaching Patriotism to Young People," Aug. 26, 1918, CBP, RG 102, 8-2-1-0-4.

26. U.S. Children's Bureau, *Sixth Annual Report of the Chief* (1918), pp. 17-21.

27. Ruth S. Bloodgood, "The Federal Courts and the Delinquent Child: A Study of the Methods of Dealing with Children Who Have Violated Federal Laws"; U.S. Children's Bureau, *Tenth Annual Report of the Chief* (1922), p. 27; Bradbury, "Children's Bureau and Juvenile Delinquency," pp. 4-5.

28. Bradbury, "Children's Bureau and Juvenile Delinquency," pp. 6-7; U.S. Children's Bureau, *Fourteenth Annual Report of the Chief* (1926); Mennel, *Thorns and Thistles,* pp. 155-57; Grace Abbott, "The Juvenile Courts."

29. The Children's Bureau published these annual reports beginning in 1927 under the title "Juvenile-Court Statistics" (Children's Bureau publications 195, 200, 207, 212, and 222; the findings of these five years are sum-

marized in the latter, U.S. Children's Bureau, "Juvenile-Court Statistics, 1931: Based on Information Supplied by 92 Courts."

30. Ibid., pp. 4-6; Gordon, *Heroes of Their Own Lives,* esp. pp. 218-22, 240-49.

31. U.S. Children's Bureau, "Facts about Juvenile Delinquency: Its Prevention and Treatment," pp. 6-11.

32. Ibid., p. 3; the original conference committee report is entitled "The Delinquent Child," from the *White House Conference on Child Health and Protection, 1930;* Mennel, *Thorns and Thistles,* p. 180; Wickersham Commission, "Report on the Child Offender in the Federal System of Justice."

33. Mennel, *Thorns and Thistles,* pp. 199-200.

34. U.S. Children's Bureau, "Facts about Juvenile Delinquency," p. 37.

35. Lubove, *Struggle for Social Security,* p. 106; Skocpol, *Protecting Soldiers and Mothers,* pp. 424-79; Gordon, *Pitied but Not Entitled,* esp. pp. 15-51.

36. Bremner, *From the Depths,* pp. 222-23; *Proceedings 1909 White House Conference,* pp. 9-10; National Conference of Charities and Correction, *Proceedings . . . 41st Annual Session;* Bruno, *Trends in Social Work,* pp. 177-82; Mark H. Leff, "Consensus for Reform: The Mothers' Pension Movement in the Progressive Era," esp. pp. 402-4; Gordon, *Pitied but Not Entitled,* pp. 39-49.

37. Julia Lathrop, "Pension the Mothers," p. 376, cited in Covotsos, "Child Welfare and Social Progress," p. 217.

38. Edith Abbott and Breckinridge, "Administration of the Aid-to-Mothers Law in Illinois"; reprinted in *The Family and Social Service in the 1920's: Two Documents,* ed. David J. Rothman and Sheila M. Rothman, pp. 7-8. This volume also includes Bogue, "Administration of Mothers' Aid in Ten Localities."

39. U.S. Children's Bureau, "Mothers' Aid, 1931," pp. 2, 23; Leff, "Consensus for Reform," pp. 402-5; Grace Abbott, "Mothers' Aid"; Covotsos, "Child Welfare and Social Progress," pp. 217-19; Skocpol, *Protecting Soldiers and Mothers,* table 10, p. 457; Isaac Rubinow quoted in Christopher Howard, "Sowing the Seeds of 'Welfare': The Transformation of Mothers' Pensions, 1900-1940," p. 189.

40. Leff, "Consensus for Reform," pp. 408, 414; Barbara J. Nelson, "The Origins of the Two-Channel Welfare State: Workmen's Compensation and Mothers' Aid," p. 133.

41. Ethel M. Springer, "Children Deprived of Parental Care: A Study of Children Taken under Care by Delaware Institutions and Agencies," p. 85.

42. Nesbitt, "Standard of Public Aid to Children in Their Own Homes," p. 40.

43. Helen Russell Wright, "Children of Wage-Earning Mothers: A Study of a Selected Group in Chicago," pp. 16-17, 79-88; Gordon, *Pitied but Not Entitled,* pp. 114-43.

44. Edith Abbott and Breckinridge, "Administration of the Aid-to-Mothers Law in Illinois."

45. Ibid., pp. 167-71.

46. U.S. Children's Bureau, "Proceedings of the Conference on Mothers' Pensions Held under the Auspices of the Mothers' Pension Committee Family Division of the National Conference of Social Work and the Children's Bureau"; Grace Abbott, *Child and the State,* vol. 2, esp. pp. 29-38.

47. For example see Bogue, "Administration of Mothers' Aid in Ten Localities."

48. U.S. Children's Bureau, "Mothers' Aid, 1931," p. 1.

49. Lundberg and Lenroot, "Illegitimacy as a Child-Welfare Problem, Part I," pp. 13-19, 23-24, 39.

50. See ibid. and Magnusson, "Norwegian Laws concerning Illegitimate Children"; Freund, "Illegitimacy Laws of the United States and Certain Foreign Countries"; Lundberg and Lenroot, "Illegitimacy as a Child-Welfare Problem, Part II"; U.S. Children's Bureau, "Standards of Legal Protection for Children Born out of Wedlock"; Rochester, "Infant Mortality"; U.S. Children's Bureau, "Illegitimacy as a Child-Welfare Problem, Part III"; ibid., "The Welfare of Infants of Illegitimate Birth in Baltimore as Affected by a Maryland Law of 1916 Governing the Separation from Their Mothers of Children under Six Months Old"; ibid., "A Study of Maternity Homes in Minnesota and Pennsylvania"; and Donahue, "Children of Illegitimate Birth Whose Mothers Have Kept Their Custody."

51. Lundberg and Lenroot, "Illegitimacy as a Child-Welfare Problem, Part I," p. 7; Donahue, "Children of Illegitimate Birth Whose Mothers Have Kept Their Custody," pp. 5-6.

52. "Mrs." E. to Julia Lathrop, n.d. (ca. May 1915), EGAP, box 59, folder 3.

53. Mary West to Mrs. E., May 11, 1915, EGAP, box 59, folder 3.

54. Mrs. E. to Mary West, n.d. (ca. May 1915), EGAP, box 59, folder 3; Regina G. Kunzel, "The Professionalization of Benevolence: Evangelicals and Social Workers in the Florence Crittenton Homes, 1915 to 1945"; Gordon, *Pitied but Not Entitled,* pp. 21-22, 28-30, 41; Elizabeth Feder, "The Elite of the Fallen: The Origins of a Social Policy for Unwed Mothers, 1880-1930."

55. Lundberg and Lenroot, "Illegitimacy as a Child Welfare Problem, Part I" p. 8.

56. Katharine F. Lenroot, "Social Responsibility for the Protection of Children Handicapped by Illegitimate Birth," p. 124.

57. U.S. Children's Bureau, "Maternal Mortality in Fifteen States," pp. 105, 114-15; the states in this study were Alabama, California, Kentucky, Maryland, Michigan, Minnesota, Nebraska, New Hampshire, North Dakota, Oklahoma, Oregon, Rhode Island, Virginia, Washington, and Wisconsin. The average illegitimacy rate for the states included in the bureau's data was 180.7 constituting 1.8 percent of all births. The states used in the study were Alabama, Connecticut, Indiana, Maryland, Massachusetts, Michigan, Minnesota, Nevada, New Hampshire, Pennsylvania, Rhode Island, South Dakota, Utah, Vermont, and Wisconsin; ibid., pp. 23-25, 27-28. On the high infant mortality rates of babies born outside of marriage see the following Children's Bureau publications: Rochester, "Infant Mortality"; U.S. Children's Bureau, "The Welfare of Infants of Illegitimate Birth in Baltimore"; and Robert Morse

Woodbury, "Causal Factors in Infant Mortality: A Statistical Study Based on Investigations in Eight Cities."

58. U.S. Children's Bureau, "Standards of Legal Protection for Children Born out of Wedlock"; Lundberg, "Progress toward Better Laws for the Protection of Children Born out of Wedlock," pp. 111-15; Covotsos, "Child Welfare and Social Progress," pp. 226-27; Leff, "Consensus for Reform," p. 405.

59. Carp, *History of Secrecy and Openness in Adoption,* esp. chap. 1.

60. U.S. Children's Bureau, "Mental Defectives in the District of Columbia," pp. 20-21.

61. Alice Channing, "Employment of Mentally Deficient Boys and Girls," p. 96.

62. Glenn Steele, "Care of Dependent and Neglected Children"; and Nesbitt, "Standards of Public Aid to Children in Their Own Homes."

63. Lubove, *Struggle for Social Security,* pp. 110-12; Nesbitt, "Standards of Public Aid to Children in Their Own Homes," p. 38.

64. Grace Abbott, "The Child in 1879 and 1929," CBP, RG 102, 0-1-0.

Chapter 7: A Policy for Security

1. Grace Abbott, "Child in 1879 and 1929," CBP, RG 102, 0-1-0.

2. For a similar view of the Children's Bureau's weakened role see Robert Allen Karlsrud, "The Hoover Labor Department: A Study in Bureaucratic Divisiveness," pp. 217-28.

3. Campaign flyer, "Republican or Democrat, If You Are a Woman You Need Herbert Hoover for President. Why?" ca. 1928, included in Irwin L. Lenroot Papers, Library of Congress, box 30, file "Printed Matter"; Costin, *Two Sisters for Social Justice,* p. 166; Edith Abbott to Julia Lathrop, June 11, 1928, EGAP, box 56, folder 6; correspondence between Mabel Walker Willebrant and Julia Lathrop, Mar. 27 and Apr. 4, 1928, in JLP, microfilm reel "Correspondence 1927-28, CL-1932 to Her Death"; "The Story of the American Child Health Association," *Child Health Bulletin,* (Sept.-Nov. 1935); reprint in ACHAP, box 1, file "American Child Health Association Publications, Histories of ACHA, 1927-1935."

4. Muncy, *Creating a Female Dominion,* p. 102.

5. Elizabeth Lowell Putnam to Alice Robertson, June 8, 1928, ELPP, MC 360, box 30, file 484.

6. Julius Rosenwald to Grace Abbott, Apr. 24, 1930, and Grace Abbott to Julius Rosenwald, Apr. 28, 1930, both in EGAP, box 36, folder 10; Costin, *Two Sisters for Social Justice,* p. 168.

7. Memorandum, "Interview with the President," Aug. 29, 1929, EGAP, Addenda II, box 3, folder 6; William John Cooper to the secretary of the interior, Sept. 11, 1929, HHP, Presidential Papers, file "Maternity Legislation,"; both also cited in Costin, *Two Sisters for Social Justice,* p. 167; Hugh S. Cumming, *Memorandum,* 1930, HHP, Presidential Papers, box 97, file "Child

Health Conference." See also Chepaitis, "First Federal Social Welfare Measure," pp. 278-366; and Karlsrud, "Hoover Labor Department," pp. 204-9.

8. James Couzens to Herbert Hoover, Mar. 5, 1929, and response from Hoover Mar. 6, 1929, HHP, Presidential Papers, box 96, file Child Health and Protection Conference, correspondence, 1929; see also Ray Lyman Wilbur to George Akerson, Apr. 25, 1929, same box and file.

9. Herbert Hoover to Edgar Rickard, ACHA, May 21, 1929, ACHAP, box 47, file "White House Conference on Child Health; Edgar Rickard to Ray Lyman Wilbur, May 28, 1929, box 47, file "White House Conference on Child Health"; and copy of ACHA Directors' Meeting Minutes, Feb. 18, 1931 (approval of further funds for follow-up conferences), ACHAP, box 47, "White House Conference, Continuing Committee, 1931."

10. Laurence Vesey, "Ray Lyman Wilbur," 4:891-95; "Secretary of the Interior," *Washington Star,* Mar. 10, 1929, clipping in HHP, Presidential Papers, box 93, file "Cabinet"; "Biographical Sketch of Ray Lyman Wilbur, Secretary of the Interior," typed memo in HHP, Presidential Secretary File Papers, box 935; "Ray Lyman Wilbur Dies at Stanford at 74"; Ray Lyman Wilbur, M.D., *The March of Medicine: Selected Addresses and Articles on Medical Topics, 1913-1937.*

11. Grace Abbott to Julius Rosenwald, Apr. 30, 1920, EGAP, box 36, folder 10; members of the executive committee of the conference planning committee were Ray Lyman Wilbur, M.D., chair; H. E. Barnard, Ph.D., Washington, D.C., director; Grace Abbott, secretary; Hugh S. Cumming, M.D. (surgeon general); French Strother (administrative assistant to the president); "Planning Committee," memo, n.d., HHP, Presidential Papers, box 97, file "Child Health Conference."

12. Grace Abbott to Julius Rosenwald, Apr. 28, 1929.

13. The six child health committees were Growth and Development, Prenatal and Maternal Care, Medical Care for Children, Public Health Organization, Communicable Disease Control, and Milk Production and Control.

14. In 1947 Eliot was the first woman elected president of the American Public Health Association. During 1949-50 she served as president of the National Conference of Social Work. From 1951 to 1956 Eliot was chief of the Children's Bureau. In 1956 she joined the faculty of the Harvard Medical School, a position she held until 1960 (Joseph B. Treaster, "Martha Eliot; Worked in Child Care"); U.S. Children's Bureau, "Background Information on Dr. Martha M. Eliot," memorandum in MMEP, MC 229, box 12, file 162.

15. Memorandum prepared by S. J. Crumbine sent to Herbert Hoover from Ray Lyman Wilbur, July 25, 1929, HHP, Presidential Papers, box 93, file "Child Health and Protection Conference, Correspondence, 1929"; Grace Abbott to Julius Rosenwald, Apr. 30, 1930, EGAP, box 36, folder 10; "Martha May Eliot," interview, COHP, part 4, pp. 28-32. The members of the Special Committee on Public Health Organization were E. L. Bishop, chair; Earl G. Brown, M.D.; Chester Brown, M.D.; Theodore B. Appel, M.D.; Henry F. Vaughan, M.D.; Anna Rude, M.D.; John A. Ferrell, M.D.; C. E. A. Winslow, M.D.; and Sadie Orr Dunbar (no occupational identification);

"Statement of General Principles Relative to Public Health in the United States Adopted by the Committee on Public Health Organization of the White House Conference on Child Health and Protection," Nov. 7, 1929, HHP, Presidential Papers, box 97, file "Child Health Conference."

16. "Clara Beyer, 98, Dies; Key New Deal Official"; "The Clara Mortenson Beyer Collection," biography with the collection, A-159, CMBP.

17. Information concerning the effort to nominate Grace Abbott as secretary of labor is in included in MMEP, MC 229, box 11, file 151, EGAP, C.A. Addenda and box 58, and CMBP, A-159, box 8, file 117; Costin, *Two Sisters for Social Justice,* pp. 176-77, 216; Karlsrud, "Hoover Labor Department," pp. 258-61; Grace Abbott quotation from Corrine Frasier, "Grace Abbott for the Cabinet," *Woman's Journal,* Aug. 1930, typed version in MMEP, MC 229, box 11, file 151.

18. Clara Beyer to Helen Bary, CMBP, A-159, box 8, file 117; Julia Lathrop to Grace Abbott, Dec. 16, 1930, EGAP, box 58, folder 4. On Doak see Karlsrud, "Hoover Labor Department," pp. 263-69.

19. Paul U. Kellogg to Haven Emerson, Dec. 23, 1929, Survey Papers, Social Welfare History Archives, box 68, folder 511, cited in Costin, *Two Sisters for Social Justice,* pp. 169-70.

20. Address by H. E. Barnard before the Indiana League of Women Voters, Indianapolis, Mar. 21, 1930, copy included in HHP, Presidential Papers, box 97, file "Child Health Conference."

21. "Statement of General Principles Relative to Public Health in the United States," Nov. 7, 1929, HHP, Presidential Papers, Box 97, file "Child Health Conference."

22. Hugh S. Cumming to Herbert Hoover, Feb. 1, 1930, HHP, Presidential Papers, box 97, file "Child Health Conference."

23. Grace Abbott, "Minority Report to Accompany Report of Committee I of Section II of the White House Conference Entitled 'Statement of General Principles Relative to Public Health in the United States Adopted by the Committee on Public Health Organization of the White House Conference on Child Health and Protection,'" n.d. (ca. Nov. 1929), HHP, Presidential Papers, box 97, file "Child Health Conference."

24. Herbert Hoover, "Address of President Hoover at the Opening Session of the White House Conference on Child Health and Protection," Nov. 19, 1930 (Washington, D.C.: Government Printing Office, 1930); copy in HHP, Presidential Papers, box 97, file "Child Health Conference," pp. 1-2, 6; for a summary of the conference proceedings see *Report of the White House Conference on Child Health and Protection;* Karlsrud, "Hoover Labor Department," pp. 238-45.

25. Hoover, "Address," p. 6.

26. Lillian D. Wald, "Shall We Dismember the Child?"

27. "Martha May Eliot," COHP, part 4, pp. 28-32; see also Costin, *Two Sisters for Social Justice,* pp. 171-72; Goldmark, *Impatient Crusader,* p. 110; Muncy, *Creating a Female Dominion,* pp. 147-48; *Proceedings of the 1930 White House Conference on Child Health and Protection,* Friday, Nov. 21, 1930,

p. 34, copy in HHP, Presidential Papers, box 98, file "Child Health Conference, Printed Matter." Lathrop quotation in Julia Lathrop to Grace Abbott, Dec. 16, 1930, EGAP, box 58, folder 4.

28. "The White House Conference," *Nation,* 131 (Dec. 3, 1930): 595; U.S. Children's Bureau, *Annual Report of the Chief* (1931), p. 121.

29. Grace Abbott, *From Relief to Social Security,* pp. 21-22, 121-22; Josephine Chapin Brown, *Public Relief 1929-1939,* pp. 68-71; Albert U. Romasco, *The Poverty of Abundance: Hoover, the Nation, the Depression,* pp. 143-49.

30. Grace Abbott, "Improvement in Rural Public Relief: The Lesson of the Coal-Mining Communities"; Covotsos, "Child Welfare and Social Progress," p. 262.

31. U.S. Children's Bureau, *Relief Expenditures, January through September, 1931;* and ibid., "Emergency Food Relief and Child Health."

32. Ray Lyman Wilbur, "Children in National Emergencies," p. 27.

33. Grace Abbott, *From Relief to Social Security,* pp. 121-22; Grace Abbott, "Memorandum," Oct. 27, 1930, EGAP, box 37, folder 11; and "Advisory Committee to the Secretary of Labor," memorandum: "Welfare Statistics of the Children's Bureau," Mar. 9, 1935, Records of the Department of Labor, RG 174, box 18, file CB, 1935.

34. Grace Abbott, "Address," *Report of the White House Conference on Child Health and Protection;* Grace Abbott interview in *New York Times Magazine.*

35. Memorandum from Grace Abbott to Frances Perkins, Mar. 15, 1933, EGAP, Addenda, box 5, folder 9.

36. "President Hoover," *Congressional Record,* 72d Cong., 1st sess., pp. 116-23; Trattner, *From Poor Law to Welfare State,* pp. 252-53.

37. U.S. Bureau of the Census, *Historical Statistics of the United States,* p. 57.

38. Emma Octavia Lundberg, "Unemployment and Child Welfare: A Study Made in a Middle-Western and an Eastern City during the Industrial Depression of 1921 and 1922," pp. 1-4.

39. Grace Abbott, *From Relief to Social Security,* pp. 22, 121-160; Senate, *Further Unemployment Relief through the Reconstruction Finance Corporation: Hearings before a Subcommittee of the Committee on Banking and Currency, S. 5336,* 72d Cong., 2d sess., Feb. 2-3, 1933.

40. U.S. Children's Bureau, "Effects of the Depression on Child Health and Child Health Services," *Congressional Record,* 72d Cong., 1st sess., pp. 3095-99; see also Bremner et al., *Children and Youth in America,* 2:1091-92; "The Health of Children in the United States during the Depression."

41. Senate, *Congressional Record,* 72d Cong., 1st sess. (Feb. 1932), pp. 3584-88, 2751; see also Karlsrud, "Hoover Labor Department," pp. 328-37; Josephine Chapin Brown, *Public Relief 1929-1939,* pp. 103-23; Adelaide R. Hasse, "Congressional Relief Programs: A Record in the Congress of the United States, 1803-1933," Senate, *Congressional Record,* 72d Cong., 1st sess. (Feb. 1932), pp. 4016-17.

42. "Martha May Eliot," COHP, part 4, p. 31; and Karlsrud, "Hoover Labor Department," pp. 238-39.

43. Katharine F. Lenroot to Grace Abbott, n.d., EGAP, Addenda, box 5, folder 7; Susan Ware, *Beyond Suffrage: Women in the New Deal,* p. 156.

44. Julia Lathrop to Grace Abbott, Dec. 16, 1930, EGAP, box 58, folder 4; "Katharine F. Lenroot," COHP, part 3, pp. 33, 83.

45. Acceptance speech by Grace Abbott at awarding of medal by the National Institute of Social Sciences in 1931, MMEP, MC 229, box 23, file 331.

46. "The Wrong Place to Save."

47. "Arthur J. Altmeyer," COHP; "Katharine F. Lenroot," COHP, part 4, pp. 34, 84-85, 39-40; Edith Abbott, *Public Assistance, American Principles and Policies,* pp. 660-61, n. 21; the Children's Bureau collected all relief statistics for the FERA and other New Deal agencies (Glenn Steele, "Family Welfare: Summary of Expenditures for Relief, General Family Welfare and Relief, Mother's Aid, Veteran's Aid").

48. "Grace Abbott Finds in Undernourishment, Delinquency, and Loss of Homes a Menace to Be Met by Greater Relief Efforts"; and "How Have Children Fared as a Whole? The Chief of the United States Children's Bureau Deals with These Questions." On children and the depression see Grace Abbott, *From Relief to Social Security,* pp. 161-97. The Children's Bureau published an overview examining the trend from private to public relief in Emma A. Winslow, Ph.D., "Trends in Different Types of Public and Private Relief in Urban Areas, 1929-35."

49. Charles H. Trout, "Frances Perkins," pp. 535-39; Perkins obit.; George Martin, *Madame Secretary: Frances Perkins;* "Frances Perkins," COHP.

50. "Memorandum to Perkins" from Grace Abbott, Aug. 10, 1933, CBP, RG 102, 4-9-0-4, also cited in Covotsos, "Child Welfare and Social Progress," p. 278; no report exists, but files concerning this meeting and the resulting program are located in the Children's Bureau papers, boxes 4-9-0-4 and -5; see also "The Child Health Recovery Conference"; "Conference on Child Health and Nutrition"; and U.S. Department of Labor, *Twenty-Second Annual Report of the Secretary of Labor,* pp. 80-82.

51. "White House Conference," p. 595; U.S. Children's Bureau, *Annual Report of the Chief* (1931), p. 121; Martha M. Eliot, M.D., "Child Health Recovery Program," unpublished report (May 1934), CESP, National Archives, RG 47, box 5, file "Misc."; Martha M. Eliot, "Child Health Recovery Program," cited in Covotsos, "Child Welfare and Social Progress," p. 278; "Child Health Recovery Conference," p. 499.

52. Grace Abbott, "Child Health Recovery"; Grace Abbott, *From Relief to Social Security,* pp. 181-82; Eliot, "Child Health Recovery Program."

53. Grace Abbott, "The Social Services a Public Responsibility," in *From Relief to Social Security,* p. 27; see also Eliot, "Child Health Recovery Program," pp. 4, 7.

54. Grace Abbott, "What about Mothers' Pensions Now?"; Grace Abbott, *From Relief to Social Security,* pp. 182-83.

55. "Edwin Emil Witte," 6:705-6; on CES see Witte, *Development of the Social Security Act;* Thomas H. Eliot, *Recollections of the New Deal;* Arthur J.

Altmeyer, *The Formative Years of Social Security;* Robert B. Stevens, ed., *Income Security,* pp. 95-166; W. Andrew Achenbaum, "Social Security," pp. 391-92.

56. Committee on Economic Security, "Committee on Economic Security," 1934, CESP, RG 47, box 1, file "Members of the Committee on Economic Security"; "Information Primer," p. 1, CESP, RG 47, box 1, file "General, n.d.,"; "Announcement of Creation of President's Committee on Economic Security and the Advisory Council to the President's Committee on Economic Security," July 24, 1934, FDRP, OF1086, box 1, file "Committee on Economic Security, 1934."

57. Hilmar Robert Baukhage, "What Will the New Deal Do for Children?" pp. 18-20, 54; "Minutes of the National Conference on Economic Security," Nov. 14, 1934, CESP, RG 47, box 4, p. 1; Witte, *Development of the Social Security Act,* p. 21; "Katharine Lenroot," part 4, COHP, pp. 34-35, 84-85.

58. Telegram from Mary Dewson to Franklin Roosevelt, June 9, 1933, FDRP, OF, OF15e, box 7; memorandum from Frances Perkins to Grace Abbott, May 8, 1934, MMEP, MC 229, box 18, file 253; Katharine Lenroot to Martha Eliot, n.d., MMEP, MC 229, box 18, file 251.

59. Memo to J. V. Fitzgerald from Edwin E. Witte quoting Perkins, Nov. 19, 1934, CESP, RG 47, box 2, file "Medical Advisory Committee"; Public Employment and Relief was the other committee formed at the time.

60. Letter of resignation, Grace Abbott to Franklin Roosevelt, June 13, 1934, FDRP, OF15e, box 7, file "a-al, 1934"; Grace Abbott to Mrs. A. M. Tunstall, July 6, 1934, EGAP, box 37, folder 2.

61. Eleanor Roosevelt to Grace Abbott, June 13, 1934, ERP, series 100, box 1283, file "a-al, 1934."

62. Grace Abbott to Eleanor Roosevelt, ERP, 70, box 600, file "a-ak, 1934"; Katharine Lenroot to Eleanor Roosevelt, Jan. 5, 1939, ERP, 70, box 75, file Lenroot, 1939; same, Jan. 23, 1929; a note from Eleanor Roosevelt to Lenroot, Oct. 13, 1938, says that she would "pass on" one of Lenroot's letters to the president.

63. Letter of resignation, Grace Abbott to Franklin Roosevelt, June 13, 1934.

64. Franklin D. Roosevelt to Grace Abbott, June 14, 1934, FDRP, OF15e, box 7, file "a-al, 1934."

65. J. Prentice Murphy, July 5, 1934, EGAP, box 37, folder 1; Molly Dewson to Grover Powers, M.D. (Yale), MMEP, MC 229, box 11, file 152; Grace Abbott to J. Prentice Murphy, July 6, 1934, and Murphy to Abbott, July 14, 1934; Katharine Lenroot to Grace Abbott, Aug. 6, 1934; all in EGAP, box 37, folder 1; and correspondence between Grace Abbott and Grover Powers, M.D., (Yale), June 1934-Dec. 1934, MMEP, MC 229, box 11, file 152; Irwin Lenroot to Clara Lenroot, Irwin L. Lenroot Papers, n.d. box 9, file "Katharine Lenroot."

66. Grace Abbott, "A New Horizon for Children in the Post-Depression Period," an address on the "The Economic Basis of Child Welfare," delivered at the commencement exercises of the New Jersey College for Women, June

3, 1934, reprinted in Grace Abbott, *From Relief to Social Security,* p. 189; Thomas H. Eliot, *Recollections of the New Deal,* p. 97.

67. Lenroot, COHP, pp. 87, 104; Eliot, COHP, p. 49.

68. "Katharine F. Lenroot," COHP, p. 89.

69. Social Security Board, "Part III: Security for Children," pp. 234-35; Katharine F. Lenroot, "Origin of the Social Welfare Provisions"; Bell, *Aid to Dependent Children,* pp. 1-19, 29-59, 188; Ashby, "Partial Promises and Semi-Visible Youths," pp. 496-97.

70. Grace Abbott, *Child and the State,* 1:229.

71. Social Security Board, "Part III: Security for Children," p. 233; Grace Abbott, *From Relief to Social Security,* pp. 182-88.

72. Social Security Board, "Part III: Security for Children," p. 241; Cincinnati Bureau of Governmental Research, *Children's Aid and Child Care in Cincinnati and Hamilton County, Ohio,* 4:2.

73. "Security for Children: Summary of the Recommendations of the U.S. Children's Bureau, prepared at the request of the Committee on Economic Security, in Cooperation with the Advisory Committee on Child Welfare," Dec. 1, 1934, typed report, CESP, RG 47, box 23, file "Security for Children Katharine F. Lenroot"; Social Security Board, "Part III: Security for Children," p. 249.

74. Katherine [*sic*] Lenroot, "Appendix E: Special Measures for Children," n.d. (ca. fall 1934), CESP, RG 47, box 23, file "Special Measures for Children's Security, Grace Abbott," p. 3.

75. Gordon, *Pitied but Not Entitled,* p. 270; Witte, *Development of the Security Act,* p. 139; Josephine Chapin Brown, *Public Relief 1929-1939,* p. 309; "Lenroot," COHP, p. 110.

76. U.S. Committee on Economic Security, *Report to the President,* pp. 35-37; "The Committee on Economic Security explains need for ADC," in Bremner et al., *Children and Youth in America,* 3:528.

77. Witte, *Development of the Social Security Act,* pp. 64, 70; Social Security Board, "Part III: Security for Children," p. 289; Howard, "Sowing the Seeds of 'Welfare,'" p. 212; interview conducted with Marshall Dimock by the author at the University of Cincinnati, Jan. 19, 1990.

78. Lenroot, "Origin of the Social Welfare Provisions," p. 130. See also "The Provisions of the Social Security Act Relating to Child Welfare Services," Title V, Part III, of the Social Security Act; and Child Welfare Division, "Progress Reports of the Child Welfare Services of Three States. Child Welfare Services in Rural Areas Provided under the Federal Social Security Act, Title V, Part 3," both in Grace Abbott, *Child and the State,* 2:646-68.

79. Social Security Board, "Part III: Social Security for Children," p. 251.

80. Ibid., pp. 256-57; "Minutes of the National Conference on Economic Security," p. 23.

81. Katharine F. Lenroot to Morris Sheppard, June 19, 1935, CBP, RG 102, 13-0-1; Social Security Board, "Part III: Security for Children," pp. 269-76; Martha M. Eliot, M.D., "The Origins and Development of the Health Services"; Duffy, *Sanitarians,* pp. 256-59.

82. "Martha Eliot," COHP, p. 46; at the time Abbott was fifty-six and Eliot was forty-two.

83. For example see U.S. Children's Bureau, "Mental Defectives in the District of Columbia," and Walter L. Treadway and Emma O. Lundberg, "Mental Defect in a Rural County: A Medico-Psychological and Social Study in Sussex County, Delaware."

84. Katharine Lenroot, "Facts about Crippled Children," report prepared for Eleanor Roosevelt, Aug. 21, 1935, ERP, 70, box 656, file "Le 1935."

85. "Martha Eliot," COHP, pp. 47-48; Katharine Lenroot to Frances Perkins, Nov. 9, 1955, Frances Perkins Papers, Columbia University Library, New York City, box 160-a, file "Katharine Lenroot"; Jane Deuel to Franklin Roosevelt, Apr. 10, 1933, FDRP, OF452, box 1, file "Crippled Children"; Hugh Gregory Gallagher, *FDR's Splendid Deception;* Witte, *Development of the Social Security Act,* p. 171; "Address by the President of the United States," in U.S. Children's Bureau, "Proceedings of the White House Conference on Children in a Democracy, January 18-20, 1940," p. 71.

86. U.S. Children's Bureau, "A Study of Crippled Children in Thirteen States"; Social Security Board, "Part III: Security for Children," p. 7. Thirty-seven states provided some funds for programs for handicapped children in 1930. The eleven states without such funds in 1934 were Arizona, Colorado, Delaware, Georgia, Idaho, Louisiana, Nevada, New Mexico, Rhode Island, Utah, and Washington; Lenroot, "Facts about Crippled Children," p. 2.

87. "Katharine Lenroot," COHP, p. 93; Social Security Board, "Part III: Security for Children," pp. 284-86.

88. "Katharine F. Lenroot," COHP, p. 100; "Arthur Altmeyer," COHP, part 4, pp. 29-32; "Committee on Medical Care of the Technical Board of the Committee on Economic Security, Minutes of Meeting—September 26, 1934," CESP, RG 47, box 1, file "Reports and Minutes on Committee on Medical Care," p. 1.

89. Medical Advisory Committee, "A Statement of General Principles," n.d. (ca. Dec. 1934), CESP, RG 47, box 2, file "Speeches, recommendations"; Robert J. Lampman, ed., *Social Security Perspectives: Essays by Edwin E. Witte,* pp. 314-21, 322-81; Daniel S. Hirshfield, *The Lost Reform: The Campaign for Compulsory Health Insurance in the United States from 1932-1943;* for a discussion of the AMA's opposition to this effort see Burrow, *AMA;* and Oliver Garceau, *The Political Life of the American Medical Association.*

90. Medical Advisory Committee, "Abstract of a Program for Social Insurance against Illness: Preliminary Draft," n.d., CESP, RG 47, box 2, file "Speeches, recommendations," pp. ii-4; "Abstract of a Program from Public Medical Services: Preliminary Draft," n.d., CESP, RG 47, box 2, file "Speeches, recommendations," p. 1.

91. Morris Fishbein, M.D., "Sickness Insurance and Sickness Costs"; R. G. Leland, M.D., and A. M. Simmons, M.D., "Do We Need Compulsory Public Health Insurance? No"; Walter Bierring, M.D., to Edwin Witte, Feb. 4, 1935, CESP, RG 47, box 2, file "Medical Advisory Committee, General Correspondence"; Burrow, *AMA,* pp. 189-98.

92. "Arthur Altmeyer," COHP, pp. 28-30; Altmeyer, *Formative Years,* pp. 57-60; Witte, *Development of the Social Security Act,* pp. 173-89; Thomas H. Eliot, *Recollections of the New Deal,* p. 111; for the final CES recommendations concerning health care and medical insurance see Witte, ibid., pp. 205-10.

93. For an overview of these health programs see Social Security Board, "Social Security Act," pp. 315-42; on the PHS and new health programs under the New Deal see Duffy, *Sanitarians,* pp. 256-72.

94. Witte, *Development of the Social Security Act,* p. 91; House Committee on Ways and Means, *Hearings on H.R. 4120,* 74th Cong., 1st sess., pp. 650, 1140.

95. Witte, *Development of the Social Security Act,* pp. 68-91; the bill was introduced in the House by Robert L. Doughton (D-N.C.) and David J. Lewis (D-Md.) (Thomas H. Eliot, *Recollections of the New Deal,* p. 104).

96. House Committee on Ways and Means, *Hearings on H.R. 4120;* Witte, *Development of the Social Security Act,* pp. 162-63; on the purpose and role of the Social Security Board see McKinley and Frase, *Launching Social Security,* pp. 382-472; Thomas H. Eliot, *Recollections of the New Deal,* p. 110; Gordon, *Pitied but Not Entitled,* pp. 283-85; Howard, "Sowing the Seeds of 'Welfare,'" pp. 188-227.

97. Works Progress Administration, *Trends in Relief Expenditures, 1910-1935,* p. 3; Josephine Chapin Brown, *Public Relief 1929-1939,* p. 21; "Katharine Lenroot," COHP, pp. 98-99; Witte, *Development of the Social Security Act,* pp. 163-64; Grace Abbott, *Child and the State,* 1:241-42; 49 *Stat.* 620, pp. 627-29.

98. Thomas H. Eliot, *Recollections of the New Deal,* p. 105; Witte, *Development of the Social Security Act,* pp. 164-65.

99. Studies that discuss the programs leading to the Social Security Act but pay little attention to the children's welfare aspects include Lubove, *Struggle for Social Security;* Daniel Nelson, *Unemployment Insurance;* Bremner, *From the Depths,* pp. 263-64; Graebner, *History of Retirement;* Berkowitz and McQuaid, *Creating the Welfare State,* pp. 96-113. On the development and implementation of the early program see McKinley and Frase, *Launching Social Security;* Achenbaum, *Social Security;* Trattner, *From Poor Law to Welfare State,* and see also Patterson, *America's Struggle against Poverty,* pp. 65-77. Some exceptions are Witte, *Development of the Social Security Act;* Bell, *Aid to Dependent Children;* Ashby, "Partial Promises and Semi-Visible Youths"; Howard, "Sowing the Seeds of 'Welfare,'" pp. 188-227; and Gordon, *Pitied but Not Entitled,* esp. pp. 253-85; but even the latter studies concentrate on mainly on one aspect, aid to dependent children, rather than providing an overview of the Social Security Act's programs offering benefits to children.

100. Budget statistics calculated from the annual reports of the secretary of labor, fiscal 1930-40; and Hilda Kessler Gilbert, "The United States Department of Labor in the New Deal Period," esp. tables 2 and 3.

101. Social Security Board, Bureau of Public Assistance, "Effect of Federal Participation in Payments for Aid to Dependent Children in 1940"; Howard, "Sowing the Seeds of 'Welfare,'" p. 215; survivors' insurance and death

benefits were also added to the Social Security Act by its 1939 amendments; for a discussion of these new programs for children see Arthur J. Altmeyer, "The New Social Security Program," reprinted in Bremner et al., *Children and Youth in America,* 2:536-38.

102. National Child Labor Committee, *Child Labor Facts,* p. 5; "Frances Perkins Letter to the Editor" (drafted by Katharine F. Lenroot), *New York Times,* June 13, 1933, reprinted in Bremner et al., *Children and Youth in America,* 3:324-35.

103. Katharine F. Lenroot, "Child Welfare 1930-40," p. 5.

104. Trattner, *Crusade for the Children,* p. 189.

105. U.S. Children's Bureau, memorandum, "Effect of NRA codes on Child Labor," June 5, 1935, CBP, RG 102, EMF, box 6, file 6; for an extensive examination of the NRA codes and their effect on child employment see "NRA, Summary," typed report, CBP, RG 102, EMF, box 10, file 3; "Samuel McCune Lindsay and Courtney Dinwiddie to Frances Perkins, May 26, 1933, Records of the Secretary of Labor," reprinted in Bremner et al., *Children and Youth in America,* 3:326-27.

106. Solomon Barkin, "Child Labor Control under NRA," typed report, Office of National Recovery Administration, Division or Review, Mar. 1936, CBP, RG 102, EMF, box 21, file 5, "Summary." For a discussion of the NRA codes and child labor see Trattner, *Crusade for the Children,* pp. 190-95. For an examination of children and industrial homework under the NRA see Mary Skinner, "Industrial Home Work under the National Recover Administration"; the cotton textile code is reprinted in Bremner et al., *Children and Youth in America,* 3:327-28; on the impact of the N.R.A. on child labor see Merritt, "Child Labor under the N.R.A. as Shown by Employment Certificates Issued in 1934," pp. 1477, 1490-91, reprinted in Bremner et al., *Children and Youth in America,* 3:337-38.

107. Barkin, "Child Labor Control under NRA," p. 202; *Schechter v. United States,* 295 U.S. 495 (1935).

108. Mary "Molly" Dewson to Franklin Roosevelt, Dec. 20, 1933, FDRP, OF58A, box 3, OF58a CL 1933-36; on Roosevelt and child labor reform in 1933-34 see, for example, Franklin Roosevelt to Governor of Utah, Apr. 13, 1933, FDRP, OF, OF15e, box 7, file "15e Children's Bureau."

109. Frances Perkins to presidential secretary McIntyre, Dec. 29, 1936; and copies of letters sent by Franklin Roosevelt to governors of nineteen states, Jan. 4 and 6, 1937, FDRP, OF, OF58a, all in box 3, file "OF58a child labor 1937." States which had not ratified by Jan. 1937 were Connecticut, Delaware, Florida, Georgia, Kansas, Kentucky, Maryland, Massachusetts, Missouri, Nebraska, Nevada, New Mexico, New York, North Carolina, Rhode Island, South Carolina, South Dakota, Tennessee, and Texas.

110. National Child Labor Committee, *Child Labor Facts,* p. 12.

111. Trattner, *Crusade for the Children,* pp. 197-99.

112. Grace Abbott, Katharine Lenroot, Courtnay Dinwiddie (NCLC general secretary), Lucy R. Mason (National Consumers' League), and Homer Folks (NCLC chair) participated in the development of the Fair Labor Stan-

dards bill (Trattner, *Crusade for the Children,* pp. 203-8); Karis, "Congressional Behavior at Constitutional Frontiers," pp. 377-406; George Edward Paulsen, "The Legislative History of the Fair Labor Standards Act"; Orme Wheelock Phelps, *The Legislative History of the Fair Labor Standards Act;* and *United States v. Darby Lumber Company* decision 312 U.S. 100 (1941).

113. Lenroot, "Child Welfare 1930-40," p. 7; for a discussion of children in agricultural labor after the 1937 Sugar Act see Trattner, *Crusade for the Children,* pp. 210-12; exemptions included: (1) any child under sixteen employed in agriculture outside of school hours or where the child was "employed" by his parent or "a person standing in the place of his parent on a farm owned or operated by such parent or person"; (2) any child employed as an actor or performer in motion pictures or theatrical productions, or in radio or television productions; (3) no child engaged in the delivery of newspapers to the consumer (52 *Stat.,* Section 13, pp. 1060-69); child labor restrictions reprinted in Bremner et al., *Children and Youth in America,* 3:341-43.

114. Lenroot, "Child Welfare 1930-40," p. 1.

115. For example see Bernard Flexner, Reuben Oppenheimer, and Katharine F. Lenroot, "The Child, the Family, and the Court: A Study of the Administration of Justice in the Field of Domestic Relations"; U.S. Children's Bureau, "Child Labor Facts and Figures"; Nettie P. McGill, "Child Labor in New Jersey, Part III: The Working Children of Newark and Paterson"; Alice Channing, "Employed Boys and Girls in Milwaukee"; Ellen Nathalie Matthews, "The Illegally Employed Minor and the Workmen's Compensation Law"; U.S. Children's Bureau, "Facts about Juvenile Delinquency"; Alice Channing, "Employed Boys and Girls in Rochester and Utica, New York"; U.S. Children's Bureau, "Children Engaged in Newspaper and Magazine Selling and Delivering"; ibid., "Juvenile-Court Statistics and Federal Juvenile Offenders, 1933, Based on Information Supplied by 284 Juvenile Courts and by the United States Department of Justice"; Ella Oppenheimer, M.D., "Infant Mortality in Memphis"; Skinner, "Industrial Home Work under the National Recovery Administration"; U.S. Children's Bureau, "Juvenile-Court Statistics Year Ended December 31, 1934 and Federal Juvenile Offenders Year Ended June 30, 1935, Based on Information Supplied by 334 Juvenile Courts and by the United States Department of Justice"; ibid., "Child Welfare Legislation, 1937"; Winslow, "Trends in Different Types of Public and Private Relief in Urban Areas"; U.S. Children's Bureau, "A Historical Summary of State Services for Children in New York, Part 2"; Emma O. Lundberg, "The Public Child-Welfare Program in the District of Columbia"; Elizabeth C. Tandy, D.Sc., "Infant and Maternal Mortality among Negroes"; Elizabeth S. Johnson, "Welfare of Families of Sugar-Beet Laborers: A Study of Child Labor and Its Relation to Family Work, Income, and Living Conditions in 1935"; Helen Wood, "Young Workers and Their Jobs in 1936: A Survey in Six States"; U.S. Children's Bureau, "Children in the Courts: Juvenile-Court Statistics Year Ended December 31, 1937 and Federal Juvenile Offenders Year Ended June 30, 1937"; ibid., "Child-Welfare Legislation, 1938"; and

Kathryn H. Welch, "The Meaning of State Supervision in the Social Protection of Children."

116. Dorothy Bradbury, "Five Decades of Action for Children," pp. 44-45; on the implementation of Title V, Part I, from 1936 through 1939, see U.S. Children's Bureau, "Maternal and Child-Health Services under the Social Security Act, Title V part I, Development of Program, 1936-39"; on the implementation of the services for handicapped children see ibid., "Services for Crippled Children under the Social Security Act, Title V part II, Development of the Program, 1936-39"; on child welfare services see ibid., "Child-Welfare Services under the Social Security Act, Title V part III, Development of the Program, 1936-38."

117. U.S. Children's Bureau, "Proceedings of Conference on Better Care for Mothers and Babies."

118. Ibid., p. 46; Conference on Better Care for Mothers and Babies, "Memorandum on Recent Material Concerning Need for Medical Care, with Special Reference to Mothers and Babies," Mar. 17, 1938, MMEP, MC 229, box 13, file 186.

119. Tandy, "Infant and Maternal Mortality among Negroes."

120. Patterson, *America's Struggle against Poverty,* esp. chap. 4; Howard, "Sowing the Seeds of 'Welfare.'"

121. Jane M. Hoey, "Aid to Families with Dependent Children," pp. 74-76.

Chapter 8: "Children in a Democracy"

1. U.S. Children's Bureau, "Proceedings of the White House Conference on Children in a Democracy, Washington, D.C., January 18-20, 1940"; for a brief summary of the conference's recommendations see Katharine F. Lenroot, "A Defense Program for the Children of the United States," copy in KLP, box 15, file "KL-Children and Defense."

2. U.S. Children's Bureau, "Proceedings of the 1940 White House Conference," p. 3.

3. Ibid., pp. 1-3, 10, 12-28.

4. Richard A. Reiman, *The New Deal and American Youth: Ideas and Ideals in a Depression Decade,* esp. pp. 31-35.

5. U.S. Office of Education, "Statistical Summary of Education, 1935-36," p. 7; "Report of the Library Extension Board of the American Library Association for the Year Ending July 31, 1939"; both cited in U.S. Children's Bureau, "Proceedings of the 1940 White House Conference," pp. 32-42.

6. U.S. Children's Bureau, "Proceedings of the 1940 White House Conference," pp. 1-3, 24-28, 84-85; ibid., "Standards of Child Health, Education, and Social Welfare: Based on Recommendations of the White House Conference on Children in a Democracy and Conclusions of Discussion Groups," p. 2.

7. Hawes, *Children's Rights Movement,* p. 9.

8. U.S. Children's Bureau, "Proceedings of the 1940 White House Conference," pp. 29-31.

9. U.S. Children's Bureau, "Standards of Child Health, Education, and Social Welfare," p. vi.

10. Franklin D. Roosevelt, "Radio Address before the White House Conference on Children in Democracy," Washington, D.C., Jan. 19, 1940, in *Public Papers and Addresses of Franklin D. Roosevelt,* 10:52-60.

11. Kathleen McLaughlin, "'Action' Program to Back Child Aid: White House Conference Ends with Expressions of Zeal for a National Drive," p. 5.

12. "Conference on Children in a Democracy."

13. Bradbury, "Five Decades of Action for Children," p. 54.

14. Elsa Castendyck, memorandum, "Summary of Report of Visit to Organizations and Camps Caring for Refugees in Switzerland, France, Belgium, Holland, and England," n.d. (ca. 1939), ERP, series 70, box 755, file "Lenroot 1939."

15. Kathryn Close, "When the Children Come," reprinted in Bremner et al., *Children and Youth in America,* 3:131-36.

16. Letter and attached memorandum from Katharine F. Lenroot to Harold D. Smith, director, the Bureau of the Budget, July 13, 1940, KLP, box 17; United States Committee for the Care of European Children, "Report of the Executive Director to the Board of Directors," Jan. 1941, copy sent from Katharine F. Lenroot to Eleanor Roosevelt, Jan. 21, 1941, ERP, series 70, box 812, file "Lenroot 1941," pp. 1-9.

17. Raymond Clapper, "Let's Save the Children," *Washington Daily News,* July 7 or 8, 1940; memorandum from Franklin Roosevelt to Stephen Early, July 8, 1940, to be forwarded to Clapper; both in FDRP, President's Official File, OF3186 Political Refugees, box 3, file "July to September 1940."

18. Edward J. Shaughnessy, acting commissioner of Immigration and Naturalization, press release, July 13, 1940, FDRP, Presidential Office Files, box 3, file "July-September 1940," pp. 1-6; Close, "When the Children Come," p. 133.

19. Close, "When the Children Come," pp. 37-39; and Bradbury, "Four Decades of Action for Children," p. 61.

20. Roger Daniels, "American Refugee Policy in Historical Perspective"; Roger Daniels, *Coming to America: A History of Immigration and Ethnicity in American Life,* pp. 296-302; Henry L. Feingold, *The Politics of Rescue: The Roosevelt Administration and the Holocaust, 1938-1945;* Judith T. Baumel, "The Jewish Refugee Children from Europe in the Eyes of the American Press and Public Opinion, 1934-1945"; Judith T. Baumel, "The Transfer and Resettlement in the United States of Young Jewish Refugees from Nazism, 1934-1945."

21. United States Committee for the Care of European Children, "Report of the Executive Director to the Board of Directors," p. 34.

22. Bradbury, "Four Decades of Action for Children," p. 62.

23. Ibid., p. 63.

24. Ibid., pp. 62-63, 83-84.

25. Letter and memorandum from Katharine F. Lenroot to Eleanor Roosevelt, Dec. 20, 1940, ERP, 70, box 782, file "Lenroot 1940."

26. "Excerpts from Field Reports and Reports from States," Dec. 19, 1940, memo attached to Katharine Lenroot to Eleanor Roosevelt, Dec. 20, 1940, ERP, 70, box 782, file "Lenroot 1940."

27. Martha M. Eliot, M.D., "Civil Defense Measures for the Protection of Children: Report of Observations in Great Britain, February 1941," p. ix; other members of the Mission were Lt. Col. Eugene Ridings, General Staff Corps, U.S. War Department; Thomas Parran, M.D., surgeon general, Public Health Service, Federal Security Agency; Geoffrey May, associate director, Bureau of Public Assistance, Social Security Board, Federal Security Agency; and Frederick C. Horner, consultant to Transportation Commissioner, National Defense Advisory Commission.

28. Eliot, "Civil Defense Measures for the Protection of Children," pp. 151-52, 157-77.

29. The Office of the Coordinator of Health, Welfare, and Related Defense Activities was renamed the Office of Defense Health and Welfare Services on Sept. 3, 1941. It existed for the war's duration and shared responsibilities with the better-known Office of Civilian Defense (U.S. Children's Bureau, "Proceedings of the Conference on Day Care of Children of Working Mothers: With Special Reference to Defense Areas, Held in Washington, D.C., July 31 and Aug. 1, 1941," pp. 2-3.) Unfortunately I have been unable to locate any biographical information on Schottland in the Children's Bureau personnel files or in other possible sources.

30. Maxine Margolis, *Mothers and Such: Views of American Women and Why They Changed,* p. 211; U.S. Women's Bureau [Mary-Elizabeth Pidgeon], "Employed Mothers and Child Care," partially reprinted in Bremner et al., *Children and Youth in America,* 3:677-78; on the alternate view of WPA preschools as good for children see Edna Ewing Kelley, "Uncle Sam's Nursery Schools," pp. 24-25, 48-49; and U.S. Federal Works Agency, "Final Report on the WPA Program, 1935-43," both reprinted in Bremner et al., *Children and Youth in America,* 3:679-81.

31. Susan M. Hartmann, *American Women in the 1940s: The Homefront and Beyond,* p. 78; Tuttle, *"Daddy's Gone to War,"* pp. 70-72.

32. Katharine F. Lenroot, "Review of Children's Bureau Position with Reference to Day Care Services," unpublished report, Aug. 6, 1945, included in KLP, box 15 10-1, file "Child Welfare Laws Act of 1945."

33. U.S. Children's Bureau, "Proceedings of the Conference on Day Care of Children of Working Mothers," pp. 13-14, 20; Hartmann, *American Women in the 1940s,* p. 78; Bradbury, "Four Decades of Action for Children," p. 53.

34. Mintz and Kellogg, *Domestic Revolutions,* pp. 162-64; mothers were also condemned for "oversolicitousness" or what Philip Wylie called in 1942 "momism" (*Generation of Vipers,* pp. 46-51, 184-204); Hartmann, *American Women in the 1940s,* pp. 176-79.

35. U.S. Children's Bureau, "Standards for Day Care of Children of Working Mothers," p. vii; on the day care conference see ibid., "Proceedings of the Conference on Day Care."

36. Bradbury, "Four Decades of Action for Children," pp. 54-55.

37. Hartmann, *American Women in the 1940s,* pp. 84-85; D'Ann Campbell, *Women at War with America: Private Lives in a Patriotic Era,* pp. 1-41; Mintz and Kellogg, *Domestic Revolutions,* pp. 162-64; Howard Dratch, "The Politics of Child Care in the 1940's."

38. Henry L. Zucker, "Working Parents and Latchkey Children."

39. Kathryn Close, "Day Care up to Now"; reprinted in Bremner et al., *Children and Youth in America,* 3:684-90.

40. U.S. Children's Bureau, "Homemaker Service: A Method of Child Care," p. 3; Sherna Berger Gluck, *Rosie the Riveter Revised: Women, the War, and Social Change,* pp. 23-24; "Care of Infants Whose Mothers Are Employed: Policies and Recommendations by the Children's Bureau," reprinted in Bremner et al., *Children and Youth in America,* 3:692-94.

41. National Commission on Children in Wartime, "A Children's Charter in Wartime"; National Commission on Children in Wartime, "Children's Bureau Commission on Children in Wartime, Mar. 16 to 18, 1942," U.S. Children's Bureau, undated memo, copy in ERP, 70 ER, box 840, file "Lenroot, 1942," p. 1.

42. U.S. Children's Bureau, "A Children's Charter in Wartime," pp. 2-4.

43. Bradbury, "Five Decades of Action for Children," p. 47.

44. For example see the following U.S. Children's Bureau publications: "The Child-Health Conference: Suggestions for Organization and Procedure"; "Occupational Hazards to Young Workers: Report No. 1, The Explosives-Manufacturing Industries"; ibid., Report No. 2, Motor-Vehicle Drivers and Helpers"; ibid., "Report No. 3, The Coal-Mining Industry"; ibid., "Report No. 4, The Logging and Sawmilling Industries"; ibid., "Report No. 5, Woodworking Machines"; "Wartime Employment of Boys and Girls under 18"; "Guides to Successful Employment of Non-Farm Youth in Wartime Agriculture: For Use in Victory Farm Volunteer Program"; "Protecting the Health of Young Workers in Wartime"; "Standards and Recommendations for Hospital Care of Newborn Infants, Full-Term and Premature"; "Community Action for Children in Wartime"; "The Selection and Training of Volunteers in Child Care"; Emma O. Lundberg, "Our Concern—Every Child: State and Community Planning for Wartime and Post-War Security for Children"; "Goals for Children and Youth in the Transition from War to Peace Adopted by the Children's Bureau Commission on Children in Wartime, March 18, 1944"; "If Your Baby Must Travel in Wartime." On the WJZ radio broadcasts see Bradbury, "Children's Bureau and Juvenile Delinquency," p. 13.

45. U.S. Children's Bureau, "To Parents in Wartime," pp. 1-2, 8-15, 20.

46. Richard M. Ugland, "Viewpoints and Morale of Urban High School Students during World War II—Indianapolis as a Case Study," pp. 150-51; James Gilbert, *A Cycle of Outrage: America's Reaction to the Juvenile Delinquency in the 1950s,* p. 65; for a contemporary discussion of the effect of wartime

conditions on adolescents and the accompanying perceived dangers to society see the special issue of *Annals of the American Academy of Political and Social Science* entitled "Adolescents in Wartime."

47. Mintz and Kellogg, *Domestic Revolutions,* p. 165.

48. U.S. Children's Bureau, "Juvenile Delinquency in Certain Countries at War"; the St. Paul study was conducted from 1937 through 1943, see ibid., "Children in the Community: The St. Paul Experiment in Child Welfare," and ibid., "Helping Children in Trouble"; Eliot, "Civil Defense Measures for the Protection of Children," pp. 35-36.

49. Bradbury, "Children's Bureau and Juvenile Delinquency," p. 15.

50. Ibid. p. 14; Bradbury, "Four Decades of Action for Children," pp. 51-52; Mintz and Kellogg, *Domestic Revolutions,* p. 165; J. Edgar Hoover, "Wild Children," pp. 40, 105, cited in Tuttle, *"Daddy's Gone to War,"* p. 70.

51. Eliot, "Civil Defense Measures for the Protection of Children," pp. 35-36.

52. U.S. Department of Labor, Frances Perkins, "Address of the Secretary of Labor at the Opening Session of the Children's Bureau Commission on Children in Wartime," Mar. 16, 42, p. 3, DLP, RG 174, box 121, file "Children's Bureau, 1942;" U.S. Children's Bureau, "Controlling Juvenile Delinquency: A Community Program," p. 1.

53. U.S. Children's Bureau, "Understanding Juvenile Delinquency," pp. 1-3.

54. The ten cities included in the report were: Birmingham, Ala.; Cleveland, Ohio; Columbus, Ga.; Detroit, Mich.; Gary, Ind.; Jacksonville, Fla.; Mobile, Ala.; Portland, Maine; San Antonio, Tex.; and Sparta, Wis. (Genevieve Gabower, "A Look at Ten Communities," pp. 86-90, 104); the entire March 1944 issue of the *Survey* was devoted to juvenile delinquency.

55. For example see Mintz and Kellogg, *Domestic Revolutions,* p. 166; Gluck, *Rosie the Riveter,* p. 6; Richard Polenberg, *War and Society: The United States, 1941-1945,* pp. 150-52; John D'Emilio and Estelle B. Freedman, *Intimate Matters: A History of Sexuality in America,* pp. 260-61; Alan M. Brandt, *No Magic Bullet: A Social History of Venereal Disease in the United States since 1880,* pp. 164-68.

56. Bradbury, "Children's Bureau and Juvenile Delinquency," p. 15; "Children's Services in Newport News and Pulaski, Virginia," mimeographed report, CBP, RG 102; Gabower, "Look at Ten Communities," pp. 86-87.

57. Camille Kelley, *A Friend in Court,* p. 257; it is possible that black girls were more likely to be charged with crimes other than sex delinquency than white girls, who were probably let go when caught committing other types of behaviors.

58. Quotations from D'Emilio and Freedman, *Intimate Matters,* pp. 260-61, 288-91.

59. For example see U.S. Children's Bureau, "Facts about Juvenile Delinquency," pp. 4-6.

60. U.S. Children's Bureau, "Controlling Juvenile Delinquency," p. 14.

61. Mary Skinner and Alice Scott Nutt, "Adolescents Away from Home" (Skinner and Nutt worked in the Children's Bureau's Social Service Division); reprinted in Bremner et al., *Children and Youth in America,* 3:140-43.

62. U.S. Children's Bureau and the Bureau of Public Assistance, "A Community Plans for Its Children: Final Report, Newport News, Va. Project," pp. 1, 9, 11.

63. Ibid., pp. 9-13.

64. U.S. Children's Bureau, "Understanding Juvenile Delinquency," p. 6.

65. Tuttle, *"Daddy's Gone to War,"* is to date the most comprehensive and well-documented analysis of children's experiences on the American home front; historians have generally paid little attention to the experience of children during World War II. Another notable exception is Richard M. Ugland, "The Adolescent Experience during World War II: Indianapolis as a Case Study." For a sampling of contemporary views on children and the war see Charlotte Towle, "The Effect of the War upon Children."

66. Elizabeth S. Magee, "Impact of the War on Child Labor."

67. Katharine Lenroot to Eleanor Roosevelt, Apr. 6, 1945, ERP, series 70, box 42, file "j-l 1945."

68. U.S. Senate, Committee on Education and Labor, "A Bill to Provide for the Termination of the National Youth Administration and the Civilian Conservation Corps," Mar. 23-Apr. 17, 1942, 77th Cong., 2d sess., S. 2295; and Reiman, *New Deal for American Youth,* pp. 178-81.

69. "Radio Address, October 12, 1942," *Public Papers and Addresses of Franklin D. Roosevelt,* 11:421.

70. U.S. Children's Bureau, "Wartime Employment of Boys and Girls under 18," pp. 7-8.

71. Magee, "Impact of the War on Child Labor," pp. 104-5.

72. U.S. Children's Bureau, "Five Years of Federal Control of Child Labor"; Magee, "Impact of the War on Child Labor," pp. 105-6.

73. Magee, "Impact of the War on Child Labor," pp. 105-6; and Polenberg, *War and Society,* p. 79.

74. U.S. Children's Bureau, "Wartime Employment of Boys and Girls under 18," pp. 7-9; see also *American Child,* 23 (Feb. 1942): 4 and (Dec. 1943): 3, 5; both reprinted in Bremner et al., *Children and Youth in America,* 3:356-58.

75. Warren S. Thompson, "Adolescents according to the Census."

76. U.S. Children's Bureau, "Wartime Employment of Boys and Girls under 18," pp. 7-9; the total rejection rate was 39.2 per 100, 36.0 for whites and 56.9 blacks, which constituted 217,000 men; 58 percent of those were rejected for physical defects ("Selective Service Rejections," memo, Mar. 3, 1945; MMEP, MC 229, box 18, folder 242, pp. 5-6).

77. U.S. Children's Bureau, "Wartime Employment of Boys and Girls under 18," pp. 14-15; see also ibid., "Statement of Policy on Employment of Youth under 18 Years of Age," and "Protecting the Health of Young Workers in Wartime."

78. U.S. Children's Bureau, "Boys and Girls Employed in Agricultural Programs—1943," based on surveys conducted in California, Colorado, New Jersey, New York, Oregon, Washington, and Wisconsin; Beatrice McConnell, "Child Labor in Agriculture."

79. U.S. Children's Bureau, "Guides to Successful Employment of Non-Farm Youth in Wartime Agriculture: For Use in Victory Farm Volunteer Program," pp. 1-11.

80. McConnell, "Child Labor in Agriculture," p. 9.

81. Amber Arthun Warburton, Helen Wood, and Marian M. Crane, M.D., "The Work and Welfare of Children of Agricultural Laborers in Hidalgo County, Texas."

82. U.S. Children's Bureau, "Protecting the Health of Young Workers in Wartime," p. 1. For a list of federal and state government references relating to children's wartime employment see p. ii of this publication; for a summary of circumstances and recommendations near the end of the war see U.S. Children's Bureau, "Building the Future for Children and Youth."

83. For example, two of the most important works about life on the home front generally ignore the contributions of children to the war effort: John Morton Blum, *V Was for Victory: Politics and American Culture during World War II;* and Allan M. Winkler, *Home Front U.S.A.: America during World War II.*

84. For a clear explanation of this program see Katharine Lenroot to Eleanor Roosevelt, Dec. 1, 1942, and attached memorandum from Dr. Daily to Lenroot, Nov. 10, 1942, ERP, series 70, box 840, file "Lenroot 1942," p. 1.

85. U.S. Children's Bureau, "Maternity Care for Wives of Men in Military Service and Medical Care for Their Children," flyer, Oct. 1942, DLP, RG 102, box 209, 13-0-1-12.

86. Ibid., pp. 58-59; Sinai and Anderson, *EMIC,* pp. 21-22; and U.S. Children's Bureau, "Maternity Care for Wives of Men in Military Service and Medical Care for Their Children," memorandum, Nov. 30, 1942, copy sent to Eleanor Roosevelt from Katharine F. Lenroot, copy included in ERP, series 70, box 840, file "Lenroot 1942."

87. Mary Helen Terrell, "'Some Kind of Social Doctor': Historical Study of Martha May Eliot's Policies for Maternal and Child Health," p. 228.

88. U.S. Children's Bureau, "Maternity Care for Wives," memorandum; and Sinai and Anderson, *EMIC,* pp. 22-24.

89. U.S. Children's Bureau, Katharine F. Lenroot, "Federal Cooperation with the States in Meeting Wartime Needs for Maternal and Child Health and Child Welfare Services," Oct. 5, 1942, copy in ERP, series 70, box 840, file "Lenroot 1942"; memorandums from Katharine F. Lenroot to Frances Perkins and Frances Perkins to President Roosevelt, Dec. 1942, same file.

90. House Committee on Appropriations, *Hearings before the Subcommittee on the First Deficiency Appropriation Bill for 1943, H.R. 1975,* 78th Cong., 2d sess., Feb. 11, 1943, p. 326.

91. House Committee on Appropriations, *H.R. Report 170,* 78th Cong., 1st sess., Feb. 24, 1943, p. 6; for a summary of the discussions surrounding the bill and the House committee report see Sinai and Anderson, *EMIC,* pp. 25-27.

92. Sinai and Anderson, *EMIC,* pp. 28-29; for an examination of subsequent hearings concerning reappropriation of EMIC through 1946 see Mulligan, "Three Federal Interventions on Behalf of Childbearing Women," pp. 73-85.

93. Katharine Lenroot to Eleanor Roosevelt, Mar. 18, 1943, ERP, series 70, box 875, file "Lenroot 1943."

94. Sinai and Anderson, *EMIC,* pp. 56-58; for an expanded version of the development of rules and regulations see ibid., pp. 55-79.

95. Ibid., p. 87; Martha M. Eliot, M.D., and Lillian R. Freedman, "Four Years of the Emergency Maternal and Infant Care Program."

96. Bradbury, "Five Decades of Action for Children," p. 57.

97. Memorandum from Daily to Lenroot and Eliot, "First Thoughts on Some Post-war Plans for Extending and Improving Obstetric and Pediatric Services in the United States," July 15, 1942; U.S. Bureau of the Census, *Historical Statistics of the United States,* p. 57.

98. Senate, Subcommittee of the Committee on Education and Labor, *Hearings for the Investigation of the Educational and Physical Fitness of the Civilian Population Related to National Defense,* 78th Cong., 2d sess., beginning Nov. 30, 1943.

99. Sinai and Anderson, *EMIC,* pp. 112-48; on the rift between the AMA and the Children's Bureau concerning EMIC see Terrell, "'Some Kind of Social Doctor,'" pp. 252-58.

100. Franklin P. Gengenbach, M.D., to Allan M. Butler, M.D. (copy sent to Martha May Eliot), Sept. 15, 1944, and Joseph S. Wall, M.D., to Claude Pepper (copy sent to Martha May Eliot), Aug. 13, 1945, in MMEP, MC 229, box 18, file 246 and box 23, file 330.

101. On the controversy between the American Academy of Pediatrics and the Children's Bureau see a collection of letters located in the MMEP, MC 229, box 18, file 246.

102. House Committee on Appropriations, *Hearings before the Subcommittee on the Department of Labor-Federal Security Agency Appropriation Bill for 1946, Part I,* 79th Cong., 1st sess., Mar. 14, 1945, p. 594, cited in Sinai and Anderson, *EMIC,* p. 48.

103. Duffy, *Sanitarians,* p. 277.

104. Mulligan, "Three Federal Interventions on Behalf of Childbearing Women," pp. 89-90.

105. Articles in the *American Journal of Public Health* show physicians' support for EMIC but opposition to the expansion of national health insurance after the war. For example see Stuart W. Adler, M.D., "Medical Care for Dependents of Men in Military Service," and "The Wagner-Murray Bill."

106. Katharine F. Lenroot to Eleanor Roosevelt, Oct. 26, 1940, and reply Dec. 10, 1940, ERP, box 782, file "Lenroot 1940."

107. House Committee on Appropriations, *Hearings on the Department of Labor—Federal Security Agency Bill for 1943,* 77th Cong., 2d sess., p. 374, cited in Tuttle, *"Daddy's Gone to War,"* p. 25; for an overview of Title V, Part II, see U.S. Children's Bureau, "Facts about Crippled Children."

108. "Confidential Memorandum," Katharine Lenroot to Secretary Frances Perkins, subject: "Problems in connection with Japanese evacuation and war relocation program," Aug. 4, 1942; DLP, RG 74, box 122, file CB 1942; Roger Daniels, Sandra C. Taylor, and Harry H. L. Kitano, eds., *Japanese*

Americans: From Relocation to Redress, pp. 22-72; Tuttle, *"Daddy's Gone to War,"* pp. 167-74.

Conclusion

1. Richard Polenberg, *Reorganizing Roosevelt's Government: The Controversy over Executive Reorganization, 1936-1939.*

2. Correspondence and report, Nov. 7, 1939, ERP, series 70, box 755, file "Lenroot 1939."

3. *Congressional Record,* vol. 90, Apr. 25, 1944, 78th Cong., 2d sess., p. 3707; the PHS had been transferred from the Department of the Interior to the FSA on Apr. 11, 1940.

4. Katharine F. Lenroot to Eleanor Roosevelt, June 14, 1944, series 70, box 917, file "Lenroot 1944."

5. Memorandum on interview conducted by Katharine Lenroot with President William Green of the American Federation of Labor, Nov. 11, 1944, MMEP, MC 229, box 11, file 159.

6. Drexel Godfrey, Jr., *The Transfer of the Children's Bureau,* pp. 20-22.

7. Ibid., pp. 24-25.

8. Ibid., pp. 22-27; for an overview of the reorganization plan see memorandum from Watson Miller, July 12, 1946, attached to letter to Edith Abbott, dated July 25, 1946, copy in MMEP, MC 2T29, box 23, file 331; for his long-term view see Watson B. Miller, "Health Education and Security—Some Post-war Perspectives."

9. Drexel, *Transfer of the Children's Bureau* p. 27.

10. Martha May Eliot," COHP, part 4, 1969, pp. 62-64.

11. Interview with Marshall Dimock at the University of Cincinnati, Jan. 19, 1990; notes in the author's possession; U.S. Department of Labor, *The Anvil and the Plow,* pp. 275-93.

12. Typed copy of address before National Conference of Social Work, Milwaukee, Wis., June 29, 1921, Julia C. Lathrop, "Our Nation's Obligation to Her Children," CBP, RG 102, 0-1-0; Grace Abbott, *From Relief to Social Security,* p. 224; Katharine F. Lenroot, "Children of the Depression: A Study of 259 Families in Selected Areas of Five Cities."

13. Eleanor H. Bernert, *America's Children,* p. 1.

14. "Advances in Federal Health Legislation and Organization"; the journal had similarly agreed with the AMA's philosophy and praised the transfer of the PHS to the FSA (effective Apr. 11, 1940, under Reorganization Plan No. 4) in an editorial, "Transfer of the Public Health Service."

15. For example, the National Consumers' League and the National Child Labor Committee were still in existence, but passage of the 1938 Fair Labor Standards Act diminished their membership rolls and influence. Another important ally, the National League of Women Voters, increasingly focused its attention on American foreign policy; for example see Louise M. Young, *In the Public Interest: The League of Women Voters, 1920-1970,* pp. 141-78.

16. Elizabeth Lowell Putnam, "Address to Sentinels of the Republic"; Mrs. William Lowell Putnam, "NO," editorial, *Boston Globe,* Oct. 5, 1924, n.p., clipping in ELPP, MC 360, box 16, file 294; and Elizabeth Lowell Putnam to Alice Robertson, Jan. 22, 1927, MC 30, box 30, file 484.

17. The most comprehensive study examining women's role in the Children's Bureau and among child welfare reformers is Muncy, *Creating a Female Dominion;* on Sellers: "Thirteen Years as Juvenile Judge Completed by Judge Sellers," *Washington Post,* Oct. 15, 1931, n.p., clipping in CMBP, A-159, box 2, file 40; correspondence from Clara Beyer to Courtney Dinwiddie, Dec. 8, 1920; Beyer to Miriam Van Waters, Dec. 1, 1920; and Beyer to John Lord O'Brian, Mar. 1, 1931; all in CMBP, A-159, box 2, file 40; Grace Abbott to Charles P. Sisson, Assistant Attorney General, Jan. 15, 1931, EGAP, box 36, folder 11.

18. Bernert, *America's Children,* p. 21; although published over fifteen years ago, Beatrice Gross and Ronald Gross, *The Children's Rights Movement: Overcoming the Oppression of Young People,* provides a good overview of how state laws and federal policies have favored the rights of adults over children; for a more recent examination of current federal policy for children see the final report of the National Commission on Children, *Beyond Rhetoric: A New American Agenda for Children and Families.*

19. Carp, *History of Secrecy and Openness in Adoption,* chap. 1.

20. The Bureau of the Census reports the 1915 infant mortality rate for the official death registration area as 99.9 (U.S. Bureau of the Census, *Historical Statistics of the United States,* p. 57).

21. On the failures of government policy concerning women and children see Mimi Abramovitz, *Regulating the Lives of Women: Social Policy from Colonial Times to the Present;* Ruth Sidel, *Women and Children Last: The Plight of Poor Women in Affluent America;* and Gordon, *Pitied but Not Entitled.*

22. Trattner, *From Poor Law to Welfare State,* p. 196; Zelizer, *Pricing the Priceless Child,* p. 209.

23. National Commission on Children, *Beyond Rhetoric;* the U.S. infant mortality rate for 1990 (the most recent year available) was 9.2; however, the infant mortality rate ranked behind twelve other "modern" nations in a 1921 comparative study conducted by the Children's Bureau; the 1990 U.S. infant mortality rate fell behind that of nineteen other countries; Japan's rate of 5.0 ranked first (Robert Pear, "Study Says U.S. Needs to Battle Infant Mortality"); "Rate of Infant Deaths Declines to New Low"; Keith Bradsher, "Low Ranking for Poor American Children: U.S. Youth among Worst Off in Study of 18 Industrialized Nations"; other nations in the study ranking 1-15 were Switzerland, Sweden, Finland, Denmark, Belgium, Norway, Luxembourg, Germany, Netherlands, Austria, Canada, France, Italy, Britain, and Australia.

24. Stephen R. Graubard, "Preface to the Issue 'America's Childhood,'" p. xii.

Selected Bibliography

Manuscript Collections

Columbia University, New York City
- Katharine F. Lenroot Papers
- Frances Perkins Papers
- Lillian D. Wald Papers
- Social Security Project, Columbia Oral History Project

Herbert Hoover Presidential Library, West Branch, Iowa
- American Child Health Association Papers
- Herbert Hoover Papers

Library of Congress, Washington, D.C.
- Irwin L. Lenroot Papers
- National Consumers' League Papers
- National Child Labor Committee Papers
- National League of Women Voters Papers, microfilm
- Theodore Roosevelt Papers, microfilm
- William Howard Taft Papers, microfilm

National Archives, Washington, D.C.
- Records of the Committee on Economic Security, RG 47
- Records of the U.S. Children's Bureau—manuscript collection and microfilm reels, RG 102
- Records of the U.S. Department of Labor, RG 174
- U.S. Film and Still Pictures Archives, RG 102

Newberry Library, Chicago
- Graham Taylor Papers

Ohio Historical Society, Columbus
- Warren G. Harding Papers

Regenstein Library, University of Chicago, Chicago
- Edith and Grace Abbott Papers

Rockford College Library, Rockford, Ill.
- Julia Lathrop Papers

Franklin D. Roosevelt Presidential Library, Hyde Park, N.Y.
- Marshall Dimock Papers
- Eleanor Roosevelt Papers
- Franklin D. Roosevelt Papers
- Records of the Interdepartmental Committee to Coordinate Health Activities in the Federal Government
- Women's Division, Democratic Party Papers

Arthur and Elizabeth Schlesinger Library, Radcliffe College, Cambridge, Mass.
Clara M. Beyer Papers
Martha May Eliot Papers
Frances Perkins Papers
Elizabeth Lowell Putnam Papers

Government Publications

Abbott, Edith, and Sophonisba P. Breckinridge. "The Administration of the Aid-to-Mothers Law in Illinois." Children's Bureau pub. no. 82. Washington, D.C.: Government Printing Office, 1921.

Allen, Nila F. "Infant Mortality: Results of a Field Study in Saginaw, Mich., Based on Births in One Year." Children's Bureau pub. no. 52. Washington, D.C.: Government Printing Office, 1919.

Bailey, William B. "Children before the Courts in Connecticut." Children's Bureau pub. no. 43. Washington, D.C.: Government Printing Office, 1918.

Belden, Evelina. "Courts in the United States Hearing Children's Cases: Results of a Questionnaire Study Covering the Year 1918." Children's Bureau pub. no. 65. Washington, D.C.: Government Printing Office, 1920.

Berolzheimer, Ruth, and Florence Nesbitt. "Child Welfare in New Jersey, Part 2—State Provision for Dependent Children, the Work of the Board of Children's Guardians of the New Jersey State Department of Institutions and Agencies." Children's Bureau pub. no. 175. Washington, D.C.: Government Printing Office, 1927.

Bird, Francis Henry, and Ella Arvilla Merritt. "Administration of Child-Labor Laws: Part 3, Employment Certificate System, Maryland." Children's Bureau pub. no. 41. Washington, D.C.: Government Printing Office, 1919.

Blackburn, William J. "Child Welfare in New Jersey, Part 1—State Supervision and Personnel Administration." Children's Bureau pub. no. 174. Washington, D.C.: Government Printing Office, 1927.

Bloodgood, Ruth. "The Federal Courts and the Delinquent Child: A Study of the Methods of Dealing with Children Who Have Violated Federal Laws." Children's Bureau pub. no. 103. Washington, D.C.: Government Printing Office, 1922.

Bogue, Mary F. "Administration of Mothers' Aid in Ten Localities: With Special Reference to Health, Housing, Education, and Recreation." Children's Bureau pub. no. 184. Washington, D.C.: Government Printing Office, 1928.

Bradbury, Dorothy E. "The Children's Bureau and Juvenile Delinquency: A Chronology of What the Bureau Is Doing and Has Done in This Field." Washington, D.C.: Government Printing Office, 1960.

———. "Five Decades of Action for Children." Children's Bureau pub. no. 358. Washington, D.C.: U.S. Government Printing Office, 1962. Reprinted in *The United States Children's Bureau, 1912-1972,* edited by Robert H. Bremner et al. New York: Arno Press, 1974.

———. "Four Decades of Action for Children: A Short History of the Children's Bureau, 1903-1946." Children's Bureau pub. no. 358. Washington, D.C.: Government Printing Office, 1956.

Bradley, Frances Sage, M.D., and Margaretta A. Williamson. "Rural Children in Selected Counties of North Carolina." Children's Bureau pub. no. 33. Washington, D.C.: Government Printing Office, 1918.

Breckinridge, Sophonisba P., and Helen R. Jeter. "A Summary of Juvenile-Court Legislation in the United States." Children's Bureau pub. no. 70. Washington, D.C.: Government Printing Office, 1920.

Burke, Dorothy Williams. "Youth and Crime: A Study of the Prevalence and Treatment of Delinquency among Boys over Juvenile-Court Age in Chicago." Children's Bureau pub. no. 196. Washington, D.C.: Government Printing Office, 1930.

Channing, Alice. "Employed Boys and Girls in Milwaukee." Children's Bureau pub. no. 213. Washington, D.C.: Government Printing Office, 1932.

———. "Employed Boys and Girls in Rochester and Utica, New York." Children's Bureau pub. no. 218. Washington, D.C.: Government Printing Office, 1933.

———. "Employment of Mentally Deficient Boys and Girls." Children's Bureau pub. no. 210. Washington, D.C.: Government Printing Office, 1932.

Chute, Charles L. "Probation in Children's Courts." Children's Bureau pub. no. 80. Washington, D.C.: Government Printing Office, 1921.

Claghorn, Kate Holladay. "Juvenile Delinquency in Rural New York." Children's Bureau pub. no. 32. Washington, D.C.: Government Printing Office, 1918.

"County Organization for Child Care and Protection." Children's Bureau pub. no. 107. Washington, D.C.: Government Printing Office, 1922.

Curry, H. Ida. "Public Child-Caring Work in Certain Counties of Minnesota, North Carolina, and New York." Children's Bureau pub. no. 173. Washington, D.C.: Government Printing Office, 1927.

Dart, Helen M. "Maternity and Child Care in Selected Rural Areas of Mississippi." Children's Bureau pub. no. 88. Washington, D.C.: Government Printing Office, 1921.

Deardorff, Neva R. "Child-Welfare Conditions and Resources in Seven Pennsylvania Counties." Children's Bureau pub. no. 176. Washington, D.C.: Government Printing Office, 1927.

Dempsey, Mary V. "Infant Mortality: Results of a Field Study in Brockton, Mass., Based on Births in One Year." Children's Bureau pub. no. 37. Washington, D.C.: Government Printing Office, 1919.

Donahue, A. Madorah. "Children of Illegitimate Birth Whose Mothers Have Kept Their Custody." Children's Bureau pub. no. 190. Washington, D.C.: Government Printing Office, 1928.

Duke, Emma. "Infant Mortality: Results of a Field Study in Johnstown, Pa., Based on Births in One Calendar Year." Children's Bureau pub. no. 9. Washington, D.C.: Government Printing Office, 1915.

Duncan, Beatrice Sheets, and Emma Duke. "Infant Mortality: Results of a Field Study in Manchester, N.H. Based on Births in One Year." Children's Bureau pub. no. 20. Washington, D.C.: Government Printing Office, 1917.

Eliot, Martha M., M.D. "Civil Defense Measures for the Protection of Children: Report of Observations in Great Britain, February 1941." Children's Bureau pub. no. 279. Washington, D.C.: Government Printing Office, 1942.

Flexner, Bernard, and Reuben Oppenheimer. "The Legal Aspect of the Juvenile Court." Children's Bureau pub. no. 99. Washington, D.C.: Government Printing Office, 1922.

Flexner, Bernard; Reuben Oppenheimer; and Katharine F. Lenroot. "The Child, the Family, and the Court: A Study of the Administration of Justice in the Field of Domestic Relations." Children's Bureau pub. no. 193. Washington, D.C.: Government Printing Office, 1929.

Freund, Ernst. "Illegitimacy Laws of the United States and Certain Foreign Countries: Analysis and Index." Children's Bureau pub. no. 42. Washington, D.C.: Government Printing Office, 1919.

Haley, Theresa S. "Infant Mortality: Results of a Field Study in Akron, Ohio, Based on Births in One Year." Children's Bureau pub. no. 72. Washington, D.C.: Government Printing Office, 1920.

Hanks, Ethel E. "Administration of Child-Labor Laws: Part 4, Employment Certification System, Wisconsin." Children's Bureau pub. no. 85. Washington, D.C.: Government Printing Office, 1921.

Healy, William, M.D. "The Practical Value of Scientific Study of Juvenile Delinquents." Children's Bureau pub. no. 96. Washington, D.C.: Government Printing Office, 1922.

Hughes, Elizabeth. "Infant Mortality: Results of a Field Study in Gary, Ind., Based on Births in One Year." Children's Bureau pub. no. 112. Washington, D.C.: Government Printing Office, 1923.

Hunter, Estelle B. "Infant Mortality: Results of a Field Study in Waterbury, Conn., Based on Births in One Year." Children's Bureau pub. no. 29. Washington, D.C.: Government Printing Office, 1918.

Jeter, Helen Rankin. "The Chicago Juvenile Court." Children's Bureau pub. no. 104. Washington, D.C.: Government Printing Office, 1922.

Johnson, Elizabeth S. "Welfare of Families of Sugar-Beet Laborers: A Study of Child Labor and Its Relation to Family Work, Income, and Living Conditions in 1935." Children's Bureau pub. no. 247. Washington, D.C.: Government Printing Office, 1939.

Lenroot, Katharine F., and Emma O. Lundberg. "Juvenile Courts at Work: A Study of the Organization and Methods of Ten Courts." Children's Bureau pub. no. 141. Washington, D.C.: Government Printing Office, 1925.

Lundberg, Emma O. "Children of Illegitimate Birth and Measures for Their Protection." Children's Bureau pub. no. 166. Washington, D.C.: Government Printing Office, 1926, 1928.

———. "Our Concern—Every Child: State and Community Planning for Wartime and Post-War Security for Children." Children's Bureau pub. no. 303. Washington, D.C.: Government Printing Office, 1944.

———. "Public Aid to Mothers with Dependent Children: Extent and Fundamental Principles." Children's Bureau pub. no. 162. Washington, D.C.: Government Printing Office, 1926.

———. "The Public Child-Welfare Program in the District of Columbia." Children's Bureau pub. no. 240. Washington, D.C.: Government Printing Office, 1938.

———. "State Commissions for the Study and Revision of Child-Welfare Laws." Children's Bureau pub. no. 131. Washington, D.C.: Government Printing Office, 1924.

———. "Unemployment and Child Welfare: A Study Made in a Middle-Western and an Eastern City during the Industrial Depression of 1921 and 1922." Children's Bureau pub. no. 125. Washington, D.C.: Government Printing Office, 1923.

Lundberg, Emma O., and Katharine F. Lenroot. "Illegitimacy as a Child-Welfare Problem, Part I: A Brief Treatment of the Prevalence and Significance of Birth out of Wedlock, the Child's Status, and the State's Responsibility for Care and Protection." Children's Bureau pub. no. 66. Washington, D.C.: Government Printing Office, 1920.

———. "Illegitimacy as a Child-Welfare Problem, Part II: A Study of Original Records in the City of Boston and in the State of Massachusetts." Children's Bureau pub. no. 75. Washington, D.C.: Government Printing Office, 1921.

Magnusson, Leifur. "Norwegian Laws concerning Illegitimate Children." Children's Bureau pub. no. 31. Washington, D.C.: Government Printing Office, 1918.

Matthews, Ellen Nathalie. "The Illegally Employed Minor and the Workmen's Compensation Law." Children's Bureau pub. no. 214. Washington, D.C.: Government Printing Office, 1932.

McGill, Nettie P. "Child Labor in New Jersey, Part III: The Working Children of Newark and Paterson." Children's Bureau pub. no. 199. Washington, D.C.: Government Printing Office, 1931.

———. "Children in Agriculture." Children's Bureau pub. no. 187. Washington, D.C.: Government Printing Office, 1929.

———. "Children in Street Work." Children's Bureau pub. no. 183. Washington, D.C.: Government Printing Office, 1928.

Meigs, Grace L. "Maternal Mortality from All Conditions Connected with Childbirth in the United States and Certain Other Countries." Children's Bureau pub. no. 19. Washington, D.C.: Government Printing Office, 1917.

Mendenhall, Dorothy Reed. "Milk, the Indispensable Food for Children." Children's Bureau pub. no. 35. Washington, D.C.: Government Printing Office, 1918.

———. "Milk, the Indispensable Food for Children." Children's Bureau pub. no. 163. Washington, D.C.: Government Printing Office, 1926.

Moore, Elizabeth. "Maternal Mortality and Infant Care in a Rural County in Kansas." Children's Bureau pub. no. 26. Washington, D.C.: Government Printing Office, 1917.

National Commission on Children. *Beyond Rhetoric: A New American Agenda for Children and Families.* Washington, D.C.: Government Printing Office, 1991.

National Commission on Children in Wartime. "A Children's Charter in Wartime." Children's Bureau pub. no. 283. Washington, D.C.: Government Printing Office, 1942.

Nesbitt, Florence. "Standards of Public Aid to Children in Their Own Homes." Children's Bureau pub. no. 118. Washington, D.C.: Government Printing Office, 1923.

Oppenheimer, Ella, M.D. "Infant Mortality in Memphis." Children's Bureau pub. no. 233. Washington, D.C.: Government Printing Office, 1937.

Oppenheimer, Reuben, and Lulu L. Eckman. "Laws Relating to Sex Offenses against Children." Children's Bureau pub. no. 145. Washington, D.C.: Government Printing Office, 1925.

Paradise, Viola I. "Maternity Care and the Welfare of Young Children in a Homesteading County in Montana." Children's Bureau pub. no. 34. Washington, D.C.: Government Printing Office, 1919.

Report of the White House Conference on Child Health and Protection. Washington, D.C.: Government Printing Office, 1931.

Rochester, Anna. "Infant Mortality: Results of a Field Study in Baltimore, Maryland, Based on Births in One Year." Children's Bureau pub. no. 119. Washington, D.C.: Government Printing Office, 1923.

Sherbon, Florence Brown, M.D., and Elizabeth Moore. "Maternity and Infant Care in Two Rural Counties in Wisconsin." Children's Bureau pub. no. 46. Washington, D.C.: Government Printing Office, 1919.

Skinner, Mary. "Industrial Home Work under the National Recovery Administration." Children's Bureau pub. no. 234. Washington, D.C.: Government Printing Office, 1936.

Springer, Ethel M. "Children Deprived of Parental Care: A Study of Children Taken under Care by Delaware Institutions and Agencies." Children's Bureau pub. no. 81. Washington, D.C.: Government Printing Office, 1921.

Steele, Glenn. "Care of Dependent and Neglected Children." Children's Bureau pub. no. 209. Washington, D.C.: Government Printing Office, 1932.

———. "Family Welfare: Summary of Expenditures for Relief, General Family Welfare and Relief, Mother's Aid, Veteran's Aid." Children's Bureau pub. no. 209. Washington, D.C.: Government Printing Office, 1932.

———. "Infant Mortality in Pittsburgh: An Analysis of Records for 1920 with Six Charts." Children's Bureau pub. no. 86. Washington, D.C.: Government Printing Office, 1921.

———. "Maternity and Infant Care in a Mountain County in Georgia." Children's Bureau pub. no. 120. Washington, D.C.: Government Printing Office, 1923.

Sumner, Helen L., and Ethel E. Hanks. "Administration of Child-Labor Laws: Part I, Employment-Certificate System, Connecticut." Children's Bureau pub. no. 12. Washington, D.C.: Government Printing Office, 1915.

———. "Administration of Child-Labor Laws: Part 2, Employment Certificate System, New York." Children's Bureau pub. no. 17. Washington, D.C.: Government Printing Office, 1917.

Sumner, Helen L., and Ella A. Merritt. "Child Labor Legislation in the United States." Children's Bureau pub. no. 10. Washington, D.C.: Government Printing Office, 1915.

Tandy, Elizabeth C., D.Sc. "Infant and Maternal Mortality among Negroes." Children's Bureau pub. no. 243. Washington, D.C.: Government Printing Office, 1937.

Treadway, Walter L., and Emma O. Lundberg. "Mental Defect in a Rural County: A Medico-Psychological and Social Study in Sussex County, Delaware." Children's Bureau pub. no. 48. Washington, D.C.: Government Printing Office, 1919.

U.S. Bureau of the Census. *Historical Statistics of the United States, Colonial Times to 1970, Bicentennial Edition, Part I.* Washington, D.C.: Government Printing Office, 1976.

——— [Frank Alexander Ross]. "School Attendance in 1920." Washington, D.C.: Government Printing Office, 1924.

U.S. Bureau of Labor Statistics [Lewis Meriam]. "Insane and Feebleminded in Institutions, 1910." Washington, D.C.: Government Printing Office, 1915.

———. "An Investigation of Woman and Child Wage-Earners in the United States." 19 vols. Washington, D.C.: Government Printing Office, 1910-13.

——— [Lewis Meriam]. "Marriage and Divorce." Washington, D.C.: Government Printing Office, 1914. pub. no. 96.

——— [Lewis Meriam]. "Paupers in Almshouses, 1910." Washington, D.C.: Government Printing Office, 1912.

U.S. Children's Bureau. "Administration of the First Federal Child-Labor Law." Children's Bureau pub. no. 78. Washington, D.C.: Government Printing Office, 1921.

———. "Advising Children in Their Choice of Occupation and Supervising the Working Child." Children's Bureau pub. no. 53. Washington, D.C.: Government Printing Office, 1919.

———. "Annual Report of the Chief." 1914-38. Washington, D.C.: Government Printing Office.

———. "Baby-Saving Campaigns: A Preliminary Report on What American Cities Are Doing to Prevent Infant Mortality." Children's Bureau pub. no. 3. Washington, D.C.: Government Printing Office, 1914.

———. "Baby-Week Campaigns: Suggestions for Communities of Various Sizes." Children's Bureau pub. no. 15. Washington, D.C.: Government Printing Office, 1915.

———. "Birth Registration: An Aid in Protecting the Lives and Rights of Children." Children's Bureau pub. no. 2. Washington, D.C.: Government Printing Office, 1914.

———. "Boys and Girls Employed in Agricultural Programs—1943." *Child* 8 (Feb. 1944).

———. "Building the Future for Children and Youth." Children's Bureau pub. no. 310. Washington, D.C.: Government Printing Office, 1945.

———. "The Child-Health Conference: Suggestions for Organization and Procedure." Children's Bureau pub. no. 261. Washington, D.C.: Government Printing Office, 1941.

———. "Child Labor Facts and Figures." Children's Bureau pub. no. 197. Washington, D.C.: Government Printing Office, 1930.

———. "Child Welfare in New Jersey, Part 4—Local Provisions for Dependent and Delinquent Children in Relation to the State's Program." Children's Bureau pub. no. 180. Washington, D.C.: Government Printing Office, 1927.

———. "Child Welfare Legislation, 1937." Children's Bureau pub. no. 236. Washington, D.C.: Government Printing Office, 1938.

———. "Child-Welfare Legislation, 1938." Children's Bureau pub. no. 251. Washington, D.C.: Government Printing Office, 1939.

———. "Child-Welfare Services under the Social Security Act, Title V part III, Development of the Program, 1936-38." Children's Bureau pub. no. 257. Washington, D.C.: Government Printing Office, 1940.

———. "Children Engaged in Newspaper and Magazine Selling and Delivering." Children's Bureau pub. no. 227. Washington, D.C.: Government Printing Office, 1935.

———. "Children in the Community: The St. Paul Experiment in Child Welfare." Children's Bureau pub. no. 317. Washington, D.C.: Government Printing Office, 1946.

———. "Children in the Courts: Juvenile-Court Statistics Year Ended December 31, 1937 and Federal Juvenile Offenders Year Ended June 30, 1937." 10th annual report. Children's Bureau pub. no. 250. Washington, D.C.: Government Printing Office, 1940.

———. "Children Indentured by the Wisconsin State Public School." Children's Bureau pub. no. 150. Washington, D.C.: Government Printing Office, 1920.

———. "Children's Bureau Publications: An Index to Publications, 1912-June 1967." Washington, D.C.: Government Printing Office, 1967.

———. "Children's Year: A Brief Summary of Work Done and Suggestions for Follow-up Work." Children's Bureau pub. no. 67. Washington, D.C.: Government Printing Office, 1920.

———. "Children's Year Working Program." Children's Bureau pub. no. 40. Washington, D.C.: Government Printing Office, 1918.

———. "Community Action for Children in Wartime." Children's Bureau pub. no. 295. Washington, D.C.: Government Printing Office, 1943.

———. "Controlling Juvenile Delinquency: A Community Program." Children's Bureau pub. no. 301. Washington, D.C.: Government Printing Office, 1943.

———. "Dependent and Delinquent Children in Georgia: A Study of the Prevalence and Treatment of Child Dependency and Delinquency in Thirty Counties with Special Reference to Legal Protection Needed." Children's Bureau pub. no. 161. Washington, D.C.: Government Printing Office, 1926.

———. "Dependent and Delinquent Children in North Dakota and South Dakota: A Study of the Prevalence, Treatment, and Prevention of Child Dependency and Delinquency in Two Rural States." Children's Bureau pub. no. 160. Washington, D.C.: Government Printing Office, 1926.

———. "Emergency Food Relief and Child Health." Washington, D.C.: Government Printing Office, 1931.

———. "Employment-Certificate System: A Safeguard for the Working Child." Children's Bureau pub. no. 56. Washington, D.C.: Government Printing Office, 1921.

———. "Facts about Crippled Children." Children's Bureau pub. no. 293. Washington, D.C.: Government Printing Office, 1943.

———. "Facts about Juvenile Delinquency: Its Prevention and Treatment." Children's Bureau pub. no. 215. Washington, D.C.: Government Printing Office, 1935.

———. "Five Years of Federal Control of Child Labor." *Child* 8 (Dec. 1943): 83-92.

———. "Goals for Children and Youth in the Transition from War to Peace Adopted by the Children's Bureau Commission on Children in Wartime, March 18, 1944." Children's Bureau pub. no. 306. Washington, D.C.: Government Printing Office, 1944.

———. "Guides to Successful Employment of Non-Farm Youth in Wartime Agriculture: For Use in Victory Farm Volunteer Program." Children's Bureau pub. no. 290. Washington, D.C.: Government Printing Office, 1943.

———. "Handbook of Federal Statistics of Children." Part 1. Children's Bureau pub. no. 5. Washington, D.C.: Government Printing Office, 1914.

———. "Helping Children in Trouble." Children's Bureau pub. no. 320. Washington, D.C.: Government Printing Office, 1947.

———. "A Historical Summary of State Services for Children in New York, Part 2." Children's Bureau pub. no. 239. Washington, D.C.: Government Printing Office, 1937.

———. "Homemaker Service: A Method of Child Care." Children's Bureau pub. no. 296. Washington, D.C.: Government Printing Office, 1946.

———. "If Your Baby Must Travel in Wartime." Children's Bureau pub. no. 307. Washington, D.C.: Government Printing Office, 1944.

———. "Illegitimacy as a Child-Welfare Problem, Part III: Methods of Care in Selected Urban and Rural Communities." Children's Bureau pub. no. 128. Washington, D.C.: Government Printing Office, 1924.

———. "Infant Mortality, Montclair, N.J.: A Study of Infant Mortality in a Suburban Community." Children's Bureau pub. no. 11. Washington, D.C.: Government Printing Office, 1915.

———. "Juvenile-Court Standards: Report of the Committee Appointed by the Children's Bureau, August, 1921, to Formulate Juvenile-Court Standards. Adopted by a Conference Held under the Auspices of the Children's Bureau and the National Probation Association, Washington, D.C., May 18, 1923." Children's Bureau pub. no. 121. Washington, D.C.: Government Printing Office, 1923.

———. "Juvenile-Court Statistics: A Tentative Plan for Uniform Reporting of Statistics of Delinquency, Dependency, and Neglect." Children's Bureau pub. no. 159. Washington, D.C.: Government Printing Office, 1926.

———. "Juvenile-Court Statistics, 1927, Based on Information Supplied by 42 Courts." Children's Bureau pub. no. 195. Washington, D.C.: Government Printing Office, 1929.

———. "Juvenile-Court Statistics, 1928, Based on Information Supplied by 65 Courts." 2d report. Children's Bureau pub. no. 200. Washington, D.C.: Government Printing Office, 1930.

———. "Juvenile-Court Statistics, 1929, Based on Information Supplied by 96 Courts." 3d annual report. Children's Bureau pub. no. 207. Washington, D.C.: Government Printing Office, 1931.

———. "Juvenile-Court Statistics, 1930, Based on Information Supplied by 92 Courts." 4th annual report. Children's Bureau pub. no. 212. Washington, D.C.: Government Printing Office, 1932.

———. "Juvenile-Court Statistics, 1931, Based on Information Supplied by 92 Courts." 5th annual report. Children's Bureau pub. no. 222. Washington, D.C.: Government Printing Office, 1933.

———. "Juvenile-Court Statistics and Federal Juvenile Offenders, 1933, Based on Information Supplied by 284 Juvenile Courts and by the United States Department of Justice." 7th annual report. Children's Bureau pub. no. 232. Washington, D.C.: Government Printing Office, 1936.

———. "Juvenile-Court Statistics Year Ended December 31, 1934 and Federal Juvenile Offenders Year Ended June 30, 1935, Based on Information Supplied by 334 Juvenile Courts and by the United States Department of Justice." 8th annual report. Children's Bureau pub. no. 235. Washington, D.C.: Government Printing Office, 1937.

———. "Juvenile Delinquency in Certain Countries at War: A Brief Review of Available Foreign Sources." Children's Bureau pub. no. 39. Washington, D.C.: Government Printing Office, 1918.

———. "Juvenile Delinquency in Maine." Children's Bureau pub. no. 201. Washington, D.C.: Government Printing Office, 1930.

———. "List of Psychiatric Clinics for Children in the United States." Children's Bureau pub. no. 191. Washington, D.C.: Government Printing Office, 1929.

———. "List of References on Juvenile Courts and Probation in the United States and a Selected List of Foreign References." Children's Bureau pub. no. 124. Washington, D.C.: Government Printing Office, 1923.

———. "Maternal and Child-Health Services under the Social Security Act, Title V part I, Development of Program, 1936-39." Children's Bureau pub. no. 259. Washington, D.C.: Government Printing Office, 1940.

———. "Maternal Deaths, a Brief Report of a Study Made in Fifteen States." Children's Bureau pub. no. 221. Washington, D.C.: Government Printing Office, 1933.
———. "Maternal Mortality in Fifteen States." Children's Bureau pub. no. 223. Washington, D.C.: Government Printing Office, 1934.
———. "Mental Defectives in the District of Columbia: A Brief Description of Local Conditions and the Need for Custodial Care and Training." Children's Bureau pub. no. 13. Washington, D.C.: Government Printing Office, 1915.
———. "Mothers' Aid, 1931." Children's Bureau pub. no. 220. Washington, D.C.: Government Printing Office, 1933.
———. "Occupational Hazards to Young Workers: Report No. 1, The Explosives-Manufacturing Industries." Children's Bureau pub. no. 273. Washington, D.C.: Government Printing Office, 1942.
———. "Occupational Hazards to Young Workers: Report No. 2, Motor-Vehicle Drivers and Helpers." Children's Bureau pub. no. 274. Washington, D.C.: Government Printing Office, 1941.
———. "Occupational Hazards to Young Workers: Report No. 3, The Coal-Mining Industry." Children's Bureau pub. no. 275. Washington, D.C.: Government Printing Office, 1942.
———. "Occupational Hazards to Young Workers: Report No. 4, The Logging and Sawmilling Industries." Children's Bureau pub. no. 276. Washington, D.C.: Government Printing Office, 1942.
———. "Occupational Hazards to Young Workers: Report No. 5, Woodworking Machines." Children's Bureau pub. no. 277. Washington, D.C.: Government Printing Office, 1942.
———. "Physical Standards for Working Children." Children's Bureau pub. no. 79. Washington, D.C.: Government Printing Office, 1921.
———. "Proceedings of Conference on Better Care for Mothers and Babies." Children's Bureau pub. no. 246. Washington, D.C.: Government Printing Office, 1938.
———. "Proceedings of the Conference on Day Care of Children of Working Mothers: With Special Reference to Defense Areas, Held in Washington, D.C., July 31 and Aug. 1, 1941." Children's Bureau pub. no. 281. Washington, D.C.: Government Printing Office, 1942.
———. "Proceedings of the Conference on Juvenile-Court Standards Held under the Auspices of the U.S. Children's Bureau and the National Probation Association, Milwaukee, Wisconsin, June 21-22, 1921." Children's Bureau pub. no. 97. Washington, D.C.: Government Printing Office, 1921.
———. "Proceedings of the Conference on Mothers' Pensions Held under the Auspices of the Mothers' Pension Committee Family Division of the National Conference of Social Work and the Children's Bureau, U.S. Department of Labor, Providence, R.I., June 28, 1922." Children's Bureau pub. no. 109. Washington, D.C.: Government Printing Office, 1922.
———. "Proceedings of the Third Annual Conference of State Directors in Charge of the Local Administration of the Maternity and Infancy Act, Act

of Congress of November 23, 1921, Held in Washington, D.C., January 11-13, 1926." Children's Bureau pub. no. 157. Washington, D.C.: Government Printing Office, 1926.

———. "Proceedings of the White House Conference on Children in a Democracy, Washington, D.C., January 18-20, 1940." Children's Bureau pub. no. 266. Washington, D.C.: Government Printing Office, 1940.

———. "Promotion of the Welfare and Hygiene of Maternity and Infancy: The Administration of the Act of Congress of November 23, 1921, for the Period March 20, 1922, to June 30, 1923." Children's Bureau pub. no. 137. Washington, D.C.: Government Printing Office, 1924.

———. "The Promotion of the Welfare and Hygiene of Maternity and Infancy: The Administration of the Act of Congress of November 23, 1921, Fiscal Year Ended June 30, 1924." Children's Bureau pub. no. 146. Washington, D.C.: Government Printing Office, 1925.

———. "The Promotion of the Welfare and Hygiene of Maternity and Infancy: The Administration of the Act of Congress of November 23, 1921, Fiscal Year Ended June 30, 1925." Children's Bureau pub. no. 156. Washington, D.C.: Government Printing Office, 1926.

———. "Promotion of the Welfare and Hygiene of Maternity and Infancy: The Administration of the Act of Congress of November 23, 1921, Fiscal Year Ended June 30, 1926." Children's Bureau pub. no. 178. Washington, D.C.: Government Printing Office, 1927.

———. "Promotion of the Welfare and Hygiene of Maternity and Infancy: The Administration of the Act of Congress of November 23, 1921, Fiscal Year Ended June 30, 1927." Children's Bureau pub. no. 186. Washington, D.C.: Government Printing Office, 1928.

———. "Promotion of the Welfare and Hygiene of Maternity and Infancy: The Administration of the Act of Congress of November 23, 1921, Fiscal Year Ended June 30, 1928." Children's Bureau pub. no. 194. Washington, D.C.: Government Printing Office, 1928.

———. "Promotion of the Welfare and Hygiene of Maternity and Infancy, the Administration of the Act of Congress of November 23, 1921, Fiscal Year Ended June 30, 1929." Children's Bureau pub. no. 203. Washington, D.C.: Government Printing Office, 1931.

———. "Protecting the Health of Young Workers in Wartime." Children's Bureau pub. no. 291. Washington, D.C.: Government Printing Office, 1943.

———. *Relief Expenditures, January through September, 1931.* Washington, D.C.: Government Printing Office, 1931.

———. "Save 100,000 Babies: Get a Square Deal for Children." Children's Bureau pub. no. 36. Washington, D.C.: Government Printing Office, 1918.

———. "Scholarships for Children." Children's Bureau pub. no. 51. Washington, D.C.: Government Printing Office, 1919.

———. "The Selection and Training of Volunteers in Child Care." Children's Bureau pub. no. 299. Washington, D.C.: Government Printing Office, 1943.

———. "Services for Crippled Children under the Social Security Act, Title V part II, Development of the Program, 1936-39." Children's Bureau pub. no. 258. Washington, D.C.: Government Printing Office, 1940.

———. "Standards and Recommendations for Hospital Care of Newborn Infants, Full-Term and Premature." Children's Bureau pub. no. 292. Washington, D.C.: Government Printing Office, 1943.

———. "Standards for Day Care of Children of Working Mothers." Children's Bureau pub. no. 284. Washington, D.C.: Government Printing Office, 1942.

———. "Standards of Child Health, Education, and Social Welfare: Based on Recommendations of the White House Conference on Children in a Democracy and Conclusions of Discussion Groups." Children's Bureau pub. no. 287. Washington, D.C.: Government Printing Office, 1942.

———. "Standards of Legal Protection for Children Born out of Wedlock: A Report of Regional Conferences Held under the Auspices of the U.S. Children's Bureau and the Inter-City Conference on Illegitimacy, Chicago, Ill., February 9-10, 1920." Children's Bureau pub. no. 77. Washington, D.C.: Government Printing Office, 1921.

———. "Standards of Prenatal Care, an Outline for the Use of Physicians." Children's Bureau pub. no. 153. Washington, D.C.: Government Printing Office, 1925.

———. "Statement of Policy on Employment of Youth under 18 Years of Age." Washington, D.C.: Government Printing Office, 1943. Reprinted from *Child* 7 (Mar. 1943).

———. "A Study of Crippled Children in Thirteen States." Children's Bureau pub. no. 230. Washington, D.C.: Government Printing Office, 1935.

———. "A Study of Maternity Homes in Minnesota and Pennsylvania." Children's Bureau pub. no. 167. Washington, D.C.: Government Printing Office, 1926.

———. "To Parents in Wartime." Children's Bureau pub. no. 282. Washington, D.C.: Government Printing Office, 1942.

———. "Understanding Juvenile Delinquency." Children's Bureau pub. no. 300. Washington, D.C.: Government Printing Office, 1943.

———. "Wartime Employment of Boys and Girls under 18." Children's Bureau pub. no. 289. Washington, D.C.: Government Printing Office, 1943.

———. "The Welfare of Infants of Illegitimate Birth in Baltimore as Affected by a Maryland Law of 1916 Governing the Separation from Their Mothers of Children under Six Months Old." Children's Bureau pub. no. 144. Washington, D.C.: Government Printing Office, 1925.

U.S. Children's Bureau and the Bureau of Public Assistance. "A Community Plans for Its Children: Final Report, Newport News, Va. Project." Children's Bureau pub. no. 321. Washington, D.C.: Government Printing Office, 1947.

U.S. Committee on Economic Security. *Report to the President.* Washington, D.C.: Government Printing Office, 1935.

U.S. Department of Labor. *The Anvil and the Plow.* Washington, D.C.: Government Printing Office, 1963.

———. *Annual Report of the Secretary of Labor.* 1914-38. Washington, D.C.: Government Printing Office.

U.S. Federal Works Agency. "Final Report on the WPA Program, 1935-43." Washington, D.C.: Government Printing Office, 1947.

U.S. Office of Education. "Statistical Summary of Education, 1935-36." Washington, D.C.: Government Printing Office, 1937.

U.S. Social Security Board. "Part III: Security for Children." In *Social Security in America: The Factual Background of the Social Security Act as Summarized from Staff Reports to the Committee on Economic Security.* Washington, D.C.: Government Printing Office, 1937.

———, Bureau of Public Assistance. "Effect of Federal Participation in Payments for Aid to Dependent Children in 1940." *Social Security Bulletin* 4 (May 1941): 27-29.

U.S. Women's Bureau [Pidgeon, Mary-Elizabeth]. "Employed Mothers and Child Care." Women's Bureau pub. no. 246. Washington, D.C.: Government Printing Office, 1953.

Warburton, Amber Arthun; Helen Wood; and Marian M. Crane, M.D. "The Work and Welfare of Children of Agricultural Laborers in Hidalgo County, Texas." Children's Bureau pub. no. 298. Washington, D.C.: Government Printing Office, 1943.

Welch, Kathryn H. "The Meaning of State Supervision in the Social Protection of Children." Children's Bureau pub. no. 252. Washington, D.C.: Government Printing Office, 1940.

West, Mrs. Max (Mary). "Infant Care." Children's Bureau pub. no. 8. Washington, D.C.: Government Printing Office, 1915.

———. "Prenatal Care." Children's Bureau pub. no. 4. Washington, D.C.: Government Printing Office, 1914.

Whitney, Jessamine S. "Infant Mortality: Results of a Field Study in New Bedford, Mass., Based on Births in One Year." Children's Bureau pub. no. 68. Washington, D.C.: Government Printing Office, 1920.

Wickersham Commission. "Report on the Child Offender in the Federal System of Justice." Report no. 6. Washington, D.C.: Government Printing Office, 1931. Reprint, Montclair, N.J.: Patterson Smith, 1968.

Winslow, Emma A., Ph.D. "Trends in Different Types of Public and Private Relief in Urban Areas, 1929-35." Children's Bureau pub. no. 237. Washington, D.C.: Government Printing Office, 1937.

Wood, Helen. "Young Workers and Their Jobs in 1936: A Survey in Six States." Children's Bureau pub. no. 249. Washington, D.C.: Government Printing Office, 1940.

Woodbury, Helen Sumner. "Administration of Child-Labor Laws: Part 5, Standards Applicable to the Administration of Employment Certificate Systems." Children's Bureau pub. no. 133. Washington, D.C.: Government Printing Office, 1924.

Woodbury, Robert Morse. "Causal Factors in Infant Mortality: A Statistical Study Based on Investigations in Eight Cities." Children's Bureau pub. no. 142. Washington, D.C.: Government Printing Office, 1925.

Works Progress Administration. *Trends in Relief Expenditures, 1910-1935.* Washington, D.C.: Government Printing Office, 1937.

Wright, Helen Russell. "Children of Wage-Earning Mothers: A Study of a Selected Group in Chicago." Children's Bureau pub. no. 102. Washington, D.C.: Government Printing Office, 1922.

Books, Articles, Theses, and Papers

Abbott, Edith. "Child Labor in America before 1870." In Grace Abbott, *The Child and the State: Legal Status in the Family, Apprenticeship, and Child Labor.* 2 vols. Chicago: University of Chicago Press, 1938.

———. *Public Assistance, American Principles and Policies.* Chicago: University of Chicago Press, 1940.

———. "A Sister's Memories." *Social Service Review* 13 (Sept. 1939): 351-407.

[———?]. "Champion of Women and Children: The Story of Grace Abbott." *World Tomorrow* 14 (Sept. 1931): 294-97.

Abbott, Grace. "Case Work Responsibility of Juvenile Courts." *Social Service Review* 3 (Sept. 1929): 395-404.

———. "Child Health Recovery." *Survey* 69 (Oct. 1933): 349-50.

———. "The Child Labor Amendment." *North American Review* 220 (Dec. 1924): 223-37.

———. "The Federal Government in Relation to Maternity and Infancy." *Annals of the American Academy of Political and Social Science* 151 (Sept. 1930).

———. *From Relief to Social Security.* Chicago: University of Chicago Press, 1941.

———. "Improvement in Rural Public Relief: The Lesson of the Coal-Mining Communities." *Social Service Review* 6 (June 1932): 183-222.

———. "The Juvenile Courts." *Survey* 72 (1936): 131-33.

———. "The Midwife in Chicago." *Journal of Sociology* 20 (Mar. 1915): 684-99.

———. "Mothers' Aid." In *Social Work Yearbook, 1935: A Description of Organized Activities in Social Work and Related Fields,* edited by Fred S. Hall. New York: Russell Sage Foundation, 1935.

———. "Ten Years Work for Children." *North American Review* 218 (Aug. 1923): 189-200.

———. "What about Mothers' Pensions Now?" *Survey* 70 (Mar. 1934): 80-81.

———, ed. *The Child and the State: Legal Status in the Family, Apprenticeship, and Child Labor.* 2 vols. Chicago: University of Chicago Press, 1938.

Abramovitz, Mimi. *Regulating the Lives of Women: Social Policy from Colonial Times to the Present.* Boston: South End Press, 1988.

Achenbaum, W. Andrew. *Shades of Gray: Old Age, American Values, and Federal Policies since 1920*. Boston: Little, Brown and Company, 1983.

———. "Social Security." In *Franklin D. Roosevelt: His Life and Times An Encyclopedic View,* edited by Otis L. Graham, Jr., and Meeghan Robinson Wander. New York: G. K. Hall, 1985.

———. *Social Security: Visions and Revisions.* Cambridge: Harvard University Press, 1986.

Addams, Jane. *My Friend Julia Lathrop.* New York: Macmillan, 1935.

———. *The Second Twenty Years at Hull House: September 1909 to September 1929, With a Record of Growing World Consciousness.* New York: Macmillan and Company, 1930.

———. *Twenty Years at Hull House.* New York: Macmillan and Company, 1910.

Addams, Jane, et al. *The Child, the Clinic and the Court: A Group of Papers by Jane Addams et al.* New York: New Republic, 1925.

———, et al. "TR—Social Worker." *Survey* 41 (Jan. 18, 1919): 523-31.

"Address to Sentinels." *Woman Patriot* 11 (Jan. 13, 1927).

Adler, Stuart W. "Medical Care for Dependents of Men in Military Service." *American Journal of Public Health* 33 (June 1943): 645-50.

———. "The Wagner-Murray Bill." *American Journal of Public Health* 33 (Oct. 1943): 1274-77.

"Adolescents in Wartime." *Annals of the American Academy of Political and Social Science* 236 (Nov. 1944).

"Advances in Federal Health Legislation and Organization." *American Journal of Public Health* 36 (Oct. 1946): 1165.

"Again, the Sheppard-Towner Bill." *Ohio State Medical Journal* 17 (Oct. 1921).

Alexander, John K. *Render Them Submissive: Responses to Poverty in Philadelphia, 1760-1800.* Amherst: University of Massachusetts Press, 1980.

Altmeyer, Arthur J. *The Formative Years of Social Security.* Madison: University of Wisconsin Press, 1966.

———."The New Social Security Program." *School Life* 25 (Jan. 1940): 103-4.

Antler, Joyce, and Daniel M. Fox. "The Movement toward a Safe Maternity: Physician Accountability of New York City, 1915-1940." *Bulletin of the History of Medicine* 50 (1976): 569-95

Apple, Rima D. *Mothers and Medicine: A Social History of Infant Feeding, 1890-1950.* Madison: University of Wisconsin Press, 1987.

Ashby, Leroy. "Partial Promises and Semi-Visible Youths: The Depression and World War II." In *American Childhood: A Research Guide and Historical Handbook,* edited by Joseph M. Hawes and N. Ray Hiner, pp. 489-532. Westport, Conn.: Greenwood Press, 1985.

———. *Saving the Waifs: Reformers and Dependent Children, 1890-1929.* Philadelphia: Temple University Press, 1984.

Baker, S. Josephine. *Fighting for Life.* New York: Macmillan, 1939.

Barton, Sam B. "Factors and Forces in the Movement for the Abolition of Child Labor in the United States." Ph.D. dissertation, University of Texas-Austin, 1938.

Baukhage, Hilmar Robert. "What Will the New Deal Do for Children?" *Parents Magazine* 8 (Dec. 1933).

Baumel, Judith. "The Jewish Refugee Children from Europe in the Eyes of the American Press and Public Opinion, 1934-1945." *Holocaust and Genocide Studies* 5 (1990): 293-312.

———. "The Transfer and Resettlement in the United States of Young Jewish Refugees from Nazism, 1934-1945." *American Jewish History* 77 (1988): 413-36.

Baumgartner, Leona. "Sara Josephine Baker." In *Notable American Women: The Modern Period.* Cambridge: Harvard University Press, Belknap Press, 1980.

Beales, Ross W., Jr. "In Search of the Historical Child: Miniature Adulthood and Youth in Colonial New England." In *Growing Up in America: Children in Historical Perspective,* edited by N. Ray Hiner and Joseph M. Hawes. Urbana: University of Illinois Press, 1985.

Bell, Winifred. *Aid to Dependent Children.* New York: Columbia University Press, 1965.

Berkowitz, Edward D. *America's Welfare State: From Roosevelt to Reagan.* Baltimore: Johns Hopkins University Press, 1991.

———. *Disabled Policy: America's Programs for the Handicapped.* New York: Cambridge University Press, 1987.

Berkowitz, Edward D., and Kim McQuaid. *Creating the Welfare State: The Political Economy of Twentieth-Century Reform.* New York: Praeger, 1980.

Bernert, Eleanor H. *America's Children.* New York: John Wiley and Sons, 1958.

Blair, Karen. *The Clubwoman as Feminist: True Womanhood Redefined, 1868-1914.* New York: Holmes and Meier, 1980.

Blum, Carol. "Women's Culture and Urban Culture: Cincinnati's Benevolent Women's Activities and the Invention of the 'New Woman' 1815-1895." Ph.D. dissertation, University of Cincinnati, 1987.

Blum, John Morton. *V Was for Victory: Politics and American Culture during World War II.* New York: Harcourt Brace Jovanovich, 1976.

Blumberg, Rose. *Florence Kelley: The Making of a Social Pioneer.* New York: Augustus M. Kelley, 1966.

Borst, Charlotte G. "The Professionalization of Obstetrics: Childbirth Becomes a Medical Specialty." In *Women, Health, and Medicine in America: A Historical Handbook,* edited by Rima D. Apple, pp. 197-216. New York: Garland Publishing, Inc., 1990.

Bradsher, Keith. "Low Ranking for Poor American Children: U.S. Youth among Worst Off in Study of 18 Industrialized Nations." *New York Times,* Aug. 14, 1995, p. A7.

Braeman, John. "Albert J. Beveridge and the First National Child Labor Bill." *Indiana Magazine of History* 60 (Mar. 1964).

Brandt, Alan M. *No Magic Bullet: A Social History of Venereal Disease in the United States since 1880.* New York: Oxford University Press, 1985.

Breckinridge, Sophonisba P. "Government's Role in Child Welfare." *Annals of the American Academy of Political and Social Science* 212 (Nov. 1940): 42-50.

Breckinridge, Sophonisba P., and Edith Abbott. *The Delinquent Child and the Home.* Chicago: University of Chicago Press, 1912.

Breen, William J. *Uncle Sam at Home: Civilian Mobilization, Wartime Federalism, and the Council of National Defense, 1917-1919.* Westport, Conn.: Greenwood Press, 1984.

Bremner, Robert H. *From the Depths: The Discovery of Poverty in the United States.* New York: New York University Press, 1956.

Bremner, Robert H., et al., eds. *Children and Youth in America: A Documentary History.* 3 vols. Cambridge: Harvard University Press, 1971.

——— et al., eds. *The United States Children's Bureau, 1912-1972.* New York: Arno Press, 1974.

Brown, Anne Kruesi. "Opposition to the Child Labor Amendment Found in Trade Journals, Industrial Bulletins, and Other Publications for and by Business Men." M.A. thesis, University of Chicago, 1937.

Brown, Josephine Chapin. *Public Relief 1929-1939.* New York: Henry Hold and Company, 1940.

Bruno, Frank J. *Trends in Social Work, 1874-1956: A History Based on the Prodeedings of the National Conference of Social Work.* 1948; New York: Columbia University Press, 1957.

Burner, David. *The Politics of Provincialism: The Democratic Party in Transition, 1918-1932.* New York: Alfred A. Knopf, 1968.

Burrow, James G. *AMA: Voice of American Medicine.* Baltimore: Johns Hopkins University Press, 1963.

———. *Organized Medicine in the Progressive Era: The Move toward Monopoly.* Baltimore: Johns Hopkins University Press, 1977.

Campbell, D'Ann. "Judge Ben Lindsey and the Juvenile Court Movement, 1901-4." In *Growing Up in America: Children in Historical Perspective,* edited by N. Ray Hiner and Joseph M. Hawes, pp. 149-60. Urbana: University of Illinois Press, 1985.

———. *Women at War with America: Private Lives in a Patriotic Era.* Cambridge: Harvard University Press, 1984.

Campbell, O. J. "Woman Suffrage and Social Welfare." *Woman Patriot* 1 (Sept. 1912): 10.

Caputo, Richard K. "Welfare and Freedom American Style: A Study of the Influence of Segmented Authority on the Development of Social and Child Welfare Reform through an Examination of the Role and Activities of the Federal Government, 1900-1940." Ph.D. dissertation, University of Chicago, 1982.

"Care of Infants Whose Mothers Are Employed: Policies and Recommendations by the Children's Bureau." *Child* 9 (1945): 131-32.

Carp, E. Wayne. *The History of Secrecy and Openness in Adoption.* Cambridge: Harvard University Press, forthcoming.

Carson, Mina. *Settlement Folk: Social Thought and the American Settlement Movement, 1885-1930.* Chicago: University of Chicago Press, 1990.

Cavallo, Dominick. *Muscles and Morals: Organized Playgrounds and Urban*

Reform, 1880-1920. Philadelphia: University of Pennsylvania Press, 1981.

Chambers, Clarke A. *Seedtime of Reform: American Social Service and Social Action, 1918-1933.* Ann Arbor: University of Michigan Press, 1963.

Chepaitis, Joseph B. "Federal Social Welfare Progressivism in the 1920's." *Social Service Review* 46 (June 1972): 213-30.

———. "The First Federal Social Welfare Measure: The Sheppard-Towner Maternity and Infancy Act, 1918-1932." Ph.D. dissertation, University of Chicago, 1976.

"The Child Health Recovery Conference." *School and Society* 38 (Oct. 14, 1933): 498-99.

Child Labor Bulletin 7 (Nov. 1918).

"The Children's Bureau Bill." *Survey* 28 (Apr. 13, 1912).

"The Children's Bureau Bill." *Survey* 28 (May 7, 1912).

"Children or Parsimony. Which Shall Prevail." *American Federationist* 21 (Apr. 1914): 313-15.

Cincinnati Bureau of Governmental Research. *Children's Aid and Child Care in Cincinnati and Hamilton County, Ohio.* Vol. 4. Cincinnati: Cincinnati Bureau of Government Research, 1935.

"Clara Beyer, 98, Dies; Key New Deal Official." *New York Times,* Sept. 27, 1990.

Clement, Priscilla Ferguson. "The City and the Child, 1860-1885." In Joseph M. Hawes and N. Ray Hiner. *American Childhood: A Research Guide and Historical Handbook,* pp. 235-72. Westport, Conn.: Greenwood Press, 1985.

Close, Kathryn. "Day Care up to Now." *Survey* 79 (July 1943): 194-97.

———. "When the Children Come." *Survey* 75 (1940): 283-86.

Coben, Stanley. *A. Mitchell Palmer: Politician.* New York: Columbia University Press, 1963.

Cohen, Ronald D. "Child Saving and Progressivism, 1885-1915." In Joseph M. Hawes and N. Ray Hiner. *American Childhood: A Research Guide and Historical Handbook,* pp. 273-309. Westport, Conn.: Greenwood Press, 1985.

"Conference on Child Health and Nutrition." *Monthly Labor Review* 37 (Nov. 1933): 1084-85.

"Conference on Children in a Democracy." *American Journal of Public Health* 30 (Mar. 1930): 313-14.

"Controversy Develops over Alleged Coolidge Support." *Woman Patriot* 10 (Feb. 1, 1927).

Conway, Jill Kerr. "Grace Abbott." In *Notable American Women.* Vol. 1. Cambridge: Harvard University Press, Belknap Press, 1971.

———. "Women Reformers and American Culture, 1870-1930." In *Our American Sisters: Women in American Life and Thought,* edited by Jean E. Friedman et al. 4th ed., pp. 399-413. Lexington, Mass.: D. C. Heath and Company, 1987.

Costin, Lela B. *Two Sisters for Social Justice: A Biography of Grace and Edith Abbott.* Urbana: University of Illinois Press, 1983.

Cott, Nancy F. *The Grounding of Modern Feminism.* New Haven, Conn.: Yale University Press, 1987.

Covotsos, Louis J. "Child Welfare and Social Progress: The United States Children's Bureau, 1912-1935." Ph.D. dissertation, University of Chicago, 1976.

Cravens, Hamilton. "Child Saving in the Age of Professionalism, 1915-1930." In *American Childhood: A Research Guide and Historical Handbook,* edited by Joseph M. Hawes and N. Ray Hiner, pp. 415-88. Westport, Conn.: Greenwood Press, 1985.

Critchlow, Donald T., and Ellis W. Hawley, eds. *Federal Social Policy: The Historical Dimension.* University Park: Pennsylvania State University Press, 1988.

Daniels, Roger. "American Refugee Policy in Historical Perspective." In *The Muses Flee Hitler: Culture Transfer and Adaptation 1930-1945,* edited by Jarrell C. Jackman and Carla M. Borden, pp. 65-71. Washington, D.C.: Smithsonian Institution Press, 1983.

———. *Coming to America: A History of Immigration and Ethnicity in American Life.* New York: Harper Collins, 1990.

———. *The Politics of Prejudice: The Anti-Japanese Movement in California and the Struggle for Japanese Exclusion.* Berkeley: University of California Press, 1962.

Daniels, Roger; Sandra C. Taylor; and Harry H. L. Kitano, eds. *Japanese Americans: From Relocation to Redress.* Rev. ed. Seattle: University of Washington Press, 1991.

Davis, Allen F. *Spearheads for Reform: The Social Settlements and the Progressive Movement, 1890-1914.* New York: Columbia University Press, 1987.

Deardorff, Neva R. "Bound Out." *Survey* 56 (July 15, 1926).

Degler, Carl N. *At Odds: Women and the Family in America from the Revolution to the Present.* New York: Oxford University Press, 1980.

Delle Donnie, Carmen R. "Two-Handed Engine at the Door: Social Workers and the Agitation for a National Children's Bureau." M.A. thesis, Catholic University of America, 1967.

D'Emilio, John, and Estelle B. Freedman. *Intimate Matters: A History of Sexuality in America.* New York: Harper and Row, 1988.

Demos, John. *Past, Present, and Personal: The Family and the Life Course in Historical Perspective.* New York: Oxford University Press, 1986.

Devine, Edward T. "Congress and the Children." *Charities and the Commons* 15 (Feb. 3, 1906): 588.

———. "The Message." *Charities and Commons* 17 (Dec. 15, 1906): 449-50.

Devitt, Neal. "The Statistical Case for the Elimination of the Midwife: Fact versus Prejudice, 1890-1935." *Women and Health* 4 (Spring 1979): 81-96 and (Summer 1979): 169-86.

Dick, Kriste Lindenmeyer. "Saving Mothers and Babies: The Sheppard-Towner Maternity and Infancy Act 1921-1929, with Emphasis on Its Effects in Ohio." M.A. thesis, University of Cincinnati, 1987.

———. "The Silent Charity: A History of the Cincinnati Maternity Society." *Queen City Heritage* 43 (Winter 1985): 29-33.

Dinnerstein, Leonard. *America and the Survivors of the Holocaust*. New York: Columbia University Press, 1982.

Dratch, Howard. "The Politics of Child Care in the 1940's." *Science and Society* 38 (Summer 1974): 175-77.

Drew, John Clayton. "Child Labor and Child Welfare: The Origins and Uneven Development of the American Welfare State." Ph.D. dissertation, Cornell University, 1987.

Dublin, Louis I. *After Eighty Years: The Impact of Life Insurance on the Public Health*. Gainesville: University of Florida Press, 1966.

Duffus, Robert L. *Lillian Wald, Neighbor and Crusader*. New York: Macmillan, 1939.

Duffy, John. *The Sanitarians: A History of American Public Health*. Urbana: University of Illinois Press, 1990.

Dwork, Deborah. *War Is Good for Babies and Other Young Children: A History of the Infant and Child Welfare Movement in England, 1898-1918*. London: Travistock, 1987.

"Editorial." *JAMA* 76 (Feb. 5, 1921).

Edwards, Newton. "Youth as a Population Element." *Annals of the American Academy of Political and Social Science* 194 (1937): 8.

"Edwin Emil Witte." *Dictionary of American Biography*. Vol. 6. New York: Charles Scribner's Sons, 1980.

Eliot, Martha M. "Child Health Recovery Program." *Public Health Nursing* 26 (Apr. 1934): 178-80.

———. "Child Health Recovery Program." *Child Health Bulletin* 10 (Mar. 1934): 41-45.

———. "The Origins and Development of the Health Services." *Children* 7 (July-Aug. 1960): 135-37.

Eliot, Martha M., and Lillian R. Freedman. "Four Years of the Emergency Maternal and Infant Care Program." *Yale Journal of Biology and Medicine* 19 (Mar. 1947): 621-35.

Eliot, Thomas H. *Recollections of the New Deal: When the People Mattered*. Edited by John Kenneth Galbraith. Boston: Northeastern University Press, 1992.

Evans, Sara M. *Born for Liberty: A History of Women in America*. New York: Free Press, 1989.

Feder, Elizabeth. "The Elite of the Fallen: The Origins of a Social Policy for Unwed Mothers, 1880-1930." Ph.D. dissertation, Johns Hopkins University, 1991.

"Federal Care of Maternity and Infancy: The Sheppard-Towner Bill." *JAMA* 76 (Feb. 5, 1921).

Feingold, Henry L. *The Politics of Rescue: The Roosevelt Administration and the Holocaust, 1938-1945*. Newark, N.J.: Rutgers University Press, 1970.

Felt, Jeremy. *Hostages of Fortune: Child Labor Reform in New York State*. Syracuse, N.Y.: Syracuse University Press, 1965.

Finkelstein, Barbara. "Uncle Sam and the Children: A History of Government Involvement in Child Rearing." In *Growing Up in America: Children in Historical Perspective,* edited by N. Ray Hiner and Joseph M. Hawes, pp. 255-68. Urbana: University of Illinois Press, 1985.

Fishbein, Morris. *A History of the American Medical Association, 1847-1947.* Philadelphia: W. B. Sanders Company, 1947.

———. "Sickness Insurance and Sickness Costs." *Hygeia* 12 (Dec. 1934): 1070-76.

"Five Years of Federal Control of Child Labor." *Child* 8 (Dec. 1943): 83-92.

Flanagan, Maureen A. "Gender and Urban Political Reform: The City Club and the Woman's City Club of Chicago in the Progressive Era." *American Historical Review* 95 (Oct. 1990): 1032-50.

Folks, Homer. *The Care of Destitute, Neglected, and Dependent Children.* New York: Macmillan, 1902.

Gabower, Genevieve. "A Look at Ten Communities." *Survey Midmonthly* 80 (Mar. 1944): 86-90, 104.

Gale, Zona. "Great Ladies of Chicago." *Survey* 67 (Feb. 1, 1932): 479-82.

Gallagher, Gregory. *FDR's Splendid Deception.* New York: Dodd, Mead and Company, 1985.

Garceau, Oliver. *The Political Life of the American Medical Association.* Cambridge: Harvard University Press, 1941.

Gilbert, Hilda Kessler. "The United States Department of Labor in the New Deal Period." Ph.D. dissertation, University of Wisconsin, 1942.

Gilbert, James. *A Cycle of Outrage: America's Reaction to Juvenile Delinquency in the 1950s.* New York: Oxford University Press, 1986.

Gluck, Sherna Berger. *Rosie the Riveter Revised: Women, the War, and Social Change.* New York: Penguin Books, 1987.

Godfrey, Drexel, Jr. *The Transfer of the Children's Bureau.* New York: Harcourt, Brace and Company, 1952.

Goldin, Claudia. "Family Strategies and Family Economy in the Late Nineteenth Century: The Role of Secondary Workers." In *Philadelphia: Work, Space, Family and Group Experience in the Nineteenth Century: Essays toward an Interdisciplinary History of the City,* edited by Theodore Hershberg. New York: Oxford University Press, 1981.

Goldmark, Josephine. *Impatient Crusader: Florence Kelley's Life Story.* Urbana: University of Illinois Press, 1953.

Gordon, Linda. *Heroes of Their Own Lives: The Politics and History of Family Violence, Boston 1880-1960.* New York: Penguin Books, 1988.

———. "The New Feminist Scholarship on the Welfare State." In *Women, the State, and Welfare,* edited by Linda Gordon. Madison: University of Wisconsin Press, 1990.

———. *Pitied But Not Entitled: Single Mothers and the History of Welfare, 1890-1935.* New York: Free Press, 1994.

Gordon, Michael, ed. *The American Family: Past, Present, and Future.* New York: Random House, 1978.

———. *The American Family in Social-Historical Perspective.* 3d ed. New York: St. Martin's Press, 1983.

"Governor Wilson and the Social Worker." *Survey* 29 (Feb. 8, 1913): 639-40.

"Grace Abbott Finds in Undernourishment, Delinquency, and Loss of Homes a Menace To Be Met by Greater Relief Efforts." *New York Times,* Dec. 18, 1932, p. 9.

"Grace Abbott Hull House, 1908-21." *Social Service Review* 24 (Sept. 1950): 374-94.

Grace Abbott interview. *New York Times Magazine,* Nov. 9, 1930, p. 11.

Graebner, William. *A History of Retirement: The Meaning and Function of an American Institution, 1885-1978.* New Haven, Conn.: Yale University Press, 1980.

Graubard, Stephen R. "Preface to the Issue 'America's Childhood.'" *Daedalus* 122 (Winter 1992).

Griswold, Robert L. *Family and Divorce in California, 1850-1890: Victorian Illusions and Everyday Realities.* Albany: State University of New York Press, 1982.

Gross, Beatrice, and Ronald Gross. *The Children's Rights Movement: Overcoming the Oppression of Young People.* Garden City, N.Y.: Anchor Press, 1977.

Grossman, Jonathan. *The Department of Labor.* New York: Praeger, 1973.

Hall, Fred S. *Social Work Yearbook, 1935: A Description of Organized Activities in Social Work and Related Fields.* New York: Russell Sage Foundation, 1935.

Hall, G. Stanley. *Adolescence: Its Psychology and Its Relations to Physiology, Anthropology, Sociology, Sex, Crime, Religion, and Education.* 2 vols. New York: D. Appleton and Company, 1904.

Hall, Kermit L. et al., eds. *The Oxford Companion to the Supreme Court of the United States.* New York: Oxford University Press, 1992.

Halpern, Sydney A. *American Pediatrics: The Social Dynamics of Professionalism, 1880-1980.* Berkeley and Los Angeles: University of California Press, 1988.

Hanlon, John J. *Principles of Public Health Administration.* St. Louis: C. V. Mosby, 1964.

Hareven, Tamara K. "Family Time and Historical Time." In *The Family,* edited by Alice S. Rossi et al. New York: W. W. Norton and Company, 1977, 1978.

Hartmann, Susan M. *American Women in the 1940s: The Homefront and Beyond.* Boston: Twayne, 1982.

Hawes, Joseph M. *Children in Urban Society: Juvenile Delinquency in Nineteenth-century America.* New York: Oxford University Press, 1971.

———. *The Children's Rights Movement: A History of Advocacy and Protection.* Boston: Twayne Publishers, 1991.

Hawes, Joseph M., and N. Ray Hiner, eds. *American Childhood: A Research Guide and Historiographical Handbook.* Westport, Conn.: Greenwood Press, 1985.

Hawley, Ellis W. "Social Policy and the Liberal State in Twentieth-Century America." In *Federal Social Policy: The Historical Dimension,* edited by Donald T. Critchlow and Ellis W. Hawley, pp. 117-40. University Park: Pennsylvania State University of Press, 1988.

"Health and Happiness Number." *Southern Textile Bulletin* 18, no. 17 (1919).

"The Health of Children in the United States during the Depression." *School and Society* 36 (Dec. 3, 1932): 712.

Hiner, N. Ray, and Joseph M. Hawes, eds. *Growing Up in America: Children in Historical Perspective.* Urbana: University of Illinois Press, 1985.

Hirshfield, Daniel S. *The Lost Reform: The Campaign for Compulsory Health Insurance in the United States from 1932-1943.* Cambridge: Harvard University Press, 1970.

Hoey, Jane M. "Aid to Families with Dependent Children." *Annals of the American Academy of Political and Social Sciences* 202 (Mar. 1939).

Hoff-Wilson, Joan. *Herbert Hoover: Forgotten Progressive.* Boston: Little, Brown Company, 1975.

Honey, Maureen. *Creating Rosie the Riveter: Class, Gender, and Propaganda during World War II.* Amherst: University of Massachusetts Press, 1984.

Hoogenboom, Ari Arthur. *Outlawing the Spoils: A History of the Civil Service Reform Movement, 1865-1883.* Urbana: University of Illinois Press, 1961.

Hoover, J. Edgar. "Wild Children." *American Magazine* 136 (July 1943).

"Horace Mann Towner." In *Biographical Directory of the American Congress, 1774-1961.* Washington, D.C.: Government Printing Office, 1961.

"How Have Children Fared as a Whole? The Chief of the United States Children's Bureau Deals with These Questions." *New York Times,* Nov. 26, 1933, p. 8.

Howard, Christopher. "Sowing the Seeds of 'Welfare': The Transformation of Mothers' Pensions, 1900-1940." *Journal of Policy History* 4 (1992): 188-227.

"Immediate Work of the Children's Bureau." *Survey* 24 (Nov. 16, 1912): 189-90.

"Is Woman's Own Work So Well Done?" *Woman Patriot* 3 (Aug. 1913): 5.

Jambor, Harold A. "Theodore Dreiser, the *Delineator* Magazine, and Dependent Children: A Background Note on the Calling of the 1909 White House Conference." *Social Service Review* 32 (Mar. 1958): 33-40.

Josephson, Hannah. *Jeannette Rankin: First Lady in Congress, a Biography.* Indianapolis: Bobbs-Merill Company, 1974.

Johnson, James. "The Role of Women in the Founding of the United States Children's Bureau." In *Women in American History,* edited by Carol V. R. George. Syracuse, N.Y.: Syracuse University Press, 1975.

Jones, Jacqueline. *Labor of Love, Labor of Sorrow: Black Women, Work, and the Family from Slavery to the Present.* New York: Basic Books, 1985.

Karger, Jacob. *The Sentinels of Order: A Study of Social Control and the Minneapolis Settlement House Movement, 1915-1950.* Lanhan, Md.: University Press of America, 1987.

Karis, Thomas George. "Congressional Behavior at Constitutional Frontiers: From 1906, the Beveridge Child-Labor Bill, to 1938, the Fair Labor Standards Act." Ph.D. dissertation, Columbia University, 1951.

Karlsrud, Robert Allen. "The Hoover Labor Department: A Study in Bureaucratic Divisiveness." Ph.D. dissertation, University of California-Los Angeles, 1972.

"Katharine Lenroot." *National Cyclopedia of American Biography.* Vol. G. New York: White and Company, 1946.

Katz, Michael B. *In the Shadow of the Poorhouse: A Social History of Welfare in America.* New York: Basic Books, 1986.

Kelley, Camille. *A Friend in Court.* New York: Dodd, Mead, and Company, 1942.

Kelley, Edna Ewing. "Uncle Sam's Nursery Schools." *Parents Magazine* 11 (Mar. 1936).

Kelley, Florence. "The Children's Amendment," *Good Housekeeping* Feb. 1923.

———. "Obstacles to the Enforcement of Child Labor Legislation." *Proceedings of the Third Annual Meeting of the National Child Labor Committee, December 13-15, 1906.* In *Child and the State: Legal Status in the Family, Apprenticeship, and Child Labor,* edited by Grace Abbott. 2 vols. Chicago: University of Chicago Press, 1938.

———. *Some Ethical Gains through Legislation.* New York: Macmillan, 1905. Reprint, New York: Arno Press, 1969.

Kemp, John R., ed. *Lewis Hine: Photographs of Child Labor in the New South.* Jackson: University Press of Mississippi, 1986.

Kemplen, Tilda H. *From Roots to Roses: The Autobiography of Tilda Kemplen.* Edited by Nancy Herzberg. Athens: University of Georgia Press, 1992.

Kessler-Harris, Alice. *Out to Work: A History of Wage Earning Women in the United States, 1820-1980.* New York: Oxford University Press, 1982.

———. *A Woman's Wage: Historical Meanings and Social Consequences.* Lexington: University of Kentucky Press, 1982.

Kevles, Daniel. *In the Name of Eugenics: Genetics and the Uses of Human Heredity.* New York: Alfred A. Knopf, 1985.

Klaus, Alisa C. "Babies All the Rage: The Movement to Prevent Infant Mortality in the United States and France, 1890-1920." Ph.D. dissertation, University of Pennsylvania, 1986.

———. "Perfecting American Babyhood: Race Betterment and the Baby Health Contest." Paper presented at the Mar. 1990 meeting of the Organization of American Historians.

Kleinschmidt, H. E. "Leaves from the Diary of a Healthmobile." *Hygeia* 4 (Mar. 1926).

Kobrin, Frances E. "The American Midwifery Controversy: A Crisis in Professionalization." In *Women and Health in America: Historical Readings,* edited by Judith Walzer Leavitt, pp. 318-26. Madison: University of Wisconsin Press, 1984. Reprinted from *Bulletin of the History of Medicine* 40 (July-Aug. 1966): 350-63.

Kolko, Gabriel. *The Triumph of Conservatism: A Reinterpretation of American History, 1900-1916.* Chicago: Quadrangle Books, 1963.

Koven, Seth, and Sonya Michel. "Womanly Duties: Maternalistic Politics and the Origins of the Welfare States in France, Germany, Great Britain, and the United States." *American Historical Review* 95 (Oct. 1990): 1076-1114.

Kraditor, Aileen S. *The Ideas of the Woman Suffrage Movement, 1890-1920.* New York: W. W. Norton and Company, 1981.

Kunzel, Regina G. "The Professionalization of Benevolence: Evangelicals and Social Workers in the Florence Crittenton Homes, 1915 to 1945." *Journal of Social History* 22 (Fall 1988): 21-43.

Ladd-Taylor, Molly. "'Grannies' and 'Spinsters': Midwife Education under the Sheppard-Towner Act." *Journal of Social History* 22 (Winter 1988): 255-76.

———. *Mother-Work: Women, Child Welfare, and the State, 1890-1930.* Urbana: University of Illinois Press, 1994.

———. *Raising a Baby the Government Way: Mothers' Letters to the Children's Bureau, 1915-1932.* New Brunswick: Rutgers University Press, 1986.

———. "Women's Health and Public Policy." In *Women, Health, and Medicine in America: A Historical Handbook,* edited by Rima D. Apple, pp. 391-410. New York: Garland Publishing, 1990.

Lampman, Robert J., ed. *Social Security Perspectives: Essays by Edwin E. Witte.* Madison: University of Wisconsin Press, 1962.

Lane, James B. *Jacob A. Riis and the American City.* Port Washington, N.Y.: Kennikat Press, 1974.

Larsen, Charles. *The Good Fight: The Life and Times of Ben B. Lindsey.* Chicago: Quadrangle Books, 1972.

Lasch, Christopher. *Haven in a Heartless World: The Family Besieged.* New York: Basic Books, 1977.

Lathrop, Julia. "The Children's Bureau." *Proceedings of the National Conference of Charities and Correction, 39th Annual Session, June 12-19, 1912.* Fort Wayne, Ind.: Fort Wayne Printing Company, 1912.

———. "The Children's Bureau." General Federation of Women's Clubs. *Biennial Convention. Official Report,* pp. 447-48.

———. "Children's Bureau in Wartime." *North American Review* 206 (Nov. 1917): 734-46.

———. "Income and Infant Mortality." *American Journal of Public Health* 9 (Apr. 1919): 270-74.

———. "Mothers and Babies First!" *Woman Citizen* 7 (Dec. 1926).

———. "Pension the Mothers." *Journal of Education* 72 (Oct. 20, 1910).

———. "Public Protection of Maternity." *American Labor Legislation Review* 7 (Mar. 1917): 27-35.

———, et al., eds. *The Child, the Clinic and the Court.* New York: New Republic, 1925.

Lazerson, Marvin. *Origins of the Urban School: Public Education in Massachusetts, 1870-1915.* Cambridge: Harvard University Press, 1971.

Leavitt, Judith Walzer. *Brought to Bed: Birthing Women and Their Physicians, 1750-1950.* New York: Oxford University Press, 1986.

———. *The Healthiest City: Milwaukee and the Politics of Reform.* Princeton, N.J.: Princeton University Press, 1982.

———. "Medicine in Context: A Review Essay of the History of Medicine." *American Historical Review* 95 (Dec. 1990): 1471-84.

———. ed. *Women and Health in America.* Madison: University of Wisconsin Press, 1984.

Leavitt, Judith Walzer, and Ronald C. Numbers. "Sickness and Health in America: An Overview." In *Sickness and Health in America,* edited by Judith Walzer Leavitt, pp. 3-10. Madison: University of Wisconsin Press, 1978.

Leff, Mark H. "Consensus for Reform: The Mothers' Pension Movement in the Progressive Era." *Social Service Review* 47 (Sept. 1973): 397-417.

Leiby, James. *A History of Social Welfare and Social Work in the United States.* New York: Columbia University Press, 1978.

Leigh, Robert D. *Federal Health Administration in the United States.* New York: Harper and Brothers, 1927.

Leland, R. G., and A. M. Simmons. "Do We Need Compulsory Public Health Insurance? No." *Annals of the American Academy of Polical and Social Sciences* 170 (Nov. 1933): 121.

Lemons, J. Stanley. "The Sheppard-Towner Act: Progressivism in the 1920's." *Journal of American History* 55 (Dec. 1969): 776-86.

———. *The Woman Citizen: Social Feminism in the 1920s.* Urbana: University of Illinois Press, 1973.

Lenroot, Katharine F. "Child Welfare 1930-40." *Annals of the American Academy of Political and Social Science* 212 (Nov. 1940): 1-11.

———. "Children of the Depression: A Study of 259 Families in Selected Areas of Five Cities." *Social Service Review* 9 (June 1935): 212-42.

———. "A Defense Program for the Children of the United States." Pamphlet. Washington, D.C.: Government Printing Office, Nov. 1941.

———. "Origin of the Social Security Provisions." *Children* 7 (July-Aug. 1960): 128-29.

———. "The Place of the Juvenile Court in a Community Program for Child Welfare." *Annals of the American Academy of Political and Social Science* 121 (Sept. 1925): 60-69.

———. "Social Responsibility for the Protection of Children Handicapped by Illegitimate Birth." *Annals of the American Academy of Political and Social Science* 98 (Nov. 1921).

Leuchtenburg, William E. *Franklin D. Roosevelt and the New Deal 1932-1940.* New York: Harper and Row, 1963.

Lewis, W. David. "Katharine Bement Davis, (1860-1935)." In *Notable American Women.* Vol. 1. Cambridge: Harvard University Press, Belknap Press, 1971.

Lindenmeyer, Kriste. "Dorothy Reed Mendenhall." In *Great Lives,* vol. 2: *Women in American History.* Englewood Cliffs, N.J.: Salem Press, 1995.

———. "Saving Mothers and Babies: The Sheppard-Towner Act in Ohio, 1921-1929." *Ohio History* 99 (Summer/Autumn, 1990): 105-34.

———. "Taking Birth Control to the Hinterland: Cincinnati's First Birth Control Clinic as a Test Case, 1929-1931." *Mid-America* 77 (Spring-Summer 1995): 145-73.

———. "'To Begin with Babies': The Early Years of the Babies' Milk Fund Association of Cincinnati, 1880-1929." Paper presented at the Ohio Academy of History's spring meeting, Apr. 19, 1986.
Lindsay, Samuel McCune. "Child Labor—A National Disgrace." *Annals of the American Academy of Political and Social Science* 28 (July-Dec. 1906): 301-3.
———. "Exploring the New World for Children." *Pedagogical Seminary* 16 (Dec. 1909): 459-63.
———. "Seventh Annual Child Labor Conference." *Survey* 26 (Apr. 22, 1911): 124.
Link, Arthur S. *Woodrow Wilson and the Progressive Era, 1910-1917.* New York: Harper, 1954.
Lipschultz, Sybil. "Social Feminism and Legal Discourse: 1908-1923." *Yale Journal of Law and Feminism* 2 (Fall, 1989): 131-60.
Lissak, Rivlen Shpak. *Pluralism and Progressives: Hull House and the New Immigrants, 1890-1919.* Chicago: University of Chicago Press, 1989.
Litoff, Judy Barrett. "Midwives and History." In *Women, Health, and Medicine in America: A Historical Handbook,* edited by Rima D. Apple, pp. 443-58. New York: Garland Publishing, 1990.
Lombardi, John. *Labor's Voice in the Cabinet: A History of the Department of Labor from Its Origin to 1921.* New York: AMS Press, 1968.
Lovejoy, Owen R. "In the Shadow of the Coal Breaker." Pub. no. 61. New York: National Child Labor Committee, 1907.
———. "Letter to the Editor." *American Child* 29 (Feb. 1947): 4.
———. "What Remains of Child Labor." *New Republic* 9 (Nov. 11, 1916).
Lubove, Roy. "James E. West." *Dictionary of American Biography.* Supplement 4. New York: Charles Scribner's Sons, 1974.
———. *The Struggle for Social Security, 1900-1935.* Cambridge: Harvard University Press, 1968. 2d ed. Pittsburgh: University of Pittsburgh Press, 1986.
Ludmerer, Kenneth M. *Genetics and American Society: A Historical Appraisal.* Baltimore: Johns Hopkins University Press, 1972.
Lumpkin, Katharine DuPre, and Dorothy Wolff Douglas. *Child Workers in America.* 2d ed. New York: International Publishers, 1937.
Lundberg, Emma O. "Progress toward Better Laws for the Protection of Children Born out of Wedlock." *Proceedings of the National Conference of Social Work, 1920.* Fort Wayne, Ind.: Fort Wayne Printing, 1920.
———. *Unto the Least of These: Social Services for Children.* New York: D. Appleton-Century Company, 1902. Reprint, 1947.
Mack, Julian W. "The President's Address." *Proceedings of the National Convention of Charities and Correction, 39th Annual Session, June 12-19, 1912.* Fort Wayne, Ind.: Fort Wayne Printing Company, 1912.
Magee, Elizabeth S. "Impact of the War on Child Labor." *Annals of the American Academy of Political and Social Sciences* 236 (Nov. 1944): 101-2.
Magie, William J. "Civilization Based upon the Family." *Woman Patriot* 10 (Feb. 1917): 9.
Mangold, George B. *Problems of Child Welfare.* 3d ed. New York: Macmillan Company, 1936.

Margolis, Maxine. *Mothers and Such: Views of American Women and Why They Changed.* Berkeley: University of California Press, 1984.

Markham, Edwin; Benjamin B. Lindsey; and George Creel. *Children in Bondage: A Complete and Careful Preservation of the Anxious Problem of Child Labor—Its Causes, Its Crimes, and Its Cure.* New York: Hearst's International Library Company, 1914.

Martin, George. *Madame Secretary: Frances Perkins.* Boston: Houghton Mifflin Company, 1986.

Mason, Jan. "An Historical Policy Analysis of United States Child Welfare Policy." Ph.D. dissertation, University of New South Wales, Australia, 1986.

"Maternity Act Extension Seekers Claim President's Support." *Woman Patriot* 10 (Feb. 1, 1926): 18.

May, Elaine Tyler. "The Pressure to Provide: Class, Consumerism, and Divorce in Urban America, 1880-1920." In *The American Family in Social-Historical Perspective,* edited by Michael Gordon. 3d ed. New York: St. Martin's Press, 1983.

McAhren, Robert Willard. "Making the Nation Safe For Childhood: A History of the Movement for Federal Regulation of Child Labor, 1900-1938." Ph.D. dissertation, University of Texas, 1967.

McCleary, George F. *The Early History of the Infant Welfare Movement.* London: H. K. Lewis and Company, 1933.

McConnell, Beatrice. "Child Labor in Agriculture." *Annals of the American Academy of Poltical and Social Science* 236 (Nov. 1944): 92-100.

McDonald, Austin F. *Federal Aid: A Study of the American Subsidy System.* New York: Thomas Y. Crowell Company, 1928.

McGerr, Michael. "Political Style and Women's Power, 1830-1930." *Journal of American History* 77 (Dec. 1990): 864-85.

McKinley, Charles, and Robert W. Frase. *Launching Social Security: A Capture-and-Record Account.* Madison: University of Wisconsin Press, 1970.

McLaughlin, Kathleen. "'Action' Program to Back Child Aid: White House Conference Ends with Expressions of Zeal for a National Drive." *New York Times,* Jan. 21, 1940.

McQuade, Vincent. *The American Catholic Attitude on Child Labor since 1891.* Washington, D.C.: Catholic University, 1938.

Meckel, Richard A. *Save the Babies: American Public Health Reform and the Prevention of Infant Mortality, 1850-1929.* Baltimore: Johns Hopkins University Press, 1989.

Mellett, Lowell. "The Sequel of the Dagenhart Case." *American Child* 6 (Jan. 1924): 3.

Melvin, Patricia Mooney. "Milk to Motherhood: The New York Milk Committee and the Beginning of Well Child Programs." *Mid-America Journal* 65 (Oct. 1983): 111-13.

Mennel, Robert M. *Thorns and Thistles: Juvenile Delinquents in the United States, 1825-1940.* Hanover, N.H.: University Press of New England, 1973.

Meriam, Lewis. "The Aims and Objects of the Federal Children's Bureau." *Proceedings of the National Conference of Charities and Correction, 40th An-*

nual Session, July 5-12, 1913. Fort Wayne, Ind.: Fort Wayne Printing Company, 1913.

———. "A Great Bureau Chief." *Illinois Voter* 12 (June 1932): 7.

Merritt, Ella A. "Child Labor under the N.R.A. as Shown by Employment Certificates Issued in 1934." *Monthly Labor Review* 41 (Dec. 1935).

Meyerowitz, Joanne. *Women Adrift: Independent Wage Earners in Chicago, 1880-1930*. Chicago: University of Chicago Press, 1988.

Michel, Sonya Alice. "Children's Interests/Mothers' Rights: Women, Professionals, and the American Family, 1920-1945." Ph.D. dissertation, Brown University, 1986.

Miller, Elissa. "A History of Nursing Education in Arkansas." Ph.D. dissertation, Memphis State University, 1989.

Miller, Watson B. "Health Education and Security—Some Post-war Perspectives." *American Journal of Public Health* 36 (July 1944): 762-68.

Mintz, Steven, and Susan Kellogg. *Domestic Revolutions: A Social History of American Family Life*. New York: Free Press, 1988.

"Misplaced Priorities." *Time*, Apr. 8, 1991, p. 28.

Moldow, Gloria. *Women Doctors in Gilded-Age Washington: Race, Gender, and Professionalization*. Urbana: University of Illinois Press, 1987.

Morantz-Sanchez, Regina Markell. "Physicians." In *Women, Health, and Medicine in America: A Historical Handbook*, edited by Rima D. Apple, pp. 477-96. New York: Garland Publishing, 1990.

———. *Sympathy and Science: Women Physicians in American Medicine*. New York: Oxford University Press, 1985.

"Morris Sheppard." In *Biographical Directory of the American Congress, 1774-1961*. Washington, D.C.: Government Printing Office, 1961.

Mowry, George Edwin. *The Era of Theodoore Roosevelt and the Birth of Modern America, 1900-1912*. New York: Harper, 1958.

———. *Theodore Roosevelt and the Progressive Movement*. Madison: University of Wisconsin Press, 1946.

Mullan, Fitzhugh, M.D. *Plagues and Politics: The Story of the United States Public Health Service*. New York: Basic Books, 1989.

Mulligan, Joan Elizabeth. "Three Federal Interventions on Behalf of Childbearing Women: The Sheppard-Towner Act, Emergency Maternity and Infant Care, and the Maternal and Child Health and Mental Retardation Planning Amendments of 1963." Ph.D. dissertation, University of Michigan, 1976.

Muncy, Robyn. *Creating a Female Dominion in American Reform, 1890-1935*. New York: Oxford University Press, 1991.

Nasaw, David. *Children of the City: At Work and at Play*. New York: Oxford University Press, 1985.

National Child Labor Committee. "Changes and Trends in Child Labor and Its Control." Pub. no. 375. New York: National Child Labor Committee, 1938.

———. "Child Labor Facts." New York: National Child Labor Committee, 1938.

———. *Twenty-fifth Anniversary of the National Child Labor Committee, 1904-1929.* New York: National Child Labor Committee, 1929.

———. "Why Conserve Our Natural Resources and Not the Generations That Are to Use Them?" New York: National Child Labor Committee, 1910.

National Conference of Charities and Correction. *Proceedings . . . 39th Annual Session, June 12-19, 1912.* Fort Wayne, Ind.: Fort Wayne Printing Company, 1912.

———. *Proceedings . . . 40th Annual Session, July 5-12, 1913.* Fort Wayne, Ind.: Fort Wayne Printing Company, 1913.

———. *Proceedings . . . 41st Annual Session, May 8-15, 1914.* Fort Wayne, Ind.: Fort Wayne Publishing Co., 1914.

Nelson, Barbara J. "The Origins of the Two-Channel Welfare State: Workmen's Compensation and Mothers' Aid." In *Women and the Welfare State,* edited by Linda Gordon, pp. 123-51. Madison: University of Wisconsin Press, 1990.

Nelson, Daniel. *Unemployment Insurance: The American Experience, 1915-1935.* Madison: University of Wisconsin Press, 1969.

Numbers, Ronald L. "The Third Party: Health Insurance in America." In *The Therapeutic Revolution: Essays in the Social History of American Medicine,* edited by Morris J. Vogel and Charles E. Rosenberg, pp. 177-200. Philadelphia: University of Pennsylvania Press, 1979.

O'Neill, Lois Decker, ed., *The Women's Book of World Records and Achievements.* Garden City, N.Y.: Anchor Press, 1979.

Padgett, Alice Elizabeth. "The History of the Establishment of the United States Children's Bureau." M.A. thesis, University of Chicago, 1936.

Parker, Graham. "The Juvenile Court Movement." *University of Toronto Law Journal* 26 (1976): 140-72.

Parker, Jacqueline K., and Edward M. Carpenter. "Julia Lathrop and the Children's Bureau: The Emergence of an Institution." *Social Service Review* 55 (Mar. 1981): 60-77.

Patterson, James T. *America's Struggle against Poverty, 1900-1985.* Cambridge: Harvard University Press, 1981. 2d ed., 1986.

Paulsen, George Edward. "The Legislative History of the Fair Labor Standards Act." Ph.D. dissertation, Ohio State University, 1959.

Pear, Robert. "Study Says U.S. Needs to Battle Infant Mortality." *New York Times,* Aug. 6, 1990, pp. A1, A14.

Perkins obit. *New York Times,* May 15, 1965.

"The Perpetuation of the Sheppard-Towner Idea." *JAMA* 91 (Nov. 27, 1928).

"A Petition to the United States Senate." *Woman Patriot* 10 (Aug. 1, 1926).

Phelps, Edward Bunnell. "A Statistical Study of Infant Mortality." *Quarterly Publications of the American Statistical Association* 11 (Sept. 1908): 233-72.

Phelps, Orme Wheelock. *The Legislative History of the Fair Labor Standards Act.* Chicago: University of Chicago Press, 1939.

Pickens, Donald K. *Eugenics and the Progressives.* Nashville: Vanderbilt University Press, 1968.

Pisciotta, Alexander W. "Benjamin Barr Lindsey." In *Biographical Dictionary of Social Welfare in America,* edited by Walter I. Trattner. Westport, Conn.: Greenwood Press, 1986.

Platt, Anthony. *The Child Savers: The Invention of Delinquency.* 2d ed. Chicago: University of Chicago Press, 1977.

Polenberg, Richard. *Reorganizing Roosevelt's Government: The Controversy over Executive Reorganization, 1936-1939.* Cambridge: Harvard University Press, 1966.

———. *War and Society: The United States, 1941-1945.* Philadelphia: J. B. Lippincott Company, 1972.

Porter, Kirk H., ed., *National Party Platforms.* New York: Macmillan and Company, 1924.

Porter, Kirk H., and Donald Bruce Johnson. *National Party Platforms 1840-1968.* 4th ed. Urbana: University of Illinois Press, 1970.

"The President and the Sheppard-Towner Act." *JAMA* 91 (Dec. 18, 1928).

Preston, Samuel H., and Michael R. Haines, *Fatal Years: Child Mortality in Late Nineteenth-Century America.* Princeton, N.J.: Princeton University Press, 1991.

Pringle, Henry F. *The Life and Times of William Howard Taft: A Biography.* 2 vols. New York: Farrar and Rinehart, 1939.

Provenzo, Eugene F. "The Photographer as Educator: The Child Labor Photo-Stories of Lewis Hine." *Teachers College Record* 83 (Summer, 1982): 593-612.

"The Public School as a Social Agency." *Annals of the American Academy of Political and Social Science,* part C, 98 (Nov. 1921).

Putnam, Elizabeth Lowell. "Address to Sentinels of the Republic." Reprinted in *Woman Patriot* 11 (Feb. 1, 1927): 23.

Rachford, Benjamin K. "A Reliable Milk Supply for Babies." *Lancet Clinic* 29 (July 2, 1892): 12.

"Rate of Infant Deaths Declines to New Low." *Cincinnati Enquirer,* Feb. 7, 1992.

"Ray Lyman Wilbur Dies at Stanford at 74." *New York Times,* June 27, 1949, p. 21.

Reiman, Richard A. *The New Deal and American Youth: Ideas and Ideals in a Depression Decade.* Athens: University of Georgia Press, 1992.

"Report of the Library Extension Board of the American Library Association for the Year Ending July 31, 1939." *Bulletin of the American Library Association* 33 (Sept. 1939): 552-57.

Riis, Jacob. *The Children of the Poor.* New York: Charles Scribner's Sons, 1892.

———. *How the Other Half Lives: Studies among the Tenements of New York.* 1890; New York: Hill and Wang, 1957.

Robinson, Caroline Hadley. *Seventy Birth Control Clinics.* Issued by the National Committee on Maternal Health. Baltimore: Williams and Wilkins Company, 1930.

Robinson, Margaret C. "Discriminating against Mother." *Woman Patriot* 10 (Apr. 1917): 9.

Robinton, Elizabeth D. "Dorothy Reed Mendenhall." In *Notable American Women: The Modern Period.* Cambridge: Harvard University Press, Belknap Press, 1980.

Romanosfsky, Peter. "Emma Octavia Lundberg." In *Notable American Women: The Modern Period.* Cambridge: Harvard University Press, Belknap Press, 1980.

Romasco, Albert U. *The Poverty of Abundance: Hoover, the Nation, the Depression.* New York: Oxford University Press, 1965.

Roosevelt, Franklin D. *The Public Papers and Addresses of Franklin D. Roosevelt.* Edited by Samuel Rosencamp. 4 vols. New York: Macmillan Company, 1941.

Rosen, George. *A History of Public Health.* New York: MD Publications, 1958.

———. *Problems of Child Welfare.* 3d ed. New York: Macmillan and Company, 1936.

Rosenberg, Charles E., et al. *The Family in History.* Philadelphia: University of Pennsylvania Press, 1975.

Rothman, David J. *The Discovery of the Asylum: Social Order and Disorder in the New Republic.* Boston: Little, Brown and Company, 1971.

Rothman, David J., and Sheila M. Rothman, eds. *The Family and Social Service in the 1920's: Two Documents.* New York: Arno Press and the New York Times, 1972.

Rothman, Sheila M. *Woman's Proper Place: A History of Changing Ideals and Practices, 1870 to the Present.* New York: Basic Books, 1978.

———. "Women's Clinics or Doctors' Offices: The Sheppard-Towner Act and the Promotion of Preventive Health Care." In *Social History and Social Policy,* edited by David J. Rothman and Stanton Wheeler. New York: Academic Press, 1981.

Rude, Anna E. "The Children's Year Campaign." *American Journal of Public Health* 9 (May 1919).

Salem, Dorothy. *To Better Our World: Black Women in Organized Reform, 1890-1920.* New York: Carlson Publishing, 1990.

Saveth, Edward N. "Patrician Philanthropy in America: The Nineteenth and Early Twentieth Centuries." *Social Service Review* 54 (Mar. 1980): 76-91.

Schlabach, Theron F. *Edwin E. Witte: Cautious Reformer.* Madison: State Historical Society of Wisconsin, 1969.

Schlesinger, Edward R. "The Sheppard-Towner Era: A Prototype Case Study in Federal State Relationships." *American Journal of Public Health* 57 (June 1967): 1034-40.

Schoff, Mrs. Frederick. "Children's Bureau Absolutely Unnecessary." *Woman Patriot* 11 (Feb. 1, 1927).

Scott, Anne Firor. "Most Visible of All: Black Women's Voluntary Association." *Journal of Southern History* 56 (Feb. 1990): 3-22.

Scott, Mrs. William Forse. "Women and Government." *Woman Patriot* 1 (May 1912): 4.

Selden, Charles A. "The Most Powerful Lobby in Washington." *Ladies Home Journal* 39 (Apr. 1922).

Sidel, Ruth. *Women and Children Last: The Plight of Poor Women in Affluent America*. New York: Penguin Books, 1986.
Siefert, Kristine. "An Exemplar of Primary Prevention in Social Work: The Sheppard-Towner Act of 1921." *Social Work in Health Care* 9 (Fall 1983): 87-102.
Simms, L. Moody, Jr. "Alexander McKelway." *Biographical Dictionary of Social Welfare in America,* edited by Walter I. Trattner. Westport, Conn.: Greenwood Press, 1986.
Sinai, Nathan, and Odin W. Anderson. *EMIC: A Study of Administrative Experience*. Bureau of Public Health and Economics, Research Series no. 3. Ann Arbor: School of Public Health, University of Michigan, 1948.
Skinner, Mary, and Alice Scott Nutt. "Adolescents Away from Home." *Annals of the American Academy of Political and Social Science* 235 (Nov. 1944): 51-59.
Sklar, Kathryn Kish. "A Call for Comparisons." *American Historical Review*. 95 (Oct. 1990): 1109-14.
———, ed. *Notes of Sixty Years: The Autobiography of Florence Kelley*. Chicago: Charles H. Kerr Publishing Company, 1986.
Skocpol, Theda. *Protecting Soldiers and Mothers: The Political Origins of Social Policy in the United States*. Cambridge: Harvard University Press, 1992.
Solomon, Barbara. *In the Company of Educated Women: A History of Women and Higher Education in America*. New Haven, Conn.: Yale University Press, 1985.
Spargo, John. *The Bitter Cry of the Children*. New York: Macmillan Company, 1906. Reprint; New York: Quadrangle Books, 1968.
Spring, Joel. *Education and the Rise of the Corporate State*. Boston: Beacon Press, 1972.
Stansell, Christine. *City of Women: Sex and Class in New York, 1789-1860*. Urbana: University of Illinois Press, 1987.
Starr, Paul. *The Social Transformation of American Medicine*. New York: Basic Books, 1982.
Steere, Geoffrey H. "Changing Values in Child Socialization: A Study of United States Child-Rearing Literature, 1865-1929." Ph.D. dissertation, University of Pennsylvania, 1964.
Stefano, Carolyn J. "Pathways to Power: Women and Voluntary Associations in Denver, Colorado, 1876-1893." Ph.D. dissertation, Duke University, 1987.
Steinfels, Margaret O'Brien. *Who's Minding the Children? The History and Politics of Day Care in America*. New York: Simon and Schuster, 1973.
Stevens, Robert B., ed. *Income Security*. Vol. 4 of *Statutory History of the United States*. New York: Chelsea House Publishers, 1970.
Stevens, Rosemary. *In Sickness and in Wealth: American Hospitals in the Twentieth Century*. New York: Basic Books, 1989.
Taylor, Eleanor. "The Story of the Children's Bureau." Washington, D.C.: Child Welfare Committee of the National League of Women Voters, 1930.
Taylor, Graham. "Personals." *Survey* 28 (Apr. 27, 1912): 176-77.

Terrell, Mary Helen. "'Some Kind of Social Doctor': Historical Study of Martha May Eliot's Policies for Maternal and Child Health." Ph.D. dissertation, Brandeis University, 1990.

Thompson, Walter. *Federal Centralization.* New York: Harcourt, Brace and Company, 1923.

Thompson, Warren S. "Adolescents according to the Census." *Annals of the American Academy of Poltical and Social Science* 236 (Nov. 1944): 17-25.

Tiffin, Susan. *In Whose Best Interest? Child Welfare Reform in the Progressive Era.* Westport, Conn.: Greenwood Press, 1982.

Tillman, Elvena Bage. "The Rights of Childhood: The National Child Welfare Movement, 1890-1919." Ph.D. dissertation, University of Wisconsin, 1968.

Tobey, James A. *The Children's Bureau: Its History, Activities, and Organization.* Baltimore: Johns Hopkins University Press, 1925.

Towle, Charlotte. "The Effect of the War upon Children." *Social Service Review* 17 (June 1943): 149-50.

Trachtenberg, Alan. *Reading American Photographs: Images as History, Mathew Brady to Walker Evans.* New York: Hill and Wang, 1989.

"Transfer of the Public Health Service." *American Journal of Public Health* 30 (July 1940): 827.

Trattner, Walter I. *Crusade for the Children: A History of the National Child Labor Committee and Child Labor Reform in America.* Chicago: Quadrangle Books, 1970.

———. *From Poor Law to Welfare State: A History of Social Welfare in America.* 4th ed. New York: Free Press, 1974.

———. *Homer Folks: Pioneer in Social Welfare.* New York: Columbia University Press, 1968.

———. ed. *Biographical Dictionary of Social Welfare in America.* Westport, Conn.: Greenwood Press, 1986.

Treaster, Joseph B. "Martha Eliot; Worked in Child Care." *New York Times,* Feb. 23, 1978, p. 2.

Trolander, Judith. *Professionalism and Social Change: From the Settlement House Movement to Neighborhood Centers, 1886 to the Present.* New York: Columbia University Press, 1987.

Trombley, Stephen. *The Right to Reproduce: A History of Coercive Sterilization.* New York: Weidernfeld and Nicolson, 1988.

Trout, Charles H. "Frances Perkins." In *Notable American Women: The Modern Period.* Cambridge: Harvard University Press, 1980.

Tucker, Helen A. "The Negroes of Pittsburgh." *Charities and Commons* 21 (Jan. 2, 1909).

Tuttle, William M., Jr. *Daddy's Gone to War: The Second World War in the Lives of America's Children.* New York: Oxford University Press, 1993.

Ugland, Richard M. "The Adolescent Experience during World War II: Indianapolis as a Case Study." Ph.D. dissertation, Indiana University, 1977.

———. "Viewpoints and Morale of Urban High School Students during World War II—Indianapolis as a Case Study." *Indiana Magazine of History* 77 (Winter 1981): 150-65.

Urofsky, Melvin I. "*Massachusetts v. Mellon.*" In *The Oxford Companion to the Supreme Court of the United States,* edited by Kermit L. Hall et al. New York: Oxford University Press, 1992.

Van Horn, Susan Householder. *Women, Work, and Fertility, 1900-1986.* New York: New York University Press, 1988.

Van Waters, Miriam. "Juvenile Delinquency and Juvenile Courts." In *Encyclopedia of the Social Sciences,* edited by Edwin R. A. Seligman, pp. 528-33. New York: Macmillan Company, 1937.

Vesey, Laurence. "Ray Lyman Wilbur." *Dictionary of American Biography.* Vol. 4. New York: Charles Scribner's Sons, 1974.

Wade, Louise C. *Graham Taylor: Pioneer For Social Justice, 1851- 1938.* Chicago: University of Chicago Press, 1964.

———. "Julia Clifford Lathrop." *Notable American Women.* Vol. 2. Cambridge: Harvard University Press, Belknap Press, 1971.

"The Wagner-Murray Bill." *American Journal of Public Health* 33 (Oct. 1943): 1274-77.

Wald, Lillian. "The Idea of a Federal Children's Bureau." *Proceedings of the National Conference of Social Work.* Philadelphia: n.p., 1932.

———. "The Right Woman in the Right Place." *American City* 6 (June 1912).

———. "Shall We Dismember the Child?" *Survey* 63 (Jan. 15, 1930): 458.

Walkowitz, Daniel J. "The Making of a Feminine Professional Identity: Social Workers in the 1920's." *American Historical Review* 95 (Oct. 1990): 1051-70.

Ware, Susan. *Beyond Suffrage: Women in the New Deal.* Cambridge: Harvard University Press, 1981.

Wegner, Beth W. "Jewish Women and Voluntarism: Beyond the Myth of Enablers." *American Jewish History* 79 (Autumn, 1989): 16-36.

Weiner, Lynn. *From Working Girl to Working Mother: The Female Labor Force in the United States, 1820-1980.* Chapel Hill: University of North Carolina Press, 1985.

Weiss, Nancy Pottishman. "Mother, the Invention of Necessity: Dr. Benjamin Spock's *Baby and Child Care.*" In *Growing Up in America: Children in Historical Perspective,* edited by N. Ray Hiner and Joseph M. Hawes, pp. 283-303. Urbana: University of Illinois Press, 1985.

———. "Save the Children: A History of the Children's Bureau, 1903-1918." Ph.D. dissertation, University of California, Los Angeles, 1974.

Weissberg, Ned. "The Federal Child Labor Amendment—A Study in Pressure Politics." Ph.D. dissertation, Cornell University, 1942.

Wertz, Richard W., and Dorothy C. Wertz. *Lying-in: A History of Childbirth in America.* New York: Schocken Books, 1977.

"The White House Conference." *Nation* 131 (Dec. 3, 1930): 595.

Wiebe, Robert. *The Search for Order, 1877-1920.* New York: Hill and Wang, 1967.

Wiggins, David K. "The Play of Slave Children in the Plantation Communities of the Old South, 1820-60." In *Growing Up in America: Children in Historical Perspective,* edited by N. Ray Hiner and Joseph M. Hawes. Urbana: University of Illinois Press, 1985.

Wilbur, Ray Lyman. "Children in National Emergencies." *Proceedings of the National Conference of Social Work*. Chicago, 1932.

———. *The March of Medicine: Selected Addresses and Articles on Medical Topics, 1913-1937*. Stanford: Stanford University Press, 1938.

———. *Memoirs*. Stanford: Stanford University Press, 1960.

Wilbur, Ray Lyman, and Arthur Mastick Hyde. *The Hoover Policies*. New York: Charles Scribner's Sons, 1937.

Williams, L. R. "Correlation of Federal Health Agencies." *JAMA* 85 (Nov. 7, 1925).

Williams, Ralph Chester. *The United States Public Health Service, 1798-1950*. Washington, D.C.: Commissioned Officers Association of the United States Public Health Service, 1951.

Winkler, Allan M. *Home Front U.S.A.: America during World War II*. Arlington Heights, Ill.: Harlan Davidson, 1986.

Witte, Edwin E. *The Development of the Social Security Act*. Madison: University of Wisconsin Press, 1962.

Wood, Stephen B. "*Bailey v. Drexel Furniture Co.*" In *The Oxford Companion to the Supreme Court of the United States*, edited by Kermit L. Hall et al. New York: Oxford University Press, 1992.

———. *Constitutional Politics in the Progressive Era*. Chicago: University of Chicago Press, 1968.

———. "*Hammer v. Dagenhart*." In *The Oxford Companion to the Supreme Court of the United States*, edited by Kermit L. Hall et al. New York: Oxford University Press, 1992.

Wright, Helen. "Three against Time: Edith and Grace Abbott and Sophonisba P. Breckinridge." *Social Service Review* 28 (Mar. 1954): 41-53.

"The Wrong Place to Save." *Survey* 68 (Apr. 15, 1933): 68-69.

Wylie, Philip. *Generation of Vipers*. New York: Rinehart and Co., 1942.

Yellowitz, Irwin. *Labor and the Progressive Movement in New York State*. Ithaca, N.Y.: Cornell University Press, 1965.

Young, Louise M. *In the Public Interest: The League of Women Voters, 1920-1970*. Westport, Conn.: Greenwood Press, 1989.

Zelizer, Viviana A. *Pricing the Priceless Child: The Changing Social Value of Children*. New York: Basic Books, 1985.

Zimand, Gertrude Folks. "Child Labor Facts." New York: National Child Labor Committee, 1940.

Zimand, Savel, ed. *Public Health and Welfare: the Citizen's Responsibility. Selected Papers of Homer Folks*. New York: Macmillan and Company, 1958.

Zucker, Henry L. "Working Parents and Latchkey Children." *Annals of the American Academy of Political and Social Science* 236 (Nov. 1944): 43-50.

Index

After a ten-year career in business, Kriste Lindenmeyer returned to the University of Cincinnati and earned a Ph.D. in American history in 1991. She is currently an associate professor of American history at Tennessee Technological University in Cookeville, Tennessee. At TTU she teaches history courses on U.S. social history and social welfare, immigration policy, and women and gender. Lindenmeyer has also developed a general historical methods course incorporating computer technology. She has given a variety of papers and published articles examining the evolution of social policy affecting women, children, and families. Her current research traces adolescent pregnancy in the United States during the twentieth century.